D1233755

4

INQUIRIES

KARL RAHNER

INQUIRIES

Inspiration in the Bible
Visions and Prophecies
The Church and the Sacraments
The Episcopate and the Primacy
On Heresy

HERDER AND HERDER

1964

HERDER AND HERDER NEW YORK

232 Madison Avenue, New York 16, N. Y.

Nihil Obstat: Joannes Barton, S. T. D., L. S. S.

Carolus Davis S. T. L.

Censores deputati

Imprimatur: Patricius Casey, Vic. Gen.

Westmonasterii, die 16 Julii, 1964

Library of Congress Catalog Card Number: 64-20435

First published in West Germany © 1964 Herder KG

Printed in the United States of America

CONTENTS

INSPIRATION IN THE BIBLE

V

VISIONS AND PROPHECIES

THE CHURCH AND THE SACRAMENTS

THE EPISCOPATE AND THE PRIMACY

ON HERESY

VIII

ACKNOWLEDGEMENTS

INSPIRATION IN THE BIBLE: Quaestiones Disputatae 1.
Freiburg, New York, London, Montreal.
Original edition "Über die Schriftinspiration", Herder, Freiburg;
First English edition translated by Charles H. Henkey;
Second English edition revised by Martin Palmer.

VISIONS AND PROPHECIES: Quaestiones Disputatae 10.
Freiburg, New York, London, Montreal.
Original edition "Visionen und Prophezeiungen", Herder, Freiburg;
English edition translated by Charles H. Henkey and Richard Strachan.

THE CHURCH AND THE SACRAMENTS: Quaestiones Disputatae 9.
Freiburg, New York, London, Montreal.
Original edition "Kirche und Sakramente", Herder, Freiburg;
English edition translated by W. J. O'Hara.

THE EPISCOPATE AND THE PRIMACY: Quaestiones Disputatae 4.
Freiburg, New York, London, Montreal.
Original edition "Episkopat und Primat", Herder, Freiburg;
English edition translated by Kenneth Barker, Patrick Kerans, Robert Ochs
and Richard Strachan. [The first part of this work also appeared in Karl
Rahner's "Sendung und Gnade", Tyrolia, Innsbruck; English edition "Mis-
sion and Grace" volume 2, Sheed & Ward, London.]

ON HERESY: Quaestiones Disputatae 11.
Freiburg, New York, London, Montreal.
The original edition "Was ist Häresie?" formed part of "Häresien der Zeit"
edited by A. Böhm (Herder, Freiburg).
The English edition of this extract is translated by W. J. O'Hara.

ABBREVIATIONS

AAS	=	*Acta Apostolicae Sedis* (Rome, since 1909)
AASS	=	*Acta Sanctorum* (The Bollandists, Antwerp, 1663 ff.)
ASS	=	*Acta Sanctae Sedis* (Rome, 1865—1908)
CJC	=	*Codex Juris Canonici*
CChL	=	*Corpus Christianorum Latinorum* (Turnhout — Paris, 1953 ff.)
DThC	=	*Dictionnaire de Théologie Catholique* (Paris)
Dz., Denz. Denzinger	=	Denzinger, H., *Enchiridion Symbolorum* (Freiburg — Barcelona)
LThK	=	*Lexikon für Theologie und Kirche* (Freiburg, 1st ed. 1930 to 1938; 2nd ed. 1957 ff.)
NRTh	=	*Nouvelle Revue Théologique* (Tournai)
RAC	=	*Reallexikon für Antike und Christentum*
RAM	=	*Revue d'Ascétisme et de Mystique* (Toulouse)
RHE	=	*Revue d'Histoire Ecclésiastique* (Louvain, 1950 ff.)
StdZ	=	*Stimmen der Zeit* (Freiburg)
ThWNT	=	*Theologisches Wörterbuch zum Neuen Testament* (Stuttgart, 1933 ff.)
ZAM	=	"Geist und Leben". *Zeitschrift für Askese und Mystik*
ZKTh	=	*Zeitschrift für Katholische Theologie* (Innsbruck and Vienna)

AUTHOR'S PREFACE

This book contains a number of individual theological studies which appeared separately in the series *Quaestiones Disputatae*, of which Heinrich Schlier and myself are the editors. They should not therefore be thought of as a regular unity, although they do indeed belong together in so far as they all deal with individual aspects of ecclesiology. This is true even of the first study, since the nature of inspiration in the Bible is seen from an ecclesiological viewpoint; in "Visions and Prophecies" an attempt is likewise made to bring out their positive meaning for the Church. That the other three studies belong to ecclesiology is quite evident. I would not, of course, wish to claim that this book presents a complete and proportioned ecclesiology; nevertheless each treatment here strives after one and the same reality, a reality which forms a main theme of the Second Vatican Council, namely the Mystery of the Church.

Munich, June 1964   Karl Rahner S. J.

INSPIRATION IN THE BIBLE

INTRODUCTION

THERE is no need to furnish an apologia for dealing with the subject of this essay. Its importance within the Christian and Catholic religion is obvious. The characterization of Christianity as a "book religion", false and misleading as it would be if understood as an essential exclusive definition, expresses a truth of great importance.

Our topic is of concern to both dogmatic theologian and exegete. It touches upon a point of defined doctrine, the very essence of the books and writings to which we daily recur for guidelines in the work of theology as well as for light and practical direction in our pilgrimage here on earth.

On the other hand, we could hardly maintain that theological interest among Catholics today is focused upon the problem of the inspiration of the Scriptures. To be honest, we must admit that the average Catholic exegete, while not denying or questioning the inspiration of the Bible, simply leaves it aside in his exegetical work; he seems unable to make it relevant to his own labours. For him, the fact that the Bible is inspired means little more than that the inerrancy of the Bible, which is a corollary of its inspiration, constitutes a negative norm for his exegesis. We may ask if it is only the exegete and the rationalistic and historical atmosphere of his studies that are responsible for this state of affairs, or whether there is not a real need for re-thinking the whole problem of inspiration.

Our approach will be that of the dogmatic, not the biblical, theologian. Our starting-point is not the Bible itself and whatever it may have to say about inspiration; rather it is the doctrine of inspiration as established in its basic outlines by the teaching authority of the Church and further explained and expanded by the theologians. Such an approach, if not the only possible one, is certainly legitimate. Whether it is to be recommended in this particular case will have to be judged by the results.

To treat so extensive a subject in such a short essay as this is not without its risks. We are aware of this, and hence feel compelled to preface our study with the following observations: surely it is reasonable to hold that in theology, as in any other science, there is a place for the tentative proposal, for the hypothesis presented with the understanding that it may in the end turn out to be unworkable (even in the judgment of its originator) once it is subjected to the critical scrutiny of friends and fellow-workers in the field of theology. Theology is anything but a settled, dry-as-dust affair; it offers ever new challenges to mind and heart, if we have but the courage to take them up, and both the courage and the humility to retrace our steps as soon as we become aware of having erred. This remark is made in all earnestness. No one who really believes that theology, like any science, can be confronted with real problems demanding better, clearer, more comprehensive and possibly simpler solutions, will begrudge seeing such problems raised. Nor, should a proposed solution prove inadequate or even erroneous, will he imagine that the role of the fraternal critic is the same as that of the ecclesiastical censor.

To pose questions about some reality which is the object of a defined doctrine is not tantamount to doubting or contesting that doctrine; it is the unavoidable business of the theologian who refuses to find comfortable support for his own mental laziness in the definitions of Denzinger.* The man who insists that, even in the most restricted circles, only final and absolute solutions ought to be proposed, is, one suspects, incapable of recognizing a new problem or a new answer in theology.

In this essay we plan first to expose some interrelated problems concerning the traditional concept of inspiration; secondly, we shall submit the outline of a systematic structure, which, in the third part, will have to prove itself as an answer to the problems raised in the first part.

The relationship between "old" and "new" in our case is the same as it is generally in theology; the matters we shall look at will be familiar ones, things known to everyone and offering no surprises. But we shall try to look at the old truths in a new perspective, one which will point up certain relations among them which have hitherto been neglected, and which may reveal to us a simple structural principle by which the whole and all its individual elements are organized.

* Denzinger, H., *Enchiridion Symbolorum,* 32nd edition, Freiburg-Barcelona 1963. This work will be referred to by the siglum D.

I

THE PROBLEMS

WE SHALL here touch only a few among the many problems which could be raised about biblical inspiration. We do not claim that the ones treated here are those of greatest moment. The only reason for our focusing on these is that they are the ones which led us to the hypothesis we shall present in the second part.

We assume the acceptance of the traditional concept of inspiration, as found partly in definitions or other pronouncements of the Church's teaching authority and partly in the common teaching of theologians. We intend neither to criticize this concept nor to propose to change it. Our only aim is to raise some questions which will point out that this concept, correct as it is, possesses a certain abstractness and formality which is easily overlooked. The result is that this abstract concept is often taken for an adequate material description of inspiration. Closer examination, however, will show that a material content still remains to be given to this abstract notion of inspiration, and we shall suggest the lines along which this might be done.

We thus assume the traditional teaching of the Church as binding: the Scriptures have God as their originator; he is their originator in a literary sense, and therefore their "author". He is author of the Scriptures because he has inspired them. This inspiration does not consist in the fact that the Scriptures have been accepted as canonical by the Church,[1] nor solely in the fact that they inerrantly record the divine revelation. Rather, inspiration consists in God's supernaturally enlightening the human

---

[1] This statement contains, of course, more problems than is generally realized. We must recall that, according to the Church's teaching and the testimony of the Scriptures themselves, an inspired author may make use of sources in his work. How far can this go? In plain language, how much is the author allowed to "copy"? May he employ sources to such an extent that his "authorship" (meaning his own work exclusive of the contributions of his sources to the inspired text) would actually consist in no more than the approbation and appropriation of his sources?

According to the moral view prevalent nowadays, an author who only copies would not be a true author at all; for our moral concept of authorship today includes the claim to originality. But does such copying (of which the technical performance may take various forms) necessarily prevent the copyist from saying: "This work is an expression of my thoughts, produced by me (through copying), and therefore, unoriginal as it may be, it is my own work"? Must we say, for example, that the original author of a religious hymn such as a psalm is necessarily inspired? Or could we maintain that the inspiration pertains to the man who introduced this psalm into the official worship of the synagogue after examining it and deciding that it was an authentic expression of his own and the community's religious conviction? Could he not then claim it as his own, albeit unoriginal, work?

If we answer this second question in the affirmative, then the act of appropriation, by a competent person or persons, of a given writing as a more or less official expression of the community's or the Church's thought might provide a sufficient basis for true authorship and thus for inspiration as well. Yet this comes quite close to the phenomenon of ecclesiastical approbation of a writing. This is not yet to say that such a form of authorship is simply identical with that "subsequent approbation" in which Catholic dogma refuses to see the essence of inspiration or its vehicle. If, for example, the Pope issues an encyclical, he unquestionably deserves to be reckoned its author, even though he may only be giving his approval to writings actually composed by his theologians, but which nevertheless serve as the expression of his own authoritative teaching. He even remains the true author although he may not have changed a single word in the text.

In such a case, of course, we might distinguish between a literary and an

author's mind in the perception of the content and essential plan of the book, and moving his will to write no more and no less than what God himself wants written, God providing him the

"authoritative" authorship. But the question would remain, how to distinguish accurately between these two types of authorship, and whether the second kind can be designated as true authorship in any proper sense. If it can be (and why not, even though it differs from what we normally understand by "author"?), then we may well ask whether this second type of authorship could not suffice as a basis for inspiration.

In the last analysis, the answer would seem to depend upon the will and intention of the person giving his approval. He may approve the work inasmuch as it expresses the ideas of the original author, or as an expression of his own views. In the first case, he could not be the subject of inspiration, whereas in the second, he might be. If, for example, St Paul "wrote" the Epistle to the Hebrews, as is generally believed, by approving the theological treatise of one of his disciples, who then was actually the inspired author? It would seem that we must reply that it was St Paul. For the Church recognizes the inspired character of this essay as a letter of Paul. But how can St Paul, following this (perhaps contestable) view, become the author of Hebrews unless he could become such through the simple approbation of a work, by approving it as an expression of *his own* mind (and not merely declaring it to be in accordance with his thought)? But if this is possible, then it would be at least useful to have a more exact formulation of the doctrine on the difference between approbation by the Church and inspiration.

Pesch (*De inspiratione,* no. 412) holds that there is nothing to prevent us from maintaining that a man can be inspired to write something which has already been written by someone else without any inspiration. (We leave aside the question of plagiarism, since in this respect conditions vary according to the literary forms and changing views of each age.) If Pesch is correct, then such an authorship could consist precisely in the appropriation of someone else's writings, while God's inspiration would then consist in bringing about this appropriation. God would therefore become the author of the work through this act of appropriation, and not through his causing the earlier and original work to be written. It is further conceivable that this human act of appropriation might itself be performed with the prior intention of making this appropriated piece of writing a book of the holy community or Church.

We do not mention all this here in order to present a thesis right at the outset of our discussion. We are only attempting to point out, by means of

while with special assistance to ensure that the work, thus conceived and willed, be correspondingly carried into effect. We presuppose the validity and dogmatic foundations of this concept, and move immediately to the problems which interest us here.

1. The Two Authors

God is the literary originator of the Scriptures, he is their author. This is stated in the dogmas of Trent and Vatican I, at least if we understand the expression *Deum habent auctorem* (D 1787; see D 783) in the light of tradition, and take into consideration the phrases *Spiritu Sancto dictante* (D 783) and *Spiritu Sancto inspirante* (D 706), which occur in this context.[2] Now according to the common view of theologians, these pronouncements do not imply that the human author of an inspired book is not a true literary

a tentative 'exercise' of this sort, that a difference can exist between the formal sense of certain statements about inspiration (which alone is covered by the teaching authority) and the material content which we often tend spontaneously to give then without any authorization thereto either from the Church's magistery or from the realities themselves.

[2] On this matter see A. Bea, "Deus auctor Sacrae Scripturae. Herkunft und Bedeutung der Formel" in: *Angelicum* 20 (1943), pp. 16-31. I would like to add at this point that the identification of *auctor* ("originator", German *Urheber*) with "author", in the literary sense, in such studies in dogmatic history, often seems to me somewhat hasty and facile. We can, after all, speak of the *auctor* of a given book in a sense which is quite different from the concept of literary authorship. The concept of inspiration, again, may be distinguished from both of these senses. This distinction is theoretically acknowledged in most treatises, but I think it does not receive sufficient attention in historical works. If we must also admit a kind of prophetic inspiration, perhaps we should examine more carefully whether, when the Church Fathers speak of the inspiration of the Bible, they do not often mean prophetic inspiration; such inspiration does not constitute God a literary author, though it may make him in some sense responsible for the

author.[3] It is here that we find a first approach to our problem. The human authors of the Bible are not mere secretaries taking down divine dictation; they are not mere secretaries even in the sense that they receive that to which God enlightens and prompts them with understanding and free consent. They are true authors. Indeed, it is permissible to say that they are no less authors of the Scriptures than other men are of their own writings.[4] The divine

books in which the inspired prophecy is deposited. On the other hand, a little reflection on the nature of theological concepts will make it obvious that the concept of authorship as we know it in our own experience cannot be transferred to God without qualifications and precisions. We need only consider the relationship between the special literary character of any writing and the particular intellectual make-up of its author, which is a determining element in our normal concept of authorship. This certainly cannot be applied to God; in respect of the particular literary character of the biblical books, he can be *auctor,* but not "author" in the literary sense. However, we cannot go into all these questions at this point. We must also here leave the question open whether the insistence, customary since Franzelin's time, that inspiration makes God a strictly literary author (as over against any other form of originatorship — for example merely authoritative — even of a book) is really no more than an explicitation of the dogma that God is *auctor* of Holy Scripture, or whether it does not go beyond this and assert something that cannot be considered defined. In this essay, we simply assume that God is the literary author of Scripture.

[3] See A. Bea, *De Scripturae Sacrae inspiratione,* 2nd ed., Rome 1935, n. 37 (pp. 41 et seq.); S. Tromp, *De Sacrae Scripturae inspiratione* 3rd ed., Rome 1936, p. 55. The magisterial statements of the Church also speak without hesitation of men as the authors of Holy Scripture.

[4] On this particular point we do not have, to my knowledge, any statement from the teaching authority of the Church. We are helped here by the analogy of faith. Recalling the Church's rejection of monophysitism and monothelitism, we can appeal to our Lord himself (using the well-known analogy between incarnation in flesh and in word) and make the following assertion: just as the free spontaneity of Christ's humanity was not diminished because of its assumption by the divine Logos, but rather was thereby raised to a supreme and otherwise unattainable height of vitality (cf. K. Rahner, *Theological Investigations,* I, London 1960, pp. 194-200, *passim*), so the same will be true of the biblical writers (assuming, as we do, that they

authorship neither competes with, nor derogates from the human authorship; the latter is not diminished, it is not reduced to a mere secretarial function. It would be a mistake to understand the notion of the "instrumentality" of the human author — which notion frequently recurs in ecclesiastical pronouncements — as meaning that the human author is merely an instrument of the divine author. He is a true human author whose own authorship remains whole and inviolate at the same time as it is permeated and embraced by that of God. Only in this sense can he be called God's "instrument". In this form of instrumentality, God's authorship does not merely tolerate full human authorship, it demands it. Making man a mere amanuensis would not enhance the divine authorship at all.

Now it cannot be said that the usual descriptions of the inspiration by which God is author of the Bible also makes clear that the human author remains, and must remain, a true author.[5]

remain true authors, not merely secretaries); their own authorship is greater, not less, than in the normal case. Divine inspiration frees rather than limits human individuality. It does not imply some unexplainable compromise between God and man, but is rather an instance of the basic relationship between God and his creatures: the two factors, dependence upon God and personal autonomy, vary in direct, not inverse proportion to one another. This holds true in the economy of salvation no less than in creation.

[5] Pius XII's encyclical *Divino afflante Spiritu* rightly emphasizes the sacred writer's instrumentality in relation to God, and concludes from it that the special character of a biblical book will reflect both its human author and his individuality (*Ench. Bibl.,* n. 556). However, this does not answer our question. For it is obvious that any instrumentality in a work will reflect the peculiar nature of the instrument; on this showing, the individuality of Matthew, Luke, and so on, would be discernible, at least to some degree, even if they had been mere (conscious and willing) secretaries. Hence the instrumentality of the sacred writers must be conceived and interpreted in such a way that it not only explains the particular literary form of the

On the contrary, they tend to give the impression that inspiration would then be most perfect, if the human writer were a mere secretary. At best, the customary descriptions do not clearly exclude a purely secretarial function for the human writer; they could quite well accommodate such a conception of his role.

Moreover, how is it possible to conceive of two literary authors working together, not as a team, but in such a way that each of them is author of the whole work (*totalitate effectus* if not also *totalitate causae*)? It is not enough, in order to solve this problem, to appeal to God's transcendent causality in the preservation of the world and his *concursus* with its operations. It is true that this is a case of double causality of a single act (although — or because — the two causes operate on different levels). But God's acting as *literary* cause of the Bible, as its author, puts him, if we may so formulate it, on the level of categorical, not transcendent, causality; that is, not only the thing caused, but also the causal operation itself, must be within the dimension of created existence and operation. God's transcendental causality of the Bible alone is not sufficient to make him its author; if he is to be truly its author, his operation itself must be within the world, within salvation history, as it is in the case of prophetic inspiration and the Incarnation. Both of these represent a miraculous activity of God which, in a certain sense, possesses — precisely as *divine* activity and not merely in its effects — a place in space and time.

writings, but also makes clear that the writers are not mere secretaries of God, but true human authors, in the exact and literal sense. This holds true even though these authors must be called *auctores secundarii* because of the simultaneous divine authorship, since this qualification does not imply any lessening of their authorship but only its subordination to the divine, which does not weaken, but actually makes the human authorship all the more perfect.

16

But the fact that in these last-named cases the person who originally acts and speaks is God and God alone seems to imply that the authorship of the Bible must also be assigned exclusively to him, that he cannot tolerate any other author beside him for the very reason that his own "authorship" is within the created dimension within which the human writer exists — and there cannot be two authors of the same book within the same dimension. In other words, a single effect can have, in any given respect, only a single cause;[6] the Bible cannot have two causes in the same respect, namely that of literary authorship.

Notice: we do not deny that the same effect can have both a divine and a human cause. What we are denying is that there can be two causalities both possessing, within the same dimension and in the same respect, the modality of literary authorship. Such a situation would involve two causes producing a single effect in the same respect, which is impossible.[7]

[6] It does not help to refer, as some authors seem to do, to the axiom of St Thomas: *idem effectus totus attribuitur instrumento et principali agenti etiam totus* (*Summa contra Gent.* III, 70) and conclude therefrom that in our case also the instrument (the human author) could call his own the whole effect (the book) and on that account be its author, although (we should have to say in this context "because") he is only an instrument of God, the primary author. Whatever the precise meaning of St Thomas's axiom might be (it is used only to illustrate the transcendent causality of God), it cannot apply here. If it were applicable, there could never be any mere secretary at all; any secretary of God, on this showing, would by that very fact be an author. This would even be true of the pen employed as an instrument in writing the book; it too would be an author.

[7] Theologians are not unaware of this difficulty. Attempts have been made to get around it by appeal to the relationship between God and creature in the *concursus*. But this does not indicate sufficient awareness that in our case the very thing requires explanation is lacking in the *concursus*: namely, that through the subordination of the created to the divine causality, the effect of *both* is ascribed properly to God. This is precisely what is excluded

On the other hand, to say that the human author is an author only in an instrumental sense raises the following questions: (a) Why does the human author not *eo ipso* cease to be an author at all, since to be, in the composition of a literary work, the instrument of another who is actually the author, seems to be the very definition of the secretary's role ? (b) Must not the role of the human author thereby be at least diminished?

It is clear that if this difficulty is not to remain unanswered, God must be shown to be the author of the Bible (a) in a sense which makes him truly (though analogously) a literary author, yet in some respect[8] which distinguishes his authorship from that of the human author, and (b) in such a way that this distinguishing quality of the divine authorship not only can be shown (by some arbitrary evasion) to tolerate the presence of a human author, but positively to require it.

2. Some Problems Concerning the Concept of Inspiration

We have already shown how inspiration, which is to explain how God is author, is traditionally interpreted. This interpretation is not to be contested. But, as we have already indicated, close examination reveals that it (correctly enough) understands inspiration quite formally and abstractly. In practice, there is a danger that this can lead to its being uncritically supplied with

in the *concursus*. Moreover, the literary individuality of the individual biblical books is not adequately explained if we merely say that God dealt with his instrument in such a way that it acted "freely and personally" (P. Benoit in A. Robert - A. Tricot, *Guide to the Bible,* New York, 2nd ed. 1960, I, p. 21). For that would be the case even if the "instrument" were a mere secretary.

[8] "Respect" is here meant in an objective-ontological sense and not merely in a gnoseological sense, i. e., *quoad se* and not merely *quoad nos*.

a material content which is by no means necessarily part of the dogmatic aspect of inspiration. We shall elucidate this further, for it will provide us with a new formal lead in our quest for the right material understanding of the concept.

When most people hear of God's illuminating the mind and moving the will of the inspired writer, they tend to form involuntarily a specific concrete image of this. This concrete understanding can be defended, but nothing compels us to accept it. There have long been theologians who have held that inspiration by no means necessarily implies a communication of hitherto unknown intellectual contents, even less so an infusion of images. Indeed, according to them, the inspired hagiographer, unlike the inspired prophet, need not be at all conscious of his inspiration.[9]

[9] Cf. M. Nicolau, *Sacrae Theologiae Summa*, 2nd ed., Madrid 1952, I, p. 1005; B. Mariani, "Ispirazione" in: *Enciclopedia Cattolica*, Rome 1951, VII, p. 324: "Non é necessario che l'agiografo sia consapevole della sua ispirazione"; Lercher-Schlagenhaufen, *Institutiones theol. dogm.*, Innsbruck 1939, I, n. 586 (pp. 345 et seq.); P. Benoit, *op. cit.*, p. 20 (Caiaphas was able to prophesy the death of Jesus, Jn 11:51, without realizing it). Lercher-Schlagenhaufen adds in this connection: "Communiter tamen assumitur, de facto hagiographos conscientiam inspirationis habuisse", and refers to Suarez, *De fide,* disp. 8, sect. 4 (Vives XII, pp. 232 et seq.). We shall prescind here from the question whether this reference to Suarez is valid. St Thomas seems "with greater probability" to have held that awareness is not a necessary element of inspiration, as Bea says in his *De inspiratione* 2nd ed., Rome 1935, n. 52.

In any case, we may state with Bea *(loc. cit.)*: "Recentiores auctores plerique partem negativam tenent." Bea quotes on behalf of the claim for consciousness of inspiration S. M. Zarb alone among modern authors: "Num hagiographi sibi conscii fuerint divinae inspirationis" in: *Angelicum,* 11 (1934), pp. 228-44. Further, it is difficult to see how a sacred writer's definite and reflex awareness of his own inspiration can be squared with statements such as we find in Lk 1:1-4, 2 Cor 7:8, 2 Macc 15:38-39 ("Here then I will make an end of my writing; if it has been done workmanly and

But what about the "illumination" of the intellect? As this word is normally understood, an illumination which communicates nothing, or even remains unconscious, is no illumination at all.[10] We may of course reply that the illumination sheds light

in historian's fashion, none better pleased than I; if it is of little merit, I have done as well as I could.").

[10] Naturally one could answer by claiming that a strengthening of the writer's judgment regarding the propositions to be written constitutes an "illumination" (cf. Bea, *op. cit.,* n. 45-9: "Haec motio in eo consistit, quod Deus . . . intellectum hagiographi ita tangit, ut hac motione elevatus iudicia in libro exprimenda eliciat; simul ipsa objecta in clariore luce ponuntur et facultas intellectiva maiorem accipit potentiam illuminativam maiusque robur, ut haec iudicia sint vera et certa ea veritate et certitudine, quae est cognitionis divinae": 2.2 q. 171, a 6); but the question still remains — how does such an illumination affect the book itself? If we could imagine an "illumination" which failed to add any new material elements to the author's knowledge, yet increased the firmness of his judgment (which is by no means clear), several questions still remain: a) Must not this "illumination" be conscious after all; for how could a *clarior lux* be unconscious? This at least demands some explanation; we do not maintain that such a "light" must necessarily be accompanied by a reflex *objective* consciousness, but we do think that an entirely unconscious "mental light" is a contradiction in terms. b) How does this illumination influence the work otherwise than as a mere *assistentia per se negativa?* It would seem that the only way the certainty furnished by such an illumination could get into the written sentences would be if they were thereby to receive some new *content* that would not otherwise be present, since only a content can be put into writing. This special certainty would seem to be unable to affect the sacred writer as *writer* unless it could somehow directly influence not only his mind, but his book as well. It is no good saying that the magisterial teaching on inspiration requires such an illumination even if it should make no difference for the authorship as such. For it is precisely from the elements of God's inspiring activity that the dogmatic sources derive his authorship: because a book is inspired, therefore it has God as its author. c) How does this illumination make for authorship? Or why is it demanded over and above the prophetic inspiration which is present directly or indirectly in all the books of the Bible even though as such it seems to have no bearing on authorship as such? In other words, is it certain that such an illumination really is demanded by the sources?

20

on already acquired mental contents, makes them clearer, lends them a greater certainty. One can also say that such an illumination need not necessarily be conscious, or that, even if marginally conscious, it need not be conscious precisely as inspiration. Even so, the question still remains, whether so circumscribed an inspiration really suffices to make God an author.[11] Nevertheless, we must agree with the theologians who hold that inspiration, despite the element of illumination connected with it, can be unconscious. There are many good reasons which show that the formal concept of inspiration, taken in itself and in a general sense, does not contain a change of consciousness of which the human author need be aware. "Illumination" here can mean only that God acts effectively in such a way that the

---

[11] An illumination in this sense would be more a subsidiary help in enunciating the content of some knowledge, in giving it written form, than something through which one would become the author of the knowledge thus illuminated. One might reply to this that the illumination is to be understood as accounting for God's authorship only in connection with the movement of the writer's will by God, and that it is not claimed that the illumination alone suffices to make God an author. But what might this illumination mean for the divine *authorship,* even in conjunction with God's moving of the will, if taken in itself it cannot make a meaningful contribution? One could of course end the discussion by claiming that this is the way in which tradition has always understood inspiration, and that we must take these positive sources into account, regardless of whether or not their statements can be derived from the concept of literary authorship. However, we may then ask the further question whether these positive sources actually propose this interpretation as matter beyond any dispute, or whether the merely employ these expressions ("illumination", etc.) to clarify the essential fact, namely, that God is the author of Holy Scripture, without affirming at the same time that such clarifications must also be regarded as irrevocable articles of faith. Further, are all the limitations on this illumination (its not having to be conscious, and so on) which are imposed without contradiction on the traditional concept as found in the older sources also covered by the positive sources of faith?

human author's mind receives a specific certain knowledge — and this alone — which God wills him to have. How God achieves this can remain an open matter whether, through some modification of the writer's psychic processes, or in any number of other conceivable ways. Obviously, it is sufficient that the effect be attained. The human author perceives something because God effectively wills him to do so, with a will which is not merely permissive and co-operative, but rather predefining — what is called in technical theology a *praedefinitio formalis*.[12]

As for the moving of the inspired writer's will, many, though not all, theologians[13] hold that inspiration does not of itself

---

[12] We shall have to discuss at greater length and in a later context the fact that a formal, efficacious predefinition is not of itself sufficient (though it is indeed necessary) to make God an author. We might remark at this point that theologians rightly point to the parallel between inspiration and efficacious grace. But at least the Molinist theologian would have to grant that the element of efficaciousness in actual grace, which is the point of the analogy, need not reside in some property of the grace by which it is "interior". The determining factor in an efficacious (as distinct from a merely sufficient) grace can consist in some external circumstance which, as God foresees through his *scientia media,* will be decisive in a man's coming to his choice, and is willed by God as such. Why should we not assume this also to be the case in inspiration, both in regard to the sacred writer's reason and his will? For it is this *de facto,* and as such absolutely willed efficaciousness (that is, predefining efficaciousness) which is required for God to be the author of the Scriptures. Furthermore, does the idea of the efficacy of inspiration being exerted immediately upon the sacred writer's mind, to the extent that this idea is found in the dogmatic sources, really amount to a statement about the reality itself, or is it merely a manner of speaking which serves only to express the fact that God has a predefining, efficacious influence upon the origin of the Scriptures?

[13] Cf. Lercher-Schlagenhaufen, *op. cit.,* n. 565: "Motio voluntatis potest concipi ad modum influxus immediate physici in voluntatem . . . Sed motio voluntatis, ut videtur, eodem modo explicari poterit per influxum divinum mediatum: . . . sive mediante impulsu externo (iussione divina: Apoc 1, 10 Is 8, 1; Jer 20, 1–2; vel iussione angelorum: Apoc 19, 9f.) immo potest

require an immediate divine intervention into the interior of the human will; it is possible for the will to be moved mediately, by means of created impulses arising within the realm of the author's concrete empirical experience. This again points up how formally one must understand the traditional description of inspiration, and how great is the danger of giving it a material psychological content which it may not demand at all. Indeed, such an interpretation has a bit of the mythological about it — if it does not simply betray a confusion between scriptural inspiration and the prophetic inspiration of the bearer of a new revelation. Provided, then, that it is God's absolute will (which he therefore unfailingly executes), God can move the inspired author to write simply by having others ask him to do so. This asking, and the writer's compliance with it, must of course also be objects of a divine formal predefinition.

Thus the question, "How does God become the real author of the Scriptures?" cautions us against ignoring the formal character of the doctrinal teaching on inspiration, and against furnishing it with a meaning which in some cases might be correct *de facto,* but which cannot be postulated generally *a priori* wherever divine inspiration occurs.

We may now summarize our two initial considerations in the following heuristic statement: we must find an activity of God

Deus ex absoluta intentione libri perficiendi causas externas (preces aliorum) per specialem providentiam supernaturalem ita dirigere, ut hagiographus reapse scribere velit. Motio voluntatis differt a gratia, quae datur ad modum actus supernaturalis indeliberati: haec enim per se non infallibiliter movet ad actum salutarem, illa infallibiliter movet ad scribendum." Nicolau (*op. cit.* no. 96, 97) holds the opposite view (following Bea) to be only more probable. This is therefore an open question among theologians. If so, we should be able to say the same about the influence of the divine inspiration upon the writer's intellect.

23

which will make him literary author of the Bible, while at the same not merely tolerating — in some inexplicable way — the authorship of the human writer, but positively requiring such a human authorship; thus the two authorships must be formally different. This activity of God may be conceived in any way whatever, provided only that it conceives,[14] wills, and accomplishes the book by formal predefinition.

3. How the Inspiration of the Bible is Ascertained by the Church

We now turn to a third problem which should point the way to a correct and adequate understanding of inspiration. How does the Church know which books are inspired? For methodological reasons, we shall confine ourselves at this point to the New Testament,[15] and pose our question only about the Church, not about individuals. We assume as proved that the individual can

---

[14] To "conceive", we must repeat, is to be taken in the sense that God "conceives" this book precisely *as* the book of the human author, that is, as the expression and objectivization of the human author's mind. We should always keep in mind that, as Benoit says (*op. cit.,* p. 28), "God cannot be an author after the manner of a man. Attributing to him 'thoughts' which he communicates to a secretary . . . is an anthropomorphism which can only mislead research."

[15] We shall return later to the particular question of whether the results of the insights attained with respect to the New Testament are also applicable to the inspiration of the Old Testament. Although inspiration is formally the same in both Testaments, we are entitled to proceed according to this methodology, because, as will be seen later, an ultimate understanding of inspiration and fixing of the Canon is, in fact, possible only in the New Testament; in other words, the writings of the Old Testament are inspired precisely to the extent that the Old Testament is the preparation for the coming of the fulness of time, so that the nature, fact, and extent of inspiration can be finally and unequivocally understood only from the New Testament.

know which books are inspired only through the Church's teaching authority. This implies that the Bible itself possesses no objective qualities which, taken in themselves, would found a certain judgment on the part of an individual concerning their inspiration and canonicity. But what of the Church herself? How does the Church know it? This cannot be established, it seems, from the books themselves. At least in most cases, it is not to be supposed that the authors themselves have attested to it, for we cannot even assume *a priori* that they themselves knew of it. Is it, for instance, historically conceivable that St Paul himself would have declared his note to Philemon to be inspired, claiming for it the rank and status of the Old Testament Torah, or that St Luke would have done the same for his own writings which he so laboriously compiled from collected documents and diaries?

And even if they had been able to testify concerning their own inspiration, it still has to be shown that they in fact did so, and that their testimony was duly handed down, and it still has to be demonstrated why and on what grounds we should or must give credence, in the case of those who were not apostles, to their subjective impressions that they were inspired. And yet the inspiration of certain specific books is part of the revealed truths which are entrusted to the Church only for custody, which she herself cannot add to, and which must have been consigned to the Church before the death of the last apostle and cannot have been revealed at a later date. Nor can the inspiration of these books have been revealed by purely logical implication in some other statement; it is impossible to conceive of a more universal statement which would contain, *formaliter implicite,* the revelation, that for example, the Epistle to Philemon

25

is inspired. Or are we, in order to get over the difficulty, to lay down that everything written by an apostle must be inspired? Even though there may be more truth to this statement than is generally admitted,[16] there still remain questions which present-day theology is unable to answer satisfactorily. For how are we to prove this statement? Unless it is deducible from some other dogma, how can it be shown historically to have always been a part of the Church's faith? And would this mean that the lost epistles of Paul were also inspired and had God for their author? Can a book written by God perish totally? What of the writings of Luke and Mark, who were only disciples of the apostles? We certainly cannot hold *a priori*, without further proof, the canonicity of everything produced by men who were, after all, not apostles.

---

[16] Later we will point out the truth contained in this idea; truth there is in it, but the truth needs proving. For it is not immediately obvious that an apostle must be inspired at all times, nor is it true that only an apostle can be inspired. We must show why the Church, at least in a general and inarticulated fashion, has always perceived an intrinsic connection between inspiration and the apostolic office. This connection is pointed up by the fact that we do not possess any apostolic writing which the Church does not *de facto* recognize as inspired. Surely the Church feels this to be more than a mere accident. (The Letter of Barnabas, in spite of Tertullian [*De pudic.*, 20] and Jerome [*De viris illustribus*, 6] is no argument to the contrary.) The objections of Pesch, Dorsch, Bea, and Nicolau seem to attribute to the statements of the Fathers a distinction which was foreign to their minds. The Fathers' statements do not, at any rate, indicate that they reckoned with the possibility of a non-inspired apostolic writing. Incidentally, if we take seriously the distinction between the Church and the Synagogue in the matter of indefectibility, then we cannot simply equate the Old Testament prophets with the apostles, as though, if all apostolic writings were inspired, the same would *a priori* be true of everything written by the prophets. For the literature on this question, see the references in Bea *(loc. cit.)*, Perrella in *Divus Thomas* 35, Piacenza 1932, p. 51, and Nicolau *(loc. cit.)* on Ubaldi, Schanz, Joüon, Zarb, M.-J. Lagrange, and Durand on the one side, and Pesch, Dorsch, Bea, Ogara, *et al.* on the other.

It is of no avail to answer that the apostles could have approved their disciples' work and thus made it their own, so that even these writings could be truly attributed to the apostles and are therefore (according to the principle stated above) inspired. Merely to approve another's work does not make one its author.[17] And in the case of Luke's writings it is quite evident that their author is Luke, not Paul.

In order to get out of this dilemma, it is sometimes argued that the apostles (or an apostle, perhaps the last one in the Church) left behind a formal and explicit revelation concerning the inspiration of the individual books of the New Testament in the form of a direct statement to that effect. But is this historically probable? Is it likely, for example, that in the case of certain smaller writings (such as the Epistle to Philemon) one apostle was ignorant of his own inspiration while another received an explicit propositional revelation that the same writing was inspired? If the inspiration of at least some of Paul's letters (such short private letters as Philemon, Romans 16:1–23) was unknown to Paul himself, it is difficult to believe that there was some other apostle (which one?) who knew these letters and actually testified to their inspiration.

So far we have not even touched upon the history of the Canon. What historically plausible explanation can be given to the Church's long hesitation about the canonicity or non-

---

[17] If however, we were to argue that apostles had given their approval to the writings of, say, Mark or Luke in such a way as to make these works the apostles' own (a possibility which cannot be dismissed *a priori*), then we would be forced to conclude that these writings, to the extent that they were inspired, were not the writings of Mark or Luke. But this would go counter to the whole of tradition, which has always regarded them as "evangelists" and inspired authors.

canonicity (and hence inspiration or lack of it) of so many writings, if it is true that one of the apostles had already delivered to the Church a formal and explicit statement of divine revelation on this matter before his death? Does what we know of the history of the Canon really support the view that the Church's recognition of the canonicity and inspiration of certain books — gradual process that it was — was based upon awareness of an explicit testimony to that effect dating not merely from apostolic times but from one of the apostles themselves? Was it not rather that the Church recognized, in the case of certain books dating from the period of the Apostolic Church, that they belonged to that period in the proper sense and as such — in other words, that they were written by an apostle and (or) represented the original faith of the Church?[18]

[18] "Apocryphal", in contrast to the inspired canonical books, does not mean in the early patristic era "not having God as the inspiring author, whose authorship is revealed whenever it is present", but rather, "not written by the apostle to whom it is ascribed, and contrary to the Church's teaching, although stemming more or less from the first generation of the Church"; or simply, "as a matter of fact not belonging to the Apostolic Church". And the primary original sense of the term "canonical" is "that which serves as a rule of faith and morals (in contrast to unorthodox or unauthoritative writings) and is *therefore* accepted into a list of such writings". We thus arrive at a distinction between the material content and formal concept of canonicity. The latter is simply inspiration recognized and ratified by the Church; a book is canonical *because* it is approved by the Church *as* inspired, and the Church so approves it because she knows that it is inspired. The material content of the term "canonical" is the recognition and ratification of a book inasmuch as it is "apostolic" (that is, written by an apostle) and (or) is a pure expression of the Church's faith in the first apostolic generation. This material concept of canonicity does not explicitly or formally include the notion of inspiration, and is thus easy for the Church to recognize as being present in a given book, at least easier than the fact of inspiration as such, as a direct datum; the latter could only be known through the explicit testimony of an apostle, which is highly improbable from an historical point of view. Of course, one still has to demonstrate

But if the latter account of the Canon's development corresponds more accurately to the historical facts, how can it be harmonized with our dogmas concerning inspiration and canonicity ? For we must hold both that there is no *inspiratio subsequens,* and that, on the other hand, the inspiration of any given biblical book is a revealed truth, which cannot therefore have been given to the Church later than the end of the apostolic era. These questions cannot be answered at this stage. These preliminary considerations are aimed only at pointing up that we need a material content for the concept of inspiration which can answer these questions without doing violence to the facts or resorting to too many historically unverifiable hypotheses. Our concept of inspiration must itself contain an explanation, without recourse to some historically unimaginable explicit testimony from apostolic times, of *how* the Church knows the inspiration of the New Testament books. Canonicity and inspiration are indeed two distinct concepts, but in view of the problem outlined above and of what we know of the history of the Canon, perhaps a deeper exploration of their close mutual relationship is called for. We must somehow explain how canonicity, in the as yet unformalized form in which it was found in the earliest Church, *de facto* applied only to the truly inspired books, so that a knowledge of their canonicity was in fact equivalent to a knowledge of their inspiration, and we must show this knowledge of their canonicity could be had without a prior explicit knowledge of their inspiration as such.

the legitimacy of the conclusion from this material conception of canonicity to the fact of inspiration, and it must be shown how inspiration can be recognized from canonicity as we have described it. This will be taken up in the second part of our paper.

4. The Inspiration of the Scriptures and the Teaching Authority of the Church

There is yet a fourth problem which can contribute to a correct and adequate understanding of inspiration. This is the relationship between inspired and canonical writings on the one hand and the teaching authority and tradition of the Church on the other. The Church has been accused of involving herself in an insoluble contradiction over this problem. It is, of course, (and rightly so) one of the favourite arguments of Catholic apologetics against the Protestant idea of the Bible and the Church, that the Bible cannot be its own interpreter, that it would be exposed to the caprice of men and unable to speak directly and authoritatively to our own historical (and therefore new) situation unless there were a living teaching authority to give it a relevant and authentic interpretation at each new stage of history. From this point of view, the familiar Catholic explanation of the relation between Bible and Church has an easy run. It presumes the existence of Scripture, and shows that it needs a teaching authority in order to fulfill its own function as living, judging Word of God to the men of each new age.

In point of fact, however, this account of the mutual relation of Bible and Church by no means settles all questions connected with it. This objection can be raised (and Protestant theologians have lately shown a growing tendency to raise it): the Church fixes the Canon of the Holy Scriptures and testifies to their inspiration. She does this by virtue of a teaching authority which claims and must claim for itself infallibility if the books are to be really canonical, serving as an absolute norm for faith and theology. Unless the teaching authority is itself "canonical" in this sense, the Bible cannot be so either.[19] Now, by herself testifying absolutely (that is through her official teaching power) that the Scriptures are absolutely authoritative, canonical, and inspired, the Church seems to involve herself in a contradiction. Either she evacuates the force of her own authoritative, "infallible" magistery in favour of the Bible, as the infallible Word of God (although she needs that very infallible magistery to certify the Bible's authority), or else she evacuates the absolute authority of the Bible at the very moment when she certifies it. For in the latter case (where she does not give up her own authority in favour of the Bible's) she subjects the Scriptures to her own magisterial interpretation; it is she who decides what the Scriptures can and do say. More briefly: why an infallible teaching authority if there is an infallible Scripture? Why an infallible Scripture if there is an infallible teaching authority? A truly infallible teaching authority ought to be able, in complete independence of the Bible, to pick out unerringly and to proclaim whatever is true and divinely revealed in the empirically given stream of opinions and human traditions handed down orally from the days when Christ wrought and revealed our salvation.[20] The Church's teaching authority has in fact made

---

[19] If, in order to get past this difficulty, we surrender with regard to both Bible and Church the absolute authority which evangelical Protestants traditionally ascribe to the Bible, and Catholics to the Bible *and* the Church, then, whether we like it or not, we shall find ourselves outside the pale of historical Christianity. Then all that is truly Christian in faith and doctrine would be the ever-new "event of faith", having no absolutely authoritative and unique origin at a determined point in space and time where salvation was wrought once for all. Faith alone would then make Scripture.

[20] It should be noted that this presupposition has been commonly made in Catholic theology since Bellarmine. It is not a certain one, as we shall show later.

infallible pronouncements without founding them in the Bible: what need has such an infallible teaching authority for an infallible Bible, if it can transmit the divine revelation inerrantly without it?

If one says, in answer to the first objection, that the Bible cannot interpret itself, that it needs an infallible interpreter, then one is in effect saying that the Bible can claim no priority over other traditions when it comes to finding out just what is of divine revelation; both are equally in need of a teaching authority if the divine revelation in them is to be unerringly discerned. The Bible would then be as little capable as tradition of fulfilling its ultimate purpose of imparting God's truth to men, without an authority superior to both, which, again, could perform the same task by itself without the support of the Scriptures. The presence of an infallible teaching authority deprives the Bible of any specific function which could not be performed equally as well without it; for the Bible to be the inerrant Word of God has little meaning, unless the Word can achieve its effect, and this power to achieve its effect must be a property of the Word of God itself. Thus, it is argued, we have to face the dilemma that, if we decide for the Scripture, we do not know where to find this authoritative Scripture; if we decide for the authority of the Church, we cannot seriously maintain authoritative writings beside it.

One opinion suggests seeking a middle path which will keep the rivalling authorities intact by separating them from each other in time: in the time of the Apostolic Church we have tradition, the oral testimony of salvation through Christ, enjoying, like all prophetic messages, authoritative character. This testimony, however, was later given such unambiguous and complete expression in the Scriptures that these replace the tradition; they become, as it were, its second self. Henceforth there remains in the Church only a teaching authority which is fully and unequivocally subordinated to the Bible, utterly dependent upon it, and possessing only as much authority (when really important decisions are at stake) as the individual Christian finds supported by the Bible. Individual protests against any decision of the Church by appeals to Scripture are possible. The individual member of the "Church ill-informed" of the present can always appeal to the future "Church better-informed" by the Bible.

Naturally we could answer this whole problem by simply asserting it has pleased God to grant to the Church an infallible teaching authority together with an inspired, holy, and inerrant Book, and that God himself will take care, through the activity of the Holy Spirit in both Bible and Church, that neither will contradict the other. To this we could add that, although it is true that the Church could get along without the Scriptures and rely solely on her infallible teaching office, this does not exclude the possibility that God could have granted her inspired books as a subsidiary (though non-essential) help for the easier performance of her proper function. The Spirit of God guides and enlightens the Church's teaching, so it is said; it need not be feared that it would ever violate the Bible. It would always understand the Bible in the sense in which it was written. Consequently it is not true that an infallible teaching authority would necessarily derogate from the authority of the Bible—even though the teaching authority apparently has no absolute need for the Bible, and is actually more independent, more extensive in the content of its teaching, and more immediate in addressing the Christian consciousness, than is the Bible. We do not dispute this argument, at least not in its general tenor. We shall point out later some needed qualifications. We would also agree that this answer to the objection we are considering is quite adequate on the level of apologetics. But it seems to us a rather dangerous theological positivism simply to assert that God has freely determined to give his Church two infallible instances, where one would have sufficed, and that there is no more to be said about it — this is God's free decision, which we have but to accept.

One may, if one wishes, renounce any attempt to explore the relation between Bible and teaching authority; one can plead that the two are simply given and that, having no objective common root, other than their common establishment by God, they have no intrinsic correlation or mutual reference to each other. But in so doing, one must ask oneself whether such a position does not involve renouncing for the dogmas of the Church that measure of intelligibility which, in the practical order at least, is needed for a solid and enduring faith on the part of the majority of men, even though the abstract possibility of faith remains. A positivism of this sort might have all the appearances of a prudent and humble faith, professing as it does, to be averse to "speculations" of any kind. In the long run, however such blind assertion generates a feeling that that which is accepted as a purely positive datum is in fact improbable, and thus paves the way for disbelief.

Naturally it is not possible, either at this stage or anywhere else in our essay, to give a comprehensive answer to this problem. We would have to deal at length with the teaching authority and the Church in general. But one other question deserves mention, not in order to discuss it in full, but to indicate what

34

a wide range of questions an exhaustive treatment of inspiration would involve. For the more a single theological question is capable of stirring up the whole of theology, the more reason we have to assume that the question has been asked correctly and is being studied in the right perspectives.

It is easy to see the connection of our problem with the old one of the sufficiency of Scripture. One might think that this question is settled for Catholic theologians, that Catholic faith demands that tradition (together with the teaching authority which bears it) be preserved as a material source of dogma alongside the Bible, and that the relation between the two must be kept sufficiently loose to be justice to this (tacitly assumed) fact. If the Church since the time of the apostles has two sources of faith to draw upon "oral tradition" which cannot be found anywhere in the Bible, then the relation between the two sources must be a loose one; there can be no question of a mutual complementary relation between them whereby they would constitute two elements of a single reality which is not complete without both of them. Without much reflection on the point, theologians in recent centuries have been accustomed to regarding tradition and Scripture as two material sources for the teaching authority, and to assume that, even after the establishment of the inspired and canonical Scriptures, "oral tradition" is still capable of furnishing explicit truths not contained in the Bible. This thesis was believed to have been proved by the teaching of Trent that Bible and tradition are to be accepted with equal respect in establishing the faith and practice of the Church, and also by the argument that, without the "oral tradition" authentically mediated by the teaching authority, we could neither know of the Bible's inspiration,

35

nor tell which books were canonical. The use of the latter argument tacitly supposed that the case of the inspiration and canonicity of the Sacred Books was one among many, and that it could be generalized. However, things take on an altogether different complexion if we recall that Trent actually made no decision at all in this sense. As regards doctrine — as distinct from discipline — the Council declared, in principle, no more than that the teaching office of the living Church is the possessor, custodian, and authentic interpreter of Scripture. The Two-Source Theory (if we may use the expression) is but one possible interpretation of the Council, and one supported by neither the unanimous opinion of the Fathers nor that of the medieval theologians. Moreover, it never claimed general consent in the post-Tridentine period, but remained only an opinion. Furthermore, it may be that the necessity of an oral tradition testifying to the Canon and inspiration of the Bible is not just one among many cases, but a unique phenomenon resulting from the peculiar nature of the relation between Church and Scripture, and therefore not susceptible of generalization. If so, then it is possible to conceive the relation of Bible and teaching authority along the following lines: the integral and full constitution of the Church, according to the plan of God, requires that she produce the Bible and perpetually testify to its inspiration. This Bible is *the* Book of the Church; it is inspired precisely as the book of the Church, and it contains a full and adequate concretization of the Church's primal memory of the days of her birth, when she first heard the revelation of God in Christ. The Church is perpetually conscious that this is her Scripture, canonical and inspired. Precisely this consciousness of the indissoluble existential bond between herself and the Scripture cannot itself be expressed in Scripture in the same way as other truths. But this is from the nature of things a unique case, and, neither in theory nor in fact, does it prove the material insufficiency of the Bible in other matters.

In the case of a human act, the subjects' concomitant self-consciousness cannot be *replaced* by the same self-consciousness grasped as object in an act of reflection. But it would be wrong to conclude from this that there must be other cases which fall outside the range of such objective consciousness. Similarly, the Scriptures, taken as the adequate objectification of the Church's primal self-consciousness, cannot be separated from the same Church's "concomitant" consciousness, itself incapable of being totally objectified in the Scriptures, that they are her Scriptures. This does not prove there must be other objects of the faith-consciousness of the Church which are not contained, even implicitly, in the Scriptures.

It is a further fact that, up to the present day, even in dogmatic definitions which contain truths apparently remote from the Bible, the teaching authority always looks for the "biblical foundation". (It is not our business here to discuss how the theologian is to explain the connection between the biblical statements and the later definitions.) This would seem to be a further justification for doubting that there are really truths of faith ("excepting", of course, the inspiration and canonicity of the biblical books) which are not in Scripture, either explicitly or implicitly, but derive solely from an "oral tradition" coming down to us as an independent source alongside the Bible.

Thus, the validity of the Two-Source Theory appears open to attack both on the theoretical and on the factual level. If this is so, then we have the possibility of rethinking the relation of

Bible and teaching authority in terms of a much more intimate interrelation between the two, and of thus furnishing our initial problem with a substantially simpler and more intelligible solution than the positivistic one mentioned above (namely, that there simply exist two instances, infallible Scripture on the one hand, and, on the other, a teaching authority, which, though it draws upon sources less pure than the Scriptures, can unerringly discern in them what is of divine revelation, and discover there truths which Scripture does not contain — while the Holy Spirit makes sure that the two instances do not come into conflict).

We have in certain points anticipated our later developments. What matters at this stage, however, is to realize that, in order to answer the questions we have raised concerning inspiration, we must be able to make clear from the nature of inspiration itself that the Bible is the Book (not *a* book) and *the* source upon which the teaching authority draws; at the same time we must show that the Bible is the *Church's* book and that the Church is for that reason able to testify to its inspiration. If we can find such an initial understanding of inspiration, then we can hope to solve the problem set forth in this chapter. We shall later be able to show that the principles set forth in this discussion of the relation between Bible and teaching authority are truly relevant to the quest for a deeper understanding of inspiration; conversely, it will become apparent how our own theory of inspiration sheds light on this question of Scripture and tradition.

The objections we have here proposed against the Two-Source Theory should not be understood to imply that the solution we shall propose is not tenable unless the Two-Source Theory is false. We aimed only at indicating some of the more general questions linked with our problem, and at suggesting how a simple and coherent solution of one theological problem may depend upon the right solution of another.

We leave aside other problems that might have been pertinent here. We might, for example, have asked how it is that we can attribute to God the literary authorship of a work, without ascribing to him the specific literary genre of the work; how it is, for instance, that God can be the literary author of the Letter to Philemon, without our having to say that God actually wrote a letter to Philemon.

II

THE THESIS

How ARE we now to answer the questions emerging from the preceding summary considerations? In order to be brief, our answer will have to be very synthetic in character. We shall not develop it immediately from the problems raised, but shall simply present a thesis in systematic form, on the basis of which the answers to our questions will then emerge.

We shall take as our starting-point certain statements from the theology of the Church.

1. God Founds the Church

God wills the Church and brings it into being. His willing of the Church is an absolute will. He wills her existence by a formal predefinition and he wills it within the context of salvation history. This is partly because his design for the Incarnation of the Logos, made absolutely and prior to any free human decision which could have been its motive, includes within itself the founding of the Church. Another reason is that the Church, as distinct from the Synagogue, is the Church of the last days, the final and irrevocable economy of salvation, the concrete representation of God's free, triumphant, unconditional design for our salvation. God does not, therefore, merely appropriate the Church to himself like other works generally of which he is the transcendent cause, and which consequently refer back to him as their author. There is a twofold distinction between God's production of the Church on the one hand, and of all his works in "nature" on the other.

(a) The Church proceeds from a will of God ("will" here means a determinate act, not the faculty) which is absolute; this will is prior to any free human action, yet includes such free action within itself. All creation, it is true, is absolutely willed by God in its simple constitution in being; however, as such this does not yet include the creature's free activity, but precedes it. When, on the other hand, something comes into being which, while remaining a free act of man or the result of such an act, is nevertheless absolutely predefined by God, in such wise that he announces beforehand this absolute will of his and miraculously puts it into effect in a way clearly set off from the normal run of things,[21] — then we no longer have to do merely with

[21] Those who hold for a formal predefinition by God of every action of a free creature (however such predefinition may be conceived) will, in order to distinguish this *(ex supposito)* universal predefinition from that involved in the founding of the Church, necessarily have to introduce into the concept of the latter this element of express prediction and historical statement, which will thus involve a miraculous positive fore-ordination to good on God's part, and not merely his permissive will. Where God formally predefines something through a miraculous prediction and historical intervention, he appropriates the predefined work in a way different from any other (possible) predefinitions of a free human act. For in the case of the latter, the ultimate moral quality of the act, whether good or evil, remains humanly unforeseeable, and thus cannot be said to be predefined by a miraculous activity of God within the world. Since this is not the place to decide

41

God's willing the world as such (and absolutely willing it in its simple constitution in being). What we then have is a qualitatively preferential will of God at certain spatio-temporal points *within* the world, within history. Since these terms of the divine action possess spatio-temporal distinctiveness within the world, they transfer this quality to the divine action itself. We thus have true salvation history: a historical action on God's part, which appropriates to God its object (namely its effect) in a qualitatively higher fashion than any other of his works. In other words: the "works" of salvation history are God's in some other, higher way than the works of nature. In the latter God acts upon the (historical) world, in the former he enacts his own history within the world.

(b) Further: this historical action of God attains its qualitatively unique climax in Christ and the Church. Before Christ it was an action which really appeared on the stage of the world — *olim loquens patribus in prophetis* —, but it reserved to itself the possibility of withdrawal. The final outcome of the dialogue between God and man (as seen from within the world) remained open and unclear before Christ; it was (objectively) still undecided whether it would end in judgment or in grace. More than that, the actual objective realizations of the divine action bore within themselves the possibility of frustration or revocation.[22] For

whether formal predefinition by God of man's free activity is something normal or something extraordinary, we add this second condition for "safety's sake". This element is, as a matter of fact, present in the founding of the Church, and even if it were not necessary, it helps explain more clearly why the Church is God's work in a special sense, in that he appropriates it to himself through this special form of his activity.

[22] From this angle precisely the positive peculiarity of the Old Testament writings can best be understood. They are *the* enduring element of the Old

example, consider the self-destruction of the Synagogue through its rejection of Christ, and of the shadowy character of the Old Testament sacraments, which could cease to be signs of grace. Both possibilities are excluded in Christ and in the Church. They are the definitive presence of God's grace in the world, an eschatological event of mercy, and end of history.

In summary: God appropriates to himself the founding of the Church in a qualitatively unique fashion, because it is the work (a) of his formal predefinition, which is (b) within the context of salvation history, and (c) eschatological in character.

2. The Apostolic Church[23]

In a further step we affirm that the Apostolic Church is subject to divine intervention in a qualitatively unique manner as distinct from the subsequent preservation of the Church through history.[24] The Apostolic Church (in the first generation) has a

Covenant, for they are the permanent crystallization of Christ's and the Church's prehistory — indeed the only element of it which still retains its validity. This points up also the negative aspect of the Old Testament: the Word as positive law of God, valid and commanding obedience (and that was the original meaning of the Old Testament), has ceased to be valid in this sense. But this possibility was contained in the Law (as imperative) from the beginning. In this there is a difference from the New Testament even as imperative; the latter was proclaimed and written from the outset as definitively valid.

[23] We shall attempt to clarify the precise meaning of this theological concept. For the time being, we shall simply define it as the Church during the time of her foundation, in the first generation, during which she is still in the process of being born.

[24] We do not thereby wish to deny the many similarities between the influence exercised by God on the Apostolic Church and that exercised on the later Church. For the most part (and rightly) it is these similarities which are emphasized, rather than the differences.

43

singular and irreplaceable function for all the rest of the history of the Church,[25] so that what has been said in the preceding section about the Church as instituted by God applies to the Apostolic Church in a special way; indeed, it applies to the Church of later ages precisely by reason of her foundation upon the Apostolic Church. This is not to deny that, in terms of the mission and powers entrusted to her, it is of the nature of the Church thus founded to last through all ages and to exist in every generation. Nevertheless, the first generation had a unique, irreplaceable function.

Precisely the Catholic conception of the nature of the Church as willed by God forbids us to think in merely actualistic terms, as if the Church were no more than the ever-recurring event of faith. The Church has, as part of her divinely given nature, an institutional character; she is a historically tangible being, and endures and perdures as such through history. This implies that she begins to exist at a given point, and then continues in existence in such a way that the quality of her continued existence is determined by the quality of her beginning. What comes later rests upon what was earlier; later forms, in spite of their evolution and development, exist only because of their derivation from the given origin (the Apostolic Church), not merely

[25] In addition to the better known modern discussions of the primacy concentrating around the extent to which Peter and the apostles may have possessed functions which were not transferable to successors, cf. also: P. Gaechter, "Die Wahl des Matthias" in *Zeitschrift für katholische Theologie,* 71 (1949), pp. 318-46 (especially pp. 318-33); E. Kredel, "Über den Apostel-begriff" in *Zeitschrift für katholische Theologie* 78 (1956), pp. 137-68; A. Vögtle, "Der Petrus der Verheißung und der Erfüllung" in *Münchener Theologische Zeitschrift,* 5 (1954), pp. 1-47; O. Cullmann, *The Early Church. Studies in Early Christian History and Theology,* ed A. J. B. Higgins, Philadelphia 1956. Obviously we cannot enter into this discussion here.

because they derive from their originating cause (God). They derive from their foundations, not merely from him who laid the foundations.

This foundation, however, is not Christ alone, but the community which he gathered around himself while here on earth, and on which he bestowed his Spirit on the first Pentecost (another essentially unique occurrence). That this is so is pointed up by the existence of juridical and sacramental apostolic succession, as well as the *paradosis* of the teaching and commission of Jesus to his disciples, together with the foundation of the credibility of this message through the transmitted testimony to the resurrection. These phenomena suggest not merely the transmitting of something, so that it is also present afterwards, but also that the reason for its being present later is precisely because it was there in the first place, because the first transmitter had something to transmit, together with the authorization to transmit it; what is present later and possesses authority remains for ever dependent on the earlier presence and authority of the first transmitter and his message; these positively and negatively determine the extent of all possible later development.

Thus it would not be correct to say that God's founding of the Church consists simply in his conserving her in existence; rather, we must say that an essential part of his conserving it in existence consists in his having founded it at a particular moment in time. God, then, as founder of the Church, has a unique, qualitatively not transmissible relationship to the Church's first generation, one which he does not have in the same sense to other periods of her history, or rather has to the latter only through the former. To contest this would be to deny implicitly that, for example, revelation was closed with the death of the last apostle; it would betray a failure to understand that Peter and the apostles were not only the first pope and bishops, but that the Bible ascribes to them unique and nontransferable qualities over and above that.

Hence, the act of the founding of the Church is ultimately qualitatively different from that of her conservation. The theologians have expressed this by labelling the preservation of the permanently constituted Church, considered as possessing its own (though not substantial) act of being, an *assistentia per se negativa*. But this cannot be said of the act of institution as such. Hence, we must say that God, in instituting the Apostolic Church and not merely conserving it, appropriates it to himself in a qualitatively unique fashion, just as the act of being born and the subsequent act of living do not have, qualitatively, the same connection with the mother.

The beginning must therefore enjoy an originality, an irreducibility and a purity in the expression of its own essence which, necessary as subsequent evolution must be, are proper only to this first phase. (This distinction does not, of course, mean that what follows the first phase is a merely human product, a Christian "history of religion", a man-made theology with its evolution; rather, it is Church history, dogmatic theology and evolution of dogma as the divinely effected unfolding through the Spirit of the virtualities of the divinely instituted beginning.) Since the Apostolic Church[26] is precisely the Church's initial

---

[26] This expression must be taken in the precise sense which we have given it: the time when revelation is still in the process of being given, before the period in which it is simply handed on; in other words, the time of the Church's coming into existence, as over against its merely continuing in existence.

moment, *out of which* later developments are subsequently to proceed, its nature is to be inchoative and thus as yet unable to direct the course of its own development. As the Church *in fieri,* it is in a very special sense God's work: *deum habet auctorem.* Conversely, this Apostolic Church is not only the first period of the Church in time, but the permanent ground and norm for everything that is to come. It reveals the principles according to which the whole further course of the Church is steered.

Naturally, two factors have to be remembered: (a) this original institution itself has a duration measurable by physical time and is not just a single instant of time. We may simply say that it is the time of the first generation, which, naturally, cannot be ended on a certain calendar date — unless one wishes to hold (as one might well do) that this first generation in our special sense ends on the day when the last apostle died. Theologically speaking, we certainly cannot hold that the Church was already complete on the day of Pentecost. The Church indeed had then visible existence as a community, a legal structure (at least in its basic traits) and the Holy Spirit. Still, she was not yet complete. There really existed, in the literal sense of Batiffol's term, an *église naissante,* the Church in the process of birth, and the process took a certain amount of time. In order to understand this point, we have only to recall that the Church, whose "only" mission, as is rightly said, is to conserve and interpret divine revelation, did not yet possess its complete being at Pentecost for the simple reason that there was further revelation after Pentecost (v. g. concerning the Canon of Scripture). The Apostolic Church had both more and less than the later Church's mission of conservation and interpretation; it had more because it was still to receive new revelation, and it had less because it

47

did not yet possess all the truths which the later Church was given to preserve, since they had not yet all been revealed.

(b) As the later Church, so also the Apostolic Church, in the course of its coming into being, had to deal with phenomena which were incompatible with its true essence and fully realized nature; one might compare the conflicts in Jerusalem, the aberrations in Thessalonica and Corinth, and so on. As the ultimate and eschatological dispensation, the Church, both in the apostolic period and later, needs the capacity to distinguish herself from elements which are foreign to her nature and yet *de facto* crop up within her. Without this capacity she could not be what she must be; she would be in danger of becoming untrue to her own nature; she could be Synagogue instead of Church.[27]

Now this capacity for clear expression of her own essence and for setting herself off from all pseudo-Christian and pseudo-Churchly phenomena must have been present in the Apostolic Church in a special measure, and must be possessed by the later Church in special dependence on the Apostolic Church. The Church must possess this capacity at all times. Otherwise time could eventually transform her into her opposite; she would cease to be a historically tangible concretization of God's grace in Christ

---

[27] This explains why there was not and could not be, in the Old Covenant, the formation of a Canon with the same definitiveness and authority which the Church possesses for both New and Old Testament. Inasmuch as it remained possible for the Synagogue to fall away from God, it could not have the same power as the Church of distinguishing infallibly between what is foreign to her nature and what is in accord with it. The Church can never lose the truth, because God has willed — *praedefinitione formali* — that in the "last times" of the irrevocable incarnation of the Logos, this should be no longer possible. We shall return to this point later.

and would be reduced to a purely "spiritual", or "ideal", form of existence. But this capacity for self-definition must bear a special connection with the Apostolic Church. For once the Church is in possession of a tangible and unambiguous Canon, available as a historically-given reality for the Church of all times, she can pursue her task of self-definition with relative ease by reference to this Canon. She then has a visible and historically tangible norm to go by. The crucial question is thus the establishment of this Canon. How accurately the norm is later applied is an important question too, of course, but of secondary importance in comparison with the question of the correctness of the norm itself. Hence, the highest point of the Church's faculty of self-possession and self-definition must occur there where the Church does not merely measure herself against the given norm, but actually produces the norm by which she is to measure herself. We must remember that the Church's formal teaching authority and the promised assistance of the Spirit have neither the purpose nor the capability of taking the place of a material norm of Christian faith and morals. It is guaranteed to her teaching and pastoral office that it will be able to apply the norm correctly, but not that it will be able to judge later phenomena without the help of a historically tangible and material norm.

3. The Scriptures as Constitutive Element of the Church

The Bible, too, belongs to the constitutive elements of the Apostolic Church which was the qualitatively unique work of God and permanent "canonical" origin of the later Church. We say "among", because the essentially constitutive elements of the

Apostolic Church must include all those things which are considered constitutive elements of the Church in general (believing possession of the transmitted revelation, the *ius divinum* of the primacy and apostolic succession, sacraments, socially organized unity of the faithful), in addition to numerous other elements peculiar to the Apostolic Church (Peter, the apostles, their function as bearers of revelation). What we mean to say is this: granted the priority within the Apostolic Church, as the Church's initial stage, of the oral *paradosis* possessing both authority and infallibility, God freely, but for reasons into which we can gain some insight, made the Bible a constitutive element of tne Apostolic Church.

The facts involved in this proposition are not open to question. For (a) the Holy Scriptures exist, and (b) they are essentially the Church's book; they are recognizable as sacred only through her, they are given to her, only she can interpret them and thus bring their inner nature to actualization. The concrete, fully realized essence of the Church includes the Scriptures; they are a constitutive element of her.

This proposition needs no further proof, but it does need some explanation. In its origin and essence the Bible is undeniably God's word to man, but it is just as fundamentally[28] the Church's self-expression of her faith, a written record of the Apostolic Church's faith and of her self-constitution. To deny this would be to deny that the New Testament writers were real authors and would be to reduce them to mere transmitters

---

[28] This "just as fundamentally" must of course be further justified; it has to be shown, in other words, how the fundamental nature of the Bible is such that it is at the same time word of God and self-expression of the Church, and both in dependence upon the other.

of a message from above. This would go counter to the concrete character of these writings: their *genus litterarium* is that of a testimonial to belief, not merely a record of revelation. It is not true that in some way and in some place or other a book was composed *Deo auctore,* and that the Church, subsequently recognizing this book as a communication coming to her from God, took it over, authenticated it, and adopted it as a textbook in the faith. The origination of the New Testament writings was a vital operation of the Church herself: they are the written embodiment of that which she transmitted and preached as her faith. They are writings which came into existence as manifestations of the Church's life, as letters, exhortations, sermons, and so on. This means that, from the very beginning, a fundamental character of the Scriptures is the fulfilment of the role which we have in general ascribed to the Apostolic Church as distinct from the later Church: to be not only the earliest phase in time, but also the permanent source, the Canon and norm for the Church of later eras. And now we see more clearly: it is precisely through the Scriptures that the Apostolic Church performs this function. The Bible is not merely an externally adopted indifferent instrument of the Apostolic Church in performing this task; her normative function for the future Church was exercised precisely by reducing to writing her *paradosis,* her faith, her self-constitution. [29]Conversely, her production of the

[29] Writing essentially implies the intention of preserving and keeping for later; the writer addresses himself to the future. Even in ancient times, writing (in which it was taken for granted, though in differing degrees, that the receiver would preserve the letter written to him) was not merely a means of bridging separation in space, but also a link with the future. Otherwise there would have been no point in keeping what was written, or in using stone and similar durable materials unsuitable for transpor-

Scriptures came about precisely as the form in which she constituted herself the normative law for the Church's future course.[30] It was by producing the Scriptures that the Apostolic Church gave evidence of that unique power of self-definition which, as we saw earlier, she needed in order to be the "canon" for the later Church.

4. The Thesis

If what has been said in the preceding sections 1–3 is correct, then we reach the following conclusion: *by the fact that* God wills and creates the Apostolic Church with a formal predefinition that is within salvation history and eschatological in character (1–2), and thereby so wills and creates her constitutive elements (3), God wills and creates the Scriptures in such a way as to

tation. We may safely assume similar intentions in both the writer and the recipient who conserves the writing: the writer, too, has more than his own contemporaries in mind.

[30] We do not necessarily wish to maintain, for our purposes, that the Apostolic Church deposited her entire oral *paradosis* in Scripture. It is possible to leave this question open and still accept our basic thesis. Whether or not there are good reasons for rejecting the sufficiency of Scripture as a material source of dogma (apart from the case of the Church's definition of the Canon), is another question. We have already suggested why this question is of some importance for the problem of the relation between the teaching authority of the Church and Scripture, and consequently for the nature of inspiration. Nevertheless the sufficiency of Scripture is not essential to our theory of inspiration. But the entire relationship between teaching authority and Scripture would be much clearer and simpler if we could assume that the tradition of the Apostolic Church, to the extent that it is to serve the later Church as an authoritative norm to which she has access as a definite and tangible reality, was deposited in the Scriptures. This would certainly make our thesis even clearer, but, as we have said, the thesis does not necessarily involve it. We shall return later to this question.

become through his inspiration their originator, their author. The important phrase is "by the fact that". The Scriptures are not produced merely "on the occasion of" or "in the course of" God's production of the Apostolic Church; rather, the active inspiring activity of God is an inner moment in the formation of the Apostolic Church and derives from this fact its peculiar character. God wills the Bible together with his own authorship of it, and he posits both because, and to the extent that, he actively and effectively wills his own authorship of the Church. Assuming what was said above in section 3, the inspiration of Holy Scripture is nothing else than God's founding of the Church, inasmuch as this applies to precisely that constitutive element of the Apostolic Church which is the Bible.

5. Inspiration and the Old Testament

We have not yet broached the question of whether our proposed thesis can also explain the inspiration of the Old Testament. For reasons of method we have until now used data which pertained primarily to the Church and to the New Testament. Perhaps our whole theory breaks down at this point. The Old Testament is inspired no less than the New, and in the same way. How can our theory of inspiration be extended to the Old Testament? It seems we must either assume that the Old Testament has a different species of inspiration than the New (which is unacceptable), or else that it is not inspired at all (which is heretical). Hence we must perforce confront this problem.

Before doing so, however, let us first consider a few points which are often overlooked. Although inspiration and canonicity are two conceptually and really different matters, they are not therefore independent of each other. And this not merely because canonicity presupposes the inspiration of the book which it attests for the Church. There is also a certain relation of mutual dependence. Without making canonicity an intrinsic element in the concept of inspiration, it is true to say that inspiration, in its fullest meaning, is present only when it is authentically attested, that is when its canonicity is recognized. God does not write books for his own benefit; whatever God writes must necessarily be adressed to someone and makes sense only if it "arrives". It must be recognized *as* having been actually written by God, and this recognition must have that certainty which is required in order that the writing may be truly effective as God's authoritative word. Hence inspiration is meaningless without canonicity.

Now the Synagogue, unlike the Church, does not have the authority to testify infallibly to the inspiration of the Scriptures. Even prior to the death of Christ, there existed no authoritative teaching *office* in the Old Testament, in the sense of a permanent institution formally endowed with inerrancy. There were individual prophets, but no infallible Church, for the eschatological event, the final and irreversible salvation act of God, had not yet occurred. It was possible for the Synagogue to apostatize from God, to turn a "No" to him and to his "Anointed" into its own official "truth", thus bringing about its own end as a divine institution. Not that the Old Testament period was altogether without knowledge of inspired and canonical sacred books. There were writings which were recognized as inspired, and, more decisively, these ideas about the meaning and extension of canonicity were recognized and ratified for themselves by Jesus, the apostles, and the Church. If, in the pre-Christian era, there appeared prophets commissioned by God to deliver his message and call men to faith, then there is no reason why there should not have existed a knowledge — ultimately grounded in the prophetic charism itself — of the inspiration of Holy Scripture and of its essential relation to the Jewish religious community (its canonicity). Such knowledge was in fact present. But it must be remembered that neither the extent not the certainty of the Canon was, or even could be, definitively established in pre-Christian times. Sacred books were written after the time when prophets existed no longer: the sacred writer need not have been a prophet himself; certainly the writers of much of the late wisdom literature would hardly have laid claim to a prophetic commission which bears witness to itself without needing any support or certification from the Synagogue or other external authority. Yet the Synagogue, as distinct from the prophets who appeared in it from time to time, was not, as a religious institution, empowered to give definitive testimony to the inspiration and canonicity of sacred books. If this is so, a final definition of the Canon was impossible before the time of the Church. An inchoative knowledge of inspiration and a start on the formation of a Canon was there possible, because (and to the extent that) prophetic charism was there to support it. But no more than that. It is not surprising, therefore, that the Church, even in the case of the Old Testament, herself completed the formation of the Canon and did not simply take over the Jewish canon as final and definitive.[31]

---

[31] The rejection by Protestants of the inspiration and canonicity of the deutero-canonical books, on the grounds that they were not recognized by the Synagogue, contradicts the fact that all the writings of the Old

There is a more important conclusion: given that the whole process of the formation of the Old Testament writings was brought to completion only in the New Testament (as regards its canonicity, and hence, as we have said earlier, as regards the perfection of inspiration involved in its "arriving" at its hearers), then it follows that ultimately God effected the production of the Old Testament books to the extent that they were to have a certain function and authority in the New Testament. The Old Testament is then not merely *de facto* an account of the Church's prehistory and the truths communicated in the course of it; if the completion of the Old Testament could be reached only in the New, then the Old Testament is by its very essence *pre*-history.

Then, along the line of our thesis, we may make the following

Testament (even apart from the reasons we have just mentioned) are directed towards Christ and the New Testament, and are a part of salvation history only because of this direction, and can be recognized as such only by virtue of it. This is not to say that no Old Testament book could be recognized as canonical until after Christ; even earlier, to the extent that they were grasped as essentially prophetic, incomplete, and open to some future revelation, the Old Testament books were already recognized as "pre-Christian" — indeed this is the only sense in which they could have been understood as the work of God. If this reference to the future belongs to the essence of the Old Testament, we may ask whether this essence is preserved and respected if an historical gap is introduced between the canonical Old Testament history and Christ of such dimensions as to constitute a real hiatus between that history and its fulfilment in Christ. If such a break is inadmissible, then we must ask: after the "cessation" of prophecy, where are we to locate the influence of God by which post-exilic history continued to be true salvation history ordered toward Christ? Against Marcionism and similar tendencies in the early Church, the Church has declared the Old Testament to be truly her own prehistory, and hence a part of her own as yet hidden life (the "Church since Adam and Abel," etc.); this prehistory cannot have come to a close long before the appearance of the Church, or have been reduced for a long interval to a merely human religious evolution.

statement: to the extent that God produces for the Church the Old Testament as the authentic crystallization of her prehistory and of her experience with God and his dealings with men in that prehistory, God inspires the Old Testament and makes himself its author. Or: because, and to the extent that, the Old Testament itself belongs to the constitution of the Church (and not merely of the Synagogue) as an element of the Church's prehistory — precisely that element which retains its vitality, in contrast with the elements which were abrogated, since it is the record of the events of that prehistory and the permanently valid truths communicated by God in the course of it —, to that extent what is true of the New Testament is also true of the Old: it is inspired as an element in God's formally predefining production of the Church.

Thus our thesis concerning the inspiration of the New Testament is not refuted by the inspiration of the Old Testament. On the contrary, the facts mentioned above (and others omitted for the sake of brevity) make it apparent that the Old Testament and its writings bear an essential dynamic relation to the New Testament and are thus subject to the same forming principles as the New Testament. A conclusion which follows from this insight was already mentioned by way of anticipation in Footnote 22.

III

CONCLUSIONS

OUR THESIS once explained, two tasks still await us: first, to show, briefly but explicitly, how our conception safeguards the essential elements traditionally postulated for divine authorship and inspiration, and secondly (and this is our main concern here), to point out in somewhat greater detail how our approach to inspiration paves the way for a more satisfactory solution to the problems raised in the first part of our investigation.

1. Given our thesis, it follows immediately that God is the originator of the Bible, its author. This being so, the Church's dogma of God's authorship of the Bible at least does not contradict our theological thesis.

We argue as follows:

With a formal predefinition which is within the context of salvation history and eschatological in character, God wills and produces the Scripture as a constitutive element in the foundation of the Apostolic Church,[32] because and to the extent that it is

---

[32] God's activity is here considered in terms of three properties which have to be taken in conjunction before we arrive at the precise form of divine activity discussed here. a) It is a formally predefining activity (analogous to efficacious grace). b) It belongs as such to the visible history

in precisely this way that he wills and effects the Apostolic Church's existence.

But: whoever effects a book in this way is its author in the proper sense, for in our limited human language there is no other word than "authorship" to designate such a form of influence upon the production of a book, even granting that

of salvation. It operates within the historical, tangible, categorical dimension of this world, and both the divine activity and its predefining character are expressly revealed and foretold within this historical dimension. A *merely* transcendent and, as it were, anonymously operating predefinition of a human act would be insufficient to make the result of that act in any special way appropriated to God.

For this, more is needed than simply the transcendent predefining act whereby God directs the world as a whole and everything that happens in it (abstracting from the question of whether this *always* involves formal predefinition); the act must have a particular point of insertion at a certain especially suitable place in space and time (in preference to any such place), that is, it must be miraculous and historical. Only thus can the result of such an act pertain to God in such a way that it can be attributed to him (by analogy, of course) in a categorical sense, as when we say that God is the *author* of Scripture. c) This predetermining activity within salvation history has the same eschatological and final character for Scripture as we claimed for the foundation of the Church, in contrast to pre-Christian salvation history. This is not contradicted by the fact that there were inspired writings before Christ. For these were willed by God from the beginning as books of the eschatological community of the redeemed, and are for that reason the only remainder from the Old Testament which is a living and valid reality in the Church.

These three factors taken together bring the origin of the Scriptures into an incomparably close relationship of dependence upon God, one that can best be expressed by calling God their originator and author. We must remember that the relation between an author and his book is a fluid thing even in the human realm, and not as *in indivisibili* as is normally presumed in the theology of inspiration. The human author can be more or less original; he may range from the creative thinker down almost to the merely transcribing "secretary" of his environment and his times, simply repeating the current clichés of speech and thought. Hence there should be no difficulty in characterizing God's authorship, as developed in our essay, as authorship in the eminent sense.

certain peculiarities inevitably associated with human authorship are not present in God's case, so that the concept can be applied to both God and man only by analogy.

Therefore: God is the author of the New Testament writings.

After what we have said in the second part of this essay, the major and minor of our syllogism hardly need further comment. We would add only one remark. We have shown earlier that the official concept of inspiration, as explained by recognized theologians, may be taken in a very abstract and formal sense. How the elements of the concept are concretely realized by God is left largely open. We have said that inspiration requires no more than that God, willing the production of a certain definite book, influence the human writer in such wise as efficaciously to ensure that he will actually form a correct conception of what he is to write *(iudicium speculativum et practicum)*, will effectively decide to write down what he has so conceived, and will actually execute this decision. This is all that is required for the divine authorship, regardless of how we suppose that God concretely carries out this divine predefinition. But in case this conception should be found disturbing by some, we may add the following consideration.

The highly complex process, by which God brings the Apostolic Church into being, while possessing according to the divine plan a uniformity of structure, becomes specific in each single constituent (for instance Scripture) which takes place within the total result (Apostolic Church) which at any one time is intended. It would certainly not be irreconcilable with our basic idea to require a special kind of divine activity for the realization of a particular constituent (v. g. the composition of the Church's Book) which would not be needed for the realization of another

60

constituent. If then, for some reason, more is thought to be needed for an adequate concept of inspiration than what we have set forth as necessary, this would not contradict our fundamental idea that God's inspiration of the sacred books is an intrinsic constituent of his founding of the Church.

Moreover, the divine impulse which is inseparable from his will to establish the Church must, in the case of his inspiration of the Scriptures, necessarily reach into the human author's mind and will; otherwise no *book* could be written. In this sense, at least, we must affirm the interiority of inspiration. Still, that this impulse operates within the spiritual faculties of the human writer does not necessarily imply that it must also have its initial point of impact there. (The ultimate hearth from which this impulse radiates is God's miraculous, "categorical" action in salvation history; in our case the radiation of the impulse from this centre is itself directed by a formal predefinition of God.) We also know that every book necessarily bears an intrinsic dependence upon the vital context in which it arises, both with respect to the occasion of its writing and its contents; if this were not so, no one would be able to understand it. Hence, it is really an enhancement of the divine inspiration if it can be inserted into the context of salvation history. The life-situation within which, and out of which, the Scriptures arise is God's astonishing and mighty work of manifesting himself in human history through the prophets and through his Son. The Scriptures' (formally predefined) emergence from this vital context is what makes them Scriptures.

2. Finally we come to the task of showing why our theory of inspiration offers a better solution than others to the many problems indicated in the first part of our investigation. This

will also make clear that more is here at stake than the relatively meaningless logical feat of subsuming a narrower concept (God's inspiration of the sacred books) under a broader one (his active, predefining establishment of the Church) by pointing out that the two concepts have certain formal elements in common (*praedefinitio formalis*), and linking them in a part-whole relationship.

a) Our theory makes it easier to understand how both God and man can be authors of the same writing. First of all, it becomes clear that the two authorships by no means effect the same result. In a certain sense, God does not *want (intentione prima et per se)* to be a "writer"; he is one only because what he does want cannot otherwise be realized. The execution of his primary and ultimate purpose can be attained only through making a *human being an author*. The common understanding of inspiration would have it that God's purpose would be achieved most perfectly if the human author were a mere secretary. We hold exactly the opposite. The human writer himself truly wills the writing of a book, and that he should so will is ultimately what God intends. God wills the establishment of a supernatural and historical community of salvation, objectifying itself (and thus attaining full self-realization) in a book. But by willing this efficaciously and absolutely, and in the historical and eschatological order (so that his willing of it involves strictly divine interventions *within* the created historical process), God is *eo ipso* an author in the true sense of the word. Therefore the two authorships are ultimately distinct, and can therefore both be predicated of the same book; there is no need to reduce either of them to a merely nominal authorship, or mistakenly combine them into a kind of teamwork.

If the term "principal author" is used of God, and "second-ary" or "instrumental author" used of the human writer, then, according to our theory, this cannot be taken to mean that this is simply one among many cases of this form of relationship. This case is unique. Apart from the instance of inspiration, a "principal author" is an impossibility: either the "instrumental author" will be a mere secretary and thus no author at all, or, if he is an author, the "principal author" will be only the "stimu-lator" or "promoter" of the writing, not its author.

We shall also be able to understand more easily why the his-tory of God's authorship has no further continuation. In the formal concept of inspiration there is no reason why this should not happen. And merely to appeal to God's free positive will is theology's easiest way out and should be used only sparingly. Neither is it sufficient reason to say that revelation is closed, for new books could easily be written even about a completed revelation, and God could be their author. But if God appears as "author" only where the Church is yet in the process of birth (God so acting as to constitute the Church in existence and causing the production of books as a part of this), then his authorship will naturally cease once the establishment of the Church is completed.[33]

We can also better understand why God's authorship, while

---

[33] The closing of revelation and the completion of the Church's founding are obviously related. What is to be understood by "the closing of reve-lation" I have suggested in the article, "The Development of Dogma" in *Theological Investigations,* I, pp. 39-77, esp. pp. 48 *et seq.* When we realize that God's revelation does not cease "because he decides to stop speaking, though he could say more", but because the eschatological salvific event, which is the only subject of God's speaking, is now fully present, then it becomes apparent why it is the completion of the Church's founding that must be appealed to here, and not the closing of revelation.

remaining authorship in a true and not merely metaphorical sense, is nonetheless *sui generis,* necessarily possessing certain peculiarities which are proper to it alone. No one but God can become an author by making someone else an author. For no one but God can arouse and direct a man's free activity in such wise that his freedom is thereby not diminished, but actually constituted and made most itself. We might say that the human authorship has a *potentia oboedientialis* towards the divine activity, so that God can make it his own and yet not diminish it in the process but rather bring it to its greatest perfection — just as the free and intellectual self-possession which constitutes man as "nature" has the *potentia oboedientialis* of achieving its ultimate perfection in assumption by a divine Person.[34]

It cannot be claimed that all this also holds true in the traditional view of inspiration, inasmuch as this conceives of inspiration analogously with the nature of efficacious grace, just as we do. It is true that this comparison does help to explain how the human writer remains a true author — although the analogy with efficacious grace is generally adduced with opposite intent: namely, to give a sufficient explanation of how *God* is author.[35]

[34] Cf. K. Rahner, "Current Problems in Christology" in *Theological Investigations,* I, pp. 149-200.

[35] If God, for example, were to cause someone, by a formal predefinition such as is had in efficacious grace, to construct a box, God would not by that reason alone become a carpenter, even though the same could be said of this as was said of inspiration: God directs the intellect in the conception and planning of the design, then moves the will to decide on the execution of this design; lastly, he directs the execution itself, so that the finished product matches the original design. Hence, a further element is needed: God must also act upon the *earthly* sphere in such wise that his directing influence takes place *from within* it.

The preceding criticism is based on the common understanding of efficacious grace found in the schools. We certainly do not deny that it

But in fact this comparison alone is not able to show how God, by means of such predefining motion, could become a true author. For this to happen, we must show how God's action, while retaining the quality of the transcendent causality by which it liberates man's autonomy, also takes place within the categorical dimension, within the framework of salvation history.[36] The traditional theory must face the problem of explaining what it conceives this categorical element in inspiration to be, and how this element not only does not degrade the human authorship

would be possible to deepen this concept of efficacious grace, as it is found in the concrete order in which we exist, so that it would also include the element of salvation history (grace, as grace which is always the grace of the incarnate Word; grace which always includes a relation to faith, which comes from "hearing" in a historical context; grace which is always the grace of the Church, proceeding from her and tending towards her). Assuming that this notion of grace, deepened by its relation to salvation history, can (or must) be applied also to efficacious grace *as efficacious,* and using this deepened concept of efficacious grace as a model for explaining the *gratia gratis data* of inspiration, then the question presents itself: where is the factor of salvation history in inspiration? Thus the traditional parallel between inspiration and efficacious grace might itself lead us to the theory we have been proposing in this study.

[36] Not every action of God which has an effect in space and time is thereby an historical action of God. For example, the moving of the sun through the divine *concursus* does not constitute a historical action on God's part, even though the sun's movement occurs in space and time and is therefore itself historical. In miracles and formal self-revelations, God *himself* acts in history; his own action is inserted into the historical chain of events, he does not merely support the chain as a whole. However, God can only accomplish this — we must affirm this, without giving any further reason here — if the event is also manifested to us, if it bears the character of a sign, so that its occurrence and its manifestation are one. A miracle which could in principle remain completely unknown to everybody would really be open to the rationalist's objection to a God who goes about tinkering with the operations of the world he has created.

These considerations alone might suggest to us that canonicity and inspiration are indeed more closely linked than is usually admitted.

to a mere word, but actually permits, nay even demands, its full reality.

b) Our theory also permits a more nuanced approach to the problem of whether the sacred writer is necessarily conscious of his inspiration. If we focus on the abstract concept of inspiration and simply equate it with the whole concrete reality of the process, then the answer will be negative, inspiration is not *per se* conscious. But if we conceive the reality of inspiration concretely as we have tried to do, then our answer will be a qualified "yes".

Certainly the concrete life of the Apostolic Church, as it experienced its own coming into being and objectified this in Scriptures, was conscious (with a consciousness, indeed, possessing supernatural and miraculous components). On the other hand, this conscious vital experience is itself an element in inspiration and its consciousness, at least to the extent that the sacred authors were conscious of their activity as a function of the life of the Church in the process of its self-constitution in the Holy Spirit. Of course this awareness did not have to amount to a direct and reflex equivalent of our formal concepts of inspiration and divine authorship. A New Testament writer according to our view, could to this extent be unaware of his own inspiration, that he did not have to say to himself that *he* was writing *this* (perhaps small and insignificant) section under a special influence from God. Yet he could have been concomitantly conscious of a special "inspiration" by God (of an intellectual and voluntary nature) inasmuch as he knew that the real core of his utterance was given through God's self-revelation in Christ, which occured in his own generation, and was witnessed to by the holy community, to which he belonged and which was now in the process of constituting itself as the norm for its future faith and practice.

Whether such a consciousness would even implicitly contain all the elements involved in inspiration can be left as an open question; we have already seen that there is no difficulty in admitting that inspiration can be altogether unconscious. However, in our theory the conscious elements we have described belong in the concrete order, to the essence of inspiration, and are merely its remote conditions. And to that extent, at least, we may say that inspiration *is* a conscious process. The only one of the above elements which might be lacking in some cases (but not in all!) is awareness of the *permanent* validity of the document being written as a divinely produced testimony of the Church to her *future*. But where this element is in some way present (as, for example in the Gospels), our theory allows us to say that inspiration is in that case *fully* conscious — though perhaps in a sense not common nowadays.

c) We may now also gain a deeper understanding of the way in which the Church recognizes the inspiration of Scripture. It is quite true to say that the inspired nature of a writing can ultimately be known only through a revelation; all other paths of knowledge are of no avail on this point. The only question is how this revelation is actually to be conceived, so that its occurrence and first formulation (both of which are necessary and interrelated) can be conceived with real historical plausibility. Some theologians hold that the apostles must have stated: "This or that writing (or collection) is inspired." It is doubtless true that actual occurrence of this revelation (disregarding for the moment the question of the degree to which this revelation has been consciously perceived) must have come "before the death of the last apostle", as it is somewhat oddly expressed. But how are we to imagine this "statement" by a particular apostle so that his action would seem historically probable?[37] One seems unable to say more than that something like this *must* have happened.[38] But is this postulated process, in the form presented above, historically probable, when we recall the delays and fluctuations in the history of the Canon?

Such historical difficulties are usually explained by stating that the tradition concerning the inspiration of a particular book was first handed down only in an individual community, and that it took a considerable time before the news spread to the

---

[37] A. Bea, *op. cit.,* n. 114, says simply: "Quomodo et cui illa prima revelatio facta sit, plerumque ignoramus." True, the living and authoritative magistery of the Church vouches for the actual occurrence of this revelation, as Bea rightly emphasizes. And that may suffice for the ordinary Christian. But if the teaching authority of the Church contains no new revelation, but only continues to witness, albeit infallibly, to what it has heard, then the *theologian* cannot simply rest satisfied with the testimony of the teaching authority; he must attempt to explain, as far as he can, whence the present magistery derives its doctrine. He must try to show just how this doctrine was first delivered through the lips of an apostle, or is contained in some other doctrine, and so on. But how can this be done, if Bea's proposition is correct and is all that can be said on the subject? It seems unlikely, that at the period when the faith-consciousness of the Church and her teaching authority were reaching clarity on the canonicity of the biblical books, there would have been anyone present who still knew "quomodo et cui illa prima revelatio (of the inspiration of a given book) facta sit".

[38] We do not contest that the bulk of the New Testament writings were transmitted in the apostolic Churches from earliest times as canonical (in a sense which, of course, needs further elucidation). But this does not lessen the problem in regard to the other New Testament writings. And this leads us to ask whether the same problem of recognizing the canonicity may not also have applied to the bulk of the New Testament books and in their case was only solved earlier, at a time which we can no longer penetrate without our having to assume for each writing an explicit and formal tradition going back to an explicit declaration by an apostle, which supposition would lack all historical probability.

whole Church and was universally accepted. But what about those traditional "opinions" in other communities, in which certain writings were accepted as canonical and inspired which actually were not (The Epistle of Barnabas, The Shepherd of Hermas, etc.)? How were the right and wrong traditions differentiated? What was the norm for making such a distinction? It is hard to make it historically plausible that in the one case there was historical evidence that the tradition really stemmed from the express declaration of an apostle, while in the other evidence was found that this was not true. If this objection is valid, how then are we to explain the long development of the Church's knowledge of the inspiration and canonicity of individual writings?

If our proposed thesis is right, we have a way out of this deadlock. We have only to distinguish between the fundamental revelation as such (as a process) concerning the inspiration of a book on the one hand, and the reflex, propositional conception and formulation of this revelation on the other hand. The former must have occurred "before the death of the last apostle", but not the latter. Of course, the two things cannot occur at separate times if, as is usually presupposed, the revelation of the inspiration of a writing can only occur in the form of an explicit statement on the subject. But this is the very presupposition which must be questioned, for our theory shows that it is not at all necessary: this revelation is given simply through the fact that the writing in question is produced as a genuine ingredient of the Apostolic Church's self-realization.[39] In this way its inspiration

---

[39] "Self-realization" does not, of course, mean that in every such (even small and occasional) writing the whole essence of the Church's faith is expressed, but only that it purely reflects (actively and passively) the faith

is sufficiently revealed, unless we are to presuppose that something can only be revealed through a direct statement, and not also through some immediately perceptible fact — a much too narrow and excessively conceptualistic notion of the possibilities of revelation.[40]

This immediately present fact (itself something effected by God's supernatural activity in salvation history) can come to be grasped consciously and given expression in post-apostolic times without the occurrence of any new revelation. This is not contradicted by the necessary assumption that only the Church is endowed with the ability to tell with absolute certainty whether some particular writing dating from apostolic times is an intrinsic and homogeneous part of the Church's self-constitution. In approaching the development of doctrine, we should not imagine that the Church's discrimination of revealed truths from among the body of empirically-given traditions is strictly limited to the forms of conceptual deduction — much less as found in some individual thinker's mind. The Church, filled with the Holy Spirit, recognizes by "connaturality" that a given writing belongs among those which accord with her nature. If at the same time

of the Apostolic Church as such. This relationship obtaining between Holy Scripture and the faith which finds pure and essential expression in it, should not be conceived as if the various New Testament writings, as material-quantitative parts, could add up, piece by piece, to the basic document of faith, v. g. as the parts of a catechism, where each part deals with a new topic and all together add up to form a total catechism. Rather, each part reflects the whole essence of the Apostolic Church's faith, yet in such a way that, while no book is simply a material part, neither is any book, taken alone, the full and adequate expression of the whole. Hence it is not an argument against our view, that many New Testament books, judged from the immediate horizon of the individual human authors, are "occasional" writings.

[40] Cf. K. Rahner, *Theological Investigations,* I, pp. 39–77.

she realizes that it is also "apostolic", that is to say a part of the life process of the Apostolic Church as such, then in accordance with our theory, it is *eo ipso* inspired, and also consciously recognized as such; yet this reflex recognition can take place at a later time and does not have to be identical with the original occurrence of the revelation or even simultaneous with it.

In this way, a history of the Canon becomes a genuine possibility. As long as we continue to think of the Church's awareness of canonicity as the result of an explicit and direct testimony from an apostle, we shall not be able to understand why it took so long before the canonicity of many writings was finally accepted. In such a case one is forced to the subterfuge *(sit venia verbo)* that the whole matter was at one time clear, then through some circumstance or other became obscured, but finally, in a third phase, arrived at definitive and explicit clarity. But this really is a mere subterfuge, for there is no historical evidence for a period of clarity regarding the formal inspiration — and not merely something akin to inspiration — of a particular writing. Such a statement is therefore no more than an *a priori* postulate based on premises which are not at all certain, and which are in addition historically improbable.

If we distinguish, however, between the occurrence of the revelation of a writing's inspiration — and not in any explicit statement about it, but through the actual emergence of this book as a self-expression of the Apostolic Church — and, on the other hand, the conscious knowledge that this writing belongs to the self-constitution of the Apostolic Church, and if we discern precisely in the latter process the recognition of inspiration and canonicity, it then becomes clear that this latter process needs

71

time, and necessarily has a history of its own, while the original revelation of the inspiration (as distinguished from the conscious awareness of it) need not on that account require the same duration. The history of the Canon, with its gropings and vicissitudes, would then be freed of those bewildering aspects with which the current view of inspiration has to grapple.

We might also ask ourselves in this connection whether the essentially correct and indispensable (precisely in our theory!) teaching that an inspired work must have originated before the death of the last apostle (cf. Pesch, *De inspiratione,* no. 602) is not sometimes interpreted in too material a sense. If the "death of the last apostle" signifies the first generation of the Church, the period of her foundation as distinct from her continuation as a body constituted for all time, then the statement is intelligible and incontestable. Less obvious, however, is the assumption that this period of the Church's foundation necessarily ended on the calendar date of the last apostle's death.

At this point we might ask ourselves whether this last deduction from the statement in question is really justified. Are we to assume as an absolute certainty, prior to any detailed investigation of the literary characteristics of, let us say, the Epistle to the Hebrews, 2 Peter, or perhaps even the Pastoral Epistles, that such writings not only belong to the first generation, but also could not have been composed after that particular date? After all, is it really relevant to the knowledge of whether or not some late New Testament writing of a non-apostle is inspired, to say that in some other part of the world there was still an apostle alive (say, John), if it cannot also be made historically plausible that this apostle was acquainted with the writing in question and explicitly testified to its inspiration?

Even if we could assume this, the question would still remain, whence he knew of the inspiration of the writing under consideration. As Christians, we must believe that the men of the Apostolic Church had certain knowledge (through miracles and other means) of God's responsibility for the salvific events of which they were both objects and witnesses. But can we as easily assume that a particular apostle would receive a special and explicit divine revelation of the divine authorship of a certain minor writing? While it is not impossible to accept such an awkward assumption, is it really necessary? Or could we explain this knowledge along the lines which we have suggested? But if our explanation is correct, or at least admissible, must the bearer of the Church's knowledge of inspiration necessarily have been an apostle, or could it not also have occurred in some other way? In the latter case, there seems to be no reason why this knowledge could not apply to a writing which belonged to the first generation, and in this sense to the Apostolic Church, yet was not necessarily written before the death of the last apostle.

No doubt the concept of the "first generation", if one does not regard it as necessarily closed at the very day of the last apostle's death, becomes somewhat imprecise. But this is no great difficulty. For although there might have been a decade or so in which no one could state with absolute certainty whether or not the Apostolic Church was now a thing of the past, nevertheless the time would soon be at hand when it could be said with certainty that it was no more. (We may use the comparison of the approach of death. The fact that there are moments in which it is still impossible to say whether death has actually arrived cannot preclude the fact that there comes a moment when we can say with certainty that it has already occurred. In abstract terms, the necessity for safe criteria for the occurrence of an event — death, the end of the Apostolic Church, and so forth — does not necessarily imply that the criteria must enable one to make the decision at any moment.) Thus, for example, twenty years after the death of the last apostle (around the turn of the first century A. D.), at a time when it was already possible to look back to an earlier and "different" age, it could certainly be stated that the time of the Apostolic Church was over.

d) If the emergence of Scripture as the book of the Apostolic Church is the precise reason why it has God as its author, then the relationship between inspired Scripture and the Church's teaching authority becomes clearer. For we can now understand that these two instances do not cancel each other out, but need one another. The problem involved here has already been developed. Its solution is now to be presented, at least to the extent that this can be done in our context, that is, on the basis of our theory of scriptural inspiration.

The Church, as the institution of the "last times", as God's ultimate community of redemption, cannot be superseded by any other event in time and in the world. She awaits but the glory of God directly revealed. She is invincible and therefore infallible. For she is this Church precisely as bearer and believer of this final revelation of God, which is revealed as the definitive victory of the divine mercy. Otherwise, a new revelation of God would have to supersede her, or else the era of grace could be followed by a historical era of God's wrath and rejection. Hence, where the Church takes possession of her faith in an unconditionally authoritative manner by witnessing (teaching) and by listening (believing), the gates of Hell cannot prevail against her.

Further, if she is hierarchically structured, then the infallibility belongs in the first place to the believing and witnessing messengers of the Lord, the twelve apostles. Their infallibility must be continued, of course, as long as the "last times" perdures and the Church remains in existence. Nevertheless, it is *not only* something, which like a formal power, is freshly given to the Church at each new stage, so that the infallibility of the later time, though similar to that of the earlier, would bear no dependence whatever upon it. The power of the later period is the power of infallibly preserving what came earlier, the power of perseverance in the teaching of the apostles.

This connection with the teaching of the apostles must not be understood only as a connection with the *content* of their teaching. This is also included, but not only this. There is also a connection with the *act* of this teaching and with its infallibility. For any appeal or reference to the earlier teaching would be pointless unless this earlier doctrine is at the same time believed and proclaimed as infallible. The act of inerrant teaching, by which the Church at any given moment in time grasps herself as the community which definitively possesses the truths of salvation, and thereby constitutes herself as Church at that particular moment, is an act performed in virtue of the earlier infallible teaching and is essentially its prolongation in time. It is not merely of the same kind as the earlier act, like two embodiments of the same species; it is the extension in time of essentially the same act. This does not, of course, imply any concrete identity between the two acts, or between their performers.

Now the first act of the Church consisted at least partly in the formation of Scripture. For not only did the teaching of the Apostolic Church *de facto* find expression in Scripture, but Scripture is the canonical presentation of the Apostolic Church's teaching; it came into being precisely as the act of the Apostolic Church teaching authoritatively. While this may not be apparent from the literary form of the individual writings, nevertheless the New Testament authors *were,* on this showing, organs of the Church's self-expression at least to the extent that God intended and effected this. Recognition of this fact requires no more than that the Church still possessed the writing after the end of the apostolic era and recognized in it an authentic expression of the Apostolic Church.

Now if in the Apostolic Church, while she is still in the process of establishing herself, this act of teaching in which she constitutes herself as the norm of faith for herself and for later times (and on which every later act of infallible teaching will bear an essential dependence) takes the form of the composition of Scriptures (leaving aside here the question of whether this first act of the Apostolic Church, wherein it makes itself the norm for later times, is fully or only partially realized in the Scriptures), then it is self-evident that any later infallible teaching of the Church will also essentially appear as an act of referring to Scripture.

There is no clash between two infallible sources. For, to begin with, they are not established independently of each other. These sources do not have to come to some mutual agreement after their constitution in order to avoid cancelling one another out. From the very beginning they are interrelated as two elements in the same essential process. The problem of possible contradiction is eliminated *a priori.* In order to understand the nature of the one, the other must also be understood. The infallibility of the later Church's teaching authority is, by definition, the inerrant interpretation of Scripture, since it includes by definition the connection with the doctrine of the Apostolic Church, which is necessarily the teacher of the later Church through the Scriptures.

If we may presuppose the previously indicated view of the sufficiency of Scripture as against the Two-Source Theory, we can even go a step further and say — if not necessarily, at least as a matter of fact — that the infallible teaching authority of the Apostolic Church, in her function for the future, consists in the capacity for creating the Scriptures, while the infallible teaching authority of the later Church consists in the authentic interpretation of the Scriptures.

Of course these statements would be badly misunderstood if they were taken to mean that in practice they would furnish the individual Christian with a ready-made and sufficient criterion for judging whether the Church was right or wrong in her teaching. In reality, the very fact that the Church proclaims a teaching according to the norms of her office (and only she, not the individual Christian, can judge whether she is so doing), guarantees that the Scriptures are being rightly interpreted.

The Church does not possess the Scriptures merely as a book which she approaches, as it were, from the outside, like an unbelieving historian or exegete, in order to see what use she can make of it for the solution of some question or other. Rather the Church possesses the Scripture as a written document which she continually reads and embodies in her own life. This ever-renewed reading of the Bible in the course of the centuries is a part of her own history, so that reference to her earlier reading of Scripture is a constituent of "oral tradition" which is present without our having to assume for it a strict Two-Source Theory.

This theory has been adopted because it is widely thought that the facts of the development of dogma, as it has actually occurred could not be explained by the principle of material sufficiency of the Scripture and by the total, material dependence of the later Church on the Scriptures. But then we find ourselves in the awkward position of having a book composed by God himself and yet not sufficient — not even in regard to the book's precise function, the communication of divine revelation. In order, then, to understand the sufficiency of the Bible, we might consider the following facts:

i. The sufficiency of Scripture (even rejecting the Two-Source Theory) does not eliminate "oral tradition". Far from eliminating it, it absolutely demands the existence of "tradition" in the sense of a living and authentic teaching authority. (It is well known that difficulties are still encountered in Catholic theology with the attempt to distinguish between the teaching authority, that is "active tradition" and authoritative magistery, on the one hand, and on the other hand "tradition" in the sense of what has been handed down as the authentic teaching of earlier times. Hence, no conceptual sleight-of-hand is involved if we point out that tradition is preserved "alongside" Scripture at least in so far as Scripture itself requires a binding teaching authority on the part of the Church for its proper interpretation.) Further, oral tradition is also preserved to the extent that the Scriptures are present in the Church not only as something written, but also as read and understood, and, as it were, themselves in constant dependence upon the faith of the Apostolic Church out of which they arose, so that the earlier tradition of biblical interpretation is both a norm for the later Church and a part of oral tradition.

ii. The sufficiency of Scripture does not mean that all later unfolding of its meaning, namely development of dogma, can be thrown aside by the individual Christian with the argument that the Bible is enough for him. Precisely because the Scriptures are the expression of the *beginnings,* of the faith of the *primitive* Church, they participate in that historical and evolutionary character of the primitive Church, which is already apparent in the Scriptures themselves; even considered as sufficient, they cry out against any attempt to fossilize them and reduce them to the level of a dead letter. The Church indeed lives entirely on the basis of her beginnings, and thus on the basis of Scripture; once this beginning has been set down as the completion of the Apostolic Church, there can be no other beginning alongside it or apart from it. But it is of the essence of this beginning that it cannot also be the end. It is not the end of theology, nor the end of (the development of) the Church's faith, nor the end of her authoritative teaching.

iii. Rejection of the sufficiency of Scripture would not actually help explain the development of dogma. This becomes apparent when we get down to particular cases. What dogmas of the Church, defined in later times, can more easily be traced back to their origin in the apostolic proclamation of God's original revelation in Christ by seeking their origin in oral tradition rather than in Scripture? There will be no such examples. One could always say, of course, in the case of a dogma whose biblical foundation is hard to find, that it was and had to be contained in the oral tradition, even if this could not be proved. But the same postulate (on our presupposition) can be asserted of Scripture with even greater justification. The later dogma "must" be contained in it, even if the researches of individual theologians cannot make clear how it is contained there. Moreover, in such a case the appeal to oral tradition would be effective only if it could be shown to be a historical fact, or atn least a probability, that there really was such an oral tradition of a particular dogma beside the Scriptures. I know, of course, as an individual Christian, that if the Church defines something as revealed by God, then it must have been contained, implicitly or explicitly, in the original apostolic teaching, and therefore in Scripture or at least in the original oral tradition (either implicitly or explicitly). However, once this conclusion has been reached, it is still the task of theology to consider where and how this presence of the dogma from the beginning can be historically verified. For, conscious as the Church is and must be in her definitions of the connection between the dogma she is defining and the original oral or written tradition, still such an awareness does not have to enjoy that degree of reflection and explicitness which would make any further theological research on this subject superfluous. Now, no one will actually be able to cite any examples in which a present-day dogma can be more successfully traced back to the original tradition by assuming this tradition to be oral rather than scriptural. In other words, which modern dogma can be historically demonstrated to have been taught by the apostles and handed down as their authentic teaching, without its being contained either implicitly or explicitly in Holy Scripture? Our assertion stands: the Two-Source Theory does not make the development of dogma easier to explain.

iv. The difficulties in the area of development of dogma which are raised by the theory of the material sufficiency of the Bible stem largely from an excessively narrow conception of how dogmas are explicitated in history. If one maintains that the only way in which something implicitly contained in Scripture can be later explicitated is a formal logical deduction such that it is capable of providing an individual thinker with absolute logical certainty on the matter, then naturally one will be unable to explain the development of all dogma from the Scriptures. But he will be equally unable to derive it from oral tradition. He will be unable to do so even in such cases as the dogmas of Nicaea, Ephesus, and Chalcedon, where the whole Church recognizes a teaching as authentic and truly present in the Scriptures, without recourse to any extraneous source. He will be unable (unless he confuses mere custom with proof) to explain cases where the Church has expressly affirmed a dogma to be found in Scripture (cf. Original Sin: Rom 5; Penance: Jn 20; etc.). But if we presuppose a less narrow concept of doctrinal explicitation (the explanation of which is not our purpose here), then it is no more difficult to trace a modern dogma back to the Bible than it would be to attempt to prove, and not merely postulate, its derivation from a primitive oral tradition alone.

Our purpose in these considerations is not to prove the thesis of the sufficiency of Scripture, nor do we assert that our theory of inspiration stands or falls with this thesis. We only wish to bring out the fact that a consistent development of our theory of biblical inspiration at least leads in the direction of other interesting theological theses which deserve a thorough treatment of their own.

e) There are many other corollaries to our basic theory which we can only mention briefly here:

i. On the basis of our thesis we might arrive at a less embarrassed attitude toward the datum of comparative religion, that non-Christian religions of a high cultural level also have their holy books. It does not seem that our theological writings on inspiration have paid sufficient, serious, and unprejudiced attention to this fact. There is no reason to be afraid of the comparisons. A community will almost necessarily establish itself as historically founded and enduring into the future through the medium of books. It could even be suggested that the origin of books lies here, rather than in the need for private communication. Possession of sacred books is something to be expected *a priori* in any religion which possesses a certain level of culture and claims to be the bearer of a historical revelation. Add to this the fact that Christianity is the true and unique deed of the living God within human history (as we must indeed affirm in the face of the levelling and relativizing tendencies of comparative religion), and the rest follows naturally. The non-Christian analogies to the Christian Scriptures are no longer a cause of unease, and the picture of a book-writing God ceases to be redolent of a naive anthropomorphism.

ii. Our theory also helps explain why the particular literary *genera* of the books of the Bible do not have to be ascribed to God just because he is their author. For example, God did not write a letter to Philemon, although he is author of the letter. Why not? It is because his authorship consists precisely in his absolute and efficacious will that the Church, as a community of love, should manifest for all ages "canonically" her nature, her faith, and her love, even in such a letter. Because God wills the letter in this fashion, which is not the way of human action, though for this very reason it must involve human activity, the particular literary genre of the writing will not have the effect of specifying God's authorship.

82

iii. This might also help us to understand more easily why and to what extent the most varied literary forms are possible in the inspired writings. For once we realize that God, in becoming the author of a book, does not necessarily also appropriate to himself the book's literary genre, then the problem of what literary forms god may "fittingly" employ becomes far easier to solve. This again has its significance for scriptural inerrancy. The inerrant meaning of particular writings and sections must be determined essentially from the literary forms of the writings. If it is true that the literary form of a particular writing is not God's own work without further qualification, then the dogma of scriptural inerrancy can be applied to particular cases with considerably less difficulty. It remains true that whatever the human writer intends to affirm as true according to his con-viction and to which he requires a real assent on our part, is also God's utterance and hence free from error. Nevertheless, a consideration of the literary form, which is attributable to man alone, and not to God, may in many cases lead us to a more discreet, and possibly more restricted, estimate of what the sac-red writer intended to affirm.

iv. The relationship between inspiration and canonicity could be made clearer, and the close link between the two brought home to us. In this connection a distinction might be introduced between canonicity in the strict sense on the one hand, a concept relating to the post-apostolic Church (inspiration reflexively known and taught by the Church), and, on the other hand, the quality of being a constitutive part of the Church, a concept relating to the Apostolic Church and not simply identical with canonicity. This appertaining to the Apostolic Church is an element of the concrete concept of inspiration which we have outlined; at the same time its close connection with canonicity helps us to get a better idea of the ontological and epistemological relationship between canonicity and inspiration.

v. Light is shed on the different status of the various biblical writers. Among the authors of the constitutive writings of the Church are, in the first place, the apostles. But there are others also whose works, due to their form and period, gave expression to the Church's nature and were a means of her self-possession. We can thus understand why in the New Testament the secondary, merely "occasional" writings (private letters) are always by apostles (Philemon; Rom 16:1–23; 2 and 3 John). Other authors (Mark, Luke) can expect to exercise an exemplary function in the Church only through more formal, representative works, whereas the apostles may claim this role in all their writings (except, of course, purely secular ones).

Such a view obviously presupposes that any lost letters of an apostle must also have been inspired, even if not also canonical. There is no basic difficulty in such an assumption,[41] at least not according to our view. Whether it would also make sense to say that God could permit the disappearance of a writing which he willed and effected *prima intentione* and *per se* as his own writing is a different question. It does not seem surprising that small of a whole work which was intended by God to be, as a whole, the self-expression of the Church might be lost. It is as little surprising as the fact that within the inspired books individual sentences should have perished, a fact which no one can doubt.

vi. Our thesis might contribute some light on certain problems in the field of hermeneutics which have recently become vital

---

[41] Cf. A. Bea, *op. cit.,* n. 125.

again.[42] If the sacred writer by definition writes as a member of the Church, then a correct and adequate exegesis of his work must take two elements into account: first, that he writes as a *member* of the Church, and secondly, that he writes as a member of the *Church*.

Since he is but an individual *member* of the Church, not the mouthpiece of some abstract Church speaking always as a totality, he has his own particular gift. This gift is not simply the entirety of all the Church's charisms, her whole insight, her whole faith in its every possible development. Hence we need a biblical exegesis which will study the individual theological physiognomy of each separate writing, that is a biblical theology (in the narrower sense, as over against the use of Scripture in dogmatic theology). Such an interpretation would aim at bringing out the theological individuality of the various writings, and would not immediately reduce everything to a systematic theological system.

On the other hand, every biblical author, as member of the *Church,* was open to the whole of the Church, believed and taught within the Church; his own theology, even where he himself could not have expressly understood this, was integrated into the universal theology of the one and entire Church of his own time. Otherwise the Church would not have recognized his writing as "canonical", that is, as representing a part of her own consciousness of her faith and her essential attitude. This in no way means a falsification or levelling down of the individual author or his theology; it is something which every

---

[42] Cf., for example, A. Bea, "Bulla 'Ineffabilis Deus' et Hermeneutica Biblica" in *Virgo Immaculata. Acta Congressus Mariologici-Mariani. Romae anno MCMLIV celebrati,* III (Rome 1955), pp. 1–17.

sacred writer really lived, namely, the involvement of his own theology in the greater whole of the Church. If therefore the exegesis of a particular writing proceeds from the whole of Scripture and from the Church, deriving rules and directions from this source, we have no right to suspect it of being for that reason bad exegesis. Rather, this method follows from the very nature of things — as long as it remains aware of the distinction between itself and the other valid method described above.

Further conclusions of a similar nature might also be drawn from the thesis we have here presented.

VISIONS AND PROPHECIES

AUTHOR'S NOTE

The author is indebted to the Reverend Theodor Baumann S. J. who, in order to clarify some of the abstract principles discussed in this study, has furnished notes on and references to particular cases. These examples are not intended as expressions of opinion on the facts concerned.

I

THE POSSIBILITY AND THEOLOGICAL
SIGNIFICANCE OF PRIVATE REVELATIONS
AND VISIONS

In turbulent times, the minds of men are agitated not only by
the events themselves, but they also seek an interpretation of
present events and a promise for the future. And if they are
believers they know that the interpretation of the present and
the promise of the future ultimately can be found only in God.
Then they hope that this enlightening and auspicious word of
God may be imparted to them as clearly and unequivocally as
possible. They seek people who claim to have perceived this
special word from heaven, and they are disposed to believe in it.
Such "credulity" need not necessarily be suspect merely because
it is induced by the anguish of existence. For why should this
anguish serve only to agitate man, grubbing up from the dark
depths of his heart nothing but spectres and wish-dreams? Why
should it not also render him more receptive to the true message
from above, to which the comfortable and self-satisfied turn a
deaf ear? Both things are possible.

But weakness of faith and difficulties with regard to faith, as
well as the misery of life can drive people to excessive credulity
where visions and prophecies are concerned, as A. Brenninkmeyer
observes in his book on the pastoral care of the neurotic. In his

opinion many hope to strengthen their weakened faith in God by believing in visions, and "then defend this substitute for faith with the violence of a shipwrecked man fighting for the last plank".[1]

Since, then, all this is possible, it becomes a matter of great importance to recognize what it is in a particular case that answers the cry of the tormented heart: the empty echo in which, all unawares, one hears only oneself, or the answer in which God is perceived. Hence the problem of a criterion for the discerning of prophets, their voices and visions, will ever and again become urgent in the Church. In view of the tragic second World War and the uncertainty of our future, who would care to doubt that it is urgent today? On every hand visions are still occurring, everywhere the messages of the visionaries are attracting the attention not only of the pious and credulous, but also of detached and sceptical observers.[2]

In terms of practical results it would be largely fruitless to try to establish principles in the light of which such phenomena could be adequately evaluated:[3] sceptical minds are ready in

[1] Cf. A. Brenninkmeyer, *Traitement pastoral des névrosés* (Paris, 1947), p. 145.
[2] The proportions of this flood may be gathered from the fact that from 1945 to 1952 in the countries behind the Iron Curtain about two thousand cases of miracles were investigated, miracles belief in which was by no means confined to Catholics. In Western Europe, between 1930 and 1950, the Church investigated thirty series of apparitions of Our Lady, with about 300 cases of individual apparitions to children, both girls and boys. Cf. C. M. Staehlin, *Apariciones* (Madrid, 1954), p. 12.
[3] Three things should be noted: This short essay could not deal with all the problems connected with the subject. Thus for example almost nothing will be said about fraudulent or really pathological "apparitions". Bibliographical references will also be sparse, serving chiefly as examples. Finally the references to individual cases are only illustrative examples and do not express any attitude, favourable or not, towards particular apparitions.

advance with their reply: fraud, or hysteria, "pseudo-mysticism". These people are only incensed by all such occurrences and their indignation, according to their temperament and cast of mind, will express itself in rational or even dogmatic arguments. In dogmatic arguments as well: either a taste for apparitions represents an aberration from the piety of Christ and the Scriptures, or the messages are absurd, unworthy of God or dogmatically incorrect, or the like. Those, on the other hand, who welcome such events are put out of patience by these views, which they call rationalistic, lacking in faith, irreligious and temerarious.[4]

Nevertheless, we shall hazard the attempt to say something about visions and similiar phenomena. We shall not discuss concrete cases; for we lack necessary data and precise information of these cases and are not in a position to learn the circumstances, the details which one would have to know (they are not given in the reports, which are usually couched in enthusiastic and general terms)[5] in order to be able to form a judgment. But we shall deal with visions in general. Even this may prove helpful to some.

---

[4] Some people are incurable: When the collector of Maria Lataste's revelations was reproached with the fact that entire passages were simply translations from St. Thomas Aquinas, he replied that 'if God inspired St. Thomas to write those passages, he could repeat them to Maria Lataste'. No doubt. Cf. A. Poulain, *Graces of interior prayer: A Treatise on Mystical Theology.* Transl. Herder, St. Louis, 1950.

[5] There is no critical history as yet of the celebrated visions of Fátima and its message and no sound critical edition of the texts. C. M. Staehlin points out the omissions and textual variations in so-called "critical" studies of the visions (*op. cit.,* pp. 351—378). On p. 379 he says of the devotional literature: "We have purposely discussed only those textual alterations which any reader can verify for himself because they are found in printed books now on sale. But when publishers and editors of diaries and the like think nothing of suppressing or altering parts of the manuscript it is difficult to

We address believing Christians, and thus presuppose the convictions proper to them. We shall seek to treat the subject soberly in the light of a Christian theology and philosophy, because they are concerned in this matter. Zealous defenders of such phenomena should realize that it would be a poor recommendation for such events should they refuse to submit themselves willingly, patiently and honestly to a sober, critical examination. True mystics have never objected to such enquiry. Gemma Galgani often concludes the letters in which she related her visions and other favours to her spiritual director with such statements: "I have told you all this, because Jesus commanded me to do so. But you must not believe any of it: for it is only my cracy mind."[6] When the classic mystic, Theresa of Ávila, had to choose between a very spiritual ("pious") and a "learned" director for herself and her nuns, she had no hesitation in preferring the learned one. Of course it would have suited her best to find the two qualities united in the same man.[7]

Genuine apparitions certainly will not resort to blackmail, threatening with punishments from heaven anybody who is not prepared to yield unqualified assent to everything.[8] From

control one's anger. In such cases the reader cannot possibly discover the fraud. If we write such things it is because we have in our possession evidence which refutes whole pages of allegations in many books now in the hands of pious people."

[6] Cf. *Lettere di S. Gemma Galgani* (Rome, 1941), p. 389.

[7] *Vida,* cap. 5 (Obras edit. Silverio de S. Teresa, I: Burgos, 1915, p. 28); *Camino,* cap. 5 (III, pp. 31 f.); Moradas IV, 8 (IV, p. 159).

[8] In a vision of our day, for instance, the apparition tells the visionary: ". . . A time will come when you will be . . . horribly slandered, for the devil knows how to blind people so that even the best are deceived . . . . The Father pronounces a dreadful woe upon all who do not submit to his will." Shortly before, the Father's will had been identified with demands made by the apparition, concerning "Our Lady's Saturday" and the "Rosary

Diadochus of Photike to John and Paul of the Cross, the mystical doctors emphasize that no harm is done even though a genuine vision be rejected.[9]

Ignatius of Loyola, who certainly knew something about mysticism, grants not only faith but even reason a right to object to such revelations.[10]

Obviously, in the space at our disposal, we cannot raise every point which one might wish to see discussed. If a reader familiar with these matters should feel that this book has nothing new to offer him, we readily agree. Our general intention is only to repeat here the teaching of traditional mystical theology. If on occasion we say anything further (perhaps in the sense of still more caution) this should be regarded as a private theological opinion, worth as much as the arguments adduced in its favour, but no more. Nevertheless, two points should be noted. Firstly: even the individual theologian has a right to express his own opinion. He can critically examine and even call in question apparitions in any way "approved" by the Church, provided that he does this with due respect for the Church (which is not infallible in such questions) and for the fact itself.[11] And even

of the Immaculate Conception". — At times this blackmail assumes subtler forms. Thus Maria Ágreda has Our Lady say to her: ". . . If anybody will not believe what you write he does not despise you, but me and my words!" (Cf. *Mística Ciudad de Dios*, p. III, 1. 8, cap. 12 § 621.)

[9] For the reason, see Part II, 4, *infra*.

[10] Ignatius, *Letter of July* 27, 1549 (*Mon. hist. S. J.*, Ignatiana 1, XII, p. 632 ff.).

[11] Thus an authentic declaration of 1877 (*ASS* xi, pp. 509 ff.; in de Guibert, *Documenta Ecclesiastica christianae perfectionis studium spectantia:* Rome, 1931, n. 1005) on apparitions like those of Lourdes and La Salette states: *Eiusmodi apparitiones seu revelationes neque approbatas neque reprobatas vel damnatas ab Apostolica Sede fuisse, sed tantum permissas tamquam pie credendas fide solum humana iuxta traditionem, quam ferunt, idoneis etiam*

if a theory of visions, their possible origins and criteria, is much bound up with the hypothetical, it is not therefore superfluous and unprofitable. For where the supernatural, divine origin of a vision is alleged, this claim must be proved, not presumed. According to all the principles of theology the burden of proof rests upon him who affirms a thesis, not upon him who doubts or denies it. Hence so long as a particular apparition can be explained in natural terms according to a reasonably probable, though hypothetical, general theory of visions, its supernatural character cannot be considered to have been established.

testimoniis ac monumentis confirmatam. (The Apostolic See has neither approved nor condemned such apparitions or revelations but merely permits Catholics to believe in them — where they have the support of credible witness and documents — with a purely human faith.) The principle here expressed was not invalidated by the introduction (1907) of the Feast of the Apparitions at Lourdes, for the text above was quoted as the basic rule in the Encyclical *Pascendi* of Pius X. For the possibility of dissenting from the Church's judgment in such matters see, e. g., Benedict XIV, *De servorum Dei beatif. et beatorum canonisatione* III, cap. ultimum, n. 15 (Opera omnia: Venice, 1767, p. 277): *posse aliquem, salva et integra fide catholica, assensum revelationibus praedictis (i. e.* approved by the Church) *non praestare et ab eis recedere, dummodo id fiat cum debita modestia, non sine ratione et citra contemptum.* (Without prejudice to the integrity of Catholic faith a person may withhold his assent to such revelations provided he does this with due modesty, not without reason, and without contempt.) Similarly *op. cit.,* II, cap. 32, n. 11. This doctrine was expounded anew by the Provincial Council of Malines in 1937 on the occasion of the apparitions at Beauraing and Banneux. The acts of the Council were confirmed by the Holy See. Cf. *Acta et decreta Concilii Provincialis Mechlinensis quinti* (Malines, 1938) VIII, pp. 5 ff. For more precise distinctions in regard to the implications of ecclesiastical approbation in such matters and the various possible kinds of "faith" in such visions cf., e. g., E. Michael, "Allgemeine kritische Würdigung der Privatoffenbarungen" in *ZkTh* 25 (1901), pp. 385—400; J. Zahn, *Einführung in die christliche Mystik,* 2nd ed. (Paderborn, 1918), pp. 568—75; C. M. Staehlin, "Apariciones" in *Razón y Fe* cxxxix (1949), pp. 433—64, 546—62; cxl (1949), pp. 71—98 (a very important article). Cf. now the same

1. The Possibility of Private Revelations

The possibility of private revelation through visions and associated auditory experiences is evident in principle for a Christian. God as a free personal being can make himself perceptible to the created spirit, not only through his works but also by his free, personal word. And he can do it in such a manner that this communication of God is not simply himself in the direct vision of the Godhead, or in the dimension of a blessed intellect emptied of all that is finite, but also, and for a Christian who believes in God's Incarnation this is essential, in such a way that this communication is bound up with a particular place and time, with a concrete word or command, with a finite reality or truth, and so that it occurs with, or is connected with, the "apparition" of an object presented to the

author's book *Apariciones*, already quoted, esp. pp. 39ff. and 51ff. For more bibliography see H. Lais, *Eusebius Amort und seine Lehre über die Privat-offenbarungen* (Freiburg, 1941), p. 85; M. J. Congar, "La crédibilité des révélations privées" in *La Vie Spirituelle liii* (1937), Suppl., pp. 29—48. Against Congar, however, it could be objected with O. Karrer ("Privat-offenbarungen und Fátima" in *Schweizer Rundschau* xlvii (1947), p. 488, note 1) and with E. Dhanis *(Bij de Verschijningen en het Geheim van Fátima,* Bruges, 1945, p. 38) that his distinction between ordinary approbations by the Church, and a few special ones which would require firm assent, has not been established. — This booklet by Dhanis can now be compared with L. G. da Fonseca's criticism of it, *Fátima y la Crítica,* (Santander, 1952), Dhanis' counter-criticism, "A propos de Fátima et la critique" in *NRTh* lxxiv (1952), pp. 580—606, and the concluding article by Dhanis, "Sguardo su Fátima e bilancio di una discussione" in *Civiltà Cattolica* civ (1953, II), pp. 392—406. Here we cannot enter into this controversy, but we would note that da Fonseca seems too unsympathetic towards a sober criticim based on the results of modern psychological research. For a summary of Dhani's booklet in Flemish cf. A. Brenninkmeyer, "Zu den Erscheinungen und der Botschaft von Fátima" in *ZAM* xxi (1948), pp. 214—20.

internal or external senses,[12] which object represents and manifests God, his will, or the like.

That there are such historical apparitions of God in created symbols is witnessed by the Scriptures. God who spoke — as the Epistle to the Hebrews says (1:1 ff.) — at sundry times and in divers manners to the fathers by the prophets, last of all in

---

[12] We are well aware that this (in contrast to the direct empiricism of most visions) is to approach the concrete phenomena of a vision from the angle of God's infinitive and unlimited self-communication to man. The justification of this procedure, which at once emphasizes the relativity of visions, will be seen later. We shall be unable, of course, to pursue other questions which here suggest themselves about the relationship between the self-revealing infinite God and the "sign" (word, picture, humanity of Christ, Sacrament), and the corresponding duality of the answering human act. — One thing we would note here, however: in one sense, perhaps, this duality of God and of the sign in the realm of visions, deriving its "historical" character from the sign, is more in keeping with the basic character of Christianity than a mystical union devoid of images. For this latter constantly raises the ancient question whether such a piety of pure spiritual transcendence is really Christian. It can only remain so, certainly, if on the one hand such purely spiritual mysticism during our pilgrimage far from the Lord retains the consciousness of being entirely provisional. On the other hand, it must also conceive itself as a participation in Christ's "kenosis", for he alone experiences the true mystical "emptying" through the cross, death and the tomb. Morever, this imageless mysticism, which sets out to apprehend God in himself, must restore this venture (a gratuitous gift) to God's free disposal, to him who will one day reveal himself even to the pure mystic as the God of the transfigured earth because he is more than pure spirit. Finally it must realize that in earthly man this emptying of self will not be accomplished by practising pure inwardness, but by the real activity which is called humility, service, love of our neighbour, the cross and death. One must descend into hell together with Christ; lose one's soul, not directly to the God who is above all names but in the service of one's brethren. On the other hand this basic incarnational structure of the unconfused unity of God and his creatures gives us to understand that we can apprehend God in the sign (or in the form of a vision) only if we do not cling to the sign ("*noli me tangere*") as if it were the ultimate reality, God himself. The sign must be welcomed and passed by, grasped and relinquished.

these days hath spoken to us by his Son. This speaking, then, of the personal, transcendent God took place according to Scripture in the most diverse manners. The prophet who is to become the mouthpiece of God for men hears a voice (Ezech. 1:28 etc.), he has a vision (Is. 2:1 etc.), he sees God's revelation in pictures and in symbols (Jer. 1:13; 24:1 etc.); angels appear delivering a heavenly message (Luke 1:11; 1:26 etc.); the divine communication can happen in a dream (Matt. 1:20; 2:19 etc); it may occur whilst the seer is in an ecstasy (Acts 10:10; 11:5; 22:17; 2 Cor. 12:2—5; Apoc. 4:2). The tendency of these multifarious sorts of divine communications varies widely according to the phase of the history of salvation in which the visionary lives and which he is intended to influence. The concrete form which this divine revelation takes in man is also very various and may be conditioned in part by the historical milieu in which it occurs. We shall not now pursue this matter further (just as from this point we confine our examination to "apparitions" as they occur in Christian Church history). However, according to the testimony of Scripture so much at least is clear: the history of Christianity would be unthinkable without prophetic and visionary elements (in the broadest sense). To try to explain all these things by natural or even abnormal human causes, would be logically to deny that any historical activity of the personal God revealing himself in the Word was possible at all. But this would be to repudiate the character of Christianity as an historical supernatural, revealed religion.

On the other hand if there were such phenomena at the establishment of the Old Testament revelation and of the Christian revelation, then the possibility of similar manifestations occurring in subsequent Christian history cannot be denied *a priori* and in principle. Since we have in Christ God's final and definitive revelation and self-disclosure, these later Christian revelations must theologically, if not also psychologically, have an essentially different character (which in due course we shall have to discuss in some detail); but this is no reason for thinking that such divine manifestations are now altogether impossible. We meet these in the Church of the apostolic period, where they are considered a normal concomitant of the possession of the Spirit, and thus as a permanent gift in the Church, however secondary in comparison with charity (Matt. 10:41; Acts 11:28; 21:9 seq.; 1 Cor. 11:4 seq. and 12—14 etc.). Joseph of the Holy Ghost, a doctor of mysticism, is thus quite right in saying: *fuisse aliquando veras revelationes et prophetias maxime tempore legis scriptae certum est de fide; immo in ipsis fides nostra fundatur. Dari etiam in tempore legis gratiae. . . . Dari etiam veras revelationes et prophetias post primitivam Ecclesiam, licet non sit ita certum, non potest tamen absque temeritatis et impietatis saltem nota negari.*[13]

Therefore, anyone who absolutely rejects the possibility of special revelations offends against faith; and anyone who denies that they may occur even since the apostolic age offends against a doctrine which is theologically certain. There is nothing further to be said on the subject. Everyone, then, who wishes to be a Christian must ask himself whether he does not live in

---

[13] "It is certain *de fide* that there have been genuine revelations and prophecies in former times, especially under the written law. The same is true under the law of grace . . . . To deny that there have been genuine revelations and prophecies since the time of the primitive Church would not be heretical but would be at least temerarious and impious."
Joseph a S. Spiritu (1609—1674), *Enucleatio mystica theologiae S. Dionysii Areopagitae* (editio critica, Rome, 1927), I, q. 24 (p. 106).

dispositions which *a priori* exclude such revelations from God; and whether he does not seem to believe and approve of the visionary events in Scripture only because he is used to them, but not because they would not instantly rouse him to rationalistic protest should he encounter them for the first time.

These comments, however, do not exhaust the "theology" of apparitions, private revelations, and the like. For the understanding of what follows a distinction must be drawn, concerned not with the psychology of apparitions, but with God's intention in producing such effects through his Spirit. The distinction is not to be taken in an exclusive sense, but is one of emphasis in such phenomena. From the history of religion we shall borrow the rather problematic distinction between the (purely) mystical vision and the prophetic (as well). (By "vision" we mean of course all those extraordinary occurrences of divine origin which form our present subject matter.) We call mystical those visions the object and content of which solely concern the personal religious life and perfection of the visionary. Prophetic visions are those which in addition induce or commission the visionary to address his environment and ultimately the Church with a message, instructing, warning, requiring something, or foretelling the future. Despite their different objects both kinds of visions may follow the same psychological course, and despite their psychological similarity they must be differently assessed, especially in respect of the criteria of their authenticity, because they make essentially different demands upon the environment of the visionary. Thus the visions of St. Gemma Galgani were mystical, because they solely concerned her intimate religious life. Those of St. Margaret Mary Alacoque, by contrast, were prophetical, because they contained demands upon other people.

The necessity for a different evalution of the two types of vision will be forcefully brought home to the reader if he considers — as Staehlin does, for example[14] — the totally different hazards which practical belief in such visions entails.

2. Observations on the Theological Significance of Private Revelations

As we proceed to develop the theology of private revelations more fully, that term will signify "prophetic visions". We shall discuss those private revelations which are concerned not only with the individual visionary and his spiritual life, but which — although they are "private" — address the Church or major parts of the Church through the visionary: private revelations recommending a particular devotion, exhorting to penance, giving certain instructions, warning against certain doctrines, recommending a spiritual doctrine or manner of life, and so forth. Without any doubt, in the course of the Church's history there have continually been private revelations of this kind, and they have exercised great influence. They present not only psycholo-

---

[14] Op. cit., p. 380. Staehlin supposes the case of a visionary approaching a head of state and requiring in the name of heaven that war be declared against an atheist state, with the promise of certain victory. But there is no need to resort to imaginary cases. We have personal knowledge of a case where a very well known visionary and stigmatist, pleading the will of the "Saviour", persuaded the superior of a charitable institution to give security for a large sum, a transaction which this superior had no authority to undertake. Her conscience was quieted with the assurance that there was no risk involved and that besides it was the will of the "Saviour". Nevertheless, the security became payable, since the firm patronized by the "Saviour" went bankrupt.

gical, but also theological problems. Now when private revelations are discussed amongst Catholics it is usually in terms of the psychology of such phenomena and hence of the authenticity of the revelations and the truth of their content. We would not contest or doubt the legitimacy of this approach. We shall ourselves examine this problem at length. Nevertheless, we feel that it is one-sided. It has to be complemented by a theological approach. It may be said that we already have this: that this aspect is duly considered, partly in fundamental theology and partly in mystical theology. However, this is true only in a very qualified sense and the aspect we shall stress is not even touched upon. For mystical theology discusses nothing more than the psychological question of how such private revelations originate, their different kind, the criteria of their genuineness and truth, and so on. Beyond this, mystical and fundamental theology only add that because God can reveal himself (in the strict sense of verbal revelation) and can give the recipient of such revelation, and also other people, adequate assurance of the divine origin of his experience — in the latter case by external critera and in the former by both external and internal criteria — therefore private revelations and knowledge of their authenticity and truth are possible, and so at least the direct recipient of such a revelation may be entitled or even obliged to accept its content with the assent of faith. It is then impressed upon one that the *revelatio publica* ceased with the death of the apostles, with the result that subsequent revelations do not belong to the Church's deposit of faith, being simply "private revelations", that hence there can be no duty to believe them with "Catholic faith", and the Church can and must deal with such private revelations only insofar as she has to ascertain whether they are consistent with the deposit of faith, and consequently whether Catholics may believe in them with "human faith".

But this average view (however correct its positive enunciation may be) remains faulty in two respects. On the one hand this "theology" of private revelations is too negative; solely on the basis that public revelation is at an end, later revelations are called "private" in a purely negative sense, and thus it becomes impossible to develop a strictly theological theory of the signifiance and necessity for the Church as such, which, however, they doubtless have. The rudiments which Scripture provides for a theology of the prophetic element in the Church and for the Church are not properly developed. Indeed, it can be said with but little exaggeration that the history of mystical theology is a history of the theological devaluation of the prophetic element in favour of non-prophetic, "pure", infused contemplation.[15] People are (and with some reason, in view of practical experience) more suspicious of prophetic mysticism, which invokes revelations and instructions from above to claim a mission and right in the Church to admonish and guide the Church and her members, than of the image-free, ineffable mysticism of pure contemplation.[16]

Certainly, the former is more dangerous and more prone to

---

[15] It should be emphasized, indeed, that at least the doctrine of St. John of the Cross, if it rejects visions, is not a mere intellectualist spiritual mysticism but one based on faith and conscious that its attitude is conditioned by the historical economy of salvation. Cf., e. g., Subida II, 22 (Obras edit. Silverio de S. Teresa II: Burgos, 1929, pp. 182 ff.).

[16] This is understandable when one remembers that the widely publicized "private revelations" of Luise Piccareta, later put on the Index, were described as "a powerful message from God to humanity, greater, more momentous, more joyous than any other age has received. Divine Providence seems to have reserved these revelations for our afflicted times as the sole means of salvation for the nations". Cf. Lais, op. cit., p. 48. For the censuring of the

come into conflict with Church authority than the latter. Nevertheless prophecy has its foundation in Scripture, and in practice a great history in the Church (labour as theorists may to prove that we already know without the prophets everything that they announce), and yet orthodox theology has never paid any serious attention to the question whether there are prophets even in post-apostolic times, how their spirit can be recognized and discerned, what their rôle is in the Church, what their relationship to the hierarchy, what the import of their mission for the exterior and interior life of the Church. Obviously in such a theology of the prophetic element in the Church a good deal of general mystical theology, and especially what this theology has to say of private revelations, could well be used. But as mystical theology has hitherto regarded these phenomena solely in the light of their "private" character it cannot be said that this mystical theology is already a prophetical theology. True, the Middle Ages had a theology of the charismata, but the lack of a sense of history prevented closer enquiry into the meaning of prophecy, as the vital stirring of the Spirit, for the growth and development of the Church. But if prophecy has always existed in the Church, if there may be danger of the Spirit being "extinguished", then a theology of prophecy would not represent thought devoted unnecessarily to something which could well exist and operate without it, but a precaution lest the Spirit be extinguished and the lament be raised: *iam non est propheta* (Ps. 73:9).

On the other hand the average theology of private revelations is also too positive. It does not adequately grasp the radical

writings of L. Piccareta cf. *AAS* xxx (1938), p. 138. How often Christians act as if a private revelation heralded the dawn of an entirely new epoch in the life of the Church!

difference between revelations before and after Christ. In considering private revelations since the Incarnation this theology sees in them (mystical theology apart) only concrete cases which can be explained by the general doctrine of revelation, as developed by fundamental theology; they are treated simply as "revelation", except for the fact (quite extrinsic to the occurrence itself) that this revelation is not addressed to all men, requiring their assent. Thus this conception draws no intrinsic distinction between earlier revelations and those of post-apostolic times. The psychological process, the content, the criteria of authenticity may be identical in the two cases; only the persons addressed differ. But even this is not obvious. For according to the general principles of ordinary fundamental theology it does not appear why a private revelation (if it is not simply an imperative to an individual but, as is usually the case, also contains factual information) should not be believed by all who learn of it, and who recognize with adequate certitude (that which is required, and suffices, to establish the fact of public revelation) that it is from God. It is unjustifiable, illogical and dangerous to demand (as is often done) a degree of certitude for the divine origin of post-apostolic private revelations which, if required in the case of Christian public revelation, would make any rational foundation for Christian belief impossible. But if no more proof of the existence of post-apostolic private revelations be required than is reasonable, and is required in the case of public Christian revelation, it does not appear why they should not be recognized in many actual cases, not only by the immediate recipient but also by others, as really coming from God, thus entailing the right and duty of faith (fides divina). For the duty of faith flows connaturally from the fact that God himself speaks, and there is no need for another special act of God in order to oblige men to believe his word.

If God has spoken and the fact is established — that is, has been made sufficiently clear to me — then automatically I must listen, obey and believe insofar as the message concerns me at all. The difference, then, between the Christian revelation and private revelations would not consist in the fact that the former is for all and the latter for the individual, but only in the fact that, in the latter case, the custody of the matter revealed is not entrusted to the Church. While not *fides catholica,* therefore, the belief in private revelations which would be generally possible and mandatory would be a *fides divina.* If the theologians normally concede that the immediate recipient of a private revelation can and even (given sufficient certitude) must believe it *fide divina,* then we really do not see why this should not be true for others. In short, from this point of view no real and essential difference between public revelation and post-apostolic private revelation can be found. Yet there is such a difference. But in order to see it, another point must be considered.

Since Christ what else can be revealed? The truth revealed by God's word, because revelation itself is history, has a time element which is essential to it. Time is not a neutral dimension in which anything can happen and so anything can be revealed at any time. Before Christ, in the historical dialogue between God and man which we call the history of the world and of salvation, everything was always unsettled, everything was assigned to the free counsel of God, still shrouded from men, still to be awaited in the event of the future. Before Christ it was still possible for something unprecedented to happen in history (without terminating history) that would change man's whole relationship

105

to God. God might proclaim a new law, establish or abolish a convenant, wrath and favour (both being manifestations of God's freedom and not only his metaphysical essence) might incalculably appear. In a word: out of the infinite possibilities of his freedom (who is the God of Abraham, of Isaac, and of Jacob, not that of the philosophers) God could reveal this or that; now this, now that; and this spontaneity of the divine action was impossible for man to anticipate, but had to be accepted in constantly renewed obedience, as an inscrutable disposition of God. Man had to be ever ready for a new revelation, which might radically alter the course of his salvation; though in retrospect, once these revelations were promulgated, man could see that they were part of the hidden plan of God, and that God's later acts were based in fact upon his earlier ones.

But now, with Christ and "since" Christ, the last days have come, God's salvific action towards man has reached its definitive and final phase. With Christ the "last hour" is here, not provisionally but permanently, so that in the Christian era we may not expect anything more which would substantially alter the conditions of our salvation. Whereas before Christ such a change not only could but had to be expected, the Christian can only await the unveiling of the end of the dramatic dialogue between God and man which has already happened in Christ, the Last Judgment. The existential theology of a possible and future revelation of God in history for men before Christ has been replaced for Christian men by a theological eschatology, and this theology of revelation has only a retrospective significance (important as that is), no longer any prospective tendency: expectation of the revelation of God in history has been superseded by expectation of the revelation of God which will end history.

Nevertheless, even in these last times there are revelations of God, not only to individuals as such but also to the Church, at least in the sense that the charisma of the individual should redound to the blessing of the whole Mystical Body. But however similar these revelations may be, from the purely psychological point of view, to the revelation of God before and in Christ, still they must display an essential qualitative difference from pre-Christian revelation, if we are correct in what we have said above about the characteristics of the last days, when there can be no further revelation which would essentially change the conditions of salvation. The nature of these post-apostolic, ecclesiastical, private revelations, that are not of purely personal significance, must accordingly be defined so that they fit intrinsically into this eschatological phase of salvation. How is this possible?

We have seen that it is not enough to say: private revelations are not addressed to the Church (or humanity) as a whole and their content is not positively guaranteed by the magisterium. If we are told that the content of private revelations, as compared with Christian public revelation, is of little significance, unessential or the like, then the question arises whether anything God reveals can be "unimportant", and how one can know whether what is revealed, if added to the deposit of faith, will not mean essential changes in the conditions of salvation to date? If it be said that private revelations contain only such things as can be known independently of them from public revelation (e. g. the possibility and fruitfulness of a new devotion), then the question arises why God reveals these things instead of leaving it to the sagacity of theologians to deduce them. If we consider all this, the only satisfactory answer to our problem of the theological nature of post-apostolic, private revelations to the Church remains this: they do not reveal an objective affirmation as such which would either form an "accidental" supplement to public revelation or simply be identical with it, but private revelations are essentially imperatives showing how Christianity should act in a concrete historical situation: not new assertions but new commands. What they affirm is already known from faith and theology. Yet they are not superfluous, are not mere heavenly refresher courses in public revelation or a Socratic method used by God in order to lead us to the knowledge of what in principle could be learnt without this help. Because what God wishes to be done in certain given circumstances cannot be logically and unequivocally deduced from the general principles of dogma and morals, even with the help of an analysis of the given situation.[17] Such theoretical considerations may delimit the sphere of the correct and appropriate human action (in many cases to such an extent that it will be clear in practice what should be done) and therefore will always be necessary. Nevertheless, they are fundamentally incapable of determining which of the various decisions within this sphere is in fact the one God wills at this moment, and how this one can be found. An opposite view would wrongly reduce the concrete and unpredict-

---

[17] See *The Episcopate and the Primacy,* pp. 303—328; cf. K. Rahner, "Der Einzelne in der Kirche" in *StdZ* cxxxix (1947), pp. 260—76 (published also in K. Rahner, *Gefahren im heutigen Katholizismus,* 3rd. ed. Einsiedeln, 1955, pp. 11—38.); *id.,* "Das Charismatische in der Kirche" in *StdZ* clx (1957), pp. 161—86.

able character of free human action to universal patterns, and would degrade individual, spiritual reality to a mere instance of universal law.

St. Ignatius says that when one is seeking to know God's will for the "election", apart from and before the "rational" consideration in the light of faith there are "times of election" in which one learns the divine will by God's direct motion, and that logical and moral reflection is only a substitute should the divine motion fail to occur or not be recognized with sufficient clarity, a substitute which should not be regarded as the normal type of election. Now in the life of the Church a divine impulse analogous to this Ignation election must operate for the Church's election and cannot be replaced either by theoretical conside-rations and the deductions of theologians and moralists, or by the *assistentia Spiritus Sancti per se negativa*, which guards those considerations from error in such a way that their source remains the bare principles and the situation at hand. Closely as the charisma of the discerning of spirits in the Church is bound up with ecclesiastical authority, it does not follow a *priori* that God will impart the divine motion making known that he commands the Church, or parts of it, to do a certain thing in the changing circumstances of history, solely through members of the hierarchy. In principle the Holy Spirit can act upon the Church through any one of her members to announce what he requires of her, what command he lays upon her for the moment. It seems to us that this is the essence of post-apostolic, prophetic, "private revelations": God inspiring a member of the Church with his imperative for the Church in a concrete historical situation. How such a private revelation passes from the individual to the Church, or to the greater part of it, whether by actual preaching: *haec dicit Dominus,* by the influence of example or otherwise, is a secondary matter.

Just as the individual, according to the classic doctrine of the ancients, in making his election should not ask only: what is the reasonable thing to do here and now according to the general principles of dogma and morals, but should also seek the" impulse of the Holy Spirit", so too in the decisions of the Church it should be asked: *"non est propheta . . . ut interrogemus per eum"* (3 Kings 22:7). It should not be too readily assumed that the prophetic charisma was only a transient privilege of the primitive Church. The social and psychological forms of the prophetic charisma and its mode of influencing Church history may alter with time. Nevertheless, side by side with the office transmitted by the imposition of hands there must always be in the Church a prophetic vocation as well which is not handed down by man. Neither of these two gifts can replace the other.

All this may sound very abstract and impractical. But anyone who for instance listens to catchwords, proposals, etc., concerning the question of what is now the most urgent task facing the Church will find the most various tendencies and opinions. The most conscientious, responsible and enlightened Christians will advocate the golden mean of a Catholic synthesis in all these matters. But then arises the embarrassing question whether such a theoretical synthesis, integrating everything, gives a practical, clear imperative for action, action which can never do everything at once, but must very unsynthetically select something to do? If, then, the theory of synthesis leads to difficulties, why should the Christian not be able and obliged to choose by some other means than theory among the many theoretically legitimate possibilities? And why should the other means not include that illumination and that word of the Lord which we are too inclined to give the rather disdainful name of private revelations, and to regard as the private luxury of a few pious souls.[18] But then the theology and psychology of such revelations — indispensable for the very necessary trial of spirits — acquires a highly practical signifiance.

This imperative may not manifest itself so clearly as a milder form of the same thing. We mean that psychological help towards fulfilling the will of God with more zeal which is afforded the faithful when God repeatedly announces his will in a particular place, to the accompaniment of specially impressive apparitions. It is well known that reference to God's commanding something in a vision is more efficacious than the best exposition of general principles. Fr. Fonseca thinks it is a well established fact of history that the intervention of heaven has often given either the first idea or the last impulse for the execution of something which in other ways and for weightier reasons was already recognized as correct, useful and necessary. He refers in this connection to the consecration of the world to the Sacred Heart in 1900 which, as is well known, can be traced to the initiative of Sister Mary of the Sacred Heart (Maria Droste zu Vischering), who was given a command to this effect during a vision of Christ.[19]

The prophetic element then, despite the conclusion of public revelation, retains unique importance in the Church and can be

---

[18] It is a striking circumstance that this function of the Church has been exercised in recent times exclusively by women. Cf. Staehlin, *op. cit.*, pp. 75 ff.
[19] Cf. L. G. da Fonseca, "Il Messaggio di S. Santità nel Giubileo di N. Signora di Fátima e la consagrazione del mondo all'Immacolato Cuore di Maria" in *Civiltà Cattolica* xciv (1934, I), p. 149.

displaced neither by the general theory of theology, nor by the natural and supernatural wisdom of the hierarchy as such, nor by mysticism (in the sense of pure contemplation as devoid of images as possible). Consequently it is an urgent question how to distinguish authentic visions, heavenly messages, prophecies, from human (normal or abnormal) and diabolical ones. For this reason we must now examine the psychology of apparitions.

II

THE PSYCHOLOGICAL PROBLEMS OF VISIONS

1. The Imaginative Vision as the Normal Case

LET us assume that an authentic vision and audition of a heavenly person (of Christ, of the Blessed Virgin, etc.) has occurred, that there has been a real intervention and influence from the other world. 'What does this mean? What has happened in such a case? On our assumption the "naive" recipient who accepts the vision has no problems at all. The celestial person, who is normally beyond the sphere of our perception, has appeared — that is, has entered our sphere of perception and spoken in the same way as anyone else comes, shows himself and speaks. The objective reality of such a vision would then be measured by its exact correspondence with normal encounters among men on earth: the person seen in the vision has this build and wears that clothing, he behaves in such and such a way, the words one hears are his as the words of other people who speak to us are theirs.[20]

[20] The 'subjective residue' which is found even in ordinary natural perception might then be neglected in a vision on grounds of irrelevance, just as happens in everyday perceptions. — This naive interpretation of apparitions gives rise to such expressions as "The eyes which beheld Our Blessed Lady", "the blessed patch of ground where the Queen of Heaven appeared", etc.

The only difference would be that this person happens to come from heaven,[21] and so we cannot seek him out ourselves. This is approximately how the naive person will understand the heavenly vision, and this explanation will satisfy him.

But it will not be found satisfactory for those who have some acquaintance with mystical writers or who simply give the matter a little thought. St. Theresa of Ávila, for example, is firmly convinced that the glorified humanity of Christ has never directly shown itself on earth in its corporeal reality since his Ascension (and apparition to St. Paul).[22] The mystical doctors recognize three kinds of visions: the corporeal, the imaginative, and the purely spiritual;[23] and they regard the imaginative type as the more valuable and exalted! Theresa of Ávila expressly

[21] "She comes from Heaven; from the direction where the sun rises", said Jacinta to Canon Formigão. And Lucia: "I asked her where she came from and she answered that she came from Heaven" (cf. Visconde de Montelo [Dr. Manuel Nunes Formigão], *As grandes maravilhas de Fátima* [Lisbon 1927], pp. 67 and 74). This book is admittedly the most important source of information about events in the summer and autumn of 1917, apart from the records of the Church's judicial investigation.

[22] Relat. XV (II, p. 49). — This opinion may reflect the views of Theresa's theological advisers. At any rate it is clear that even the Saint's vast mystical experience does not contradict this perfectly legitimate theological opinion. Cf. St. Thomas, *S. Theol.* III, q. 76, a. 8. St. Thomas argues that Christ can be seen *in propria specie* only in one place, and would therefore have to leave heaven in order to appear *in propria specie* in some other place. Also III, q. 57, a. 6., where he claims for St. Paul alone an apparition of Christ such as the other apostles had. Cf. also Suárez, *De mysteriis vitae Christi,* disp. 51, sect. 4 (ed. Vivès XIX, pp. 983—86); M.-J. Ribet, *La mystique divine* II, 2nd ed. (Paris, 1895), ch. 6.

[23] Cf. John of the Cross, *Subida* II, 11; 16 (II, pp. 105 ff., 136 ff.); Joseph a. S. Spiritu, *op. cit.,* cap. I, q. 23 (p. 104 f.); Poulain, *op. cit.,* ch. 20 § 1 (pp. 311—16); Zahn, *op. cit.,* pp. 555—68. As purely intellectual visions are by definition without images, we can disregard them here, all visions which figure at all in popular and ecclesiastical piety being imaginative ones.

declares that she never had corporeal visions but only imaginative ones.[24] And she had a great abundance of visions. Thus the "authenticity" of a vision cannot be simply equated with its corporeality, its objective presence within the normal sphere of perception affecting the external human senses. Such an assumption, furthermore, would in most cases lead to impossible consequences. In such visions angels often appear, and human persons from the other world who already possess a resurrected body, together with people who have not yet risen.[25] Do we not need here an explanation which would cover all cases? Or shall

[24] *Vida* 28 (I, p. 218); *Moradas* VI, 9 (IV, p. 162). It should be noted here that in the opinion of St. John of the Cross and other mystical writers imaginative visions rank higher than corporeal ones and St. Theresa expressly mentions that she knows this to be so. Why did she have no corporeal visions though she did have the "higher" kind? We may suppose that she observed more keenly than those who took her visions for bodily ones and the latter for the normal type (cf. also note 30, p. 118, and note 47, p. 133). By saying that she does not have bodily visions Theresa means only that she does not see the object of her visions with her physical eyes, and so the question remains for her whether that object is present in its own being. But as she is convinced, e. g., that Christ never physically returned to earth after his Ascension it is, according to her interpretation, logically justifiable to conclude that the object seen in imaginative visions (seen, of course, with "the eyes of the soul") is not present in its physical reality. — If we were to infer that her visions should then be considered hallucinations, we should have to admit — as really serious Catholic scholars do — that she was at least sufficiently conscious of the "hallucinatory" character of her visions never to transport their objects into the sphere of objective perception. Consequently she did not have hallucinations in the popular sense of the word, which implies that a person falsely thinks the object of the hallucination is really present and is perceived by the senses from without.

[25] After the Queen of the Rosary disappeared at Fátima, e. g., on October 13, 1917 (according to the statements of Jacinta and Francisco) the Holy Family appeared high in the sky, grouped round the sun: on the left side of the sun was St. Joseph with the child Jesus, who presently took up a position under the sun, and Our Lady was on the right side (cf. Visconde de Montelo, *op. cit.*, pp. 114 and 119).

we postulate an apparent body assumed *ad hoc* on the one hand, whereas the others are present in their glorified bodies?[26] How, for instance, would this objectivistic conception explain the appearance in visions of Jesus as a child? Since he is not a child any more, how can he appear as such at this particular time and place before the visionary? How would one explain Our Lady under various titles — as the Sorrowful Mother, the Queen of the Rosary, the Virgin of Carmel, etc., — appearing in rapid succession, while other visionaries simultaneously see the Holy Family?[27] Or the appearance of a celestial person (the Saviour carrying his Cross, the Mother of God weeping) in a situation and frame of mind which are inappropriate to that person now? How can one explain those visions which, conveying as vivid an

[26] The assumption of an apparent body outside the visionary is, of course, not a contradiction (cf. Thomas, *S. Theol.* III, q. 76, a. 8). But an affectation of the sense organs without any corresponding external object is also conceivable according to Thomas *(ibid.)*. This second assumption is preferable because it is simpler and because it better explains a further complex of questions. Cf. on this matter Hubert Thurn, "Aussergewöhnliche religiöse Erfahrungen im Lichte der Psychologie" in *ZAM* xxi (1948), pp. 170—3.

[27] Lucia saw these various pictures of Our Lady while Francisco and Jacinta simultaneously saw the Holy Family. She also saw the bust of the Saviour as he blessed the world. Cf. Visconde de Montelo, *op. cit.,* pp. 95 f. Consequently she spoke of the *"Senhora de dois naipes"*, "Our Lady of the two playing-cards". Neither Francisco nor Jacinta saw these various pictures of Our Lady nor did they see the Saviour blessing *(ibid.,* pp. 114 and 116). — This emphatic distinction among the various Madonnas becomes more understandable if one reads Fonseca in *"Fátima y la crítica"* (Santander, 1953), p. 44: if a priest hearing confessions of pilgrims at Fátima gives a certain number of "Hail Mary's" for a penance, the penitent immediately asks "To which Blessed Virgin"? The people, especially the children, wish to know exactly whom they should address: The Queen of the Rosary, the Immaculate Conception, Our Lady of Sorrows, Our Lady of Joys, or the *Assumpta.* They know all these from the different statues. They do not know any statue of the Mother of God without a particular name.

impression of actuality as other visions, present past events as happening here and now[28] and that in a manner which contradicts the known historical facts as well as other visions of the same event,[29] (without there being any apparent reason to regard one vision as authentic and the other as illusory)? How (without arbitrarily postulating another miracle) can this naively realistic interpretation of visions explain the fact that not all present see the apparition? A naïve equation of visions with ordinary sense perception (everything being normal except the "presence" of the heavenly person) would inevitably raise the question whether the "glorified" bodies can exercise a physical influence on people not yet glorified, and whether they also have glorified "clothes" (after all, these are "seen" in the vision) like ours; and if, in both these respects the immediate impression conveyed by the vision is to be critically restricted, is there any point in continuing to maintain that the person seen is present in a spatio-temporal sense (as in the case of normal objects of sense-perception)?

[28] If one were to insist in such cases (Maria of Ágreda, Catherine Emmerick, etc.) on a direct "televisionary" connection between the seer and the historical events of the past, one could not explain the contradictions between such visions and would inevitably have to class these visions with other natural phenomena of parapsychological, profane clairvoyance (only the object being different). Thus they would lose their specific religious meaning and clear divine origin. In an isolated case or two, naturally such an explanation would be the more likely one, especially where things are seen and heard the religious or moral significance of which is not apparent, for instance hearing foreign languages which are not understood (cf., e. g., B. P. Siwek, S. J., *Une stigmatisée de nos jours: Thérèse de Konnersreuth*, Paris 1950, pp. 142 ff.). Obviously the question whether such parapsychological powers (the existence of which does not seem unlikely) might be miraculously activated by God still remains open.
[29] Examples in Poulain, *op. cit.*, ch. 21, § 1 (pp. 338 ff.); Zahn, *op. cit.*, § 41 (pp. 582 ff.).

The fact that the object seen gives the visionary an impression of reality and is even integrated into the normal dimension of sense-perception is no proof of the objectivity of the impression. For, on the one hand, we find the same thing in actual hallucinations and in eidetic phenomena,[30] and, on the other hand, this impression of accuracy is not a simple and immediate fact of consciousness, but (as in the case of the simplest and most ordinary illusions) must be regarded epistemologically as a judgment which misinterprets the perception. For that misinterpretation the visionary is responsible, not the vision and its transcendent cause. God does not deceive man, but man deceives himself.

For the same reasons it is not to be taken as a proof of the corporeality (and divine origin) of the vision if the person seen in it "speaks", "moves" — and even lets himself "be touched" (for even this happens in natural, purely imaginary processes);[31] even if the visionary has the impression of learning something surprising and hitherto unknown to him. This division of

[30] This impression may be so strong, as happened in the case of Bärbel Ruess at Pfaffenhofen (Germany), that the visionary is perfectly convinced that the others present must also have seen the person who appeared in the vision. Pastor Humpf reports: "Bärbel is firmly convinced that we too saw the Lady and heard everything. When we say that we saw nothing she gets angry and says: 'I know what I saw, I haven't taken leave of my senses.' She is quite indignant at our attitude." (From the account privately printed by Gebr. Keller at Fuessen, no date.)

[31] If the victim of hallucination changes his position the object "seen" may also shift accordingly because an hallucination frequently has some external basis; so that this normal criterion for the reality of an external object is not infallible in every case. Cf., e. g., Duret, *Les facteurs pratiques de la croyance dans la perception* (Paris, 1929), pp. 249 ff. He says of the integration of purely imaginary objects into the dimension of perception, "Il n'est au fond qu'un espace, dans lequel tantôt nous percevons et tantôt nous nous représentons les corps" (p. 29 f.). Even in pure hallucinations the condition of the pupil may alter according to the supposed distance of the object (*ibid.*, p. 251). —

118

consciousness into two personalities[32] and the sense of surprise we all experience in dreams; we do not wonder at it there because it is familiar, but the psychological explanation of the experience is far from simple.

It is always possible that the locution of a person seen in a vision may be the product of the creative subconscious of the visionary, unless its content absolutely transcends the powers of the visionary's consciousness, a fact which cannot easily be established. (Even in dreams, who has not found a person talking in a much more intelligent and impressive way than he could do in reality, where the free play of the creative imagination is subject to all sorts of inhibitions?) And though this proof were contrived, possible parapsychological explanations would still have to be considered, such as clairvoyance and second sight (which also occur in the lives of saints[33] — St. Theresa's vision

Staehlin reports experiments which were conducted to verify Duret's statements. He asked a seventeen-year old hairdresser's assistant seated in a room with white walls to look at the picture of his favourite brother on a piece of light green cardboard. Within 14 seconds the picture appeared indeed, first black and white with blurred contours, but perfectly plastic. Soon it not only took on natural colouring but protruding features, like the nose, cast appropriate shadows when a torch was trained on the cardboard in the darkened room, and when daylight was admitted into the room by opening the shutters, the picture soon conveyed so vivid an impression of reality — although the boy knew it was only an experiment — that Staehlin felt he must discontinue the test. In other experiments he observed that the people concerned engaged in conversation with their apparitions, and even "touched" their "clothes" (Staehlin, *op. cit.*, pp. 282 f.).

[32] Staehlin emphasizes the rôle played by split-personality in the case of people troubled by "the devil" (*ibid.*, pp. 248 f., 304). He tells of a student at a Jesuit college who was terrified by threatening letters which he continuously received. Investigation proved that he himself wrote the letters, and afterwards had no recollection of doing so (*ibid.*, p. 344).

[33] A. Mager, *Mystik als Lehre und Leben* (Innsbruck, 1934), p. 269, also thinks that a supernatural impulse might set the functions of a natural

of June 26, 1570 is an example),[34] at least as proximate causes.

In these circumstances is it not the most probable supposition that an apparition of Christ or of the saints is an imaginative vision? For what purpose would be served by the "objective" formation of an apparent body, or a miraculous affection of the visionary's external senses? The presence of Christ's own humanity in such a vision would be no more "objective" than it is in an imaginative vision.

In short: most visions are imaginative, above all simply because many visions (including those assumed to be genuine) cannot be corporeal ones: therefore all of them can be at least presumed to be imaginative visions.

There are, of course, cases where this rule of thumb runs into difficulties. What of several persons seeing the same vision? In that case must one not assume an object external to the visionaries, equally accessible to them all and actually perceived in common by their senses? Or what if profane observers of the proceedings think they saw other phenomena though not the figure?[35]

---

mediumistic consciousness operating. — The arguments of Thurn, *op., cit.,* on eidectic phenomena could be cited in his support.

[34] AASS Oct. VII, 1, n. 502 ff. (pp. 299 ff.). She saw the matyrdom of 40 Brazilian martyrs at the very moment when it happened. The process was so like profane clairvoyance that this latter must be presumed the proximate cause, the more as a relative of St. Theresa was amongst the martyrs. For the problem of mediumstic telaesthesia cf., e. g., F. Moser, *Der Okkultismus, Täuschungen und Tatsachen* (Munich, 1935), I, pp. 412—38; II, pp. 486 ff. (For our purpose, of course, it is immaterial whether St. Theresa's was a case of telepathy or of teleasthesia proper.) J. Rhine, *Extra-Sensory Perception* (New York, 1934); *The Reach of the Mind* (New York, 1947); Renée Haynes, *The Hidden Springs* (London, 1961).

[35] At Fátima "some persons claimed to have heard the sound of the answers (of Our Lady)" (cf. Visconde de Montelo, *op. cit.,* p. 85). These spectators

First of all we have to emphasize that the presumption of a "merely" imaginative vision is only a presumption, which in certain cases may yield to another explanation. Now it is often remarkable in apparitions to a number of persons at once that some of the visionaries do not see or hear as much as others.[36] Is this not a natural and even normal effect of what appears in other contexts as mass hypnosis,[37] or in a distorted form in the case of psychic disturbances, as induced insanity? Is the element of suggestion wholly excluded when crowds eagerly awaiting[38] a new apparition think they observe some (relatively insignificant) concomitant phenomena of the vision itself which they do

were also convinced that at each of the six apparitions (*ibid.*, p. 18) they observed some heavenly manifestation: a dimming of the sun, a shining egg (p. 59), a white cloud (on Aug. 13, when the children were not there; p. 82), a shining balloon. It is noteworthy that Canon Formigão, who was personally present on Sept. 13, tells of the report of another eye-witness, quoting a third person (also anonymous), that this person and others had seen a shower of flowers. The second eye-witness said that he was sorry not to have seen it. Canon Formigão continues: "Before concluding I must say in all candour that my impressions of what happened that day at Fátima were not enthusiastic (animadores)" (*ibid.*, pp. 59—61).

[36] Cf. note 25 on p. 115, and note 27 on p. 116.

[37] Staehlin reports an interesting experiment with six youths between 15 and 18, whom he asked to imagine a battle of medieval warriors going on above an isolated tree. Two of them merely saw it, two others saw it and also heard the noise of battle and the individual cries of the warriors, but the last two neither saw nor heard anything. Though the youths were strictly watched to prevent them talking to each other before reporting what they had seen and heard, the reports — especially of those who heard sounds — agreed in every detail (*op. cit.*, pp. 389 ff.).

[38] Canon Formigão gives us a vivid picture of the tension and deep religious absorption of the multitude even before the apparitions at Fátima: "I shall never forget the tremendous impression made upon me by seeing so many thousands of the faithful falling on their knees. In tears they prayed aloud, confidently begging the Queen of Heaven for her motherly protection" (p. 59).

not see? Must not the actual vision be considered imaginative even in such cases, when the figure seen changes during the vision and appears in the company of persons (such as the child Jesus) who do not objectively exist as they are seen? If collective hallucination on a very considerable scale can be caused by purely human suggestion,[39] if therefore a psychic mechanism can be started simultaneously in a number of people, then the possibility that God too might make simultaneous use of these psychic potentialities in a number of people cannot be rejected *a priori*.[40]

Suppose that the same seers have visions which are undoubtedly imaginative.[41] Even where a vision is purely imaginative so far as the person actually seen is concerned, there is no reason why its divine origin cannot be confirmed by phenomena of the objective order (such as cures, or the miracle of the sun at Fátima).

To sum up: in principle the possibility of corporeal visions (even apart from the "apparitions" of the Risen Christ to the Apostles) can hardly be disputed; but conclusive proof of such

[39] Consider the effect of mental suggestion on crowds watching the Indian "rope trick". Cf. Moser, *op. cit.*, I, pp. 391—6; also H. Thurston, "Limpias and the Problem of Collective Hallucination" in *The Month* cxxxvi (1920), pp. 387—98, 533—41.

[40] Dhanis, *op. cit.*, p. 31, is also inclined to interpret the childrens' vision at Fátima, for instance, as imaginative (Francisco did not hear anything at all, he did not even see the lips of the apparition moving (Visconde de Montelo, *op. cit.*, p. 115); Lucia and Jacinta do not seem to have heard quite the same thing and they certainly did not see the same thing. We should also consider that the apparitions disappeared piecemeal, first the head, then the trunk, and the feet were the last thing the children saw. Lucia explicitly stated this on Oct. 13, 1917 (Visconde de Montelo, *ibid.*, p. 100).

[41] The "vision of hell" which the children of Fátima saw can only be conceived as an imaginative vision (cf. Dhanis, *op. cit.*, p. 60).

an ocurrence will rarely be possible in a concrete case. Normally, authentic visions will be imaginative ones. However, this statement does not solve the psychological problem of the nature of these visions but only poses it and indicates the direction in which a solution must be sought.

Can we work out a more precise idea of imaginative visions? Two things can be said at the outset: on the one hand by the nature of the case such a vision must largely conform to the psychic laws determined by the intrinsic structure of the seer's spiritual faculties; and on the other hand, in order to be held authentic, the vision must be caused by God. Both propositions call for brief explanation before we can examine their implications in concrete detail.

As to the first, in principle God is certainly able to interrupt the natural functions of his creatures by his miraculous intervention. But we must first consider that for a variety of reasons, which here need not be enumerated, a suspension of natural laws is not be presumed but must be proved. Even where a miracle really occurs we can consider the laws of nature suspended only to the extent strictly required by the event; and in such cases as far as it is possible God will use the natural laws which after all he has created and willed. Then again, generally and in particular in spiritual matters a total suspension of all natural laws is not only not to be presumed but is impossible; in spite of or rather because of God's omnipotence it does not happen, because it would imply an essential contradiction. For a vision to be truly the spiritual reality of a given person it must, metaphysically speaking, be the true act of this person, not only an act produced in him by God but also an act really performed by the person himself. But this is to say that the act must express the laws of the

123

person's ontological structure, because otherwise there could be no vision at all.

Of course in an actual vision it will be almost impossible to trace the precise borderline between those psychical laws which necessarily operate and those which, though natural, are not necessary and are in fact suspended by the miraculous intervention of God. But if one considers what has been said above, namely that miracles and their multiplication are not to be presumed but must be proved, then it is to be expected that even in visions of divine origin the seer's psychical structure and the laws of his nature will remain intact and operative to the fullest extent.[42]

To the second point: it must be observed that the statement "this vision is the work of God" is in itself extraordinarily

---

[42] Cf. J. Maréchal, *Étude sur la Psychologie des Mystiques* I (Bruges - Paris, 1924), pp. 134 ff.: "Quelle que soit leur cause, le mécanisme psychologique de ces visions imaginaires n'offre rien qui les distingue foncièrement des pseudohallucinations avec ou sans spatialisation précise de l'image (p. 136) ... Les états mystiques, même supérieurs, si fortement marqués à l'estampille des individus, qui les éprouvent, plongent des racines profondes dans la zone des activités psycho-physiologiques générales, contiennent celles-ci, les prolongent en quelque façon et en étendent la portée, bien loin de leur substituer des facultés totalement 'nouvelles' et hétérogènes, peu intelligibles vraiment" (p. 185). Engl. tr. *Studies in the Psychology of the Mystics* (New York, 1927). (Whatever their cause, the psychological mechanism of these imaginary visions presents nothing that distinguishes them sharply from pseudo-hallucinations with or without precise spatialization of the image ... .The mystical states, even the higher ones, hallmarked as they are by the persons who experience them, are deeply rooted in the zone of general psycho-physiological activities, continuing these, prolonging them in some way and extending their scope and are far from substituting for them totally "new" and heterogeneous faculties — which indeed would hardly be intelligible.) Similarly Lais, *op. cit.*, p. 56; Anonymous, "Les révélations privées" in *Collationes Dioecesis Tornacensis* xxxiv (1938/39), pp. 108—18; R. Dalbiez, "Marie-Thérèse Noblet, considérée du point de vue psychologique" in *Études Carmélitaines* xxiii (1938, II), 225 f.

ambiguous. Everything (except sin, which he only permits) is the work of God. Especially where an event is of positive moral and religious significance for a man he will rightly see in the event a special favour of Providence and gratefully accept it as "God's doing" even if objectively no miracle (in·the sense of a divine intervention suspending natural physical or psychological laws) can be demonstrated and none has occurred. Indeed it could be said that from the devotional point of view it is immaterial whether the divine causality operates within or beyond the framework of natural law, since the religious man can rightly see, even in events that are capable of "natural explanation", the free graces of God given for his salvation. In this sense a vision that could be naturally explained could be considered — insofar as it conformed to genuine Christian standards of faith and morals, and did not injure the spiritual health of the visionary but contributed towards his progress in virtue and piety — "the work of God" and "a grace", even though the immediate "natural" cause of the vision were found in psychic mechanisms which ordinarily do not operate all, or at least not with the same intensity; for a phenomenon of this sort should not be summarily dismissed as pathological, or "anomalous" in a pejorative sense.[43]

[43] Why should the natural parapsychological powers of telepathy, clair-voyance, psychometry (if these exist) not be able to apprehend religious objects, just as the "normal" powers of a religious person do, and thus occasion acts of religious value? And why should not such acts (of religious contemplation, the searching of hearts, recognition of relics, etc.) be taken as "graces" of God? — conversely, natural physical and psychic occurrences, normal or extraordinary, which of themselves or a least in practice handicap, threaten or destroy the religious and moral life of man can be called "diabolical", even if nothing "queer" is involved. For it is quite scriptural to see such things, considered from a more general point of view, as effects of

But we must attribute "divine origin" in a special sense to those visions which are caused by a properly supernatural intervention of God, one, that is, which transcends the laws of physical and psychical nature. Now this supernational intervention of God can and must be distinguished.

There is first a supernatural causality of God (especially in what we call God's supernatural indwelling in the souls of the justified in "sanctifying grace") which implies an essentially new action of God superior to nature, which transforms nature but does not suspend its laws in any proper and empirically verifiable sense, which does not imply a merely sporadic divine intervention but belongs (even outside explicit Christianity) to the normal structure of concrete psychic reality. Now it would be very difficult to prove that it is wholly impossible for this supernatural reality, produced by God, in its normal development (at least in the case of certain people because of their natural character and spiritual progress) to initiate psychic processes which judged by their immediate effects must be called visions. Such visions would then, on the one hand, be produced supernaturally by God without, on the other hand, being miracles in a technical sense. These visions would be the extraordinary

diabolical activity in the fallen world (cf., e.g., 1 Thess. 2:18; 2 Cor. 12:7; 1 Cor. 5:5). From this point of view the older mystical writers were by no means mistaken in attributing to Satan those mental processes which in fact are psychically destructive or morally pernicious for the person in question, even in cases where today we primarily see hallucinations, hysteria and mental disease. The two aspects, the theological and the empirical, are not mutually exclusive, though they must be distinguished in order to avoid practical blunders in the treatment of people so afflicted. Exorcism of persons who in fact do not suffer from diabolical possession is an example. According to Staehlin (*op. cit.,* p. 291) this has the disastrous effect of intensifying the morbid symptoms.

but not preternatural psychophysical echoes of a normal development of supernatural life, and in this sense of supernatural
and divine origin.[44]

There is a second supernatural causality of God which must be
regarded as a miracle in the strict sense of the word: that is, a
divine intervention which partly suspends the laws of nature
(and therefore the normal laws of psychology as well). If a
vision is caused by such an intervention, it is of divine origin in
an eminent sense; and this is the sense, according to common
opinion, in which authentic visions are produced by God.

Clearly then, in an actual case, it will not be easy to say
whether a vision is of supernatural origin and produced by God
in the first or in the second sense, as both elements may
contribute to the same vision. Furthermore it must be borne in
mind that the religious significance of a vision which is
supernatural in the first sense may by the nature of the case be
far greater than that of one which is supernatural in the second
sense; for the technically miraculous need by no means be more
perfect, either ontologically or ethically. A quite ordinary act

---

[44] Cf. pp. 137 ff., *infra.* We must clearly understand that an intensely spiritual
life, even one characterized by superrational mystical graces, can still be
considered the final stage of the "normal development of the life of grace".
If something extraordinary occurs in the psychophysical dimension as an echo
of these mystical graces or simply as an echo of a great love of God, then
the whole process is indeed supernatural but not necessarily "miraculous" or
preternatural. Thus considered, the second case is not basically different from
the first since the first also concerns a man living in the grace of God. —
Still it must be observed that extraordinary phenomena (stigmatization,
visions) do not necessarily presuppose the state of grace, and so may appear,
as in the first case, where nothing supernatural is involved at all. Cf. Staehlin,
ibid., p. 68, with reference to St. Bonaventure's *De profectu religiosorum*,
1. 2, cap. 75: "De quattuor generibus visionum", n. 3. (*Opera omnia*, ed.
Vivès, XII, p. 434).

127

of virtue is ontologically and ethically of greater significance than an imaginative vision as such insofar as the latter is not produced by an act of supernatural virtue or does not give rise to one. These visions involving a partial or total suspension of natural laws must not on that account be considered "corporeal" visions. They too can be and are purely imaginative ones.

These various types of divine causality in an authentic vision must be noted, because when one is considering how the authenticity of a vision can be ascertained and also what the Church means when she recognizes a vision as "credible", the credibility of an authentic vision by no means necessarily implies that it is effected by a miracle in the proper sense. Why, for instance, could acknowledgment of a vision by the Church not remain meaningful (and therefore open to legitimate interpretation in this restricted sense) if it only implied that the content of the vision and its effects on the visionary and on others are wholesome and in that sense come from God, or that it is a legitimate echo of the seer's own mystical experience, consistent with faith and reason? In neither case need we presuppose a literally miraculous intervention of God, confirmed as such by the Church.

At all events it is clear that criteria of authenticity for visions which are genuine in the first and second of the three senses we have distinguished are more easily found than criteria of authenticity for a vision caused by God in the third sense of the word, and that in practice it is quite sufficient to establish authenticity in the first and second sense (even if the vision should be objectively a miracle as well). Similarly it cannot be proved *a priori* that God could not confirm the truth of a vision genuine only in the first and second sense (therefore in itself a non-miraculous vision), by a miracle subsequent or concomitant (but distinct from the vision itself) such as cures at the scene of the apparitions; so that one could not automatically conclude from this miracle that the vision itself had been technically miraculous. In other contexts, after all, God can miraculously confirm knowledge, impulses, preaching of the truth, which certainly are not of miraculous origin. Why should not God be able to do the same thing in the case of visions?[45]

This preliminary discussion was necessary to clarify the formal sense of the two propositions above; we must now examine their concrete psychological implications.

It is to be noted that we still proceed according to this method: we presuppose a genuine imaginative vision — one, that is, produced by God as a real, supernatural cause. From this point of departure three things must be considered: a) the production of a *species sensibilis* (phantasm), a picture in the imagination, b) the objectification of the same, and c) the question of the exact point at which the *species sensibilis* is elicited.

[45] If a person were unable to discover anything in the visions of Fátima that transcends the laws of nature and explained them all in natural terms, this would be far from denying divine origin. Nevertheless, most books about Fátima unfortunately set out to prove at any price that the visions defy all the laws of nature (cf. Staehlin, *ibid.*, pp. 367—79, and the publications of L. G. da Fonseca, particularly *"Fátima y la crítica"*), and to this end withhold important texts and even make false statements (see note 96, p. 156, *infra*).

2. How the "species sensibilis" is Produced

We cannot enlarge here upon experimental or speculative psychology in order to describe in detail how a vision arises. We can only state in general terms, which are not intended as a real explanation, that where a vision is not simply connected in obscure fashion with a spatio-temporal object but is presented with the object itself as spatial, that is, in its very act possesses the object as spatial, then the act of vision itself, in its own "subjective" reality, is a sense-act: its immediate faculty includes a somatic element but the act of vision is psycho-somatic. If the act is not caused by the external influence of the object in its own materiality, then the physiological stimulus (in scholastic terms, the *species sensibilis impressa)* of which the "internal" conscious aspect or correlate is the object presented to the senses, must come from elsewhere, in our case immediately or mediately from God. In any case no one should be so absurdly naïve as to imagine that the "object" of a vision has only to be personally present (in a place) in order to be seen. Before the senses can become conscious of an object they invariably require a stimulus, so that the object will be actually perceived, not merely envisaged intellectually "in itself". If this *species sensibilis impressa,* as the real prerequisite to sense-perception, is produced by God, then in principle it may appear in all the vastly different forms which it could otherwise assume: as the *species* of a perception, of a pure fancy, of an illusion, of an eidetic phenomenon, of a pseudo-hallucination, of an hallucination, and so forth. It may affect individual senses ("external" or "internal") or it may be co-ordinately present in several senses.

3. "Objectification" of the Object of Sense Consciousness

The form taken by the objectification of the object of sense consciousness will correspond to the character which this *species sensibilis* (in our supposition caused by God) happens to have. The content of sense consciousness is objectified (disregarding the question of whether, from the point of view of the metaphysics of cognition, a function of intellectual consciousness is already involved here) first of all by the fact that the content of consciousness does not appear to the consciousness (at least in the case of hearing and seeing) as a disposition of the person experiencing it but stands before the consciousness as an "object". Whether this object is felt to be "perceived" or only "imagined" will depend on the character of the psycho-physical stimulus, i. e., of the *species sensibilis*.

At all events it must be said that the consciousness of perceiving a corporeal object which, e. g., appears to be integrated in the normal field of perception, is not altered even by deliberate effort, displays the details and materiality of an ordinary object of perception, cannot be produced at will, moves apart from the conscious desire of the subject, speaks, does not accompany movements of the eyes — all these and similar features which characterize normal perception and ordinarily prompt us to a spontaneous judgment that a spatial object as such is really present — are not criteria which in every case would authorize the conclusion that what one perceives is objectively there. Such evidence of perception is a (spontaneous, implicit) judgment which could be erroneous in an individual case. Proper and unerring evidence of perception can never directly prove the nature of the object "in itself" but only our consciousness of the object. Any consciousness of objectivity which one may have in addition to this is never the result of perception but always of a judgment, and therefore in an individual case it can always be erroneous. Indeed we may encounter all the ordinary evidence for the perception of an object which is physically present, in cases where the object in itself is not present and where other causes, nevertheless, stimulate the cognitive organs of sense in the precise manner required for normal perception.[46] It must also be noted that an important workaday criterion of the reliability of perception — its obvious harmony with our whole experience hitherto and its confirmation by our subsequent experience — is automatically excluded in the case of a vision.

It is immaterial by what signs, for what reasons and by what devices the falsehood of such a judgment on a perceptional presence is discovered in a concrete case. The error may be detected in one case by closer observation, in an entirely different case by theological arguments and considerations: but it is not invincible and it is to be sought not in the senses as such but in the judgment which follows perception.

[46] Cf. note 42, *supra;* J. Froebes, *Lehrbuch der experimentellen Psychologie* I. (2end & 3rd ed., Freiburg, 1923), pp. 235—7: "(Imagination and perception) merge into one another, and passage from one to the other is not impossible" (p. 237); Thurn, *op. cit.,* pp. 172, 175; Maréchal, *op. cit.,* I, p. 77: "Le sentiment contraignant d'une réalité présente n'est donc pas l'apanage exclusif de la sensation externe; il peut se greffer sur ce phénomène purement central, qu'est l'image hallucinatoire." (The compelling feeling of the presence of a reality is thus not the exclusive attribute of external sensation; it can be grafted upon the purely central phenomenon which is the hallucinatory image.) — Staehlin, *op. cit.,* pp. 282 ff. Cf. note 31, p. 118, *supra* (the experiment with the hairdresser's assistant). We shall not enter here into the difficult metaphysical and psychological problems surrounding the nature and basis of certainty in perception. It will suffice for our purpose, at least, to grasp the simple fact that nothing the visionary is able to communicate

It follows that we cannot speak of an unavoidable deception by God if this sense impression is caused by him, "evidence of sense-perception" arises and thus a false judgment on the corporeal presence of what is perceived by the sense consciousness suggests itself (though not necessarily).[47] This holds true even where more attentive ordinary reflection on the supposedly physical perception could not establish (as is possible in many cases) that the object "seen" has not been present in its own reality, but this fact only emerges from indirect (rational) considerations.

A further consequence: the truth of a sensible (imaginative) vision does not depend on its perceptible content, at least in practice and for outsiders.[48] As the content of such a vision has its real existence primarily in the stimulation of the faculties of

to others of the experience and content of his vision will justify them in concluding beyond doubt that the object "seen" was really present. For more thorough discussion of these problems see Maréchal, op. cit., I, pp. 67—131. Cf. also K. Jaspers, *Allgemeine Psychopathologie* (Berlin, 1953), pp. 55 ff; E. de Greeff, *Psychiatrie et religion* (1958).

[47] But the impression can be so forceful that even saints are moved to form a false judgment. At a time, for example, when the apparitions of the miraculous medal had become known but not the identity of the visionary, St. Catherine Labouré said with great emphasis to one of the nuns who doubted the bodily reality of the apparitions, "Ma petite, la Sœur qui a vu la Sainte Vierge, l'a vue en chair et en os!" (My child, the Sister who saw the Blessed Virgin, saw her in flesh and blood.) Similary St. Bernadette insisted: "Je l'ai vue avec mes œuls" (!) ("I saw her with my own eyes"). (Cf. Staehlin, op. cit., p. 231.)

[48] St. Theresa does indeed say that even the sensible content of such visions (brilliance, and so on) is so powerful and so different from anything that could be produced by the imagination (e. g., Vida 28 [I, p. 219]), that this alone excludes any possible doubt of the vision's divine origin. But does she not overlook here the difference between voluntary phantasies and spontaneous eidetic or hallucinatory phenomena? For the mystical doctors declare that this criterion is by no means an infallible one. Cf., e. g., Joseph

133

sense, it is attached to and limited by the powers of those faculties. To prove the divine origin (authenticity) of an imaginative vision by its content would be possible only if it could be demonstrated that the concrete content of that vision quite exceeds the powers of the seer's sensible and intellectual faculties (memory, creative imagination, the subconscious, para-psychological faculties like telepathy, etc.). But this will be feasible, if at all, only in the rarest cases; for the content of most visions[49] is such as could be constructed out of elements already

a. S. Spiritu, *op. cit.*, I, q. 26 (114): "Possunt etiam naturaliter contingere ex aliquo humore praedominante vel ispsius imaginationis vivacitate et ingenio. Et licet dentur regulae (amongst which he lists that just mentioned) ad eas discernendas, hae non sunt infallibiles." (They can also occur naturally because of some predominant humour or the vividness and bent of the imagination. Altough there are rules by which to discern them, they are not infallible). — Cf. also John of the Cross, *Subida* II, 17, 7 (II, p. 150); II, 18, 8 (II, p. 156). It should also be added that the outside observer can never so precisely assess the difference between the sensible content of a phantasy (hallucination, etc.) and of a true vision, as to draw a firm conclusion, the more so as there are also hallucinatory experiences (e. g. the toxic) of extraordinary power.

[49] In practice the content of a vision could escape this category only if it disclosed a knowledge of the future which could be proved to be possible to God alone. For in view of the possibilities of telepathic communication, this is really the only content of which the divine origin can be strictly demonstrated. We presuppose, of course, that such a prediction of the future has been communicated to others before its fulfilment. The content of most visions can be explained by the religious knowledge of the visionary even without recourse to the possibilities of telepathy. To cite only one very recent example, there are the revelations of Sister Josefa Menéndez: *Way of Divine Love. The Message of the Sacred Heart to the World and a Short Biography of his Messenger.* (Newman Press, Westminster, Md., 1949.) The author (the Mother General Lescure) is not named, but there is a letter of recommendation by Cardinal Pacelli and an introduction by H. Monier-Vinard, S. J. The objective theological doctrine does not contain anything that would not be known by a nun properly trained in religion even without any divine communication. In particular instances, indeed, it can be shown that the

present in the visionary before the vision. This consideration seems particularly appropriate in the case of children. How could a child understand a revelation containing words (it is always a case of visions and auditions) entirely unknown to it? If it is established that immediately after the vision or audition it was communicated, especially to other children, the revelation cannot contain any words or concepts which were unknown to the children, either the seers or the ones who received the communication, because otherwise any communication would be quite impossible.[50]

To express the matter in theological terms: generally even

"words of the Lord" derive from her own subconscious mind. For instance, the Lord has her read something from the book of his heart which she had often prayed in her youth, a prayer of St. Margaret Mary Alacoque (cf. Staehlin, *op. cit.*, pp. 116 f. Other instances are adduced on pp. 114 and 117. Cf. also pp. 252 f.). We shall return later to this biography of Sister Josefa Menéndez (note 86, p. 152). In judging such lengthy revelations one should also remember what M. Meschler once said: "The mystics also observe that genuine divine allocutions are very brief and concise." "Über Visionen und Prophezeiungen" in *StdZ* xv (1878), p. 260.

[50] An example: Lucia revealed the "secret" to her cousin Francesco, as he explicitly states (cf. Visconde de Montelo, *op. cit.*, p. 105). Moreover, when questioned by Canon Formigão Francisco behaved exactly as Jacinta and Lucia did, who had learned the secret from the mouth of the apparition. He thinks, for example, that the people will be sad if they learn that the secret concerns the three children, etc. He never indicates that he did not understand at least some parts of it, as was suggested by the fact that when questioned about its content he was unwilling or forbidden to speak. If then Lucia was quite able to pass on the secret — within the limits determined by the apparition — and Francisco understood it, one cannot agree with L. G. da Fonseca that it was a great grace that the children of 1917 were not permitted to reveal anything, because "with their narrow ideas and lack of vocabulary to express themselves they would have destroyed the work of God" (cf. *Fátima y la crítica*, p. 48). Rather the fact that the secret was told to Francisco seems to show that it contained nothing which the children were unable to understand at the time. Cf. also note 104, p. 162, *infra*.

authentic visions (in regard to their content) will not be supernatural *quoad substantiam* but only *quoad modum* (as caused by God); or at least it will be impossible to prove them anything more. In short, neither experiencing its apparent or real perception nor the content itself will generally be a strict "criterion of authenticity", that is, of the imaginative vision's non-subjective causation and divine origin, because the nature of an imaginative vision as such simply cannot offer such evidence, or at least does not do so under normal circumstances.

This is not to deny that the visionary might in principle receive from God objectively valid evidence of the divine origin of his vision. There is no reason to doubt the possibility of such evidence. The imaginative vision can be conceived as accompanied by purely spiritual divine influence upon the soul which would give the visionary infallible and objectively valid evidence that here God is really at work. Two points should be noted here, however.

First, that such spiritual evidence is of its nature incommunicable to others. How could one prove to somebody else that one really had it and was not deceived? In the case of a mystic who was already accustomed to such experiences (the fact being also well known to others), one could rely on his testimony that he had had another indubitable experience of the same nature, because in these circumstances (but only these) one could assume that he was able to distinguish it from illusory experiences. But in this case we presuppose that he has already had genuine mystical experience of a strictly spiritual nature, and the question remains how this fact can be recognized by others.

Secondly, the question remains how far a concomitant (or earlier) spiritual experience of a divine influence, which the recipient may rightly accept as unquestionable evidence, is able or intended to confirm the objective accuracy of the imaginative content of an individual vision. The genuine mystics themselves emphasize that even here — for reasons we are about to discuss — great caution and reserve are in order, because even with respect to the imaginative content of the vision errors and misinterpretations may creep in.[51]

4. The Point of Contact of the Divine Action on the Visionary

An entirely different aspect of the psychology of the imaginative vision still calls for attention. We have to ask "where" the visionary receives the divine impetus to the imaginative vision which to a certain extent is the "primary effect" of the divine

---

[51] Those considerations show how questionable is the confidence with which people accept every statement made by a seer many years after her visions — acknowledged to be authentic — about these visions and later ones intended to complete them. If it be true, as is extremely probable, that true, divine visions use the same psychic mechanism as hallucinations and other eidetic phenomena, and that, moreover, true visions occur almost exclusively where saintly people have a special propensity for such things, then one is justified in assuming that true visions produce a habitus and may so foster an inclination already present that this will sometimes set the psychic mechanism operating even if there is no divine motion. This would explain the self-deceptions of canonized saints. Cf. Benedict XIV, *De servorum Dei beatificatione et beatorum canonisatione*, III, cap. 53, n. 17: "Aliquando sanctos Prophetas, dum consolantur, ex magno usu prophetandi, quaedam proferre ex suo spiritu, suspicantes, hoc esse ex spiritu prophetiae." Cf. also J. Surin, *Cathéchisme spirituel de la perfection chrétienne* (1801), vol. I, Part 3, ch. 5, p. 284: "Ce sont quelquefois des personnes vertueuses et accoutumées aux visites de Notre-Seigneur, et qui néanmoins ne peuvent pas reconnaître la tromperie" to which they fall victim in taking what comes from themselves or the devil for messages of Christ.

contact. This impetus need not necessarily be the stimulation of the sense-organs as such, which may be a mere consequence and radiation of the divine action much "deeper" in man. We can assume on principle[52] what is urged by the testimony of classic mysticism, that even in the imaginative vision it is not as a rule the vision as such (the stimulation of the sense-organs) that is primarily and directly effected by God. Rather the vision is a kind of overflow and echo of a much more intimate and spiritual process.[53]

[52] Normally then a vision presupposes and fosters the moral and religious progress of man. Now the sanctity which is the presupposition and goal of the vision primarily concerns the spiritual core of the person. If the divine motion were not first applied here, then the vision would expose the seer instead to the danger of passing the essential thing by. Even Judas "saw" the Lord. But the eyes of his spirit, of the personal core in him, were closed. Only in the case of a purely charismatic "prophetic vision", of a simple *gratia gratis data,* could one assume without great hesitation that the divine impulse directly affects the faculties of sense as such and them alone. But generally God will not use a man as Balaam's ass.

[53] Cf., e. g., John of the Cross, *Subida* II, 16, 11 (II, p. 142): the "formas, imágenes y figuras" are only the husks of the real "communicaciones espirituales"; *Subida* II, 17, 7 (II, p. 150) also assume that the proper "efecto" of the divine communication remains even if man rejects the "visiones imaginarias" — that come from God. These, then, cannot be the cause of the divine communication proper "en sustancia". The relationship is just the reverse. In the imaginative vision — to borrow a metaphor of St. John of the Cross (*Subida* II, 14, 9 [II, pp. 126 f.]) — the pure and simple light of God is refracted in the prism of sensibility. St. Theresa's description of God's "allocutions" (including imaginative "formal" ones) (Moradas VI, 3 [IV, p. 115]) shows that they irresistibly achieve in the soul what they say, and consequently are "substantial" at the same time (in the terminology of John of the Cross). Thus the "heart" of the experience is not in the senses at all. St. Theresa logically thinks it is not wrong to disbelieve locutions *(Moradas* IV, 3 [IV, p. 114]) although she also approves the opposite attitude, so she obviously has divine locutions in mind. G. B. Scaramelli, *Il direttorio mistico,* tract. IV, cap. 6, n. 84, (Tournai, 1863, vol. II, p. 65), also says that a divine imaginative vision must be accompanied by

This is not the place for a detailed description of this more central and in itself purely spiritual process, of which the imaginative vision is only a secondary phenomenon. Let us only say that this is the process which the classic Spanish mystics describe as "infused contemplation" (from the "spiritual betrothal" to "the spiritual marriage", the full mystical union). Just as ecstasy, the suspension of the activity of the senses, is only a concomitant phenomenon, a result of the central mystical process, which indeed disappears at the highest degree of perfect mystical development, and is even considered a certain weakness in the nature of the mystic, who cannot contain the abundance of God's mystical self-communication, so the imaginative vision, which presupposes such infused contemplation, is only the radiation and reflex of contemplation in the sphere of the senses, the incarnation of the mystical process of the spirit.

Hence arise a series of important insights and consequences for the nature and judgment of imaginative visions as such if they are genuine, which now means effected by God in the way we have just explained.

1. First of all it will now be understandable why classic mysticism — though with markedly slight differences — is so indifferent towards, and even critical of, imaginative visions, even in the supposition that they come from God.[54] It is explicitly

an intellectual one. — The consequences of this explanation (which can be justified independently of it) will presently confirm the view now presupposed. This conception of the origin of true visions is already found in A. Mager, *op. cit.*, pp. 192 f. and indeed as early as the mysticism of Görres if we abstract from the details which he presupposes (cf. J. Pacher, *Die plastische Kraft im religiösen Gestaltungsvorgang nach Joseph von Görres*, Würzburg, 1928).

[54] John of the Cross, *Subida* II, 12 ff. (II, pp. 113 ff.); Joseph a S. Spiritu, I, q. 26 (pp. 112 ff.); Antonius a S. Spiritu (d. 1674), *Directorium mysticum* (ed.

emphasized that no one should fear that by repelling such a vision he will resist grace and offend God. (If this is valid for the visionary, how much more so for others.) To repel or disregard even a genuine imaginative vision is neither to reject nor hinder what God is really doing; rather what is disregarded is a reflex, in the sphere of the senses, of the real thing and this attitude directs the attention of man and his personal decision to the one thing necessary, to the work which the mystical grace of God does in infused contemplation in the depths of a person, to pure faith and love of the God who transcends all images. This doctrine which runs through all the history of mysticism[55] does not originate merely or principally from a spiritual metaphysics of neo-platonic tendency, for which everything sensuous and graphic is basically suspect, but from an experience which, while it may be variously interpreted according to the metaphysical opinions prevalent in succeeding ages, must still be explained in every metaphysics of mysticism because it is a fact: that God is always greater than any image of himself and wishes to communicate himself as thus greater, in mystical experience. Here least of all, then, should man cling to his appearance, because it remains true even in the highest theology of union

Bernardus a SS. Sacr., Paris, 1904), tract. 3, disp. 5, sect. 2 (pp. 360 ff.); G. B. Scaramelli, *op. cit.*, tract. IV, cap. 4, n. 42 (II, p. 33).

[55] For Origen see: Jean Daniélou, *Origen* (London, New York, 1955); for Evagrius Ponticus: H. U. v. Balthasar, "Metaphysik und Mystik des Evagrius Pontikus" in *ZAM* xiv (1939), pp. 31—47; for Diadochus of Photike: F. Dörr, *Diadochus von Photike und die Messalianer* (Freiburg, 1937), pp. 127—9; for Philoxenus of Mabbug: J. Hausherr, "Contemplation et sainteté. Une remarquable mise au point par Ph. de M." in *RAM* 14 (1933), p. 192; for George of Sinai, N. Arseniew, *Ostkirche und Mystik*, 2nd ed., p. 21; for Denys the Areopagite: M. Viller - K. Rahner, *Aszese und Mystik in der Väterzeit* (Freiburg, 1939), pp. 236 ff.; for John of the Cross, in spite

that the God who can no longer be separated from the world of his appearance still remains unconfused with his appearance.

2. It will be understood that genuine Christian mysticism is highly suspicious of alleged imaginative visions if they occur outside the context of properly mystical graces.[56] It is quite conceivable that a psychologically untrained, simple visionary in recollecting and relating his experience might (objectively speaking) overemphasize its imaginative element just because it is much easier to describe, but this need not mean that he did not experience something more essential. But if in fact nothing else was experienced, if, for example, the heavenly person was seen as one "sees" anybody else (and was at first taken for an ordinary human being),[57] this is no argument for the authenticity of the vision, which should be treated with the greatest reserve if not rejected as a mere hallucination. On the basis of his own experience with real mystics[58] and following St. John of the Cross, K. Hock, for instance, rejects in principle all visions which occur before the mystical betrothal, and so without

of philosophical and theological shortcomings, it is still worth reading J. Baruzi, *Saint Jean de la Croix et le problème de l'expérience mystique* (Paris, 1931), pp. 449 ff.: "Une critique des appréhensions distinctes;" for St. Paul of the Cross: Gaétan du S. Nom de Marie, "St. Paul de la Croix: sa doctrine et sa pratique touchant les visions, révélations et extases" in *RAM* viii (1927), pp. 361—92.

[56] Cf. K. Hock, "Johannes vom Kreuz und die Nebenerscheinungen der Mystik" in *Theologisch-praktische Quartalschrift* lxxviii (1925), pp. 506—19, 698—705: St. John of the Cross and St. Theresa both express the opinion that true visions and revelations are not granted to a soul until it has reached the stage of mystical betrothal, and this is generally accepted by mystical authors.

[57] This was the case at Pfaffenhofen a. d. R. (cf. the account of the pastor, note 30, p. 118).

[58] Cf. A. Mager, *op. cit.*, p. 419.

ecstasy.[59] Viewing the matter from this angle, then, it is not a positive argument for its truth if the vision gives an impression of quite normal sense perception and presents itself as an object in the normal sphere of perception. Such impressions in simultaneous conjunction with an intimate mystical experience of infused contemplation are hardly conceivable. The situation is just the opposite of what the layman would think: the more peripheral the stimulation which causes the vision, the more it resembles ordinary perception, and the more it impresses the layman as "genuine" and "normal" — the more decidedly it will be rejected by St. John of the Cross.[60] In the case of distinctly "prophetic visions" the judgment may be somewhat milder, that is, in such cases it should perhaps not be postulated as a criterion of truth that they be connected with infused contemplation. But if so, and if such visions are to be acknowledged as authentic, we must demand that they accredit themselves by the only criterion left: a miracle.

[59] Hock, op. cit., p. 703: "If a soul has not yet attained the mystical betrothal, and so has never enjoyed the union of love in ecstasy even in a transitory manner, then any visions and revelations it may allege must be considered as illusions."

[60] According to him bodily visions are less perfect than imaginative ones: Subida II, 11 (II pp. 105 ff.). And this is also the opinion of those "who understand things better than I do" according to Theresa, Vida 28 (I, p. 218). Cf. G. B. Scaramelli, op. cit., tract. IV, cap. 6, n. 82 (II, p. 64). — In face of these considerations and the facts that have been adduced, can St. John of the Cross possibly have understood "bodily" visions to be literally such, involving the physical or at least the substantial presence of the holy person seen, and in this sense contrasted with imaginative visions? The term "bodily" would still be justified if it referred solely to the content of the consciousness as this conveys a much stronger impression of normal corporeality than imaginative visions; whereas these latter visions, for all their vividness (on which St. Theresa lays great stress), are clearly distinguished from bodily visions by their brilliance and transfigured quality.

3. From the assessment at which we have arrived the following important insight results. If the divine influence as such commences on a deeper level than that of sense, and if the imaginative element of the vision is a merely subsidiary function of the divine activity, then on the one hand we have here a genuine vision, but on the other hand the vision will proceed largely according to the general psychological laws of the domain of sense. To prove that this is so, that, for example, functions of the organs of sense with which we are familiar are set in motion, that amongst visionaries we find the ordinary psychological types, etc., that in non-Christian religions the same visionary phenomena occur (in the course of the imaginative experience!), all this is no argument against the authenticity of a vision (though indeed it is an argument against supposing that criteria of authenticity could be derived from the process of the sensory operation itself) because various causes can produce the same experiences in one and the same sphere.

4. One will now understand more precisely what is meant when mystical theology emphasizes "humility" and similar attitudes as a criterion of true visions. These attitudes do not so much imply a normal piety, veracity, modesty, discretion, etc., existing independently of the vision (and of course these are necessary) as a decisive transformation, a religious deepening of the person that comes with the experience and endures.[61] This, for

[61] Mélanie, the visionary of La Salette, e. g., changed religious orders four times until she was finally dismissed. Her fellow seer, Maximin, died after a varied life (seminarist, employee, medical student, Papal Zouave, etc.) just when he had finally resolved to become a priest after all. Before that he manufactured a liqueur called "Salettine", with a lable depicting himself. (Cf. L. Carlier, *Histoire de l'Apparition de la Mère de Dieu sur la montagne de la Salette,* Tournai, 1912, Appendix.)

the investigator, is much readier and simpler evidence that the imaginative experience was accompanied by God's interior work of grace in the depths of the spirit, than any psychological description by the seer of his own vision, which — especially in the case of the first such genuine experience — may be wrongly described and misinterpreted by the visionary. This happens particularly when he already has a mystical vocabulary derived from reading and other sources. One should also note here that it is not *a priori* impossible that purely psychogenic visions, due to no special divine influence, might have a saluary effect on pious and well-disposed people,[62] like our normal "good ideas", always provided that, considered impartially and from a purely psychological point of view, such an hallucinatory experience is not a product of an incipient pathological disorder and of a disintegration of the personality, which is, however, by no means always and necessarily the case.

5. If the actual "point" at which God first affects the soul lies deeper, behind the faculties of sense-perception, if it leads primarily to a contact and union of man's spirit with God and thus to the scene of the real work of grace, then it becomes understandable and natural that the echo in man's sensibility of this interior and pivotal process will not be governed exclusively by the process itself, but will also be influenced by

[62] Staehlin reports such a case. He was asked to help investigate a series of apparitions which became increasingly shameless. While these were in progress two "visionaries" appeared on the scene. The experience had been a turning point in their lives and they decided to enter a very austere religious order. This fact caused some of the investigators to accept the visions of the two girls as genuine. Staehlin, however, took the view that God could not possibly produce genuine apparitions in such a connection and he was vindicated by the Church's subsequent condemnation of these apparitions (cf. *op. cit.*, p. 280).

all the other dispositions of the visionary which are unconnected with this divine influence, such as elements of phantasy, patterns of perception, selective attitudes of expectation due to religious training, or the historical situation, or aesthetic taste, etc.[63]

The content of the imaginative vision then — although the varying proportions of the different elements will be very difficult to ascertain in any concrete case — will inevitably represent the joint effect of the divine influence plus all the subjective dispositions of the visionary. We must assume, indeed, that in the case of a prophetic imaginative vision confirmed by miracles even the imaginative element enjoys a certain divine guaranty insofar as it is revelant to the mission of the prophet as conveyed by the vision, though even here the whole imaginative content will bear traces of the visionary's subjectivity. With this exception, however, we can say that in the case of any "mystical vision" the divine influence gives no warranty that the imaginative content even of a genuine vision may not be so influenced by the subjectivity of the visionary as to betray

---

[63] We have an excellent example in the visions of St. Margaret Mary Alacoque. Almost all their thought and imagery can be found in earlier published books and especially in the traditions of her order. Sixty years earlier Anne Marie Rosset, fifty years earlier Anne Marguerite Clément, and contemporaneously with the Saint, Juana Benigna Gojos, all had visions of the Sacred Heart (cf. *Vida de Bienaventurada Margarita María Alacoque, escrita con ocasión del segundo centenario de su muerte por una religiosa del segundo monasterio de la Visitación de Santa María de Madrid,* Madrid 1890, pp. 129—32). This book points out that St. Francis de Sales originated this "tradition of the Sacred Heart" *(ibid.,* p. 127). — On June 10, 1611, St. Francis de Sales proposed to St. Jane Frances de Chantal that the arms of the new order should be a heart pierced by two arrows and surrounded by a crown of thorns. June 10, 1611, was the first Friday after the Octave of Corpus Christi (cf. François de Sales, Œuvres complètes, tom. VII, pp. 198 ff.: Lettre à Madame de Chantal sur les armoiries des monastères de la Visitation [10 juin, 1611]).

historical inaccuracy, theological distortions and errors, partiality, or bad taste.

The graphic content of a vision is not only a "picture" of the actual divine contact but also of the person who receives it; and since by definition that content cannot impinge on his consciousness until it is already a synthesis of the divine influence and the seer's subjective limitations, it will not only be very difficult in practice to undertake an "analysis" of the two sources, but even impossible in principle. Proof that the imaginative content is positively intended by God and is a correct expression of the ineffable in terms of human sensibility — that the imaginative content itself is "inspired" — could only be provided by external criteria. In practice then, much uncertainty will continue to surround the content of such visions, which must be left to the personal judgment of each enquirer.

In fact the history of visions, even in the case of canonized Saints and Beati — that is, of people whose honesty, great sanctity and true mystical experiences are beyond dispute — exhibits an abundance of errors and distortions, historical, theological and aesthetic. Let us cite a few examples, not so much because they are instructive and chastening as because they are probably the best argument for our thesis that even genuine imaginative visions are as a rule only indirectly caused by God. No one will deny that the saints of whom we shall speak had substantially genuine mystical experiences which they (to some extent) rightly held to give subjective and objective proof of divine origin. If nonetheless they were not able — as history witnesses — to distinguish truth from falsehood in the content of their imaginative visions (this must have been possible for them if the imaginative element as such had exhibited the obvious divine origin) this can only be explained by the fact that the actual experience of the divine influence (which they could not doubt) occurred deeper within them than the imaginative vision (audition, etc.), and that their conviction of the divine origin of this experience was uncritically extended to include its imaginative reflex.

When St. Theresa says,[64] therefore, that if a person has once experienced a real vision he can never again be deceived by hallucinations, then this is both true and false. True in this sense: one who has really experienced genuine infused contemplation (which is also the core of a true imaginative vision) could never mistake it again. False, because if such a genuine and obvious interior experience occurs, its effect on the imaginative sphere may still give rise to error. If a mystic who is well-balanced, theologically trained, guided by a skillful director, and uninterested in certain dangerous subjects (divination) has visions, their imaginative content will be unobjectionable. But this does not result from a greater divine influence in his case than in the case of others (even saints) who do not have the same qualifications in the same degree, but from more favourable natural conditions. The sense of authenticity will be the same in both cases; it will attest the divine origin of the actual experience in the depths of the soul, and offer no warranty for the imaginative vision (audition, etc.) because here it simply does not apply. If one does not proceed from our assumption that the imaginative vision as such is only indirectly caused by the divine influence, it will not be possible to explain how even saints who were mystics so often extended their mystical

---

[64] *Moradas* VI, 9 (IV, p. 164); VI 3 (IV, p. 118); Vida 25 (I, p. 192).

certitude to things to which this could not apply. Were this "evidence" an intrinsic element of the imaginative vision itself, it could not be so frequently confused by true mystics with (harmless or dangerous) experiences, which being distorted effects of real mystical experience, can only be called illusions and hallucinations.

Let us come now to the examples. There is plenty of historical falsehood, theological error and distortion, and subjectivity (extending even to bad taste) in these examples which require no further comment. These are all cases in which saintly people were convinced that they had learnt these things in genuine visions, though this may not be obvious to us in every instance. St. Norbert of Xanten was absolutely certain *(certissime)* that Anti-Christ would appear in his generation.[65] St. Vincent Ferrer declared on the authority of his visions that the end of the world was imminent.[66] St. Catherine of Siena believed Our Lady had revealed to her that she was not conceived immaculate.[67] Bl. Veronica of Binasco was told the same thing by Our Lady.[68] Apparitions of Christ delivered impossible etymologies to

[65] Bernard of Clairvaux, epist. 56 (PL 182, 162).
[66] P. Fages, *Histoire de Saint Vincent Ferrier,* I (Paris, 1893), esp. pp. 334—54, and the letter of the saint to Benedict XIII, pp. LXXVI—LXXXV. When Fages declares that this prophecy was a true one, but conditional (which Vincent never said), and that God postponed the destruction of the world because of the works of the saint (p. 354), his interpretation is too benevolent. We Christians pray that the coming of Christ may be hastened. The saints, then, cannot delay it but can only hasten it. We cannot enter into the question of the confirmation of this prophecy by the miracles of the saint (he believed that he had worked them in order to authenticate his prediction.).
[67] Benedict XIV, *op. cit.,* III, cap. ult., c. 16 (III, p. 277); Poulain, *op. cit.,* p. 355 f.
[68] *Vita,* lib. III, cap. 7 (*AASS,* January II, 185).

Mechthild of Hackeborn and Gertrude of Helfta.[69] Hildegard of Bingen attributed her knowledge — which was by no means always correct — to immediate divine illuminations and dictation.[70] To St. Catharine Ricci, Savonarola frequently appears as a prophet and martyr, and she works for his beatification.[71] St. Frances of Rome received information in many visions on the nature of the firmament which she believed to be situated between the starry sky and the *coelum empyreum*.[72] Blessed Alan de la Roche (1428—1475) reports fantastic revelations concerning the founder of his religious order and the origin of the Rosary.[73] The contradictions between the visions of various saints (St. Magdalene of Pazzi, St. Brigid of Sweden, St. Elisabeth of Schoenau) in regard to the life and death of Our Lord and his mother are well known.[74] The Bl. Margaret Ebner was instructed by the child Jesus "how his holy circumcision was performed",[75] and believed she heard the voice of the Lord bidding her give suck to the wooden statue of the child Jesus which she kept in a crib.[76] Bl. Lidwina (d. 1433)

[69] *Legatus divinae pietatis*, I, 16 (ed. Solesmes, Paris, 1875), pp. 51 f.; IV, 27, p. 388.

[70] *AASS*, Sept. V, 633.

[71] Cf. J. Schnitzer, *Savonarola* II (Munich, 1924), pp. 890 f.; Benedict XIV, *op. cit.*, III, cap. 25, nn. 17—20 (III, pp. 131 f.).

[72] *Vita*, lib. II, *visio* 14 (*AASS*, March II, 111).

[73] Cf. Analecta Bollandiana 22 (1903), p. 219. The Blessed said he wished to be damned if he was not speaking the truth. Cf. H. Thurston, in *The Month* (1901), p. 294.

[74] Poulain, *op. cit.*, p. 343. Cf. *AASS*, May VI, 244 ff.: "Parergon de Sanctarum ecstaticarum secundum species naturaliter praehabitas durante raptu quandoque motarum dictis factisque ad historicarum questionum decisiones non transferendis."

[75] Ph. Strauch, *Margareta Ebner und Heinrich von Nördlingen* (Freiburg, 1892), p. 100.

[76] *Ibid.*, p. 87.

believed that (without leaving her bed) she travelled almost
every night for 24 years to the Holy Places in Palestine, Rome,
etc., and there revered the relics of the saints.[77] Bl. Maria
Oignies (d. 1213) believed that the child Jesus rested all day
long on her bosom.[78] St. Mary Magdalene of Pazzi watched
Jesus write his name on her heart with the milk of the Blessed
Virgin.[79] St. Elizabeth of Schoenau (d. 1165), even on her death-
bed (strengthened by an apparition of her guardian angel)
claimed divine authorship for the book of her revelations. It
abounds in the most arbitrary phantasies.[80] Bl. Josefa Maria de
Santa Inés (d. 1696) one Shrove Tuesday played a game of ball
from her place in the choir with Christ in the tabernacle. Christ
had begun throwing her some beautiful transparent oranges.[81]
Of the fantastic revelations of Bl. Hermann Joseph about St.
Ursula and her companions Papebroch rightly says:*quid libet
toleraverim prius, quam pro caelestibus revelationibus talia
suscipiam.*[82] Finally, the theological problem raised by the
"great promise" given to St. Margaret Mary Alacoque is well
known.[83]

[77] *AASS,* April II, 280 (n. 47).
[78] *Vita,* cap. 10 (*AASS,* June V, 567).
[79] O. Karrer, *Die große Glut* (Munich, 1926), p. 135 (indicating the precise
source).
[80] *Vita,* cap. 8, c. 106 (*AASS,* June IV, 524); Poulain, *op. cit.,* pp. 347 f.
[81] P. Corro del Rosario, *Augustinos amantes de la Sagrade Eucaristía,* p. 212.
[82] "We would endure anything rather than accept such things as divine
revelations." Commentarius praevius de s. Ursula, § 7, n. 76 in *AASS,*
October IX, 93.
[83] Cf., e. g., K. Richtstaetter, *Das Herz des Welterlösers* (Freiburg, 1939),
pp. 93 f. In regard to these promises for the hour of death — and there
is one which requires even simpler conditions — Staehlin observes that no
promise offers better proof of its authenticity or is more clearly expressed
than that of Christ: "He that eateth my flesh and drinketh my blood hath

But not only the past, even our own century can offer pertinent examples. Here, to be sure — because the dates are so recent — we are not dealing with canonized saints. Nevertheless, their life was such that their elevation to the honours of the altar does not seem to be excluded. Sister Maria Anna from Cuba (born in 1882 in Havana), who died in 1903 (at Plasencia, a Spanish city in the province of Cáceres) in the odour of sanctity, mystically experienced in herself the conception, pregnancy and on August 15, 1901, about midnight, the birth of the child Jesus. When she afterwards nursed him she was soothed by Our Lady . . . .[84] Marie Sainte-Cécile de Rome, of the congregation of Jésus-Marie, in the world Gina Bélanger, was reminded by Christ almost daily for a year and a half that she would die on August 15, 1924. He would sometimes tell her the number of days that were left to her, and then affectionally bade her count them. The figure was always correct. What was incorrect, however, was the day of her death. She died in 1929 in the odour of sanctity.[85]

Now if saints could err, we must not be surprised to find self-deceptions occurring in the case of other visionaries whose sanctity is by no means established. Sister Josefa Menéndez was informed by Jesus — Jesus dictated her revelations — that the

everlasting life" (John 6, 54). Yet, he says, nobody has presumed to see in these words a firm guarantee of eternal salvation (*op. cit.*, p. 154).

[84] Staehlin, *ibid.*, p. 74, note 9.

[85] Marie Sainte-Cécile de Rome (Dina Bélanger), *Autobiographie, Cantique d'Actions de Grâces ou Chant d'Amour* (Quebec, 1949), pp. 128 ff.; L. Crenier, Marie Sainte-Cécile de Rome (Dina Bélanger). Autobiographie et Témoignages (Quebec, 1934), I, p. 211; II, pp. 22 ff. It is noteworthy that these publications relate events exactly as they happened, without any attempt to improve upon the facts. We shall see in the following note that this is not always done.

robe which his Mother made for him as a child miraculously grew with him.[86] Poulain reports several cases of very recent years where quite pious people thought they had received prophetic instructions indicating the correct attitude for the Pope to adopt in certain political crises — instructions which,

[86] Cf. (M. Lescure), *Un appel à l'amour*, p. 460. In the German edition (cf. note 49, p. 134) this has simply been omitted without comment. But this is not all. On p. 431 a passage in the French edition is missing. It is a reproduction of the crucifixion scene which is found in Maria Ágreda and Jeanne of the Incarnation (cf. Staehlin, *op. cit.*, p. 110 ff.). The closing words of St. Margaret Mary Alacoque's prayer, which Josefa read in the Sacred Heart (cf. note 49), are also missing. They were: "(You [Josefa] will be a sacrifice of atonement to me through . . .) and by hating your criminal and accursed flesh" (French ed., p. 90; German ed., p. 91). In the vision of hell, which copies St. Theresa's, there are a number of omissions in the German edition (p. 233 ff.) as compared with the French (p. 243 ff.). Other omissions in the German edition — to mention only those we have happened to discover — include note 1 on p. 90 of the French edition: "Faut-il ajouter que celle-ci (Sr. Josefa) n'avait alors aucune connaissance de la vie ni des écrits de Sainte Marguerite Marie?", and the passage on p. 240 of the text: "Josefa, qui n'avait jamais lu les révélations de sa sainte compatriote." For in the meantime Staehlin had shown (*El Padre Rubio:* Madrid, 1947, p. 247) when it was that Fr. Rubio had given his penitent, Josefa, these books to read (a prayerbook called *Oraciones de la Beata Margarita María* and the Life of St. Theresa; it is this book, not the "Révélations", which contains the vision of hell). In this case the omission is perfectly justified, but the previous categorical assertion that Josefa had not read these texts before is another matter. Is it historically or religiously justifiable to put forward an assertion so long as the contrary is not proved, and to omit words which seem less suitable for a certain audience, whilst believing — and endeavouring to convince the reader — that these words were literally dictated by the Lord and must all be carefully preserved? Cf. p. 166: "All (of these words) will be read when you are in heaven", Jesus says to Josefa. P. 275: "Josefa writes down his words exactly as they come from his divine mouth." P. 504: (Jesus dictates in such a way as to say, for example, "that will do, we shall continue tomorrow".) Can we be sure that these revelations have not been still further adapted to prevent Christ saying anything theologically incorrect? And how can this procedure be reconciled with those words of Christ to the visionary: "Nothing of what I make known to you shall ever be effaced" (p. 274)?

had the Pope followed them, would have involved him in grave difficulties.[87] This craving for heavenly directions in the political dark had to be combatted by David of Augsburg, Gerson and the Fifth Lateran Council[88] and has not died out to this day.[89] Finally we must mention the prayer which Lucia learnt from the angel. In this prayer men are to offer God the Father not only the Body and Blood but also the soul and the divinity of Our Lord Jesus Christ, which is theologically impossible.[90]

[87] Poulain, op. cit., p. 348, note 1; p. 363 f. Cf. also his personal information in RAM ii (1921), p. 68, note 1.

[88] For David of Augsburg cf. Michael, op. cit., p. 399; for Gerson his book De distinctione verarum visionum a falsis (Opera omnia, the Hague, 1728, vol. I, 2nd ed., col. 45 ff.); for the Fifth Lateran Council, which issued a bull forbidding the public preaching of prophecies: L. Pastor, History of the Popes, vol. V. (London, 1898), p. 218; Mansi XXXIII, 945.

[89] Nevertheless, particular cases are very soon forgotten, like that of the notorious Mathilde Marchat, who gave the ecclesiastical authorities, Bishops and Pope alike, a great deal of trouble from 1888 to 1894. God had given her the mission of restoring a Bourbon prince to the throne of France, who would then protect the Pope against the Italian government. In spite of repeated condemnations in 1888 and 1889 the affair dragged on until 1894. Les annales de Loigny, the periodical she founded, published the most incredible tales about the real Leo XIII, who approved of her foundation, but was held a prisoner as anti-pope by Cardinal Monaco, etc. Cf. Analecta Ecclesiastica 2 (1894), pp. 291—301.

[90] Cf. Dhanis, op. cit., pp. 42 f. and Fonseca's hardly objective criticism of this point in Fátima y la crítica, p. 31. Lucia's answer to the theological objection, according to Fonseca, was that "the angel may just not have studied any theology". — This expression "body and blood, soul and divinity of Our Lord Jesus Christ . . ." is found in the (Portuguese and Spanish) catechism not quite as a prayer but as the answer to the question: What is in the consecrated Host? Is this not another case of 'reproduction', of which Staehlin cites many examples (op. cit., pp. 109—33)? Fonseca, who also noted this coincidence, tries to get over the difficulty by suggesting that the angel's own expression was correct but that the word divinity was added later (op. cit., p. 31).

The same offertory formula is found in the revelations of Sr. Marie Faustine.[91]

These examples, which easily could be multiplied, clearly show that divine action and human subjectivity extending to the erroneous and bizarre, are intermingled even in the visions of the saints, so that even "genuine" visions cannot be regarded as exclusively God's work. Even in these human subjectivity finds expression. Even in "genuine" imaginative visions human powers are creatively at work.

Another remarkable phenomenon which would repay investigation and which could be called "the fashion in visions"[92] is

---

[91] Here the prayer is shorter: "Eternal Father, I offer thee the flesh and blood, soul and divinity of thy most beloved Son, our Lord Jesus Christ, for our sins and for the sins of the whole world. By his bitter passion have mercy on us and on the whole world." Sr. Marie Faustine heard the same prayer "in her heart" when an angel, the executioner of God's wrath, threatened the world with thunder and lightning. The angel proved to be powerless against this prayer and was not able to carry out the punishment." — Once more an angel is involved. And the prayer is infallible! It would seem that this "infallibility" must be connected with the offering of the "divinity", in view of an article in *La Voz de Fátima* xxx (13 April, 1949) quoting Father Faber (All for Jesus, ch. 7) to the effect that "many pious men offer the Lord his infinite perfections and the honour he derives from these attributes, which constitute his divinity, when they wish to obtain some extraordinary grace . . . ." Cf. Fonseca, *op. cit.*, p. 32, note 58. This apparition, i. e., the revelation of the miraculous prayer, took place on September 13, 1935, although we are not told when Sr. Marie Faustine first made it known. She died on October 5, 1938. These dates are suggestive since Lucia at about this time also spoke of an angelic visitation. For Marie Faustine and her revelations cf. J. Andreasz, *Gottes Barmherzigkeit, wir vertrauen auf dich* (Altenstadt/Vorarlberg, 1949), p. 18.

[92] E. g., we do not find in modern visions the wealth of apocalyptic imagery of St. Hildegard of Bingen. Today apparitions of the saints of antiquity, of martyrs, of older patrons of churches so frequent in the Middle Ages, have become very rare. Before Lourdes were there cases of definite series of apparitions, occurring at fixed intervals, such as happened afterwards at Fátima?

adequately explained by the fact that imaginative visions are subjectively conditioned, without any need to assume changing attitudes in God himself.

Similarly, the errors and distortions in visions which have been too indulgently called an "accommodation of God[93] to the visionary," could be more easily and more correctly conceived as an un-intentional, preconscious accommodation of divine influence (in itself unaltered) *by* the character of the visionary to this character of his. [94]

This state of affairs entails both positive and negative consequences. The positive: An experience alleged to be a vision simply cannot compel one either to accept it as accurate in every detail, or to reject it altogether as a human or diabolical illusion or fraud. Such a logical and plausible rigorism is in fact a psychological blunder. From our point of view a certain leniency and a disposition to grant the divine origin of visionary experiences even if their whole content cannot be admitted, is quite defensible. It is not absolutely impossible, indeed, that pure hallucination *and* genuine visions might occur in the same person.[95] For it is quite conceivable that a slight stimulation of the organs of sense perception, such as one observes in hallucinations,

Browe shows, for instance, that in the Middle Ages apparitions of the child Jesus were typical of, almost epidemic in, certain limited circles, but were scarcely known elsewhere, and later became very rare everywhere *(Die eucharistischen Wunder des Mittelalters,* Breslau, 1938, pp. 100—11). It has been frequently observed that there is a mutual interdependence between the changing imagery of visions and the changes in artistic styles.

[93] Poulain, *op. cit.,* pp. 342 ff.; cf. also Zahn, *op. cit.,* p. 588, who rightly rejects any idea of God "adapting" himself to the mystic.

[94] On this point cf. H. Thurn, *op. cit.,* on the typological differences among so-called intuitive images.

[95] Cf. note 51, p. 137. Dhanis considers the actual apparitions of Fátima

might also lend strength and clarity to the "echo", in the sensibility, of a genuine mystical experience, in other words might produce an imaginative vision.

The negative: Even when the authenticity of a vision as a whole is established (especially by external criteria) it does not follow that every detail of its content is accurate and must be accepted. Even a genuine vision may contain errors; the figure, the behaviour, the speech of the person who appears derive more from the subjectivity of the visionary than from the person seen in the vision. The message of a prophetic vision can also be very strongly influenced by the subjective qualities of the visionary, by the time and by the milieu he lives in, by his theological training. The prayers which in such visions seem to be spoken by a celestial person need not be accepted as necessarily composed in heaven. If we abstract from the question of the historical truth of the reports (which would of course be the first duty of the chronicler of an apparition) it is not necessarily a disrespectful interference with divine revelation if the theological narrator of such an event slightly modifies the words heard for theological or other weighty reasons.[96]

authentic (p. 32), but believes the first vague angelic apparitions to have been hallucinations (p. 45), for even according to the later statements of Lucia they first began with obscure visions (cf. "Sguardo su Fátima" in *Civiltà Cattolica* ciii [1953, II], p. 405) which seem to be identical with those which Lucia's mother spoke of in 1917 (cf. Visconde de Montelo, *op. cit.*, pp. 110—3). Lucia denied these before Canon Formigão on September 27, 1917 (p. 72). When the Canon then called Lucia's attention to the contradiction between her statement and her mother's and demanded an explanation, Lucia remained silent, although she could easily have distinguished between the apparitions of Our Lady (which she had denied) and the other revelations (of which she did not speak when first questioned on September 27 [p. 113]).
[96] The chroniclers of Fátima, for instance, have taken ample liberties in adapting its history. Cf. Dhanis, *Bij de Verschijningen . . .*, p. 63 ff. Literary

We might also add that if a subjective element must inevitably be presupposed in the vision itself, it may intrude even more powerfully after the vision, even in the case of perfectly honest people: unconscious corrections, tricks of memory, the use of pre-established mental patterns and a familiar vocabulary in the account which will imperceptibly shift the perspective, unconscious later additions,[97] psychological description and interpretation of the event which will be more or less successful according to the seer's capacity for self-analysis.

accuracy would, of course, require that the reader's attention be drawn to such revisions and ommissions. None of this is to be found in L. G. da Fonseca's *Le meraviglie di Fátima* and its translations, where he quotes the Visconde de Montelo with (pp. 66 ff. and 95 ff. in the German ed. 1952) and without acknowledgment (e. g., pp. 47 f. and 60 f.). The title of the German translation is rather more pretentious than that of the Italian, Portuguese or Spanish editions: "Mary speaks to the world. The Secret of Fátima and its historical mission to the world"; 10th ed. (Fribourg, 1952). To give one example of "adaptation": on p. 23 we read: "Francisco, however, only heard Lucia's voice, but he observed that the Lady spoke, because he saw her lips moving. Is this circumstance not a proof of the little seers' veracity?" Yet in Visconde de Montelo we read on p. 115: "Didn't you see (Francisco is addressed) that her lips moved?" — "I saw nothing!"

[97] These are probably involved in Lucia's later statements (since 1936) about the message and promise of Fátima (cf. Dhanis, *Bij de Verschijningen, pp.* 52 ff.). Lucia prefaced her final report to the Bishop on November 25, 1941 (cf. Dhanis, "Sguardo su Fátima", in *Civiltà Cattolica* civ [1953, II], p. 403) as follows: "Its seems to me, Your Excellency, that in similar cases I say or write nothing of myself. I must bless God for the assistance of the Holy Ghost, who, I feel, inspires me with what I must write or say." (Cf. Dhanis, "À propos de Fátima et la critique" in *NRTh* lxxiv [1952], pp. 601 ff.) Fonseca quotes Ms. IV, p. 2, but omits parts of the text (cf. "*Fátima y la crítica*", p. 27, note 49). To claim the assistance of the Holy Ghost in writing down supplementary material twenty-five years after the event makes any further discussion difficult.

157

III

SOME CRITERIA FOR GENUINE VISIONS

FROM what we have said, and with a few additional observations, we shall try to deduce some criteria for genuine visions and thus to some extent supply criteria for the attitude to be adopted when psychic phenomena occur which purport to be genuine visions and revelations of God.

First of all which are the unsatisfactory or at least inadequate criteria? Piety and personal honesty are absolutely perequisite before a vision can possibly claim to be considered genuine, but are no proof of its authenticity because these qualities are no protection against error. Even saints have frequently been deceived in such matters.

The same is true of (bodily and) mental health. The argument from health tacitly assumes that if the vision is not "genuine", then the visionary must be hysterical or mad. But as the visionary otherwise gives the impression of being perfectly normal and rational by conventional standards, it is concluded (unless for other reasons the question of diabolical influence arises) that the vision must be authentic. This argument, for several reasons, is false or inconclusive. For one thing it overlooks the fact that a sharply defined insanity may affect a part of mental life in isolation from the rest, which latter appears to remain quite normal.[98] Furthermore it assumes that all phenomena which do not occur in the ordinary mental life of a rational Western man must be either pathological or the effect of a transcendent cause. This presupposition, however, is false. There are phenomena which on the one hand are natural and not pathological, and, on the other hand, are not caused by any transcendent influence: spontaneous eidetic experiences, extraordinary achievements which cannot be produced at will but emerge from the subconscious, moments of brilliant intellectual accomplishment which seem literally inspired from without and from above — things, in short, beyond the ken of the average man of our time, which are neither "normal", nor really "anomalous", nor supernatural.[99] Even where no supernatural agency is involved, "extraordinary" and "pathological" are not synonymous terms. In short, merely because a visionary is sane it does not follow that he must have "authentic" visions.

We have already observed that neither clarity nor stability nor apparent objectivity conclusively prove a vision genuine, but may at times indicate the opposite. Furthermore it should be noted that elements of the total vision which belong to the realm of parapsychological, mediumistic powers must not be taken for decisive criteria. If genuine (natural) telepathy,

---

[98] This seems to have been the case with Fr. Surin (cf. E. de Greef, Succédanés et concomitances psychopathologiques de la "Nuit obscure") (Le cas du Père Surin) in Études Carmélitaines xxiii (1938, II), pp. 173—6. A classic if only "literary" case of partial insanity is that of Don Quixote. As long as his idée fixe of caballería andante is not involved he speaks and acts quite rationally.

[99] Cf. R. Dalbiez, "Marie-Thérèse Noblet, considérée du point de vue psychologique" in Études Carmélitaines xxiii (1938, II), pp. 225 f.

telaesthesia, cryptaesthesia, and even physical mediumistic powers exist (and such possibilties must at least be seriously reckoned with),[100] then we must disregard many phenomena formerly, perhaps, accepted as decisive proofs of the supernatural origin of visions. It would still be necessary, of course, to allow for the possibility of God's supernatural intervention using these mediumistic powers for his own purposes or setting them in involuntary operation as happens with other human faculties. Many extraordinary phenomena in the lives of the saints might be thus explained.

Personal integrity is continually cited as a criterion of authenticity. In fact it seems difficult, especially in personal encounter with the visionary, not to be swayed by this "test" of personal influence. Père Tonquédec, with his vast experience as an exorcist in Paris, strongly advises against concluding that a vision must be genuine if the visionary is sincere and seems incapable of deceiving anyone.[101] We have already seen that even obviously good effects are no absolute criterion.[102] Staehlin also draws attention to what is known as "transfiguration", where the features are transformed by an "unearthly" beauty. He reports a case in his own experience where he observed a girl during an ecstasy, and then withdrew because of the crowd. When she had recovered from the ecstasy he failed to recognize her. Only by

[100] Cf. H. Thurston, *Physical Phenomena of Mysticism* (London, 1951), who also mentions many "profane" examples. The author was obviously moved by books like *Phantasmas of the Living* by Gurney, Myers and Podmore to show that an incomparably greater treasury of parapsychological phenomena than these books disclose lies buried in Catholic hagiography.
[101] J. Tonquédec, *Les maladies nerveuses ou mentales et les manifestations diaboliques* (Paris 1938), p. 80.
[102] Cf. note 62, p. 144.

her clothes was he able to convince himself of her identity. Her face, destitute of radiance, was perfectly commonplace. Other onlookers even spoke of her clothes shining, and one person who had always refused to believe in apparitions before was quite convinced by this experience. Yet it was a case of ordinary hallucination.[103]

As to positive criteria, it will be well to distinguish between standards for the visionary himself and those for outside observers.

Even for the visionary the impression of real sensory perception is no apodictic criterion. However, if the imaginative vision is connected with a proper and original mystical phenomenon belonging to the realm of infused contemplation, then it is quite possible that the visionary, in the act of this experience, may be unable to doubt its divine origin, thus finding a warranty for the truth of his imaginative vision insofar as the two things are cause and effect. After such a mystical vision the seer may, by reflecting on the central mystical experience in the light of criteria which we need not discuss here, attain a secondary certitude that he has really had that experience. It would then be permissible to assume that the imaginative vision has also been a true one. Detailed analysis would still, of course, have to reckon with subjective elements in the whole content of the vision, such as possible misinterpretations and faulty recollection.

But in every case, according to the doctors of mystical theology, one should take the attitude that visions are relatively unimportant compared with the infused contemplation from which they derive, and compared with faith, charity and the

---

[103] Staehlin, *op. cit.*, pp. 387 f.

other supernatural Christian virtues, which should be our principal concern. Where there is neither infused contemplation nor an external miracle to authenticate the vision, the seer will scarcely be justified, in practice, in accepting it without qualification as genuine. If the vision contains nothing offensive to faith and Christian morals, if it fosters his spiritual progress without inducing him to give it undue importance for his personal religious life and to assume the rôle of a prophet sent to others, he must either suspend definitive judgment on the vision or else accept it in humility, in gratitude, and in silence[104] as an aid to his own devotion.

As for *us*, outside observers, if it is a matter of purely mystical visions which do not claim a prophetic mission the same criteria will apply, *mutatis mutandis,* which we have established for the visionary himself. But, as we cannot directly observe the interior, mystical experience of infused contemplation in the seer and it will be less certain or less probable (for us) that it really has occurred, our power to arrive at reasonable certainty, through the use of the same criteria, though not nullified will be seriously diminished.

[104] May not the fact that in almost all series of apparitions a secret is communicated about which absolutely nothing must be said, indicate a consciousness of the duty of silence when a person has visionary experiences? — The answer of Lucia and of the two other children to the questions of Canon Formigão gives the distinct impression that a personal secret must have been involed. It is "for the good of the three of us" (Jacinta, p. 92); it concerns "all three" (Lucia, p. 75); "it is for the good of his own soul, and for Lucia's and Jacinta's" (Francisco, p. 106). Fonseca arrived at the same conclusion in his report on Fátima for the year 1931: ". . . rivelò ai bambini un segredo personale . . ." in *Civiltà Cattolica* lxxxii (1931, III), p. 378. For the evidence that this anonymous text is by L. G. da Fonseca, see the same publication, civ (1953, II), p. 392. — Cf. note 50, p. 135.

In practice, then (failing the external evidence of a miracle) we must content ourselves with more or less probability and accord a mystical vision the respect due to the spiritual life of sane and devout people. Whether what the visionary saw does or does not have a meaning for one's own spiritual life is a matter for one's own free judgment.

Certainly there is no obligation to attach much importance to such things when classic mystical doctrine warns the visionary himself against attributing too much value or significance to these experiences. Where they are alleged by people without the properly mystical graces of infused contemplation, it can almost always be safely assumed that such visions (if not fraudulent or pathological) are parapsychological, eidetic or other hallucinatory or pseudo-hallucinatory occurrences. For, on the one hand, these phenomena can occur in people who are morally and mentally sound and, on the other hand, they adequately account for the facts of the case. The principle always remains valid that supernatural agency is not to be presupposed but must be proved. The history of mysticism justifies Poulain's judgment that even with pious and "normal" people, in three cases out of four visions are well intentioned, harmless, genuine illusions.[105] With such occurrences, therefore, there is more danger of error in credulity than in scepticism, especially in unsettled times.

---

[105] Poulain, *op. cit.*, pp. 336 f. This seems also to have been the opinion of St. Paul of the Cross: in a letter he tells the amusing little story that St. Theresa once appeared to a nun and told her: "Know that of all the visions and auditions . . . that I myself have had, only a small part, a very small part was true and good" (*RAM* viii [1927], p. 383); indeed he even writes in one letter (*ibid.*, p. 381) "amongst hundreds or perhaps thousands of these articulated auditions, scarcely one or two are true." It is well to remember that St. Paul of the Cross himself enjoyed very advanced mystical graces.

But where we encounter "prophetic" visions, which lay demands upon us the validity and binding force of which are not evident apart from these visions, the only criterion which can justify this claim is a real miracle (physical or moral) in the strict sense.

If Catholic fundamental theology can and must apply this criterion to public Christian revelation,[106] how much more must it apply to private prophetic revelations. Demands, messages — even within the framework of general revealed doctrine — directed to others than the visionary himself and based on a vision, must prove their divine origin and their binding character by miracles. But even then they will not generally call for the belief of *fides divina*[107] like public revelation (certainly not for *fides catholica*), if only because it is clear (as it is in the case of public revelation) that God is prepared to grant everybody the graces of light and strength which are necessary for such acts of faith. Without a miracle such a vision can lay no claim whatever to the assent of outsiders.[108] To reject such a revelation (always

---

[106] "Factum revelationis criteriis objective certis et externis demonstrari debet" and "criterium externum, factum sc. miraculosum est unicum criterium revelationis sufficiens et primarium" are theses, e. g., in H. Dieckmann's *De revelatione christiana* (Freiburg, 1930), pp. 258—67, 291—328.

[107] It is the common teaching of theologians that the authenticity of a private revelation may be so clear for the visionary himself that he is permitted and even bound to believe its content with divine faith. Cf., e. g., Dieckmann, *De ecclesia* II (Freiburg, 1952), pp. 150 f.

[108] These miracles, however, must not themselves raise a problem, like the miracle of the sun, which was not by any means seen by all those present. Thus Izabel Brandão de Melo writes in a letter dated October 13, 1917: "this (the report of the sun-miracle) is what people were saying next to me, and what thousands of persons claim they saw. I did not see it, although I looked at the sun and felt terribly moved to hear everybody screaming that they saw extraordinary things in the sun . . . ." Cf. L. G. da Fonseca, *Fátima y la crítica*, p. 18 and note 27. Nevertheless, this witness believed in the

conformably to our general human duty of caution, restraint, and reverence) in any case never implies resistance to divine grace, and may rather be part of man's duty to "believe not every spirit; but try the spirits if they be of God".

If the investigations and the judgment of the Church declare that a particular vision and private revelation may be believed with human faith (for the Church does no more than this),[109] this ecclesiastical approbation in itself is not necessarily infallible (for the infallible magisterium was not given to the Church, the custodian of general public revelation in Christ, for this purpose).[110] The approbation implies only that such a revelation can show good grounds for human credibility and does not contradict the deposit of faith; like all important acts of the Church's pastoral authority (to which this judgment is to be attributed rather than to the magisterium), it deserves to be respectfully obeyed by the faithful. (Nothing more is necessary, by the very nature of the judgment, which imposes virtually no activity on the faithful.) Yet a Catholic is not forbidden to think within himself, for weighty reasons, that the judgment is in fact incorrect; and if he feels it appropriate he may even express his opinion with becoming modesty, always provided this will not promote an attitude of general scepticism which ultimately would deny the possibility of any supernatural, historical revelation of God. Much more will a critical attitude be permissible towards the details of a vision which, as a whole, is recognized as genuine.

apparitions. Father Martindale in his book *The message of Fátima* (p. 82) speaks of two English ladies who did not see the sun-miracle either (cf. Fonseca, *ibid.*).

[109] Cf. note 11, p. 93.

[110] Cf., e. g., Dieckmann, *op. cit.*, p. 150, n. 823.

And even if a vision (mystical or prophetic) be recognized in itself as genuine, our attitude towards it, our reaction to it may still be wrong. One may be deaf, or refractory, to the message. Who can deny that most people do not welcome a call to penance or to a devotion that would be salutary for a given time? But the other extreme is also possible, especially among people of a piety too intuitive and unenlightened. Where private revelations (even genuine ones) are abused to gratify a spiritual sensationalism, those revelations are not correctly understood. If we crave prophecies which are so clear and definite that they take from us the burden of responsible decision and loving abandonment to God's inscrutable Providence, then what we want is sooth-saying and we are no longer capable of interpreting true prophecy aright should such emerge from a real "apparition".

Where private revelations (for example of new devotions) are taken as disclosing a spiritual trick, a method for acquiring holiness at little cost or changing the way of the Cross into pure joy; or where the entire spiritual life is reduced to revolving round one revelation (however genuine in itself), whose content, in comparison with the whole wide world of Christian truth by which we should live, is bound to be meagre — we can conclude that even genuine revelations have certainly been misunderstood and misapplied. On the other hand even the little gateway of a private revelation must be praised if by entering it people arrive at their first real grasp of Christianity, as often happens. Who would force these people of the little doors to enter God's house by the (really or supposedly) lofty portals of our great theology or of our own very private thought? On the other hand, however, one must not stop at the little door. Even the best devotion, which we should all practice, is not the whole of Christianity, and we are certainly not meant to conclude that it is if heaven recommends the devotion in a vision.

Though God speaks to us in divers ways, it is not clear *a priori* that his most important instructions will be given in visions. Rather they are contained in the Gospel and are proclaimed by the Church in her "ordinary" preaching. God's Spirit stirs — sometimes, at least — even in the Church's theologians and various "movements", even if they cannot appeal to visions. Lovers of revelations and apparitions should not forget either (as often happens) that Christ appears to us most surely in the poor and suffering. In the Sacrament and in the grace of the Holy Ghost, offered to every Christian, we have God's most real presence. The Cross is true mercy, and charity the highest of all gifts. If we do not recognize the hand that chastises us as God's merciful and healing hand, we shall not find him in "revelations" either. The only good in any spirit is what makes us better Christians, and our conscience, trained by the spirit of the Church, tells pretty plainly what does that. This criterion will enable us to cope with real life, even though it may not settle the very theoretical question of whether a mental phenomenon comes directly or indirectly from the Spirit of God. What is left of visions and revelations after this test may still contain much that is human mingled with the divine, and it will be very difficult to distinguish the one from the other. A., therefore, must not force B. to seek the divine in this particular human element, and B. must not dispute A.'s ability to find the divine in this same human element. The Church has always adopted this attitude and she will continue to do so.

In our own day, as always, the Church has gone about her

duty to try the spirits with the utmost caution and sobriety. To our knowledge only three of the many apparitions of recent decades[111] have been recognized: [112] Fátima, Banneaux and Beauraing (both these latter places in Belgium having had apparitions in the years 1932 and 1933). Numerous other apparitions have either been actually condemned by episcopal authority or by the Holy Office, or else the Church has remained reserved, awaiting events and dissuading the faithful from accepting them. As evidence of the Church's caution in these matters we shall enumerate a few scenes of alleged apparitions during the past twenty years which she has either condemned or

[111] For the following items cf. R. Ernst, *Maria redet zu uns. Marienerscheinungen seit 1830* (Wels, 1950); B. Grabinski, *Flammende Zeichen der Zeit* (Wiesbaden, 1950; uncritical concoction; cf. D. Zähringer in *Bened. Monatschrift* xxvii [1951], pp. 426 ff.); D. Zähringer, "Muttergotteserscheinungen" in *Benedektinische Monatschrift* xxvi (1950), pp. 29—40; G. J. Strangfeld, "Marienerscheinungen seit Fátima" in *Der Große Entschluß* vii (1951), pp. 82—5. Except where otherwise noted the following data are drawn from these works.

[112] The bibliography on Fátima can be omitted here; a critical survey can be found in the work of Dhanis already quoted. For Banneux cf. *Notre Dame de Banneux. Études et documents publiés par son Excellence Msgr. M. L. Kerkhofs, évêque de Liège*, Tournai 1950. The second edition of a similar volume on Beauraing is about to appear (cf. *NRTh* lxxiii [1951], p. 1087). From earlier literature: J. B. Lenain, "Les événements de Beauraing" in *NRTh* lxv (1933), pp. 327—56. It is noteworthy that ecclesiastical approval for the apparitions of Beauraing and Banneux was given only after a fully public investigation, embracing even literature which gave ample scope to dissenting opinion (approval for Beauraing by the Bishop of Namur in 1943 and 1949, for Banneux by the Bishop of Liège in 1942 and 1949). Cf., e. g., *Études Carmélitaines* xviii (1933): "Bruno de Jésus-Marie, Paul van Gehuchten, Étienne de Greeff, Les faits mystérieux de Beauraing" (also separately published, Paris, 1933). It is also remarkable that the Holy See declined to announce the approbation of Beauraing and Banneux, as the bishops desired, but gave the bishops permission to announce it of their own episcopal authority (cf. Staehlin, *op. cit.*, pp. 38 f.).

refrained from approving. In alphabetical order they are: Acquaviva Platani (Sicily), Aspang (Lower Austria), Assisi (Italy), Bouxières-aux-Dames (France), La Codesera (Spain), Elz bei Limburg (Germany), Espis (France), Ezquioga (Spain), Forstweiler bei Tannhausen (Germany), Ghiaie di Bonate (Italy), Gimigliano (Italy), Hasznos (Hungary), Heede (Germany), Heroldsbach (Germany), Hintermailingen bei Lahr (Germany), Hoesbach bei Aschaffenburg (Germany), Kayl (Luxembourg), Klausenburg (Transylvania), Le Bouchard (France), Liart (Belgium), Limpias (Spain), Lipa (Philippines), Lomnitz (Silesia), Petersberg-Rotalben (Germany), Pfaffenhofen a. d. R. (Germany), Lublin (Poland), Tre Fontane near Rome, Urucaina (Brazil).

This list could be considerably extended. It is noteworthy that these condemned apparitions often drew huge crowds (in Lublin in 1949, for instance, the weeping Madonna is said to have been visited by 100,000 people in one day; in 1939 70,000 people gathered on Mount Ezquioga in the Basque country) and that even the opposition of the faithful and of some clerics was unable to deflect ecclesiastical authority from its judgment (for instance at Heroldsbach and Bouxières-aux-Dames); that certain apparently miraculous answers to prayer on the occasion of pilgrimages etc., inspired by such apparitions, were not uncritically accepted by the Church authorities as divine confirmation of those visions (e. g. Ghiaie di Bonate); and that many such "apparitions" strongly impress one as doubles of prior apparitions in other places (a series of appearances, a "sun miracle",[113] etc.). It is also evident that even today we are not necessarily secure against attempted fraud: the "revelations" of

[113] Staehlin reports such repetitions of the sun-miracle in connection with

Maria Rafols (d. 1853) which have been published since 1926 are a modern forgery;[114] the "apparitions" at Lipa in the Philippines were deliberately staged as a hoax;[115] the visions at Gimigliano were invented by the little visionary after seeing the film on Bernadette (though many people claim to have seen the sun-miracle during those "visions").[116]

apparitions which are certainly false. In one of these cases a priest was sure that he had observed it (*ibid.*, p. 120).

[114] Cf. *LThK VIII¹*, col. 611 f.; A. Lambert, "Sur les 'Escritos postumos' de la V. M. Rafols" in *RHE* xxix (1933), pp. 96—107. (The reply of P. Dudon, "Los Escritos postumos de la V. M. Rafols" in *RHE* xxix [1933], pp. 398—406, fails to carry conviction.)

[115] Cf. J. Hofinger, "War Lipa Betrug?" in *Die Katholischen Missionen* lxx (1951), pp. 115—6.

[116] Cf. Strangfeld, *op. cit.*, p. 84.

IV

PROPHECIES

WHAT we have said of apparitions in general implicitly includes
the most important theological information on prophecies. For
such prophecies, insofar as they concern the religious sphere and
claim divine origin, almost always occur as communications
delivered by persons seen in visions, and thus claim supernatural origin in the same way as the apparitions themselves. The prophecies of La Salette [117] and of Catherine Em-

---

[117] Cf. W. Widler, *Buch der Weissagungen* (8th ed., Munich, 1950), pp. 117—
128. More bibliography in *LThK* IX (1st. ed., 1937), col. 118 f. We must
realize that the Church, and more specifically the Holy See, has repeatedly
forbidden the propagation of the prophecies of La Salette. First, by two
letters of Cardinal Caterini immediately after their publication by the
visionary in 1879 (with the imprimatur of her spiritual director, the Bishop
of Lecce). Then formally in 1901 and 1907 on the occasion of the condemnation of two books by Gilbert Combe on the secret of La Salette (*ASS* xxxiii
[1900—1901], p. 677; xl [1907], p. 271). The most explicit and severe
prohibition was issued in 1915. By this decree anyone who presumes to write
about this secret in any manner whatsoever is threatened with the gravest
penalties (*AAS* vii [1915], p. 594). Nevertheless, another book on the secret
by H. Mariayé had to be condemned in the following year (*ASS* viii [1916],
p. 178). A new edition of the secret was prohibited in 1923 (*AAS* xv [1923],
pp. 287 f.). All this did not prevent Léon Bloy publishing the secret again
in his book *Celle qui pleure*. He maintained that its first publication in
1872 had been blessed by Pius IX, while the edition of 1873 had received

merick,[118] the predictions and promises of Fátima[119] are examples. All that has been said about the possibility and psychology of such apparitions in general, about the criteria of their authenticity and the compenetration of divine and human elements in them, will also apply to the prophecies given in these apparitions. Nevertheless, it will be useful to add a few separate remarks in their regard.

What we today call prophecy, that is a prediction or a foresight of a future event which could not be known by ordinary human means, occurs in the most various forms. Therefore it is difficult even to produce a typology of such prophecies. Yet we must not neglect the effort here since nothing intelligible can be said of prophecies unless their various types have been at least in some degree distinguished. Otherwise one would risk predicating the same things of, and giving the same criteria for, totally different phenomena. If we distinguish certain types of prophecies, of course it is done with the reservation that in concrete reality they may not occur as "pure" types. Who, for instance, could exclude from the outset the possibility that in Catherine Emmerick's or Don Bosco's visions of the future[120] divine inspiration may have been combined with natural parapsychological forces? At any rate, in such cases, the supposition is not wholly impossible.

the approval of Cardinal Xyste-Riario Sforza. W. Widler holds his peace about all this (cf. Staehlin, *op. cit.,* p. 363 f. and note 29). More about La Salette in E. W. Roetheli, *La Salette. Das Buch der Erscheinung* (Olten, 1945), especially pp. 306, 308 ff.

[118] Cf. Widler, *op. cit.,* pp. 97—106. We cannot embark here on a critical discussion of the predictions of Catherine Emmerick.

[119] Cf. Dhanis, *Bij de Verschijningen,* pp. 56—89.

[120] In the case of Don Bosco (as in that of C. Emmerick) the early occurrence of such phenomena (visions in dreams) seems rather to indicate a parapsychological inclination.

In the *first* type of prophecy we would classify all those phenomena which are best and most clearly described as soothsaying, or divination in the pejorative sense of the term. In spite of the great differences there may be among them, we include here: oracular practices of classical and Germanic antiquity, astrology (insofar as it claims to be able to foretell details which depend on future free human decision), chiromancy or palmistry (insofar as it makes the same claim), fortune-telling from cards, soothsaying by questioning "spirits" at seances, necromancy (conjuration of the dead in order to penetrate the future), etc. These things, while very different from each other, all fall into the category of superstition.

Superstitions they are, not only in the sense that the means are not proportionate to the end, and thus such practice is based on error and leads to illusions, but also because these practices spring from the soil of an irreligious attitude and in many cases may even imply readiness to entertain diabolic influences and activities, and to make use of these. Such practices leave the door wide open to delusion. Simply from the point of view of mental health all these things should be avoided as highly detrimental to people who indulge in them. The results of such practices, the prophecies arising from them, are practically always infantile and primitive — befitting the intellectual and moral standards of their adepts — which of itself suffices to show that they reveal no source of "higher" knowledge. When, for instance, have the spirits at a seance ever said anything which was not as foolish and insignificant as the ideas and fancies already in the heads of the people who organized the occasion? Such superstitious divination is fundamentally irreligious, because

173

on the one hand it is "magical", that is, it claims to possess a technique for wresting God's secrets from him, and on the other hand because it dispenses altogether with the essential foundation of true religion, man's humble devotion to the sovereignty of the living God, whose ways and counsels are inscrutable; and it is in this devotion, and not in any knowledge of the future, that man finds true peace of heart. The main characteristic of such superstitious divination being an "irreligious profanity", one could say conversely that where prophecy is irreligious (in the attitude from which it arises, in the belief that one has a sure technique for prophecy that can always be applied, etc.) and profane (that is, at the service of worldly ambitions, of financial and similar advantages), the case is one of divination and must be rejected.

The *second* type of prophecy is of the "parapsychological" kind, prophetic dreams, second sight, clairvoyance, foreknowledge of the hour of death, etc. Whether genuine phenomena of this nature exist is not an easy question to answer. Even if many instances are explained as illusions or interpreted in terms of normal psychology, a residue of such phenomena can neither be frauds nor coincidences, nor yet can they be explained by ordinary psychology. They may be called "parapsychological", because though extraordinary they do not imply a special intervention of God but derive from natural faculties, even if these faculties are not — at least to any perceptible degree — at the disposal of the modern man of today. Supposing that one does not completely reject the reality of such phenomena, they must be attributed to natural powers, even if these be of an extraordinary character. For on the whole the achievements of these powers are from the religious point of view too insignificant to suggest a truly supernatural intervention of God. This does not mean, however, that they may not occur at times even in religious and saintly people, and that in them they may not serve some religious purpose. They seem often to be hereditary and endemic, associated with a certain region. If we call these prophecies "parapsychological" it is only to assert their reality (or at least admit their possibility) and to distinguish them, as natural phenomena, from prophecies of divine origin. We are far from intending to explain these phenomena. Minds great and small have tried again and again, in the course of history, to explain how such visions of the future, of themselves natural, can come about. If one wished to write a history of these attempts, the names of Aristotle, St. Augustine, St. Thomas Aquinas, Leibniz, Jung-Stilling, Schopenhauer, E. von Hartmann, Driesch, Willi Moock and many others[121] would have to be mentioned. However, it could not be said that all these attempts have shed much light on the question. For it is difficult indeed to explain how anybody could so rise above time as to encounter the future as if it were already present, if one is not to embrace an absolute determinism according to which the whole future, even free personal activity, is already fixed in present reality and therefore can be ascertained from the present.[122]

[121] Cf. Reginald Omez O. P., *Psychical Phenomena* (London, 1959); E. Osty, *La reconnaissance supranormale* (Paris, 1925); Renée Haynes, *Extrasensory Perception* (London, 1961). We cannot enter here into the history of the explanation of "divination" and of real supernatural prophecy. Material will be found, for example, in *DTC* XIII, 708—37; M. A. van den Oudenrijn, *De prophetiae charismate in populo israelitico* (Rome, 1926); A. Bouché-Leclerq, *Histoire de la divination dans l'antiquité* I-IV (Paris, 1879—81); T. Ortolan, "Divination" in *DTC* IV. 1441—55.

[122] "A telephone line to the Absolute" (E. V. Hartmann's expression), if

However desirable it might be for us to know how such a vision of the future occurs, for our purpose — which is to distinguish parapsychological prophecies from those of divine origin — this is not absolutely necessary. We can draw an approximate distinction between them, even failing a full explanation. Where, for the reasons already mentioned, we have to assume a case of natural parapsychological clairvoyance, these phenomena exhibit characteristics by which they can be clearly distinguished (at least in general; we admit that there are difficult borderline cases) from prophecies of divine origin, of which we have examples in the Bible. The former are distinguished from the latter, not only by their content (the absence of any real religious purpose and of integration into a theological interpretation of history), but also psychologically. The paraspychological vision of the future is just a vision. That is, it shows a small, random part of the future, like an incidental cut from a long film, without reference to any larger, coherent event, without any interpretation, any accompanying person to impart the revelation and personally address the visionary. The parapsychological seer in some impersonal way seizes a shred of the future, which by some "accident" is blown senselessly and blindly into the range of his observation. Whatever is seen is very clear and concrete, as if one were really there; the visionary can describe it like a reporter. But what is seen so clearly is isolated, and thus in spite of all attempts at interpretation remains unintelligible.

this Absolute is rightly understood (i. e., to mean a personal God), would amount to explaining clairvoyance by proper, supernatural revelation. A "spiritualistic" explanation would only defer the problem: How can finite spirits know a future that is not yet real and that remains free because it is not predetermined by its causes?

A divine prophecy is different. When the Lord of the world and history, transcendent over time, imparts information about the future, this is not a "vision" (at least essentially) but a "word". It does not show a picture of part of the future, but communicates something about it together with an interpretation. In its details, therefore (because, not although, it comes from God), this communication will be obscure, because it speaks rather of the meaning of the future and does not wish to be a means by which one could protect oneself from it, but wishes to leave the future obscure so as to preserve man's freedom in valourous reliance on God. Its style, consequently, is not that of a reporter miraculously transported into the future, who then narrates what he experiences on the spot. Rather it will give the man to whom it is addressed the forward look into the future which he needs in order to endure his own present now with loyal confidence in God. In short: the first is a vision; the second is a word; the first is an anticipation of the future as if it were present; the second an anticipation of the future which remains a future.

As we have said, in an individual case it will not always be easy to diagnose a prophecy as one type or the other through this general description of parapsychological and divine prophecy, the more so as an intermingling of these two types of phenomena cannot be excluded *a priori*. Still if we think, for example, of the prophecy of Muehlhiasl or that of the youth of Elz (assuming that both were true),[123] we will see the position

---

[123] Cf., for example, Widler, *op. cit.*, pp. 91—7, 86—91; E. Stemplinger, "Der Weltkrieg und Deutschlands Zukunft" in *Süddeutsche Monatshefte* xxix (1932), pp. 763—74 (more bibliography on the so-called Muehlhiasl of Apoig in the Bavarian Forest). On the youth of Elz: Kutscheit, *Sechs bisher unbekann-*

at once. Such predictions as these latter include some elements that are remarkably clear and some, at the same time, that are unintelligible; something is seen that is incomprehensible even for the seer himself. He does not know how far the vision reaches, whether it is a purely local event that may be totally unimportant for the history of the world, or whether it is the heart of future history. A religious interpretation, a theological and historical context for the vision, will at most be added by the seer on the basis of his other opinions and beliefs but is no part of the vision itself. Otherwise it would have to be given in the "word", not in a vision, because a word, a concept, can comprehend the abstract, can condense and interpret the future; which a vision of the future as it really happens could not do unless (and this is impossible for other reasons) it were to present the whole long film of the future or a great part of it. And therefore it is safe to consider such prophecies as these parapsychological, natural and not supernatural.

For where God reveals himself with his knowledge of the future by a miraculous intervention, a religious purpose and interpretation are an intrinsic element of the communication about the future and God always speaks personally to the seer. Otherwise God would not be working a miracle contrary to the laws of nature. This is the only intelligible purpose of a miraculous divine communication and automatically explains the content and psychological characteristics of a divine prophecy. Where these are not verified all visions of the future (however "true" in some sense) must be pronounced parapsychological phenomena,

te, *höchst merkwürdige Prophezeiungen*, (2nd ed., Bonn, 1848); further bibliography about him in F. Zurbonsen, *Die Sage von der Völkerschlacht der Zukunft "am Birkenbaume"* (Cologne, 1897), p. 63.

although we do not have as yet any precise and convincing theory of how they occur.

A *third* type anticipates the future (at least attemps to do so) in the light of the philosophy and theology of history. Great human minds have always looked to the future, sensed coming events, warned their contemporaries of the future consequences of the deeds of the present, consoled those who in their present had to sow in tears with the thought of the joyful harvest that coming generations would gather. Perhaps we should associate with this type the "national prophecy" which "accompanies the history of all peoples who have awakened to national conscious-ness" (J. Bernhart). Men[124] like St. Augustine, Nicholas of Cusa, Savonarola, Rousseau, Heine, Donoso Cortés, Soloviev, Nietzsche and others come to mind. However diverse their opinions and presuppositions, and consequently their anticipatory interpretations of history, these and similar "prophets" all had frequent and uncannily accurate intuitions of the future, insepa-rable indeed from their particular historical perspective and limited accordingly. Obviously a variety of causes will conspire to produce "prophecies" of this kind: the philosophical and historical perspicacity of a great mind, guidance from Scriptural prophecy and its theology of history, occasional parapsycholo-

---

[124] Cf., for example, J. Bernhart, "Das Prophetische" in *Süddeutsche Monats-hefte* xxix (1932), pp. 774—80; Widler, *op. cit.,* pp. 144—9 (Donoso Cortés); J. Schnitzer, *Savonarola II* (Munich, 1924), pp. 632—58; J.-J. Rousseau, *Contrat Social II,* 10; Widler, *op. cit.,* pp. 133—5 (Soloviev); G. Sacke, *W. S. Solovjews Geschichtsphilosophie* (Berlin-Königsberg, 1929), pp. 99—106; Nicholas of Cusa, *De concordantia catholica* (which he proposed to the Council of Basle in 1433); Donoso Cortés, *Der Abfall vom Abendland. Dokumente* (edited, with a preface by Paul Viator, Vienna, 1948; further bibliography); H. Heine, *Die Geschichte der Religion und Philosophie in Deutschland,* vol. 3; Fr. Nietzsche, *Beyond Good and Evil,* VI.

gical influences and perhaps even properly supernatural ones. Generally speaking, however, predictions of the sort will bear the hallmark of their principal cause: the insight of human genius into historical developments already in embryo which will mould the more or less distant future. Therefore they will be a mixture of truth and falsehood, light and darkness; there will be partiality, oversights, misinterpretations. Many things will happen not because they were forseen, but because they were "predicted" of a future "utopia", which will attract people as a new ideal and inspire them to realize it. Here the future is not foretold because it is going to happen, it happens because it has been foretold. The "prophet" does not foresee the future, but sets the men of the present a new goal — sometimes even by warning against it. "Talk of the devil and he is sure to appear", (as good Christians of our day who like to assume the mantle of Jeremias and talk of impending doom should remember). As such prophecies always prove to be deductions from an analysis of the present, they can be distinguished from supernatural prophecy with relative ease. They are worth as much as the evidence on which they rest, that is, the analysis of the present (correct or incorrect, balanced or unbalanced).

We shall briefly mention a *fourth* type: fabricated prophecies. We mean not simply those crude illusions and frauds which constantly recur in all the forms of superstitious investigation of the future already classified as the first type of prophecy. Rather we have in mind examples such as the prophecies concerning future popes which are ascribed to St. Malachy,[125] or the "prophe-

---

[125] Cf. F. X. Seppelt, "Die angebliche Papstweissagung des hl. Malachias" in *Süddeutsche Monatshefte* xxix (1932), pp. 750—4 (further bibliography here and in *LThK VI²*, col. 1323).

cies of Lehnin" (a Cistercian monastery in Brandenburg),[126] or those of St. Ottilia.[127] There is always a tendentious political or religious composition (often profoundly clever), which in the garb of prophecy propagates ideas on civil or ecclesiastical government and in some cases pronounces judgment on the past (which is presented as still in the future). We need say nothing more of fabricated prophecies, often as they have been believed and have swayed the thoughts and aspiration of men.

The *fifth* and last type of prophecy are genuine supernatural revelations of which God himself is the immediate cause. We shall have to discuss their real significance. A Christian who seriously believes the testimony of Scripture cannot doubt that such revelations are possible.[128] Together with miracles they are the evidence in sacred history by which God confirms his message to humanity, given through the prophets and apostles, and manifests its divine origin. The Church teaches that they are motives of credibility.[129]

The possibility of God's predicting the future is quite consistent with the Christian concept of God, difficult as it may be to see precisely how God can know the future without prejudice to its "futurity" and especially to its freedom. As the living and omniscient God he transcends time and history. As the omnipotent First Cause sustaining all creation, that is, all reality

---

[126] C. Sauter, "Die Lehninsche Weissagung" in *Süddeutsche Monatshefte* xxix, (1932), pp. 754—63; further bibliography in *LThK VI²*, col. 883 f.

[127] Investigated by M. Barth, *Die hl. Odilia, Schutzherrin des Elsass,* II (Strasbourg, 1938). This prophecy became very popular during the second World War.

[128] Cf., for example, Isa. 41:22—29; 43:12; 44:7; 45:21; 46:10—15; Deut. 18:22; 2 Pet. 1:20 f.; Joh. 13:19.

[129] Cf. *Denz.* 1707, 1790, 2145.

other than himself, he is equally close to everything that happens or is to happen in time. Time is an intrinsic modality of all "becoming" in creation but not a modality of God's relationship to the world. Therefore the future is not such for God himself. For God the future is the present. Therefore he can make it known if he wishes to do so.

We would not maintain that this classification is absolutely complete, nor that it is always easy to assign a concrete prophecy to one of our five types. One might ask, for instance, whether diabolic prophecies are possible or actually exist, a question which much engrossed the Fathers of the Church. Again one might ask how we should classify the famous prophecy of Nostradamus.[130] But we shall not pursue these matters here.

We shall now endeavour to say something about the theology of prophecy.

Divination, in the sense we have defined, is morally wrong. It is either an attempt to achieve an end by using inappropriate means, or it is an explicit or implicit attempt to invoke diabolic powers. Both are morally wrong. Here the Christian must still say: "There is no soothsaying in Jacob, nor divination in Israel" (Num. 23:23). (Cf. Lev. 19:26 and 31; Deut. 18:9—14.) According to Canon Law the bishop must combat and punish "superstition" (*CIC* can. 2325), and this is doubtless particularly applicable to divination. Catholics may not take part in spiritualist conversations and manifestations (Decree of Holy Office, April 24, 1917; *Denz.* 2182). Thus the Church forbids seances

---

[130] Cf., for example, J. Hildenbrand, "Nostradamus" in *Süddeutsche Monatshefte* xxix (1932), pp. 742—9; A. Le Pelletier, *Les oracles de Michel de Nostradame* I/II (Paris, 1867); C. Loog, *Die Weissagungen des Nostradamus* (6th to 8th ed., Pfullingen, 1921).

wherever, and insofar as, such parapsychological phenomena (real or supposed) are sought and are evoked in the hope of communications from the other world (from the dead, or "spirits", etc.), wherever these natural parapsychological phenomena are not investigated out of serious scientific interest and on the basis of an "animistic" theory, with proper scientific sobriety, but people do those things because they are supposed to elicit information from the spiritual world. This will be true especially where such spiritualistic practices are developed into a system ("Occultism", etc. Decree of the Holy Office, July 18, 1919; *Denz.* 2189). The scriptural account of a very early case of necromancy with the object of learning about the future (1 Kings 28:5—25) is still worth reading. Such "spirits" even today might well ask the participant in a spiritualist seance: "Why askest thou me, seeing the Lord has departed from thee, and is gone over to thy rival?" But where one is convinced that the results of such spiritualistic seances actually come from the subconscious of the participants, which is usually the case, the possibility of obtaining any information about the future is automatically excluded.

As to visions of the future which are really parapsychological (that is natural, though extraordinary, mental phenomena — if and so far as they exist) there is nothing more to be said from the religious and theological point of view. They occur involuntarily, and therefore the seer can have no moral responsibility for them, the less so as they seldom or never enable him to act differently in view of such knowledge than he would have done without it. As there is no really reliable method of causing these natural visions of the future, we need not broach the question of how to behave if there were.

We have already stated how the foresights of great minds

resulting from their studies of the philosophy and theology of history are to be theologically evaluated: they are worth as much as the arguments which those men adduce in their support from a rational or intuitive analysis of the present. If they invoke the revealed principles of the theology of history, or interpret a prophecy contained in revelation, it is necessary to ascertain whether these deductions and interpretations are correct, and whether they can be understood literally of the near future (which is not usually the case). Prophecies of the historical future which modern sects (Jehovah's Witnesses, Adventists, etc.) think they find in the Apocalypse of St. John are based entirely on an arbitrary misinterpretation of biblical revelation. The doctrine that Christ will visibly reign on earth for a thousand years before the last judgment and the consummation of all things has been repeatedly condemned by the Church in very recent times as a misinterpreation of the Apocalypse (Reply of the Holy Office, July 11, 1941; *Denz.* 2296).

Finally a word should be said on correctly understanding real God-given revelations of the future. Scripture testifies that genuine divine prophecy is possible and has in fact occurred. Suffice it to recall Christ's prediction of the destruction of Jerusalem. To deny the possibility of such predictions in principle would therefore offend against the Catholic faith. Prophecy is also to be a permanent endowment of the Church and a proof of her supernatural mission. Therefore the prophetic genius will never die out in the Church. There will always be men in the Church with charismatic gifts, who will look into the future like the prophets of old and warn us to make the right decisions in the present. This is not to say that all the prophecies, even of saints, must be authentic and accurate. A few examples have been cited above to show that even saints have been deceived in their visions of the future. An absolute criterion of a genuine prophecy can be found, before its fulfilment, only in what we have shown to be the sole proof of a genuine vision (for others than the seer): namely a miracle (of a different sort) which is demonstrated to be such, and is performed in such connection with the prophecy that it can really be taken as its divine confirmation. The truth of a prophecy is not confirmed, for instance, if miracles occur during a pilgrimage to the scene of a vision, but not in such connection with the prophecy as to be regarded as its divine confirmation,[131] or if such a connection cannot be proved beyond all doubt. Even if one assumes the sun-miracle of Fátima to be a true miracle, it would not prove that the seer's revelations of the future have received the divine seal. The miracle occurs to confirm the vision,[132] but it does not follow that every

[131] A distinction is therefore made between miracles of confirmation and miracles of mercy. The latter are granted by God in view of and as a reward for the great faith and confidence with which a person approaches him seeking help. They are, however, not given as a confirmation of visions which previously occurred at the place in question. Cf. J. Lhermitte, *Le problème des miracles* (Paris, 1956), pp. 57—71. The author refers here to a miracle granted at Port Royal to a niece of Blaise Pascal during the time when the nuns were in rebellion against the ecclesiastical authorities.

[132] It might be interesting to give here a brief summary of the revelations (disclosures and prophecies) of Fátima which became known before 1935 and 1941 (or more precisely, before 1927, in which year Canon Formigão's book was published). Concerning the first apparition: When Lucia asked on May 13th about the whereabouts of two girls who had recently died, the apparition answered that one of them was in heaven and the other in purgatory (L. G. da Fonseca, *Mari spricht zur Welt* [1952], p, 21). On September 27 Lucia said it had been revealed to her that St. Joseph would appear with the child Jesus on October 13 and give the world peace and that the Mother of God would work a miracle on that day (this latter only when Lucia asked what Our Lady intended to do so that people should believe Lucia) (Visconde de Montelo, *op. cit.*, p. 76). On the evening of October 13, Lucia

pronouncement of the visionary on the future is warranted, especially since this information about the future was only disclosed at a much later date.[133] Such reservations are even more

said: "She said that we should become better, that we should not insult our Lord, because he has already been insulted so much; that we should say the rosary and beg for the remission of our sins, that the war will end *today* and that we should expect our soldiers to return very soon" (*ibid.*, 99). This statement was confirmed on the 19th: "She said: 'The war will end this very day, and people here should expect their returning soldiers very soon'." And: "I said it (on October 13) exactly as Our Lady said it" (*ibid.*, p. 109). On the same 19th of October Lucia also said that the apparition revealed to her on August 19, or on the 13th of some month, that Christ would appear on October 13 in order to bless the world, and Our Lady of Sorrows as well (*ibid.*, p. 113). On November 2 Jacinta finally said that the apparition had revealed on August 19 that if the children had not been taken to Ourem on the 13th St. Joseph would have come with the child Jesus to bring peace to the world (*ibid.*, p. 121).

[133] In 1941. The books on Fátima published before that date know nothing about them. We mean the following predictions: Jesus wishes to establish devotion to the Immaculate Heart of Mary through Lucia (*Maria spricht zur Welt*, pp. 31 f., 42). Not long after the present war (1914—1918) another war will break out during the pontificate of Pius XI unless people amend their lives. An unknown light will be the sign announcing it. Then the "request that Russia be consecrated to the Immaculate Heart; if this is done Russia will be converted; if not, Russia will spread her errors and the good will suffer martyrdom. In the end will come the triumph of the Immaculate Heart and the conversion of Russia, which will be consecrated to it by the Holy Father. Several nations will be annihilated" (*ibid.*, p. 42 f.). When asked in 1946: "Is it not a pity that the secret was not revealed before the war?" — Lucia answered: "Well, if God had wanted to present me to the whole world as a prophetess then it really would have been a pity. But it seems that was not his intention . . ." (*ibid.*, p. 291; the three dots are also there). But how is it comprehensible that God should *reveal* certain matters concerning the whole world to a person, in order that this person should keep them *secret* until after their fulfilment? Or what can we say of a mission to establish a certain devotion (one should rather say, to promote a devotion; the devotion to the Immaculate Heart of Mary has been known for over a hundred years) if this mission was given as a secret with a strict order for it to be strictly guarded? Even if it be said that the time for secrecy

appropriate in the case of the prophecies which allegedly derive from the visionaries of La Salette.[134]

As to the purpose of such divine prophecies, we must first state that they cannot be intended to restrict human liberty. Being divine interventions whose purpose is human salvation, they will not take from man the burden and grace of free decision in courageous and trusting faith. They do not intend to provide man with a device for cleverly avoiding the difficult passages of his history and securing himself a safe and comfortable life (from the worldly point of view). They are not instructions for fleeing the cross of Christ. Where prophecies are so understood they are misunderstood, though genuine and of divine origin in themselves. Divine prophecy has a different sense and object; it is to manifest the living God as the Lord of history, even the history of darkness. Such prophecy would tell us that the seemingly hopeless situations of the world and the kingdom of Christ in it, do not mean that God has lost control of history, but were taken into account in the plans of his Providence from the beginning, because he wishes to triumph through our weakness. Divine prophecies will warn us against worldly optimism, against the mania for progress and against the utopian attempt to realize on this earth a kingdom of universal bliss. For this reason they constantly announce a dark future. True prophecies call us to penance, conversion, prayer, trust in the victory of Christ, hope in God eternal. What we have said

has now run out, we still are faced with a unique instance of God giving an order twenty-five years before he wishes it carried out.

[134] It is a remarkable coincidence that Mélanie made her first attempt to publish the secret — she left the Carmelite convent in Darlington for this purpose — in 1858, the year in which the apparitions occurred at Lourdes and attracted attention (cf. L. Bloy, *Celle qui pleure*, p. 112 f.).

187

earlier of visions in general will also apply here: post-apostolic prophecies must fit into the framework of scriptural prophecy if they would be acknowledged as genuine. Consequently they will tell us nothing essentially new beyond the scriptural perspective and interpretation of the future; but at the same time they will be concrete and timely imperatives for our day, deriving from the general theology of the future and of history which Scripture already gives us. Their real sense will be an imperative for the right attitude towards a future which always remains dark and threatening, which is always forfeit to death (from a worldly point of view) and yet is profitable for the salvation of those who believe and love.

Prophecy, according to 1 Corinthians 13:9, is a mere fragment in comparison to charity, which alone has the strength to embrace even the perpetual darkness of the future, which no prophecy could so illumine as to banish all dangers from it. For love alone can accept such a future from the hands of God as a gift of his wisdom and his love. There will ever be true and false prophets in the kingdom of Christ (Matt. 10:41). So the exhortation is always opportune, "extinguish not the spirit; despise not prophecies; but prove all things; hold fast that which is good" (1 Thess. 5:19—21). The good in every prophecy is ultimately shown if it awakens us to the gravity of decision in courageous faith, if it makes clear to us that the world is in a deplorable state (which we never like to admit), if it steels our patience and fortifies our faith that God has already triumphed, even if in this world we still have distress, if it fills us with confidence in the one Lord of the still secret future, if it brings us to prayer, to conversion of heart, and to faith that nothing shall separate us from the love of Christ.

THE CHURCH
AND THE SACRAMENTS

INTRODUCTION

THE subject that is to be dealt with in this *Quaestio disputata* is: the Church and the sacraments. The two concepts are intended to throw light on one another in the course of the inquiry, so that a deeper understanding of the Church may be gained by asking what the sacraments are, and greater comprehension of the sacraments, by reflecting on what the Church is. In the mind of the faithful at large, and perhaps even for theologians, the connection between Church and sacraments is not very clear. Everyone knows that the Church is empowered to dispense the sacraments because they were instituted by Christ and their administration entrusted to the Church by her founder. But that is more or less all that is thought of as connecting the two. In general, the sacraments are regarded as means of grace for the salvation of the individual, which they certainly are, of course, but as nothing else. If the sacraments are viewed in that way, the Church can only appear as the dispenser of these means of grace for the individual's salvation, as the supplier of heavenly treasures, as it were, to whom one must turn to obtain them, but from whom one turns away as soon as they have been supplied. In this way the relationship between the two remains so superficial and external that in the average view it would not be at all inconceivable that God might just as well have entrusted the administration of those means of grace to some other person or institution. The Church as Church, and the Church as dispenser of the mysteries of God, are almost only *per accidens* one and the same. If the connection between Church and sacraments is to be more clearly and deeply recognized, it will be necessary to deal first with the Church as the Church of the sacraments, so that the inquiry will proceed from the Church and a correct understanding of what she is, towards the sacraments; and secondly with the various sacraments as the living accomplishment of the Church's nature, so that the relation of each to the Church may be recognized, and as a consequence an understanding of the Church's nature achieved, with the sacraments as starting-point.

I

THE CHURCH AS
THE CHURCH OF THE SACRAMENTS

1. The Church as the Fundamental Sacrament

THE Church is not merely a religious institution, established to meet religious needs. It goes without saying that it was not created by men for that purpose. But neither was it simply founded from above by Christ as a spiritual welfare establishment. The institutional, hierarchical build of the Church with its legal and official organization, which, of course, exists and is essential to the Church and shares in the indispensability of the Church for salvation, is the juridical constitution of something that must be already there for it to be given such a constitution. The reality that has to be so organized and constituted, with a basis in a hierarchical and juridical order that is its expression, is not the amorphous mass of individual human beings in need of redemption, but the "people of God". It is because this is what it is, not what it has yet to become, that it receives in the Church as a juridical organization its institutional structure according to Christ's will at its foundation.

Can this be made more precise? A comparison may help. An actual State that has come into existence in the course of history, for all its importance for the life of a nation, is not what first brings together an amorphous mass of individual human beings into a community. It is rather the actual existence of a national group, with a common history, a common territory, a certain historic mission, a common civilization and so on, that brings about the existence of the State. Of course the two things condition one another, for the common cultural life of a single nation and the unity of its history is itself grounded in the existence of a single State, or at least may be. The State exists because logically if not necessarily in time, the nation is prior with its unity of territory, history, civilization and so on.

A similar relation holds between the Church as a juridically organized society and the reality we are calling the "people of God". What is meant by the people of God? The eternal Word of the Father, born of the virgin Mary one of the daughters of Eve, has become of one race and family with us (Heb. 2:11), not merely of the same nature in the abstract as it were. He belongs to the one human race which is not merely the logical sum of the multitude of individual human beings, but an actually real unity by the will of God. However difficult it may be to find categories to define it, this unity is manifested in the monogenetic descent of all men from the one Adam, is raised above nature by the call of all mankind in that one Adam to a supernatural destiny, and unfolds in original sin and the one history of the human race in salvation and perdition. That unity is confirmed, increased and made definitive by the incarnation of the Logos. Since he is man, a human nature is divinized, thanks to the hypostatic union, through the sanctifying grace that necessarily ensues from that union, and shares in the immediate presence of God by direct vision and love. But because this man Jesus is a member of the one human race, this itself is called to a supernatural destiny in and through him, even if it were not so called in Adam, or not called in Adam because called in Christ as first willed by God. God maintains this vocation of all humanity, despite sin, on account of Christ, who by what he is and what he does, the sacrificial death on the cross, is a member of this single human race. God sees all human beings as brothers and sisters of his incarnate Son "in the midst of the Church" (Heb. 2: 10–11), as the people of God with whom he has concluded that new and eternal covenant by that union between God and creature which we call the hypostatic union. By the gracious coming of the Logos in the flesh, in the unity of the race, in the one history of humanity, mankind as a whole has become a consecrated humanity, in fact the people of God.

Even though in biblical as well as in present-day official ecclesiastical terminology "Church" and "Body of Christ" too always signify the society comprising the whole of mankind called to supernatural salvation in Christ, with its juridical build and the hierarchical, social, organized structure given to it by Christ, that does not alter the fact that this organized association of those who are called to redemption, and the personal acceptance of the call by the individual, are in fact preceded, even chronologically, by a consecration of the whole of mankind which took place in the incarnation and death on the cross of the eternal Word of the Father. As the people of God socially and juridically organized, the Church is not a mere eternal welfare institute, but the continuation, the perpetual presence of the task and function of Christ in the economy of redemption, his contemporaneous presence in history, his life, the Church in the full and proper sense. To make this clearer, Christ's own

195

rôle in the mystery of redemption must be considered rather more closely.

Christ is the historically real and actual presence of the eschatologically victorious mercy of God. The incarnation is not merely the constituting of a subject who, if eventually he is willing, or is given the task by God, can intercede for sinful mankind before the holy majesty of God, through an atonement that gives Christ a claim to be heard as of right. If it were, nothing at all would have been determined by the incarnation itself in regard to redemption. The connection between the two realities would only consist in God's having willed the incarnation "in view of" the cross. Such a view cannot do justice to the "physical" theory of the redemption found in the Greek Fathers of the Church nor explain why the hypostatic union continued even after the crucifixion. It also makes it difficult to understand why the redemption actually took place through a sharing in the lot of sinners, suffering the death that is theirs, the very manifestation of their guilt. Rather did God by the incarnation take the world fundamentally and once and for all into his mercy. Through the incarnation the whole of redemption was already pre-formed, even if it still had to be carried out in the suffering of death, precisely because the Logos had assumed the "flesh of sin", as St. Paul says in Romans 8:3, in other words the flesh that is marked out for death, and a true human life that must be personally lived through, not merely a static "nature" that endures without a history. For the Logos redeemed by really identifying himself with the sinner.

Consequently the whole of mankind is in principle already accepted for salvation in this member and head of mankind who is irrevocably united with God in unity of person. From

196

the moment the Logos assumes this human nature from out of the unity of mankind, and as a part of it, redemption cannot be arrested or cancelled. The fate of the world has been finally decided, and in the sense of divine mercy. Before Christ, the dialogue between God and mankind in the history of eternal welfare and loss was an open one, the history of mankind as a whole could lead to salvation or ruin (though that does not imply any clear decision one way or the other for the individual). Everything was still unsettled. New, incalculable and surprising reactions of the living God who manifests himself in his actions throughout that history, could take place. Of what kind they would be, was not to be inferred from the previous course of human history with God. But now in the Word of God, God's last word is uttered into the visible public history of mankind, a word of grace, reconciliation and eternal life: Jesus Christ. The grace of God no longer comes (when it does come) steeply down from on high, from a God absolutely transcending the world, and in a manner that is without history, purely episodic; it is permanently in the world in tangible historical form, established in the flesh of Christ as a part of the world, of humanity and of its very history.

That is what we mean by saying that Christ is the actual historical presence in the world of the eschatologically triumphant mercy of God. It is possible to point to a visible, historically manifest fact, located in space and time, and say, Because that is there, God is reconciled to the world. There the grace of God appears in our world of time and space. There is the spatio-temporal sign that effects what it points to. Christ in his historical existence is both reality and sign, *sacramentum* and *res sacramenti*, of the redemptive grace of God, which through him no longer,

197

as it did before his coming, rules high over the world as the as yet hidden will of the remote, transcendent God, but in him is given and established in the world, and manifested there.

Consequently it would be totally to misapprehend the message of Christianity (yet how often it occurs in preaching), if one were to attempt to think of God's plan of salvation as opening out two possibilities, two ways, between which man's freedom, neutral and indifferent in itself, had to choose: salvation or perdition, God or damnation. Of course, each has freely to decide, and life and death are presented for choice. But God did not simply set up a fully equipped stage, for men to act out the drama of their history on their own. God himself has taken part, acted, given the drama the dénouement he himself wanted: salvation, grace and eternal life. The individual human being cannot, as long as he is a pilgrim and faced with decision, yet say whether and how this one divinely effected consummation of the whole of history will end in blessedness for him. But because he cannot tell that about himself or any other individual, speaking generally, he must not have the impression on that account that history as a whole is still at the disposition of mankind, with God awaiting the decision. History as a whole is already decided, and by God. Not that man's freedom is abolished thereby. But in Christ himself God has decided the free consent of man as a whole in regard to the God of grace and life, in faith and love. In its teaching on grace, theology must not only say, as all its schools of thought do, that God by his efficacious grace "can" decide the free consent of man to his salvation, not abolishing the free consent but constituting it. If it is to do justice to holy Scripture, theology must say, and generally forgets to say, that God has actually promised this

198

efficacious grace for history as a whole and its single end (which can be viewed as the final result and the one meaning and pattern of all human history). When we say that Christ on the cross merited incontestably and irrevocably the "grace of God", that grace is not only to be understood as a "possibility" of effecting redemption, as a mere offer of attaining forgiveness and producing works of eternal life. That grace, viewed in relation to the totality of the history of the world and mankind, is a grace which effects the acceptance of what it offers, for, of course, all is grace, the possibility and the realization of the possibility, the capacity and the act, the word of God and the answer of man. And seeing that this grace with its eschatological invincibility and conclusiveness is given in Christ, and promised to the individual in so far as he belongs to the people of God, the promise and presence of this grace, understood in this way, has a public character, and is not only a factor in the private history of the interior life of the individual.

This last-mentioned characteristic of grace is another thing that needs clarification. There is official, public history and private, individual history. The history of a nation, if it is not given an individualistic and liberalistic misinterpretation, is not simply the sum-total of the individual private lives of the human beings who compose that people. There is also the history of the nation as a nation, as a whole. The same is proportionately true of the sacred history of salvation and eternal loss which unfolds between mankind and God acting in the history of the world. There, too, there is the private history of the individual's grace and sin, and the public, official, "political" (from πόλις) history of humanity and the nations in eternal welfare and ruin, as this is effected by God and by human beings who act as spokesmen for the nations and epochs. Christ belongs to this history, but of course in a way that is his alone. In this dimension of the πολί-τευμα of salvation (citizenship, see Phil. 3:20), Christ is the primal sacramental word of God, uttered in the one history of mankind, in which God made known his irrevocable mercy that cannot be annulled by God or man, and did this by effecting it in Christ, and effected it by making it known.

Now the Church is the continuance, the contemporary presence, of that real, eschatologically triumphant and irrevocably established presence in the world, in Christ, of God's salvific will. The Church is the abiding presence of that primal sacramental word of definitive grace, which Christ is in the world, effecting what is uttered by uttering it in sign. By the very fact of being in that way the enduring presence of Christ in the world, the Church is truly the fundamental sacrament, the well-spring of the sacraments in the strict sense. From Christ the Church has an intrinsically sacramental structure. Historically visible in space and time, with its double aspect as people of God and as juridical and social organization of this people, the Church is the body and bride of Christ who abides in the Church as the presence in the world of God's historical and eschatological promise of himself, during this last of its epochs. He does not abandon the Church, and cannot do so, since he himself wills to remain forever in the flesh of the one human family.

This abiding presence of Christ in the Church is the sign that God in his merciful love identifies himself in Christ with the world. And because the Church is the sign of the grace of God definitively triumphant in the world in Christ, this sign can never — as a real possibility — become a meaningless symbol. As an historical and social entity, the Church is always and unchangeably the sign which brings with it always and inseparably what it signifies. As with Christ the distinction between his Godhead and his humanity remains without confusion though they are inseparable, sign and reality, manifest historical form and Holy Spirit, are not the same in the Church, but as in Christ, are not separable any more either. The Church is the official presence of the grace of Christ in the public history of the one human race. In its socially organized form the people of God as in fact redeemed by Christ, receives his permanent presence through history. And when we examine what this one reality implies, it means a presence, as it were an incarnation, of the truth of Christ in the Church through Scripture, tradition and magisterium; a similar embodiment and presence of Christ's will in the Church's teaching when it announces Christ's precepts in her pastoral office and her constitution; and a presence and embodiment, again analogous to the incarnation, of the grace of Christ, for the individual as such, through the sacraments. Viewed in relation to Christ, the Church is the abiding promulgation of his grace-giving presence in the world. Viewed in relation to the sacraments, the Church is the primal and fundamental sacrament.

2. Explanation of the Sacramental Structure of the Church and its Actualization in the Seven Sacraments Generally

a. Various levels of the Church's activity

The Church is not a mythical entity to be hypostasized or personified in a false way. By the will of Christ her founder she is the organized community of the people of God, established through the incarnation in the unity of the one human race. Even if such a society is represented by individual human beings, it still remains a community. Such a collectivity may in a true sense continue in being even when all its members are asleep and the common business or activity for the moment has completely ceased. But in order to exist, nevertheless, a community has to fulfil its nature, must actually function. The enduring existence of such a society can to be sure find concrete expression in the most diverse ways, and manifest itself with greater or less intensity in visible historical form. And a community of spiritual persons depends much more than a real individual person on such *actus secundi* (operations flowing from a nature and expressing it), because it is only an association. One can confidently say that once a society renounced once and for all its own actualization and functioning, it would by that very fact cease to exist altogether. That holds true of the Church too. The Church exists in the full sense, in the highest degree of actual fulfilment of her nature, by teaching, bearing witness to Christ's truth, bearing the cross of Christ through the ages, loving God in her members, rendering present in rite in the sacrifice of the mass the saving grace that is hers.

b. The actual fulfilment of the Church's essence as the sign of an individual's sanctification

If it is true to say that the Church as the continuance of Christ's presence in the world, is the fundamental sacrament of the eschatologically triumphant mercy of God, then salvation is offered and promised to the individual by his entering into positive relation to the Church. This positive relationship may possibly have very different degrees and grades of intensity, but if the individual is to attain salvation, can never entirely be lacking. God's life is offered to men plainly and once and for all in Christ, through whose incarnation the people of God exists. This has socially organized form in the Church, which is consequently the abiding and historically manifest presence of this saving grace in Christ, the fundamental sacred sign or sacrament of this grace. From this the necessity of the Church for salvation — at root it is the necessity of Christ himself — directly follows. Its necessity as a means is also clear, the kind of necessity which is presupposed by the question of a moral claim to men's obedience. We have also, of course, in the distinction between the aspect: people of God, and the aspect: juridical constitution of that people, within the one complete unity of the Church, an objective means of discerning degrees of intensity in membership of the Church, so that in fact there can be no instance of saving grace of which one would have to say, that it had no connection with the Church and with membership of the Church.[1] So though the individual, in what concerns his own personal sanctification, works out his own unique, irreplaceable salvation in personal freedom, he always

[1] See *Schriften zur Theologie* II (Einsiedeln ³1958) 7–94; cf. note 7, p. 257.

203

does so by finding his way to the Church. For the Church is the presence of saving grace in the world. To deny the ecclesiastical character of all grace and redemption would either imply that grace is not always related to the incarnation, to history and so to the Church, or else it would imply that one can attain salvation without the grace of Christ.

If, however, the means of grace, its presence, has a sacramental structure, that is, is based on the unity of grace and its historically manifest concrete embodiment, this must also be true of access to this means or fountain of grace, of entry into it, and of any further acceptance of grace by the individual from it. That does not imply that any and every conferring and acceptance of the grace present in the Church as the fundamental sacrament, has in every case the nature of a sacrament in the strictest and technical sense of the word. It has been sufficiently indicated already, and we cannot go into the matter further here, that any grace-giving event has a quasi-sacramental structure and shares in Christ's character as both divine and human. But when the Church in her official, organized, public capacity precisely as the source of redemptive grace meets the individual in the actual ultimate accomplishment of her nature, there we have sacraments in the proper sense, and they can then be seen to be the essential functions that bring into activity the very essence of the Church herself. For in them she herself attains the highest degree of actualization of what she always is: the presence of redemptive grace for men, historically visible and manifest as the sign of the eschatologically victorious grace of God in the world.

Now if the Church as the people of God in a socially organized form is the enduring historical presence of the eschatologically triumphant grace of God and of Christ in the world for the individual, the obtaining of grace by the individual cannot consist simply in his approval and consent to the mere presence of this redemptive grace. A community with an organized structure only acquires by its own act reality and validity for the individual who at first is outside it. A society must" enrol" him if he is to enter it. It is only in that way, then, that it is manifest that God's redemptive grace in Christ is a free grace, his own operation in us and not a factual reality always of necessity present, and in regard to which it is really only a question for us, of what attitude we choose to adopt towards it. The actualization or accomplishment of the eschatologically victorious redemptive grace established in the Church for the world and offered to all men, takes place, therefore, (in instances where this accomplishment is realized fully and perfectly), in an act of the Church in the individual's regard, whereby the gratuitous character of redemptive grace is proclaimed. This act of the Church in regard to man necessarily bears within it the structure of the Church's own nature. It is sacramental in accordance with the Church's character as the primal sacrament of grace. It is to be remembered here that we have called the Church the fundamental sacrament, not by a vague borrowing of the concept of sacrament known to us already from the current teaching about the sacraments, but by deriving our concept from Christology. Therefore fundamental sacrament means for us the one abiding symbolic presence, similar in structure to the incarnation, of the eschatological redemptive grace of Christ; a presence in which sign and what is signified are united inseparably but without confusion, the grace of God in the "flesh" of an historical and tangible ecclesiastical embodiment, which therefore cannot be emptied of what it signifies and renders present, because otherwise the grace of Christ (who always remains man), would also be something merely transitory and replaceable, and in the last resort we would still be under the old covenant. Consequently, because first of all and independently of the usual idea of a sacrament, we envisage the Church as the fundamental or primal sacrament, and form the root idea of a sacrament in the ordinary sense as an instance of the fullest actualization of the Church's essence as the saving presence of Christ's grace, for the individual, we can in fact obtain from this an understanding of the sacraments in general.

3. *The Nature of a Sacrament in General,* *Viewed in Relation to the Church as Fundamental Sacrament*

We have, of course, no intention of attempting to deduce in precise detail from this conception all the basic characteristics of the sacraments as they are listed in the treatises on the sacraments in general. Nevertheless a few indications must be given.

a. *Opus operatum*

Our viewpoint permits a deeper understanding of the meaning of *opus operatum*. When applied to one of these acts of the Church in regard to an individual in which her nature is accomplished, this expression simply says what we said about the Church in general when we explained that she is the definitive sign, impossible to deprive of meaning, of God's grace in the world, which is rendered present by being manifested in this way in the Church.

The concept of *opus operatum* is, of course, not as simple as might at first appear. We are leaving out of account the fact that in standard theology it is not identical with the concept of a sacrament, as there are instances of it which are not sacraments (the mass as sacrifice; indulgences too, according to a commonly held view). The idea in itself too presents considerable difficulties which can perhaps be solved more easily with the present approach than if one starts from the individual sacraments themselves and tries to build up the concept of *opus operatum* from them. In the usual account, the concept means that grace is conferred on the recipient through the positing of the sacramental sign itself, and neither the merit (holiness) of the minister nor that of the recipient is causally involved (Denzinger 849, 850f.).

It is explained that God has linked his grace once and for all to the making of this sign and that through this connection established by God himself between sign of grace and grace signified, any objection that the sacramental *opus operatum* is being understood in a magical way *ipso facto* vanishes, all the more so as the need for inner receptiveness and for appropriation in faith of the grace conferred is not only not excluded but is expressly taught by the Council of Trent (Denzinger 797 f., 819, 849). All that is correct and at first sight quite clear. But we must note that in the first place the Council teaches the necessity, if the sacrament is to be received with fruit by an adult, of a right disposition: active co-operation in the reception of the sacrament with faith and love. Consequently the sacrament in its concrete reality involves, like the *opus operantis* (the dispositions of the recipient), an element of uncertainty about grace, of doubt about its factual efficacy. With the sacrament a person knows just as little as he does with his merely "subjective" actions performed in faith, whether it has really given him God's grace. Just as little and just as much. That is after all an undeniable fact which is hidden in the popular view of the sacraments by what the average person thinks *opus opera-tum* implies. Everyone has heard Catholics say, or has himself thought, that when someone prays or repents of his sins, he is not as sure that God has heard him or forgiven him as he is if he goes to the sacraments. Since Scotus more or less, this idea has been one of the standard arguments in apologetics to show the necessity or utility of the sacrament of penance, confession, even when this is not strictly obligatory because no grave sins are in question. The idea of *opus operatum* in fact current, contains an element of what one might almost call physical certainty of functioning, which does not belong to it in more accurate theology. Conversely one can certainly affirm that God has attached the unconditional promise of grace and help to other realities as well as to the sacramental signs. If someone prays in the name of Jesus for saving grace and for nothing else (and in a particular case he knows as much or as little whether he is doing so as he does about his dispositions when he receives the sacraments), he knows with infallible certainty that God hears him, even if perhaps the precise mode of the answer remains hidden and must be left in God's hands. It is not a cogent objection to this example to say that here the prayer as *opus operantis* represents a "merit" and consequently the obtaining of grace and its measure depend on the measure of this subjective merit, whereas fortunately this is excluded in the case of the sacraments, where God acts towards men according to his own generosity and good pleasure. This does not meet the difficulty. For the measure of grace in the sacraments is dependent on the quality of the recipient's dispositions (Denzinger 799).

Furthermore, even if the prayer is meritorious, God's hearing the prayer is not based on the merit that accrues through the prayer, but as all theologians agree, on the fact that in prayer as such, appeal is made for Christ's sake to the infinite generosity of God. It is to this prayer that God has promised an absolutely certain hearing. Consequently one can say in a general way with regard to the two instances that in both of them, the sacrament and the prayer, and not only in the one where we employ the term *opus operatum,* we have occurrences to which, if they are true and genuine, God has absolutely promised his grace. Other acts could be quoted as well as prayer, that have a similar character, and we only omit them because in this connection they occupy a less prominent place in the average Catholic's awareness of his faith: reading of Scripture, listening to the word of God, and others. But in both the instances we are dealing with, grace is also conferred according to the measure of the recipient's dispositions which, of course, in the last resort are themselves a gift of grace. In both cases, too, the operative cause is not really the (supernatural) merit of man (which exists) but God's promise. So where is the real difference between the *opus operatum* of the sacraments and these other instances of grace being conferred, which we do not call sacraments?

In order to be in a position later to give as concrete an answer as possible to this question, let us illustrate once more with an example. Someone repents of his sins with genuine contrition and conversion, in his own conscience. If he does this, he knows with absolute certainty, by reason of the faithful and irrevocable words of the divine promise, that God truly forgives him his guilt. What happens then is an actual instance of grace being conferred, not a merely "subjective" desire for it to happen. Another man confesses his sins contritely in the sacrament of penance. He knows that God forgives him his guilt by the

Church's power of the keys, if he is truly and genuinely repentant. In neither case is there absolute certainty about the fulfilment of the condition. In both cases, over and above what the man does and experiences, he must also trust in God and his inscrutable judgment, seeing that in both cases he is obliged to trust firmly and unshakenly (not to know), with simple and childlike hope, (for God is greater than our heart), that God will truly have produced by his grace the necessary condition, our "good will". In the first case we speak of *opus operantis,* in the second of *opus operatum.* What is the difference between the two?

First of all it must be calmly and candidly recognized that the difference is not at all as radical as a rather mediocre theology would have it. Supernatural activity where grace is conferred and promised to us by God, infallibly on his part, and sacramental activity, are not identical. The second is only one of the possible kinds of the first. And as regards our question itself, the answer can only be that in the first case the sign (the prayer, repentance, in other words what the individual as such privately does), to which God has attached his grace, is itself intrinsically fragile, vulnerable, capable that is of becoming invalid of itself, and of being for its own part deprived of the character of visible expression of God's promise of grace. In the second case the sign has an irrevocable eschatological validity; in itself it is the sign of the eternal irrevocable covenant of God with men, a sign which so shares in the eternity and irrevocability of God's salvific will, that the sign itself can never lose the quality of being the visible expression of God's consenting answer to man. It can meet with refusal from man, who can reject the word of God and let it stand against him. But since Christ, and only since him, man can no longer prevent this word's being permanently addressed to him, calling him and not being withdrawn; or that this word summoning him to grace is irrevocably present in the sacramental sign, inseparable from it.

What that implies becomes even clearer if we reflect on the sacraments of the old Law which, according to the Church's teaching, truly existed. Since Augustine, with a few evanescent exceptions, theology has held firmly to their existence and the Church presupposes it in many doctrinal pronouncements (Denzinger 695, 711f., 845, 857). The question therefore arises whether and how they differ from the sacraments of the new covenant. In answering this question theologians got into very obvious difficulties. Particularly in view of the Epistle to the Hebrews, they could not and did not try to locate the difference in the outer form of the rites alone. Such a distinction is clearly too slight and would not do justice to the absolute originality and finality of the new and eternal covenant (Denzinger 845). On the other hand, theology could not be satisfied with the thought of the Epistle to the Hebrews alone, that the Old Testament rites only and exclusively concerned an external ritual "holiness" and were of absolutely no importance for the inner sanctification of men. Of course they were primarily and directly concerned with the "flesh", by the very fact that they had a nationally restricted and earthly import, like the old covenant in general, of which they were the visible expression and realization. As, however, that covenant despite its fleshly character had justification and redemption as its ultimate meaning, for even in the old Law, as the Epistle to the Hebrews also teaches, faith and justification were given by the Spirit of God, so that we have to follow the "father of those who believe" and the "cloud of witnesses" and attain justification and sanctification

211

thereby; and as that giving of grace and the visible covenant with its rites of circumcision and so on were not merely facts juxtaposed in time and space without intrinsic connection, for in that case there would have been no difference at all between the men of the Old Testament and the heathen in the actual workings of grace, and the visible alliance would have been a mere political and national affair, traditional theology with few exceptions has always held that for example circumcision and justification were connected in the old covenant.

On this supposition the problem arises in its full difficulty of how to determine in what the difference between the sacraments of the old Law and the new actually consists, for it is an essential difference. The question becomes even more puzzling when we recall that for a modern treatment in apologetics of the sacramental element in the Church, it is more a question of showing that there have always been sacraments everywhere in the sacred history of redemption, and for that reason theology rightly speaks of *sacramenta legis naturae,* not recognizing any period at which there were no sacraments at all in existence. There is no question of making such apologetics easier by simply referring to a free decree of God instituting as a matter of fact, though doubtless very wisely, sacraments in the new covenant although it need not have been so. Such a theology of mere divine decrees is at bottom a refusal really to think theologically, and it abandons all hope of real apologetics. Without realizing it, such an attitude attributes to the people of to-day an anthropomorphic conception of God, because it thinks of him as ordering now this, now that within the world, whereas after all he freely created a world with definite structures. Once this whole is freely set in being, it is intrinsically coherent. If it is involved in an historical process, and alters, these changes are the fulfilment of the enduring structures of the whole, even if in certain circumstances it is only from the complete accomplishment that the disposition of an earlier stage in view of a later can be recognized, and this recognition is not possible on the basis of the potentialities of the earlier stage alone.

This general consideration shows that it is not to be expected that there was once a time in which no such things as sacraments existed. Such a view or tacit assumption would inevitably make an intelligible apologetics of the sacramental aspect of Christianity extremely difficult. But if there were always things of the sacramental kind, that is, historical spatio-temporal phenomena manifesting the salvific action of God in the individual, the question becomes even more pressing how the sacraments of the new law differ intelligibly from those of pre-Christian times. From all this the answer given to an earlier question will be clearer. The old covenant as such — and the same applies *a fortiori* to all sacred signs under the "law of nature" — was intrinsically fragile; of itself it was transitory, temporary, replaceable and destructible, though capable of persisting outwardly when in truth it had ceased to exist. If it does persist outwardly, though already in fact abolished, through the defection of the nation and the conclusion of the new and eternal covenant, then the signs of grace which were the effective expressions of the alliance, circumcision, the sacrifices and so on, still exist in certain circumstances of course, but in truth are no longer promises of divine grace. That is impossible in the new and eternal covenant, which is the covenant of the visible manifestation of the final grace of God, grace which is God's eschatological victory over the inner fragility of all that is human, even what is divinely

213

established in man. Consequently the signs of grace in the new covenant are always and permanently assurances of divine grace. To be sure they can be refused by the individual as an individual. But they remain the valid and validly promulgated offer of redemption by God. They are truly *opus operatum*. They can only be so when the signs are posited as signs of the Church as such, when they are ultimately and radically the actual accomplishment of the eternal covenant, operations in which the whole nature of this is actualized, for it alone has this assurance and guarantee.

An historically tangible concrete act of a human being, a prayer for instance, does not in itself possess this, because of itself it can be empty of the content that of itself it expresses, and because it is not an act that is accomplished by the Church as such. In such instances one can always say no more than: If this concrete phenomenon really contains what it purports to contain, then the grace of God is bestowed. With the sacraments of the new law, however, one can say unconditionally: Here in all truth a manifestation of God and his salvific will is taking place. It may remain questionable whether here and now grace is received. But it is not questionable that in general grace is in fact received under these signs, for the Church as a whole has also the promise of her own subjective holiness produced and preserved by efficacious grace. Above all, it is not questionable that God here and now in the sacrament offers his grace. Consequently *opus operatum* means the unambiguous, abiding promise irrevocably made by God, and as such recognizable and historically manifest, of grace for the individual human being, a promise made by the God of the new and eternal covenant. The statement that it is a conferring of God's grace without the subjective merit of the minister or the recipient of the sign, is only the negative and therefore secondary formulation of this positive content of the concept.

b. The reviviscence of the sacraments

With our approach it is also possible to understand what theologians teach about the "reviviscence" of the sacraments. It is not a question of a coming to life again, but of a sacramental sign's becoming effective; it still persists with its signification, an irrevocable word of God addressed to the individual, because the human being actually does accept it within the span of time in which, from the nature of the sign, we must consider the proffer of grace still subsists. This varies with each sacramental sign because of the different meaning of each. By its very nature a meal lasts a shorter time than the period of validity of a rite of admission, of the conferring of an office, of the bond of marriage, of the anointing in an illness that puts a human life in jeopardy. On that basis we can understand the distinctions that theologians make concerning the reviviscence of the various sacraments in particular. The reviviscence of the sacraments is simply a property that accompanies their character of being each an *opus operatum*. And *opus operatum* is only the plainest expression in Catholic dogmatic theology to affirm that God gives his grace of himself, on his own initiative; man's answer is truly only an answer, deriving its whole meaning and existence from God's word to man. It is quite surprising that this expression has provoked such contradiction in Protestant theology. *Opus operatum* is not a concept in opposition to faith. It states that God *sola gratia,* out of pure grace, gives this faith and utters this gracious summons to man plainly and simply in the historically visible form of the sacraments. *Opus operatum,* of course, does not mean that where a human being is capable of personal faith, this grace which is offered and unconditionally promised in the sacraments, ignores the faith of the human being. On the contrary, the grace is a grace of faith and love, the grace to be able and to accomplish, a grace which is realized in the loving faith of man.

c. *Sacramentum* and *res sacramenti*

With the approach that takes the Church as starting-point, it is possible to make it clearer how in the sacraments there is the duality of sign and what it signifies, *sacramentum* and *res sacramenti*. Precisely this duality has in fact been indicated in the Church.

d. The way the sacraments cause grace

With the same approach it would be possible to make it comprehensible that the efficacy of the sacraments is precisely that of signs: by signifying, to effect what is signified. For we have already seen that the Church is the visible outward expression of grace, not in the sense that she subsequently announces as it were the presence of something already there without the announcement, but in the sense that in the Church God's grace is given expression and embodiment and symbolized, and by being so embodied, is present. With that in mind it would probably be possible to attain a viewpoint that would put into perspective the controversies, usually so inextricable, concerning the correct theory of the causal efficacy of the sacraments. This much-discussed question is not to be treated again here *in extenso*. We can only give a few indications of how an intelligible approach to a solution of the problem of the nature of sacramental causality can be discerned in the ecclesiological origin of the sacraments.

Usually the question of the kind of causality at work in the sacraments is envisaged unconsciously, as though as a matter of course, in terms of the concept of transitive efficient cause borrowed from the philosophic doctrine of the categories. God, sacramental sign and grace are envisaged from the start as quite distinct factors, almost as though they were material things. Then the causality of the sacramental signs is thought of in relation to God, as a "moral" causality, analogous to that of prayer, for example, the making good of a legal claim on someone who has contracted to perform something. Or it is thought of in terms of grace, and then the efficacy is represented on the analogy of the physical causation of an effect. In view of the difficulty of a rite "physically" causing interior grace, this view calls to its aid the proposition that the causality in question is "instrumental". But then the present-day theory, as opposed to that of some mediaeval theologians who spoke of the production of an *ornatus animae* by way of dispositions in view of the effect, no longer makes it really clear, what precisely it is that even an instrumental cause must itself contribute to the final total effect, for the co-operation of such an instrumental cause to be at all intelligible. Or else the causality of the rite viewed directly in relation to grace, is interpreted in a juridical, "intentional" sense, physical causality being rejected. The sacrament is considered to confer on the recipient a legal title, which may be identical with the sacramental "character" but need not be. It

217

may be wondered whether this theory does not really amount to the same as the *ornatus* theory of the mediaevals, or would do so, if it were interpreted in not too physical a sense.

In all these theories it is noteworthy that the fact that the sacraments are signs plays no part in explaining their causality. Their function as signs and their function as causes are juxtaposed without connection. The axiom everywhere quoted, *sacramenta significando efficiunt gratiam,* is not in fact taken seriously. Nor do these theories take into account the fundamentally human element in the sacraments as sacred rites which have a past and a background in the whole history of man's religious activity. Always and everywhere men have had the conviction that in gestures and rites and figurative representation, what is signified and pointed to, is in fact present, precisely because it is "represented", and this conviction should not be rejected off-hand as "analogy magic".[2] The intrinsic difficulties of these current theories are too well-known for them to need long discussion. "Physical" causality inevitably does most to push the symbolic character of the sacraments into the background. It explains the possibility of reviviscence of the sacraments only with the help of very intricate supplementary hypotheses. It can give no real meaning to the instrumentality of the sacraments, cannot explain what the instrument itself can contribute to the effect, grace, nor make it intelligible how precisely a "symbol" can be the physical instrument of supernatural grace. That theory overlooks that a sign itself is not a "physical" thing, especially as in the sacraments it is composed of words

[2] This rejection is false because it fails to recognize the primarily ontological nature of symbol. See K. Rahner, *Theologie des Symbols* (*Schriften zur Theologie* IV, Einsiedeln 1960).

and ritual gestures which themselves are separated in time or form an essentially juridical process, which after all by its very nature cannot be a physical instrument in the same way as water, for instance absolution, or the marriage contract. The theory of "moral" causality, whether it admits it or not, must acknowledge a causality in regard to God which is then retracted by explaining that the real nexus is that between sign and grace: God wills the grace as dependent on the sign, but does not will this grace because of that sign. But, of course, the sign is the cause of grace, not of God's decision physically to confer grace. The theory of "intentional" causality either stops where the question recurs, how the legal title conferred on the recipient of the sacraments itself produces grace, or else it relapses into the theory of moral causality, which it was designed to avoid, when it thinks of the legal title to grace as "moving" God to confer grace. Furthermore the sign in the sacrament precisely as sign is just as unrecognized as it is in the other theories. The fundamental defect that leads all these theories into conceptual difficulties, consists, as we have said, in tacitly laying down the pattern of transitive efficient causality, in which one factor adequately distinct from another must produce the latter.

With the approach we have been using, it can become clear that the sacraments precisely as signs are causes of grace, that it is a case here of causation by symbols, of the kind that belongs to what by its very nature is a symbol. By such "natural symbols" or intrinsically real symbols, we mean for our purpose here, the spatio-temporal, historical phenomenon, the visible and tangible form in which something that appears, notifies its presence, and by so doing, makes itself present, bodying forth this manifestation really distinct from itself. With natural symbols, the sign or symbol as a phenomenon is intrinsically linked

to what it is a phenomenon of, and which is present and operative, even though really distinct. In fact we must distinguish
between two aspects: the dependence of the actual manifestation
on what is manifesting itself, and the difference between the two.
To cite a comparable relationship, a spiritual being is an intellectual substance, yet only constitutes itself as such, as mind, by
there emanating from it what is not identical with itself, its
really distinct power of knowing. A proportionately similar
relation holds between phenomenon and underlying reality.
Hence it is possible to perceive why the symbol can be really
distinct from what is symbolized and yet an intrinsic factor of
what is symbolized, essentially related to it. In the same way
there holds between what we have called an intrinsic or natural
symbol and what it signifies neither a nexus of transitive efficient
causality, nor the relation of subsequent notification of something
that has already taken place and is in being, by an extrinsic announcement of the state of affairs which is quite unaffected by
it. It is a case of an intrinsic and mutual causal relationship. What
is manifesting itself posits its own identity and existence by manifesting itself in this manifestation which is distinct from itself.
An example of this relationship is available for the scholastic phi-
losopher in the relation between soul and body. The body is the
manifestation of the soul, through which and in which the soul
realizes its own essence. The sign is therefore a cause of what it
signifies by being the way in which what is signified effects itself.
The kind of causality expressed in such a conception of symbolism
occurs on various levels of human reality. In substantial being
(body as the sign or symbol of the soul); in the sphere of activity
(bodily gesture through which the inner attitude itself which is
expressed by it first attains its own full depth). On this level of

activity the informative expression, without prejudice to its essential connection with what is expressed, may be posited quite freely and take the form of a legal reality. When, for example, what is signified is itself freely posited, the sign can share this characteristic. In other words, even a sign freely posited and belonging to a juridical order can be what we have called an intrinsic or essential symbol.

This concept of the intrinsic symbol, though developed so briefly here, must now be employed if we are to grasp what characterizes sacramental causation, and if we are to do this on the basis of the ecclesiological origin of the sacraments. The Church in her visible historical form is herself an intrinsic symbol of the eschatologically triumphant grace of God; in that spatio-temporal visible form, this grace is made present. And because the sacraments are the actual fulfilment, the actualization of the Church's very nature, in regard to individual men, precisely in as much as the Church's whole reality is to be the real presence of God's grace, as the new covenant, these sacramental signs are efficacious. Their efficacy is that of the intrinsic symbol. Christ acts through the Church in regard to an individual human being, by giving his action spatio-temporal embodiment by having the gift of his grace manifested in the sacrament. This visible form is itself an effect of the coming of grace; it is there because God is gracious to men; and in this self-embodiment of grace, grace itself occurs. The sacramental sign is cause of grace in as much as grace is conferred by being signified. And this presence (by signifying) of grace in the sacraments is simply the actuality of the Church herself as the visible manifestation of grace. Consequently the converse holds. The relation between the Church as the historical visible manifestation of grace and grace itself, one of reciprocal conditioning, extends into the relation between sacramental sign and grace conferred. The sign effects grace, by grace producing the sacrament as sign of the sanctification effected. This, of course, can only be said if the Church as an entity is truly and inseparably connected with grace. Only then is her act, when it is an unconditional realization of her essence, (that is of the Church as the presence of grace), essentially and irrevocably a manifestation of grace, so that the manifestation necessarily renders present what is manifested.

This accounts for the connection between *opus operatum* and the causality of the sacraments in relation to grace. Both are rooted in the same nature of the Church as the essentially primal symbol of grace inseparable from what is symbolized (grace).

This kind of causation is sufficient in this matter. All theologians agree that one satisfies the Church's doctrine that the sacraments are a "cause" of grace, provided one holds firmly that grace is conferred "on account of" the sacramental sign. No more is defined, and even the theory that the sacraments are only *condiciones* of the conferring of grace has never been officially rejected. Our interpretation fits all this. Provided the sign is an effect of God the dispenser of grace, it is true to say: This grace is conferred here and now because embodied, and by taking concrete form, in the sacramental manifestation. This statement is not falsified by there being other instances of the conferring of grace in which such sacramental embodiment does not occur. Even in regard to the grace conferred the two kinds, sacramental and non-sacramental, are not identical.

e. The institution of the sacraments by Christ

From the principle that the Church is the primal sacrament it would be possible to see that the existence of true sacraments in the strictest traditional sense is not necessarily and always based on a definite statement, which has been preserved or is presumed to have existed, in which the historical Jesus Christ explicitly spoke about a certain definite sacrament. This would have its importance for apologetics of a less anxious and worried kind in the history of dogma, in the matter of the institution of all the sacraments by Christ. A fundamental act of the Church in an individual's regard, in situations that are decisive for him, an act which truly involves the nature of the Church as the historical, eschatological presence of redemptive grace, is *ipso facto* a sacrament, even if it were only later that reflection was directed to its sacramental character that follows from its connection with the nature of the Church. The institution of a sacrament can (it is not necessarily implied that it must always) follow simply from the fact that Christ founded the Church with its sacramental nature. It is clear too that, properly understood, the treatise *De sacramentis in genere* is not an abstract formulation of the nature of the individual sacraments, but a part of the treatise *De ecclesia*. It rightly precedes doctrine about the individual sacraments; it does not follow as a subsequent secondary generalization; for only on the basis of the doctrine about the Church, the fundamental sacrament, can the sacramentality of several sacraments be recognized at all.

In order to be clear about scope and significance of what for the moment has only been indicated here, we must ask how it is possible to demonstrate in an historically credible way the sacra-

223

mentality of matrimony, holy order, extreme unction and confirmation, that is to say, here, their institution by Christ, which
is, of course, a dogma (Denzinger 844). We have no sayings of
Jesus about these sacraments. The authorization given to the
apostles to celebrate the Lord's supper is not the institution of a
sacramental rite which confers ministry and office. For no one
can deny that in the new covenant there are official powers by
divine law, and the transmission of such powers, which are not
sacraments. One has only to think of Peter and his successors. The
sacrament of order does not therefore follow from the *anamnesis* precept, the command to commemorate. Consequently,
for four sacraments we have no words of institution from Jesus
Christ himself.

Is it historically probable that Christ actually spoke such
words though they may not have been handed down to us?
Many theologians presume so, and point to the Easter period
when the Lord spoke with his apostles concerning the kingdom
of God (Acts 1:3). Yet the question cannot be settled by such a
general presumption. As there was no general concept of a sacrament at that time, it is in the first place historically plain as a
matter of course that Jesus cannot have spoken about these other
rites in terms of the concept of sacrament as such. But then the
question arises how, if we suppose him to have spoken explicitly,
of matrimony, order, etc., he could have spoken so that grace
could be recognized as the effect of the events in question. With
baptism, for instance, the matter is easy to understand. It is expressly called re-birth, forgiveness of sins, because without these
designations it can hardly be intelligibly described even in exter-
nals. Similarly with reconciliation with the Church (binding and
loosing) and the Lord's supper as the sharing in the redemptive

death of Jesus by the *anamnesis* of his passion. In these rites, then, the mention and designation of the rite necessitates the indication of an effect, which is grace. And so a sacrament can be affirmed without more ado from the facts of the case.

But this obvious quality is not present with order and matrimony. It is possible to speak of them intelligibly without any mention of grace being conferred. For one can talk of marriage, its purpose and obligations, its dangers and other characteristics – Jesus Christ did so – without reflecting on the fact that it is an efficacious sign of grace *ex opere operato,* a sacrament. The same is true of the ecclesiastical ministry and its transmission. Ministry is not grace. Consequently it is possible to speak of ministry in the Church and its transmission without saying that the ritual transmission of ministry in the Church is a sign that confers "grace". It follows that when Jesus Christ spoke of the ministry and of marriage, the situation with regard to an explanation of their sacramental quality was different from what it was with baptism, penance and the Lord's supper. He would have had to say something himself in addition. Is it likely? If someone objects: Why shouldn't Christ have done so? two points must be made.

First, how is this supplementary explanation that the well-known ordinary occurrences of contracting marriage or of appointment to office in the community, are also things that confer grace, just like baptism, eucharist and reception back into the community of the redeemed, supposed to have been worded, in expressions that can be supposed to have been spoken by the historical Jesus? If one simply takes as starting-point the divine omniscience of the Logos, one can, of course, consider every concept and every sentence of such an assertion to have been possible for him. But if one starts with the historical Jesus, and one must if one does not wish, without realizing it, to be a theological Monophysite or Docetist, the material of concepts and ideas in which the presumed explanation is supposed to have been given must to some extent be discoverable within the surroundings, thought and manner of expression of Jesus as we know them elsewhere to have been. Otherwise the statement assumed to have been made by Jesus Christ is simply a quite unhistorical postulate. Hence until proof of the contrary, until it is shown that Jesus Christ can be thought to have expressly asserted the sacramentality of matrimony and order more or less in this or that definite way, it becomes historically improbable that Jesus could have explicitly said essentially more than we in fact know him to have done.

Furthermore, if the attempt were made to produce this missing counter-proof, if it were shown that Christ could have said more than tradition has preserved, if it were proved, for example, that his ideas about his Church, of the final and eternal covenant, of the holiness of the new community of the alliance, of the demands made by the ministry on those who share in it, imply that the transmission of ministry must be something of the kind that we nowadays call a sacrament, and that such a statement lay within the possible range of Christ's conceptions and declarations, then precisely the opposite of what was intended has been proved. For one is demonstrating that from what Jesus Christ said in so many words, provided the whole of what he actually said is taken at its full value, the sacramentality of holy order and matrimony can be recognized, and that for that very reason an explicit explanation by Jesus himself is not at all possible and therefore need not necessarily be postulated.

226

The second counter-question is even more important. What is the use of such an explicit statement of Christ about the sacramentality of order and matrimony to be? It only has point to postulate such a saying if it could make it historically likely that the Church recognized the sacramental nature of these transactions because of this saying of Christ. But this is just what cannot seriously be maintained, and must be flatly disputed. Historically speaking, it is quite a naïve way of imagining things, to suppose that these words of Jesus were handed down, orally perhaps, parallel to Scripture and without connection with it, later to become the *dicta probantia* of the explicit knowledge by the Church of the sacramentality of the two sacraments in question.

If we survey the first three or four centuries of theology in the Church, especially regarding marriage, we can quite definitely say that there is not the slightest historical reason to suppose that the Church explicitly knew more then, than is available to us today in all the sources to which we still have access. One may make, if one wishes, the supposition that the sources available to us now from a shorter period of time, the first century and the first half of the second century, for example, no longer inform us of everything that was then known, thought and taught in the Church. Even then one might ask whether it is possible for there to be missing from the sum of these indubitably fragmentary sources anything which the Church of that period taught as a binding truth of the faith; and one could give a negative answer for several reasons. But in any case, in view of the wealth of source material for the first four centuries as a whole, and considering the fact that without any calculation or planning much of the literature that did exist has survived, nothing being deliberately suppressed, we know we have a sample that can be taken as representative of the whole, and therefore it is historically quite unthinkable that any important matters of the kind that were taught as binding truths of faith received from the apostles (note the proviso), are missing for us from the literature of the first four centuries, but were once expressly contained in it. What is no longer available to us in explicit statements concerning binding truths of faith – obviously matters of importance – in this literature, was not present and available in such statements in the first four centuries either. If the attempt is made to find an explicit statement about the sacramentality of marriage in what is said explicitly about marriage in the first four centuries (the time limit is arbitrary, one could extend it much farther), it is a waste of time. A lot will be found about the meaning, divine origin and holiness of marriage, the need of grace for Christian married life, the symbolism of marriage in regard to the relation between Christ and the Church, and so on. But none of this is an explicit assertion of the sacramentality of marriage. Consequently there were no such assertions.

All attempts to give historical verisimilitude to the contrary view would amount, as in the case of the supposed words of Christ, to showing that in the actually surviving words of the Fathers, the present teaching about the sacramentality of marriage is implicitly contained, in other words all such attempts would in fact prove the opposite of what was intended. For these explanatory attempts all involve a supplementary general principle, and so the further question arises of what this principle is and how it is known to be valid. A reply to that question, however, leads to considerations which in fact point in the direction which we are following here; in other words it becomes clear that the general principles were already known all the time, and so there was no need and is no need today to argue from an explicit statement of Christ about the sacramentality of marriage.

If that is so, what would be the point of the explicit statement of Christ about the sacramentality of marriage? Historically it is not available. It has not been handed down. It had no influence on doctrine even in the early Church. Even if, contrary to all historical probability it is postulated, it contributes nothing to the purpose for which it is adduced, that is, to explain how and by what means the Church knows about the sacramentality of marriage. Even if Christ's saying existed, the Church must have recognized this sacramentality from another source.

What is said in the fifth chapter of Ephesians makes no essential difference to this state of affairs. The Council of Trent (Denzinger 969) says cautiously that Paul in that passage "suggests" (innuit) the sacramentality of marriage. But that means after all that it has to be deduced from the passage. It can only be inferred by introducing many other considerations and truths which are also contained in revelation as a whole. It can only be deduced with the help of a conceptual apparatus which had first to be formed in a slow process of historical development. If according to the Council Paul in this passage only "suggests", "hints at", it certainly does not mean that he explicitly knew more about this question and simply contented himself in this passage with a passing allusion, but in other contexts no longer available to us, said substantially more. Such an affirmation presupposes exactly the same historical improbabilities that we have noted in the similar hypothesis of a saying of Christ, once explicitly made but no longer preserved.

It will have to be left till later to discuss in greater detail how, if all this is presupposed, the sacramentality of marriage is nevertheless to be established, on the basis of the doctrine that the Church is the primal sacrament and that the character of being an *opus operatum* belongs to all her fundamental actions in regard to the individual in which she accomplishes her very nature as ultimate sacrament in situations that are decisive for the individual's spiritual life. This is best done in connection with the question of the ecclesiological aspect of marriage, that is, in the second part of this essay.

If the problem arises in the case of one sacrament, that it cannot be conceived as coming into existence through an actual formal statement of Christ instituting it, and yet must have been instituted by him, then the problem arises generally. There is no reason why the same possibility should not be reckoned with as with marriage (that is, that their institution by our Lord was of the kind we have already referred to but still have to make clear), in cases where such words of institution are perhaps less improbable, but have not really been shown to exist, and cannot positively be represented as historically probable.

That is true in the first place of holy order. Jesus established a ministry in the Church. But no word of his concerning its sacramental nature has been handed down to us. That he uttered such a word, nevertheless, is not to be deduced from the fact that in the Jerusalem community and then in Paul's churches this ministry was already transmitted by a rite of imposition of hands. That gesture was one used even before the Christian era, as a ritual for the handing on of office. It was quite a matter of course for it to be employed in handing on official Christian authority too. And it was just as much a matter of course if the transmission or conferring of office was looked upon as that and nothing else. But in our current text-books it is said that it is plain to be seen in the theology of the Pastoral Epistles that this rite of conferring the ministry is also declared to confer grace, and that this could not have been known without an explicit statement by Christ, for no one but God the giver of grace and Christ whom he sent, could link grace to a rite as its effect. Consequently it is certain that Christ instituted holy order as a sacrament by his word, that is, by an express statement to the apostles. Not all of this argument is sound. In the first place it is not at all so easy to show, if one argues only from the texts directly concerned, that the connection between the rite of conferring ministry, and grace, is meant to be as close and certain as the above argument supposes. Why should this connection not have been thought of as, to use the modern term, a "sacramental"?

In the piety of all ages there have been many rites thought to confer grace, yet without its being possible to declare that they were sacraments: imposition of hands, blessings and so on. If it is said that the more detailed correct interpretation could only be recognized unmistakably and with certainty through tradition, in other words through the later declarations of the Church's magisterium, but that this does not prevent the texts being understood as pointing in the same direction, the question must be put in return, what was the source of this supplementary knowledge displayed in later teaching and going beyond the minimum, inescapable sense of the texts? Unless one is going to answer this by alluding to the infallible assistance of the Holy Spirit (which simply amounts to declaring an answer impossible within the domain of theological argument, and so closing the debate on rather easy terms), a solution can only be looked for in the direction in which all our reflections on the establishment of some of the sacraments by Christ tend.

Secondly the preferred explanation presupposes the point to be proved, which isn't proved, and the contrary of which can be held without anxiety. It implies in fact that the linking with sanctifying grace of a ritual imposition of hands conferring office, can only be known by the apostles or the later Church, through an explicit statement of Christ concerning precisely this fact. But it is just this assumption which is unproved and incorrect, as can be seen from the possible manner of institution of a sacrament by Christ which we have suggested, namely by implicit institution of a sacrament in the explicit instituting of the Church as the historically visible form of eschatologically victorious grace. As with matrimony, we postpone to the second part of this essay the question how in these conditions the sacramentality of order, which as a "ministry" was explicitly established by Christ, can be proved, on the basis that the Church is the fundamental sacrament and that the *opus operatum* is the radical self-expression and actualization of this Church.

If one can reasonably ask in the case of marriage and also of holy order, whether it is historically probable that these two sacraments were instituted by an express statement of Christ, and incline to a negative answer because explicit words of institution of that kind are historically very unlikely in regard to the first and in the case of the second cannot be shown to have any positive likelihood, then the same question can also be put regarding confirmation and extreme unction. Not that it should be presupposed *a priori* that all the sacraments are in the same case. Indeed it is a defect in our usual theology of the sacraments that, because there are seven, they are all given the same stamp, whether it is a matter of proving their existence or of discussing their nature. And in fact with these two sacraments the situation is different when they are compared with one another or with the other sacraments. Yet on closer examination the question of how they were instituted points in the same direction as before.

As regards confirmation, its whole history indicates how closely it belongs with baptism, as a part of Christian initiation. Certainly we may not affirm, nor does history oblige us to, that confirmation is not a sacrament because it stands in particularly close connection with baptism or because in the Acts of the Apostles it looks as if confirmation had split off from baptism. (Though confirmation was administered in Samaria, one has not the impression that anything was lacking to "baptism" in Jerusalem. The Holy Spirit was received here by a man's cleansing from sins by baptism and incorporation in faith into the new people of God, in which the Holy Spirit was poured out, so that he filled everyone who was admitted.) But why should not we be able to say that the fact of incorporation into the people of the new covenant is forgiveness of sins and infusion of the Spirit? Why then could we not add that this one incorporation takes place, though it is one, through two rites, which in their duality represent and effect the two sides of the one process, death to the past and the old adam (forgiveness of sins), and new life (gift of the Spirit)? Why should each part of the one event not be called a sacrament? Why then not two sacraments be spoken of? Every theological theory speaks of a general grace common to the sacraments, without anyone thinking the plurality of the sacraments endangered thereby. The particular grace that characterizes and distinguishes each of them is reasonably understood to be, not

233

an extrinsic supplement to the general grace, but an intrinsic specialization of the one grace of the sacraments which can cause its manifold vital energies to operate in the most diverse directions. If that is correct, the sacraments are distinguished from one another not only by the outward rites but by their effects also, but this difference of effect is not a difference between things that are simply disparate. It is the difference which one and the same gift, grace, has and can have in the development of its own dynamic force. Even if it is given primarily with a certain orientation, at the same time it contains virtually the potentialities of the other dynamic forces of the one grace.

It will be noted we are speaking of sacramental grace, not of orders as such or marriage as such. So it is, for example, that the eucharist can *per accidens* give the grace of justification and extreme unction forgiveness of sins. It is therefore possible that by baptism itself (as distinct from confirmation), one is incorporated into the Church, and possesses the Spirit and yet that the giving of the Spirit in contradistinction to the forgiveness of sins is signified and effected through another rite. And the identity in the potentiality of the one grace (for all the difference in direction of its actualization) need not oppose the duality of the sacraments. That must be said quite independently of the question how explicitly or implicitly both sacraments were instituted by Christ. Everyone who knows how difficult it is, in Scripture, in tradition and in present-day dogmatic theology too, to distinguish between the sacramental grace of these two sacraments, also knows that it is really an impossible undertaking if one takes distinguishing them to imply that one of these two sacraments does not give implicitly and virtually simply what the other gives explicitly, actually and more abundantly. If one were to try to distinguish them, the gift of the Spirit in confirmation could only be understood as something very incidental, instead of being the messianic gift of possession of the Holy Spirit, as the sources after all require us to understand it. With that view of the effect of confirmation, however, one cannot, in accordance with Scripture in other contexts, refuse the same effect to baptism itself, all the more so as, if one did, one would be denying that baptism alone can be sufficient for salvation. One can be saved by baptism alone, yet no one can reach heaven who does not possess the Spirit. In any case, if the two sacraments do stand in the relation of two sacramental phases of a single process, intrinsically one yet having several aspects, and which can be articulated even in time in their visible sacramental form and their effects, without detriment to the unity of the process which washes away sins, gives the Spirit and incorporates into the community of the redeemed, then one can also say that the complete meaning of the one full initiation into the Church is represented with its two aspects in two different rites, which were distinguished by the Church of the apostles, and that both of them can be called sacraments, without its being necessary that Christ himself must have explicitly prescribed this division of the rite into two. Moreover, one will not on that account have denied that Christ instituted both sacraments in the one whole that the initiation forms.

It is not difficult to grasp how this ritual distribution of the initiation instituted by Christ (in instituting the Church and baptism), came about. "Baptism" at that time, especially with the baptism of John in men's minds, must have predominantly had the meaning of a remission of sins, a baptism of penance. One cannot, of course, assume the whole Pauline theology of death and resurrection with Christ to have been explicitly contained in their rite in the original community in Jerusalem, if only for the reason that Paul in his theology of baptism is thinking of the whole rite of initiation. From Acts 19 we can see that he very likely conferred confirmation at the same time and so in passages like Romans 6 he is including under "baptism" this part of the initiation too. Consequently when in the original Jerusalem community they wanted to say in so many words that baptism is not only received as a baptism of penance when one enters Christ's Church in accordance with his will, but that with the Church and with membership of the Church the fullness of the Spirit is given, this was best done by adding to the washing from sins an imposition of hands conferring the Spirit, in order to render explicit the positive side of the whole initiation. Perhaps in the earliest days this did not always need to be done everywhere. To this day theology says that confirmation is not absolutely necessary for salvation, implying therefore that what is given by confirmation is already in essentials conferred by baptism. It is not difficult to think it was at first only imperative to make the positive side of the initiation express and explicit in places where the outward manifestations of this gift of the Spirit (received, fundamentally speaking, in baptism itself) were not so immediately manifest as on the basis of the enthusiasm of the early Church one might have expected. It is unnecessary to overstress the fact that the apostles and not the evangelists administered confirmation in Samaria, for that is probably rather to be explained by circumstances of place and persons. Otherwise it would not be very easy to see why later on, confirmation was not kept as the exclusive privilege of the bishops.

236

In such an unfolding or articulation (division would not correctly describe the reality), the early Church could have been quite convinced that it was acting according to the mind of our Lord. She was, of course, aware from Christ himself that she possessed this grace with its two aspects; that this grace was linked to membership of the Church as the fundamental sacrament of that grace; that such membership according to Christ's will was to be imparted by a rite. There we have the institution of the rite of initiation by Christ, at least, to use the modern terminology, *institutio in genere* if not *institutio in specie mutabili*. And this rite of initiation does not cease to be instituted by Christ when it is separated into two phases. There is no argument that would prove that these two phases cannot rightly be termed sacraments. Provided one does not start with the unproven assumption that the "distance" between any two sacraments must always be equal. One can see it is not so; the Church, for example, recognizes (Denzinger 907) one sacrament as *consummativum* of the sacrament of penance, and that obviously could not be said of other sacraments in relation to the sacrament of penance.

From the fact of such a partition of the complete initiation rite, which is historically at least very probable, it can be quite correctly inferred theologically, as is done in regard to other cases of the sacramental activity of the Church, that what the Church in fact did, she could legitimately do. As regards method, it is not a question, in such instances, of first laying down a very dubious *a priori* principle in advance, namely, that the Church cannot do this and that and therefore has not done it, and of then concluding that this or that cannot have happened. A more appropriate method would be to observe as impartially as possible how in fact the early Church seems to have acted, and only then infer a theological knowledge of the extent of her possibilities. That is how the theology of the sacraments has come to see in other cases that these possibilities are much greater than had previously been thought, despite the immutability of the "substance" of the sacraments.

All this is all the more relevant, because even the defined dogma that there are seven sacraments must be interpreted with a certain caution. It will probably not be disputed nowadays, that the division of holy order into several sacramental grades of order was carried out by the Church herself and not by Christ, at least as regards the division between episcopate and priesthood, supposing one does regard the episcopate as a truly separate sacramental grade of holy order. But if there are several grades of truly sacramental nature, then it is a mere matter of judging what terminology is appropriate, as to whether in the numbering of the sacraments each grade counts by itself or all the grades form only one sacrament. For in the second case one would have to admit that in order, in sharp contradistinction to the other sacraments, one is counting a *genus* and not a *species infima*. From this, however, it follows that what is essential about the definition that there are seven sacraments, is not the number, but the affirmation that the ecclesiastical rites comprised by this number are in fact of sacramental efficacy, all these and only these. Whether one then arrives at this or that number in counting the rites so designated, is in itself a matter of indifference. If one were to say there are nine sacraments, because diaconate and episcopate are sacraments too, one would not have said anything false. And if someone asserted there are only six sacraments, because he included baptism and confirmation in the one concept of initiation, as grades of this sacrament, just as the

238

grades of order are counted as one sacrament, he would not necessarily have said anything false provided, of course, that he admitted that confirmation is a sacramental rite.

Someone might try to urge against this view that such a development of the rite of initiation certainly enriches it, perhaps more or less as the medieval rite of ordination with its *traditio instrumentorum* did, as compared with the simple imposition of hands in the early Church, but for all that "two" sacraments cannot be said to originate from it. There are two things to be said in reply. If in this development the "division" takes place so that the first "part" is regarded as sufficient for salvation and yet the second part still shares essentially in the sacramentality of the initiation as such, we have in fact two sacraments. It is not asserted that in every case the development of a rite *eo ipso* produces several sacraments, nor is it to be inferred that this is possible in no instance. Here the facts must be ascertained from experience, *a posteriori*.

This is all the more so because, as will soon be shown in more detail, it cannot be assumed as certain that what the early Church did, can always and in every case be done by the later Church, in other words that a decision of the early Church could never have absolute value and validity for all later ages, and have to be regarded as of divine law, *iuris divini*. We can therefore say that for Christ to have instituted the sacrament of confirmation, it is sufficient for him to have willed a visible form of initiation or admission to the Church, conferring on men what is essential for the Church, remission of sins and the plenitude of the Spirit. If the Church of the apostles once and for all unfolds this single initiation into two acts following one another in ritual and in time, then each act shares in the meaning and

THE CHURCH AND THE SACRAMENTS

effect of the one initiation and is a sacrament. Each of the sacraments arising in this manner can be declared to have been instituted by Christ in the one initiation.

The situation is different and more puzzling in regard to the anointing of the sick referred to in the fifth chapter of St. James' epistle. There is not the slightest historical difficulty about the origin of the procedure described and recommended there. The anointing of a sick person, accompanied by prayer, is not an unusual thing that requires a special cause or origin. It is just as little surprising that such an anointing should have taken place among Christians to the accompaniment of invocation of our Lord. That in such a case health of body and forgiveness of sins should be requested together is no problem either in view of the connection between sickness and guilt in the explicit theological views of the Judeo-Christian world of that time. Why should not James have been convinced that this prayer would be heard in one way or another when made in the name of Jesus, and why should he not have expressed this conviction? It is, therefore, impossible to say that the text manifestly describes something that would be unthinkable without an express formal prescription or authorization on the part of Christ. In view of the well-founded Christian confidence in the infallible certainty of an answer to prayer, one cannot say either that the connection of the whole ritual of prayer with the conferring of grace can only be justified if founded on an express declaration of Christ, in addition to the one he gave concerning genuine prayer in faith.[3] The ritual form of this

[3] Someone who says today, "If you call on the name of the Lord contritely and ask for forgiveness of your sins, you will unfailingly receive forgiveness and grace from God", or who says, "If you ask on someone else's

prayer in which words are linked to anointing, leads a modern Catholic theologian too quickly to see it as a sacrament.

First of all, therefore, we must observe that on purely historical grounds, we are not obliged here to assume actual words of institution by Christ in order to explain the text as it stands. Someone may reply that later exegesis and the Church's teaching about the sacramentality of extreme unction prove that the text must be interpreted sacramentally, even if this cannot strictly speaking be recognized simply from its literal tenor, and that the text at least presents no obvious obstacle to such an interpretation. Now this last is true, for one can certainly conceive of Jesus' healing the sick by anointing and an actual statement of his about such anointing consequently involves no historical impossibility or patent improbability, especially when one thinks of Mark 6:13, a text the importance of which for our present question must not be exaggerated, however, for in it it is chiefly the perhaps charismatic healing of bodily illness that is prominent and no mention is made of the forgiveness of sins or of a permanent, official, not free and charismatic institution. Yet it still would remain to be asked, as we did earlier in a similar instance, how the Church recognized this possible but not inescapable reading of the text to be in fact the only correct one, when no statement of our Lord was known to her to support this later interpretation of hers. An appeal to the infallibility of the Church as the formal guarantee that in this

behalf for the forgiveness of their sins, you will infallibly be heard, provided the other person has good will, which even with a sacrament is a condition of its efficacy", they have said something that is perfectly correct, although they have not instituted a sacrament nor referred in what they have said, to such an institution by Christ.

241

interpretation she has not erred, is not an answer to the question how the Church recognized its truth, on what pertinent considerations and on what intrinsic principles. The confusion of these two answers is at bottom always the outcome of a tacit belief, never, of course, conscious and explicit, that infallibility involves something like a new revelation. If one does not favour this conception, which is heretical as it stands, one cannot invoke the infallibility of the Church in this question any more than it would be legitimate to answer the question how a certain person knew that Charlemagne existed, by saying that the person in question was a very learned historian. It would also have to be asked whether, even if we assume a saying of our Lord with the same content as that of James, it could be plainly recognized that it concerned a sacrament. For even on this assumption, one might ask whether the promised infallible efficacy of prayer in faith made with anointing, asserted in the supposed words of Christ, was due to the instituting of a new sacrament by Jesus. And if we are to remain in the domain of historical probability, could we imagine a clearer pronouncement in the mouth of Jesus than the one we hear from James? However one turns and twists the matter, in every case one needs in addition to the text a more general principle which makes it clear that this prayer in faith with anointing is something more than any other confident prayer in a situation of great need, which can be certain of an answer.

It must be noticed that it is the presbyters of the Church who are to recite this prayer of faith; it is therefore in some way a solemn intervention of the Church as such, the organized community. And these presbyters are "brought in". Can one say that such a prayer of faith of the Church herself, as such, in this precise critical situation in regard to salvation is, *eo ipso*, a sacrament in view of the Christ-given character of the Church, because even without any further words of institution by Christ, it cannot be anything else? If it is possible to say this and to provide sufficient grounds for the assertion from the nature of the Church and the situation that is in question, it is unnecessary to have recourse to a special pronouncement by Christ instituting this sacrament, which from the historical point of view is at the least very uncertain, yet it is possible to say with truth that our Lord instituted this sacrament because he instituted all the factors which in this case necessarily come together to form a sacrament.[4]

We must simply ask, therefore, whether there is the slightest possibility of an official prayer for God's saving help remaining unheard by God, when it is uttered by the official Church, in a situation affecting the eternal welfare of a Christian, that is, a

---

[4] When it is said (Denzinger 908, 926) that Christ instituted extreme unction *(instituere)*, James promulgated it *(promulgare)*, the word "promulgated" cannot simply mean the action of the apostles or evangelists reporting the special act of institution by Christ. For such a promulgation could and would have to be expressed concerning each sacrament. Clearly the Council intends here to bring out a special feature which is not found, for example, in the case of baptism. Even something of that kind points in the direction of the idea we are trying to work out here. We might notice, too, that even though the Council of Trent avoids the expression "direct", "immediate", institution, nevertheless the teaching of the Council concerning the institution of all the sacraments by Christ is interpreted by theologians in the sense that this institution was "immediate", that is, that Christ gave no one authority to institute sacraments according to their own judgment, in such a way that Christ would then have only been indirectly or mediately the cause of the sacraments. It is to be noted that the theory we are developing here does not contradict this direct and immediate institution of the sacraments, but affirms it.

person who has been made one by God in baptism and in whose regard, as a consequence, God's actual salvific will cannot be doubted; and in view of the power promised in general to prayer, previous to any question of the human being's own attitude? If this question has to be answered with a plain No (as is indeed the case, as will be shown in rather more detail in a moment), then we have a sacrament: words and rite, infallibly linked to the gift of grace. It might be thought, at first sight, that if what has been said is correct, it would follow that any prayer of the Church for a supernatural benefit would have to be a sacrament, which is obviously false. But this is not so, and

When we say that by the very fact of instituting the Church (directly of course), Christ instituted the sacraments, any intermediary able to decide the institution or non-institution of the sacraments is already excluded by that very fact. The institution of the sacraments by Christ is, therefore, an immediate one. At most it could be objected that the concrete rite as such, in which the Church performs this action in which her nature as the primal and fundamental sacrament of grace is accomplished and actualized, is not determined by Christ himself, yet this belongs to immediate institution by Christ himself. To this it may be replied that the theory does not exclude but includes Christ's having himself determined in some cases (baptism and eucharist, for example), the concrete rite too in which such a grace-giving fulfilment of the Church's nature takes place. But that does not mean he must have done so in all cases. If in some instances as the particular case requires, this is disputed or left an open question (confirmation, order, extreme unction; the case of matrimony is different again because it is not a question of a sign fixed by authority but of a natural sign), it is not the immediate institution of all the sacraments that is disputed. It is the *institutio in genere* that is being affirmed or conceded as the case may be. This latter doctrine, of course, is expounded without objection by Lugo, Arriaga, the Salmanticenses, Gonet, Billuart, the Wirceburgenses, Hurter, Billot, Van Noort, and others. See Patres S. J. Facultatum Theologicarum in Hispania Professores, *Sacrae Theologiae Summa IV* Madrid ²1953, 110f.

reflection why it is not so shows why conversely it is correct to say that this prayer of the Church in this situation for this purpose, is a sacrament.

In the first place, from the nature of the case, a sacrament is only in question when the Church's act directly concerns an individual as such, in relation to his individual salvation. That is clear. There is an *opus operatum* which is not a sacrament in this strict sense because it does not possess this characteristic: Mass as the sacrifice of the community. The act of the Church must therefore concern the individual as such in his actual supernatural situation and also concern an actual conferring of grace. This is in contrast, for example, to an indulgence, which according to many is an *opus operatum* but not a sacrament because it is forgiveness of punishment for sin and not a grant of remission of sins, grace properly so called. Furthermore the question has to be taken into account: When is the Church as such indubitably acting? When is it certain that those characteristics which belong to the Church as the eschatological presence of the triumphant grace of God are actualized absolutely and unambiguously, that is to say, when is this nature of the Church fully engaged and committed?

Negatively it can at once be said that that is not in question in every instance of an official act done by a priest at the behest of the Church or, in particular, in the case of a prayer. When a priest celebrates the liturgy for the parish in general there is no question from the start of a sacrament, in view of what has been said. And even when a prayer of the kind we have defined is spoken by the priest as such for an individual, it is not always a sacrament. Not every such prayer can be held to engage the Church as the eschatologically victorious grace in Christ. Such

a prayer in very many cases, of course, will not really be request-
ing saving grace, and consequently there will be no unmistakable concern with God's gift of such grace on the lips of the
Church in the prayer. Mostly benefits are prayed for which are
of service in a person's salvation indirectly; so it is in blessings
for an individual for example. But even if we suppose a priest
on some order of the Church, of whatever kind, asking for
grace for an individual, forgiveness of sin, for example, such an
act is still not necessarily that absolute commitment in which
the Church either quite unmistakably (in her eyes and God's)
must manifest herself and therefore actualize her essence, or else
not be the enduring sacramental presence of the unquestionable
salvific will of God in Christ which has become public and
irrevocable, in other words, *opus operatum.*

The Church cannot be assumed to be teaching in a way that
absolutely commits her magisterium everywhere she teaches,
even though she is teaching at the behest of Christ, but only
when it is a special and radical case of her actualization as the
presence of Christ's truth. For the same reasons, which cannot
be further developed here, the same holds good of her actual
realization of her nature as the presence of the grace of Christ
for the individual. If such a lesser degree of actuality is possible
at all, it will certainly be so when it is a question of the individual
as such. For in this instance, from the very nature of the case,
the Church as Church, that is, as society of the faithful and
those who have been sanctified by grace (despite her mission to
all individuals), is essentially less immediately engaged than when
she addresses the multitude as such. For example, there is never
any question of a decision of an ecclesiastical authority in an
individual case as such being infallible. The reason is clear, for the

Church can only act with ultimate certainty and engage her full responsibility when it is a question of herself as such in her totality. Her infallibility is not, of course, limited to doctrine. It extends to the most varied sectors of her life, where it is not always referred to as infallibility, but amounts to the same characteristic of excluding contradiction and any absolute divergence between idea and reality, what should be done and what in fact is done. Now if her infallibility were to extend always as a matter of course to the individual case as such, the individual would inevitably, in the concrete detail of his life, leave the zone of uncertainty about his salvation and the ambiguity that belongs to the condition of a pilgrim. If we suppose him to have good will and be a member of the Church, he would share in the prerogatives of the Church herself. That, of course, is quite excluded. For the individual would pass into the divine sphere, he would really be in pure possession of grace like the Lord himself, not a recipient of redemptive grace in fear and trembling, in doubt and temptation, in the pure hope that what remains hidden is truly present.

So where the Church is dealing with the individual as such, it is to be presumed usually that she is acting without absolute certainty, or what amounts to the same thing, without absolute involvement, even when she is acting "officially". When she prays for the individual, comforts the individual, rouses his hope of salvation and so on, it is not *ipso facto* certain that here there is an instance of God's unconditional word to men. Such actions involve a certain ambiguity — is it the Church in her nature as such who is speaking, or is it men as representatives of the Church? Conversely, such an absolute involvement of the Church in her action regarding the individual as such is not thereby excluded. We already know, of course, that there are such actions. When in baptism the Church receives a human being into her realm, when she reconciles him anew to herself and to God, when she celebrates the eucharist as the highest actual fulfilment of her own being, and permits the individual to share in it[5], such actions are not merely actions of the Church, but really bring into actuality and functioning the very nature of the Church herself, her own self is involved totally and radically. Such activities share in the nature of the Church herself as the fundamental sacrament.

Can there then be a prayer of the Church which is infallibly heard, in which it is certain on the one hand that it truly answers to the nature of prayer, with the infallibility promised it by Christ, and on the other hand concerns directly an individual and his salvation as such, that is, grace for him? Is there a prayer of the Church that avoids the limiting condition that cannot usually be excluded from prayer, despite the genuine certainty of being answered which has been promised to it, the doubt, that is, whether the prayer really is in God's eyes what a prayer should be? Only the prayer of the Church as such can be of such a kind. And since not every prayer of the official Church is certainly of that kind, the prayer must occur, if there is any such prayer, in a situation that is of an essentially special kind. This can only be the situation of the person prayed for, for only in

[5] If the eucharist were not in the first place and essentially an act that accomplished the nature of the Church itself, but a mere action of the Church in an individual's regard, in the everyday course of his life, the reception of the eucharist, not being in such conditions a participation in the Church as such and as a whole, would not have objective certainty of effect, could not be an *opus operatum*.

this way can there be a critical situation sharply marked off from all others. Such a situation is the distress of approaching death. We do not say of the agony of death, for to view the matter for once dogmatically and purely *a posteriori,* this sacrament can be received without its being certain that the recipient is dying. But it is a matter of the distress of approaching death, though, of grave illness as the moral theologians say, words that nowadays leave the situation referred to rather vague, with its urgency, and unique quality focusing a life in its totality. James' "sickness" must indubitably be seen through the eyes of a human being of that time, with all that such a situation implied, the loneliness of helplessness, confrontation with the whole of a life now seen to be coming to its end, quite independently of the empirical question of whether it would in fact cease in the immediate future, physically speaking.

The whole person is in question, brought face to face with himself, with no more possibility of turning his mind from himself, fleeing into his job and the details of everyday life. It does not matter whether the individual human being is actually fully aware of this situation. It is there and demands to be accepted. Only someone falsely persuaded that a free person, at any moment whatsoever, can adopt any attitude he pleases quite independently of the real objective situation, not a capriciously invented one, can suppose that the personal possibilities opened out by the situation of approaching death can be coped with at will, by spontaneous asceticism, for example. The fact is that this situation is a unique one that cannot be arbitrarily constructed and in it, objectively speaking, a human being faces and is summoned to an ultimate decision, with the whole of his life in question.

Such a situation is as little susceptible as any other, concerning eternal salvation or loss as it does, of being a purely "private" concern of the Christian. If the Christian in an extremely critical situation concerning salvation and perdition, could in principle retire into a purely private individualistic domain (unless exceptionally and as a mere matter of fact), such "salvation" could have nothing to do with the Church. But if the Church as the primal sacrament of grace for the life and salvation of the individual as such, belongs to the supernatural life of the individual, this must be so above all in such a situation as this. Consequently in it the Church must be called to an action which corresponds to the unique crisis that is in question. If her own fundamentally sacramental nature can ever be involved in the circumstances of individual salvation, in certain cases if not always everywhere or arbitrarily, it must be possible here. It must be possible for her prayer to be offered here as a manifestation of the unconditional promise of salvation for the whole life of a man such as is at stake in this situation, and as a prayer that is certainly heard, because it is truly and indubitably a prayer of the Church. It must unconditionally engage the responsibility of the Church, it must radically bring into action the Church in as much as she is the fundamental sacrament of grace for the individual, as such, in critical situations, for the purpose of conferring grace on him. Therefore it is an *opus operatum* with grace as its effect. In other words it is a sacrament.

It does not, of course, follow from what has been said that one could infer all seven sacraments from the nature of the Church, by a strict deductive proof. Not does it follow that what has been said is false because such a plain and peremptory proof is simply not possible. As individual theologians we, of course, only learn from the acts proper to the Church's own life (called sacraments), and which are derived *a posteriori* from revelation, what the concrete nature of the Church is as Christ willed her to be. Complex epistemological factors are at work here which mutually condition each other, but there is no vicious circle. In the first place it must be remembered that there may be genuine abstract deductive knowledge of the nature of something, even where it is not possible without reference to the *a posteriori* experience of the individual instances actively existent and operative. For example many characteristics which Christian philosophy rightly counts as belonging to the changeless and necessary essence of man (and uses in propositions concerning the natural law), and which therefore have to be conceived as flowing of necessity from the fundamental idea of human nature, in fact would not be so deduced or recognized, if what is so deduced were not already known beforehand from actual experience. One might attempt to show, difficult as it would be, that it is necessary and essential to man, as a spiritual being endowed with a body and having a temporal life-history, who must meet other human beings in the dialogue of authentic personal relationships, to exist in two sexes, whether he wishes or not; so that his sexuality is not merely a characteristic that happens to belong to him, one that he no doubt cannot in fact abolish, but in principle a merely incidental one. It makes no difference that in fact no one presumably would undertake such an abstract deduction of sexuality as a property belonging to the essence of man, who did not already know about human sexuality as an actual fact. So too with regard to our question. We are acquainted with the sacraments; we know, because we have already experienced what they are in actual fact from their administration, that they

251

are *de facto* acts fundamentally expressive of the Church's life, even if at first it is not clear why they are so and why other actions of the Church are not. But then in these conditions we can quite definitely recognize from the nature of the Church why they must be acts fundamentally expressive of the very essence of the Church and as a consequence possess certain characteristics such as that of the *opus operatum*.

But all this holds good of the Church herself. She experiences her own nature by fulfilling it, and, of course, what Christ express-ly said about the Church belongs to that "experience", as its foundation and root. By experiencing it she perceives the differ-ent levels of her activities by the extent to which she is impli-cated in them. And so she can recognize that certain acts flowing from her nature are fundamentally and unconditionally the accomplishment of that nature and so are what we call sacra-ments. The Church could not know this, and certainly the indi-vidual theologian could not, if this nature or essence were only given in an abstract idea and not in its real fulfilment in activity; the Church could not abstractly deduce the sacraments, and especially their sevenfold number, from that idea alone. But possessing and recognizing her essence in its concrete fulfilment, she can understand that such and such definite activities which she has already carried out spontaneously in accordance with what she is – always a condition of self-analysis – are essential to her own nature, without really having to be informed of this again explicitly. It makes little sense to object that after all it would be possible to think of and construct other such acts, and so deduce more than seven sacraments. In the first place that is not at all easy to do convincingly, even theoretically as an ex-periment. Consequently one might calmly wait for the as yet untried attempt to be made, and if it were, one could then show in all probability that these imagined additional acts in which the essence of the Church found expression cannot really be unmistakably proved to be of equal rank with the seven sacraments that do exist.

Furthermore it would have to be pointed out that such acts, perhaps abstractly possible in themselves, are not in fact performed by her, so that there are in fact no more sacraments. A radical self-commitment without awareness of it, is, of course, impossible, and the Church by her affirmation that there are seven sacraments and no more, declares such an awareness to be not present even in an implicit form, and expressly excludes it. Then too it would have to be said that if such supplementary acts realizing and bringing into activity the very essence of the Church are not forthcoming, even after the Church has already attained the full actual accomplishment of her nature, the reason for this can only be that such additional fundamental activities are not possible, for otherwise they would already have been performed and manifested. This can be asserted even more readily as a matter of course, if one assumes, as one may, that in certain circumstances there could be an irreversible historical decision of the Church which by the nature of the case is to be regarded as *iuris divini,* even if before the decision was taken it was not absolutely inevitably necessary for it to be taken. Once made, however, it is irrevocable, because it derives from the divinely ordained essence of the Church. If one considers that conceivable in principle, one is still left with the possibility of maintaining the sevenfold number of the sacraments as *iuris divini,* without thereby prejudging the question whether it would not have been possible, when the Church was still at the stage of formation, for her one fundamentally sacramental essence to have unfolded in an even larger number of such basic acts expressive of her nature.

It has already been indicated that such a fact must almost inescapably be reckoned with, in at least one instance, that of holy order. It is open to any Catholic theologian to regard diaconate, priesthood and episcopate as the articulation or distribution of her one power of order derived from Christ. This is all the more so because all the great theologians of the Middle Ages conceived the lower grades of order as sacramental, and it is even now permissible to consider that they were then true sacraments, even if one wants to maintain that they are so no longer. This opinion is indeed more probable, for reasons which cannot be gone into here, but which follow from the principles we have enunciated. If one counts all the sacraments according to their *species infima* and not according to the wider *genus,* one can even today count nine sacraments, on account of the three parts of order. And one can say that this number is not and was not an absolutely necessary one. This could be said by someone who wants to hold in an intelligible manner that the Church today can no longer abolish these three grades of order because they were formed in that early Church which must be looked on in a strict theological sense as the Church still in process of being constituted in existence. Then that historical decision must almost inevitably be regarded as irreversible in the way mentioned above. It was freely made, it would appear, as we can see from the way the apostles introduced the diaconate, nevertheless cannot be abolished, as must be held by anyone for whom these three grades of order are *iuris divini* and unalterable.

In this section we have been concerned with the question whether the problem of the historical difficulty of proving the

254

institution by Christ of certain sacraments could not be given a better and easier solution if approached from the standpoint of the Church as the primal sacrament, with certain fundamental and essential acts in which her nature finds actualization, as the sacraments. The reflections showed first of all why such a question needs to be propounded anew in more acute form; historically explicit words of institution are not only not historically available, but are demonstrably improbable on historical grounds. These reflections were fully worked out on the positive side as regards extreme unction, but partly postponed to later sections of the inquiry in the cases of matrimony and order. In regard to confirmation the matter was brought, it seems to us, to a positive conclusion.

In fact traditional theology has already taught from other angles and with other concepts, the basic principle which we took as starting-point. It affirmed that in the New Testament in contrast to the old covenant, there are no signs of grace prescribed by Christ himself (we would say which Christ established with the Church, as the essential acts proper to her, whereby her nature is accomplished) which are not also true sacraments. This traditional theology then demonstrated, for example, the sacramentality of marriage precisely from this general axiom. So, for example, we find in Pesch (*Praelectiones dogmaticae* VI Prop. IX): *Omne signum quod in nova lege ex praecepto Dei hominibus applicandum est ad significandum gratiae est etiam efficax ad producendam gratiam.* For Pesch, therefore, the rites effected by the Church, which manifest God's saving action in regard to men, are necessarily efficacious causes of this grace, that is, *opus operatum,* when they are instituted as such by God and not merely determined by the Church's good pleasure. From this thesis it is not far to the theory we have been expounding here. It is only necessary to assume in addition that the indispensable prescription by God and Christ of this manifestation of grace in symbolic forms took place by being implied by the founding of the Church. Such a supposition cannot, however, have involved any insuperable difficulty for Pesch either, because he used the axiom we have quoted, and which is proved from the difference between the old covenant and the new, to show the sacramentality of marriage, without requiring a demonstration that the institution of the sign by Christ took place by an explicit declaration.[6]

f. Sacramental and personal piety

If we view the sacraments as acts in which the Church accomplishes her nature as the sign of the eschatological presence of God's grace in Christ, we can also understand more easily how in the process of sanctification of the individual, sacramental event and personal event penetrate and mutually presuppose each other, without coinciding completely. For we find the same relation in doctrine about the Church in general, between visible membership of the Church on the one hand, and on the other, the interior bond of grace linking the individual with the Spirit of the Church through personal faith and love. It would, therefore, only be necessary to show in the treatise on the Church in general what the relation is between the Church as a visible society and the Church as an interior community of faith and grace, for all the essentials to have been said about the relation, difference, and

[6] See Ch. Pesch, *Praelectiones dogmaticae* VII Prop. LIII n. 702 ed. V (Freiburg 1920).

mutual connection between sacraments as rites of the visible historical society and the personal acceptance in faith of interior grace through, under and by this ritual act, in other words, between sacramental and personal piety. We must, however, refer the reader to our earlier treatment of this question.[7]

We shall note later what follows from the principle developed here in regard to the sacramental character.

[7] See K. Rahner, *Schriften zur Theologie* II (Einsiedeln [3]1958), pp. 115–141; E.T. *Theological Investigations* II (London 1964).

II

THE VARIOUS SACRAMENTS AS ACTS
IN WHICH THE CHURCH'S NATURE IS FULFILLED

THE ECCLESIOLOGICAL ASPECT OF THE SACRAMENTS AS EVENTS
IN THE INDIVIDUAL'S SANCTIFICATION

1. General Considerations

WE HAVE already said that the Church is not a mere institute for
eternal welfare, administering powers that God happened to
entrust to her, but which he might just as well have given to
another to administer. Since the Church herself is the sign of the
presence of the grace of God in the world, because Christ continues his presence in history through her, the Church is not an
offer of God to the world of such a kind that it remains in doubt
whether it will be accepted or not; it is rather the sign of present
and victorious grace. Acceptance itself, however, can only take
place in the individual, for victorious grace is only present where
the subjective holiness of an individual is achieved through it.
(The infusion of grace at the baptism of an infant without such
acceptance in faith and works, can be left out of account here.
In the first place the Church cannot primarily consist of infants;
the purely objective nature of their Christianity prevents their
being typical Christians. Furthermore such a grace given solely

through the sacrament without the intervention of personal decision as a supernatural habitus of the theological virtues is entirely intended for personal use by the recipient, and only in that way attains the full perfection of its nature, because grace is ultimately a sharing in the actual plenitude of God's life and all merely habitual grace is only rightly to be understood as the ontological presupposition of that life.) Consequently the Church as historical sign of victorious grace only attains the highest actualization of her own nature when grace is victorious in this sense in the individual and also is tangibly expressed and really occurs for the individual's sanctification. That is exactly what happens in the sacraments.[1] This is what has now to be considered in each of the sacraments, and all along it is a matter of seeing that the sacraments, precisely as events in the spiritual life and sanctification of the individual, have an ecclesiological aspect. For it goes without saying that this aspect belongs to the sacraments as official acts of the Church who dispenses the mysteries of God.

Before we go on to consider the sacraments from this angle, another general observation might be made. It is profitable to reflect on the question why Jesus, according to the testimony of the gospels, instituted and spoke about the various sacraments

[1] It is true that from that point of view, a closer examination would show that the Church as Church which attains the highest degree of actuality in administering the sacraments, and the Church which is truly holy in her members and is manifestly holy, is necessarily one and the same Church. These two factors condition one another in her, although it cannot be absolutely certain that they coincide, if the Church is also to be the Church of those who are still pilgrims in hope, and who must work out their salvation in view of a judgment of God which has not yet been made known.

in such an apparently unsystematic and haphazard way. There is no mention in his life of several of them: confirmation, extreme unction, matrimony, order (as a sacrament). The others are referred to almost incidentally, without method and system. Penance is mentioned first (Matt. 16 and 18), unless we are to assume that baptism is first spoken about, on account of the baptism of John and because of John, chapter three. It is even possible to say that Jesus was not concerned at all about systematic arrangement, that he did not envisage under so abstract a concept as sacrament the tangible salvific acts of his love in the individual's regard in their concrete reality. But if once again we envisage the Church as the fundamental sacrament, we shall perhaps achieve an even better understanding of this striking fact. When the Church is considered in her hierarchical order as the community of redemption in Christ, in contrast to the people of the covenant of the old testament, attention will turn less to the question by what rite one enters it, than to the fact that by reason of its hierarchical constitution full membership is always subject to the control of those who in this sense can bind and loose.[2] And with that we have already got what nowadays we call the sacrament of penance. When this new community of those who believe in Jesus Christ separates itself more and more from the world which thrust out the Lord of that community,

---

[2] This is all the more so because when the entry of an individual into Christ's sacred community was in question, thoughts must have been much more occupied with belief in Christ, acceptance of the *basileia* (kingdom, rule) of God that was being manifested in him, through the *metanoia* (conversion) of the whole man, than with the particular rite of such admission to membership. There is no reason for objecting that the same must apply to penance of the individual within the community, that is

and consequently his followers, into death, we see the moment when this community grasps her own innermost nature, in the ritual celebration of that death which is her true life. That is the eucharist. It is obvious that this highest accomplishment and fulfilment by the community of its own nature, in its essence and totality, must be celebrated by the authoritative act of those whom Christ has appointed as leaders of this sacred community. It is then scarcely necessary to state that the transmission of this authority, constitutive as it is of the Church, is a sacrament, the sacrament of holy order. For it is willed by Christ, and it is a fundamental act of the Church herself who maintains her own historical existence by such an historically manifest and tangible action. When Christ gave the apostles his authority and knew and stated himself to be the redeemer of all and as the end and purpose of history, as the judge who is to come, he had already

---

to say, that in this case too attention must involuntarily have turned first of all to the personal, "subjective" change of heart and not to the sacramental rite. The objection is not pertinent, for the situation is quite different from that of a man's first conversion. One who belongs to Jesus' sacred community, who has been admitted into Christ's kingdom of God, which is at hand, must live in holiness. If he sins, therefore, he offends against the whole status which he accepted in his new existence, and against the Church. Consequently in such a case his attention must inevitably at once turn to the contradiction between his sin and Jesus' community. What then must at once be described is not the "rite" of a renewed forgiveness of sins (as such) dispensed by the Church but the correct manner in which the holy community reacts to the sin of its member. This reaction, when it is "loosing" not "binding" is in fact a sacrament, but is not looked upon as baptism is, as a symbolical rite, but as a judicial act of passing judgment (as a *krisis:* 1 Cor. 5:3–12; 2 Cor. 2:6f.). As of course dogmatic theology rightly says down to the present day, with the Council of Trent, the "form" of the sacramental sign in penance consists in a judicial act of the Church. It is something that is quite different in nature from symbolic

affirmed his Church to be final and irrevocable, and in a milieu familiar with the conferring and the handing on of office by the ritual imposition of hands, he had already said all that there was to be said about ritual transmission of ministry. That such a rite was also a sacrament will have to be shown later.

Then almost incidentally it can be stated how the rite is to take place which will first admit someone outside into that community, which until then had concentrated more on its own inner life. That would give us baptism. Only when the Church at Pentecost experiences herself to be the Church of the Spirit, endowed with the charismata, will she explicitly advert to the fact that the full rite of admission must comprise ablution of guilt and the imposition of hands for the reception of the Spirit: confirmation will be seen explicitly as a fundamental act proper to the Church which necessarily expresses her own nature in the constitution of a full citizen. That is to say, confirmation is

ritual gesture. Such small observations show what an impediment it can be to a knowledge of the precise nature of the various sacraments if their actual place in real life is passed over and they are envisaged more or less abstractly in terms of the general schema or type of a "sacrament as such". In that way many insights that are important for the pastoral administration of the sacraments become harder to attain than they need be. Perhaps, too, dialogue with Protestant theologians about controverted points of theology in regard to the number of the sacraments might be carried on with better chance of agreement if the number seven were not put at the beginning, as is commonly done in our dogmatic treatises, but was considered as a relatively subordinate consequence, which is only arrived at the end, after a calm consideration in the light of Scripture of all the individual events and activities there are in the Church, as Scripture testifies, and the nature of which can be grasped before they are subsumed under the generic concept of sacrament, the number seven being reached at that point.

a sacrament.[3] Later still the gaze of faith will be able to see that marriage, because of its character, indicated in Scripture, as type or symbol of God's love in Christ for men; of the love that brings about the new and eternal testament, must be in the Church, for the Church and for mankind, a sign of the grace of God which cannot be thought of as absent from Christian living. It is a sign that therefore belongs to the basic manifestations of Christian life, and because it is such a fundamental sign of grace in the Church, cannot be an empty sign but in the way proper to it, is a sacrament too.

It is not very difficult to understand, if we open ourselves to the Church's sense of her faith, that the Church must be at a pitch of highest actuality in her own nature when she assures an individual human being that he belongs to her not to the world, when in his mortal distress he is threatened with the loss of this world in good or ill. And with that we have the sacramentality of the prayer in faith with anointing, which we call extreme unction, without our necessarily having to postulate an explicit statement by Jesus to his apostles.

But the same *proviso* must be made in regard to these discussions which we have already expressly made earlier. Deductions of this kind are made with the concrete nature of the Church in view before our eyes. They are attempts to imitate and recapture insights in the Church's awareness of her own faith which she attained in the course of a long history guided by the Spirit, not

---

[3] These considerations are not intended to suggest that Jesus made no explicit statements about the sacraments. Our point is that we need not depend upon them as much as positivist theologians sometimes seem to think. They tend to be embarrassed when such statements cannot be discovered and, in their dilemma, postulate these somewhat too confidently.

263

absolutely self-supporting, independent, mathematical proofs. This brings us to the actual theme of this second part of our inquiry, the ecclesiological aspect of the various sacraments, not so much as official actions of the Church administering them, but as events in the individual spiritual life and sanctification of their recipient.

2. The Eucharist

We begin not with baptism, as the usual treatises on the sacraments do, but with the eucharist. It cannot simply be put on a level with the other sacraments and listed along with them. The Council of Trent points that out (Denzinger 846, 876). It follows from the real presence of the Body of Christ; from the fact that here there is not only a sacrament but also the sacrifice of the new covenant; from the teaching that sees the eucharist as the source of the other sacraments.[4] Indubitably the celebration of the eucharist is an absolutely central event in the Church. Even nowadays it needs repeatedly to be stressed that mass should not be viewed by the faithful (the danger is far from remote), as merely the production of Christ's real presence in the sacrament for the purpose of communion regarded in an extremely individualistic way. Such an idea is unacceptable, though not because the point of view of a personal, individual meeting with the "bridegroom of the soul" is false or to be disparaged, and it is not right that it should be attacked by those who want to manage without a personal spiritual life. The individualistic

[4] See M. de la Taille, *Mysterium fidei* (Paris 1931).

narrowness must not be tolerated because it mutilates the faith, if not in theory, at least in practice. For faith tells us that the mass is so much the sacrifice of the Church, that even a priest's most private mass is always the Church's sacrifice, and as far as possibility allows, must appear as such (Denzinger 944, 945). Communion is a deeper incorporation into the mystical Body of Christ, because the redeemer has left his real Body to his Church, through which he wished to have all Christians joined together (Denzinger 873a, 875).

We can and must say that participation in the physical Body of Christ by the reception of this sacrament imparts the grace of Christ to us in so far as this partaking of one bread (1 Cor. 10:14–8) is an efficacious sign of the renewed, deeper, and personally ratified participation and incorporation in that Body of Christ in which one can share in his Holy Spirit, that is to say, the Church. In other words *res et sacramentum*, first effect and intermediary cause of the other effects in this sacrament is the more profound incorporation into the unity of the Body of Christ. In support of this we might recall the passage from St. Paul quoted above, the first eucharistic prayers in the *Didache,* the eucharistic teaching of St. Augustine, who always makes this aspect so prominent that he could be suspected of an over-spiritual volatilization of the doctrine of the real presence. Indications are found in St. Thomas, who regards the eucharist as the sacrament of the Church's unity (III q. 82 a. 2 ad 2). If someone prefers to call the Body of Christ itself present under the species and becoming a sacramental sign for us through them, the *res et sacramentum* and the unity of symbol formed by species and words as *sacramentum tantum,* with all the supernatural effects in grace thought of as the *res,* which is certainly the usual

265

view (Denzinger 415), he will at least have to say that the Body of Christ is a sign of his grace, by its being in possession of the Church as a sign of her own unity, pledge of eternal life and as sacrificial offering to God. He would also have to arrange among themselves in intelligible order the various effects of the eucharist, which he comprises under the concept of *res sacramenti*. Then however, once again, union with the mystical Body of Christ whose life is the Spirit, by analogy with the other sacraments especially baptism from which the idea of *sacramentum* and *res* originally came, would still be the effect of the sacrament that is prior to all others. So it is that Innocent III in the passage just quoted only brings out *unitas* and *caritas* as the effect of the sacrament. He is still thinking quite entirely in terms of the Church (Denzinger 415).

It must further be borne in mind that the words of consecration even when physically they are past, always belong to the sacramental sign as present. Now this form of words speaks of the new and eternal covenant that was concluded in the Blood of Christ. Christ is present in the sacrament under these words. (It is not a question here whether they always require to be recited explicitly or not for consecration to be valid.) He is therefore present as bond of unity, as the foundation of the covenant between God and men, as the Church's unity therefore. Because he really gives himself in ever new sacramental manifestation as sacrifice for the Church (Eph. 5:25 f.) and as sacrifice of the Church, because he exists in the Church in visible and tangible sacramental form, there *is* the Church. She is most manifest and in the most intensive form, she attains the highest actuality of her own nature, when she celebrates the eucharist. For here everything that goes to form the Church is found

266

fully and manifestly present: her separation from the world (even today this demands and justifies a sort of discipline of the secret, *disciplina arcani*[5]); her hierarchical structure (priest and people); her attitude of dutiful receptivity to God, which forbids her to be an end in herself (sacrifice); her recitation of the efficacious words which render present what they proclaim (the *anamnesis*, the words of commemoration, are the primal constitutive words of the Church[6]); her unity (the one bread of which all eat in the sacred meal which unites all who take part in it); her expectation of the final kingdom, the glory of which is ritually anticipated in this celebration; her penitential spirit in offering the sacrifice which was offered for the sin of the world: Denzinger 875, 940: *donum paenitentiae concedens;* the invincibility of the grace of God, which was definitively given her, that she might be holy, for she has him who is the final victory and she already celebrates in advance the ultimate victory of God's kingdom, by proclaiming the death of the Lord, who is the victory, in the consciousness that she will do that until he comes again (1 Cor. II:26); her profound readiness to serve others (the sacrifice to God *pro totius mundi salute*).

In connection with this it would be possible to indicate much else that can only be alluded to rather as inquiry than as statement. It has already been briefly remarked upon that the eucharist is really the starting-point of all kerygmatic, apostolic preaching in the Church. The *anamnesis,* the words of commemoration are the very central words of the Church because in the most

[5] See *Sendung und Gnade*. E. T. *Mission and Grace* (London 1963).
[6] See K. Rahner, *Schriften zur Theologie* III (Einsiedeln ³1959), IV (Einsiedeln 1960).

real and intensive way they make present for our salvation what they signify. For that reason all other words in the Church are ultimately only preparation, exposition and defence of these words alone, in which the incarnate Word of God comes into our space and time as our salvation. Furthermore we should have to consider in what way the Church in general, the whole Church, is given with and in the single congregation or parish, by whose celebration she is rendered present as a totality in her highest degree of actuality. For it will not represent the state of affairs to which we are referring with any precision if we view the single congregation simply as a segment of the Church, comparable to an administrative district in a State, nor if the Church as a whole is hypostatized and regarded purely juridically as the subject of the celebration of mass in the individual parish.[7] On the basis of the preceding considerations regarding the historical presence of redemptive grace, it seems possible to gain some insight that where the eschatologically triumphant grace of God is present in historically tangible form, however this happens or whoever the human subject involved may be, the Church as the consecrated and socially organized people of God is manifested, and so the total Church is present. From this one could perhaps approach the Pauline conception of the Church as a whole and as individual congregation in their mutual relationship, just as in time of Christ individual groups and fraternities thought of their relation to the whole people of the covenant, from which they were distinct and of which they nevertheless felt they were representative as mediators of its promises.

[7] On this see: *The Episcopate and the Primacy,* pp. 20–30; also K. Rahner, *Zur Theologie der Pfarre,* in Hugo Rahner, *Die Pfarre* (Freiburg 1956), pp. 27–39.

In all these reflections it must never be overlooked that holy communion has this reference to the Church, even as an event in the individual's sanctification. It is the Church that gives the individual the Body of Christ, which she has in her possession as the pledge of her redemption and the presence of grace in her, and she makes the individual share, for his sanctification, in the unity, love and plenitude of the Spirit of this holy community of God's covenant, and so she fills him with all grace. Only a person who is prepared in principle to entrust himself to the whole activity of the Church that takes place in the eucharist, through which she is more consecrated to God, given over more profoundly to the death of Christ, becomes more closely one, approaches more and more the consummation of all things in the coming of the Lord, will share even in the blessings and graces of this sacrament for the individual. For ultimately these are nothing but that deeper and deeper union with the Church, her action and her lot.

3. Baptism

Little need be said about baptism, not because its ecclesiological aspect would be hard to discover, but because it is everywhere expressly stated and obvious. As is well known, baptism according to the formal teaching of the Church (Denzinger 324, 570a, 696, 864, 1413, 1936a; Cod. Iur. Can. c. 87) is at least the sacrament of incorporation into the Church. But we can go further. This incorporation, as adherence in faith to the sacred community of the Lord, in which the *protestatio fidei* is from the first not the enunciation of an individual and private view of the world, but the proclamation of acceptance of the Church's

belief, adherence to a belief already there and manifestly exercised in the Church, is not only one effect in fact of baptism, but
is itself a sacrament, a sign of the other effects of the grace of
baptism. To be incorporated into the Church is, therefore
sacramentum et res in this sacrament of Christian initiation. That
full membership of the Church as the Body of Christ vivified by
the Spirit, provided no obstacle is put in the way of the influence
of the Spirit of the Church, can bring with it all the other effects
of baptism, so that this membership can therefore be regarded as
sacramentum et res, needs no lengthy proof after what we have
said about the nature of the Church. It should also be remembered
that in the old testament and in the new, the subject of redemption to which God's mercy is addressed is in the first place
always the people, the nations, the Church as the partner in the
covenant (which the individual as such cannot be), and the
individual only shares in grace as a member of such a people of
the promise.

Now it has become customary to consider the sacramental
"character" as the first effect of baptism and as the mediating
cause of the other effects and so as *sacramentum et res* in regard to
them. What we have said should not and need not be understood as in contradiction to this common teaching. By character,
something concrete must be signified. One must ask what this
signum spirituale et indelibile (Denzinger 852), which is impressed
on the soul really means and in actual fact is. If one avoids
arbitrary mystification about this sign, and bears in mind the
origin of the doctrine of baptismal character in Augustine[8], it

---

[8] It is derived with him entirely from the knowledge that baptism cannot
be repeated and from no other theological sources, so that it is possible to
say what follows from that about the character. It is always for Augustine

will be quite possible to say that the import of the character is the Church of Christ's express and enduring claim to the baptized person, produced by a sacramental and historical event. It is, then, unimportant for our purpose whether the character is said to be identical with this condition of being claimed by the Church or that this being in duty bound to the Church is founded on an ontological state of the soul given at baptism. For if one goes on to ask in what this ontological state of the soul consists, what its meaning and function is, and if one does not arbitrarily, without examination and without reference back to the original sources, fill the formal breadth and vacuity of such a concept (ontological state, physical quality, etc.), with some conceptual scheme of one's own choosing, one cannot but come across this claim of the Church on an individual which has been expressed visibly and tangibly in time and place and therefore is a permanent one. If one does not, it is only by very artificial elaborate explanations that one can show how the character is a "sign". For if one wants to answer that question without such devices, one must point to an element that is "perceptible"[9], for without it there is no sign, and one that is lasting, even though deriving from an action, for otherwise there would be no *signum indelibile*. What could one point to except what we have described? As a fact having social duration, it is not visible like a house, for example, but it has a really historical

---

a sign of belonging to Christ's flock and militia, even when, by reason of the baptism of heretics and schismatics, the sheep may have fled and the soldier deserted.

[9] It is, to put it mildly, absurd, to say that this sign is a sign for God and the angels, simply so as to be able to maintain that it is still a sign even when it is a completely invisible reality.

and social perceptibility, just as the possession of an office which, constituted by a visible transmission, itself is concretely tangible and manifest. The teaching of St. Thomas on baptismal character does not necessarily contradict this view. It is sufficient to ask why through the baptismal character a human being shares in the priesthood of Christ and how this participation can be distinguished from the one that derives from grace. The answer must surely be that it belongs to a man in as much as he is a member of the Church and remains in relation to the Church; because the Church as the visible Church in the world of space and time (not only in the depth of the conscience sanctified by grace) continues the priestly function of Christ the high-priest.

In order not to misunderstand what has been said, it must always be remembered that even where a baptized person is no longer, as the encyclical *Mystici corporis* has it, in the full sense a member of the Church because he is a heretic or a schismatic, he always remains in relation to the Church through the enduring fact of having been baptized; and this does not belong in the same way to an unbaptized person, even if he is justified.

4. Confirmation

It is not difficult to perceive an ecclesiological aspect in confirmation either. If we reflect on what the Acts of the Apostles says about confirmation, it is clear that the Spirit conferred by the imposition of hands in this sacrament is always regarded as a Spirit that manifests itself externally in the charismata. Because the Spirit was not recognized at baptism alone, it was said at that time that the Holy Spirit had not yet been received. The Spirit that had not been received was the Spirit whose mighty sway and influence had not yet been experienced. That too had to be given. It did not necessarily have to take place in a way we today probably would think of as "charismatic", externally remarkable, and miraculous. For we see in the first epistle to the Corinthians that Paul on occasion counts quite unexciting gifts and talents among the charismata which the Spirit of God gives to individual Christians and members of the Church for the good of the whole Church.

What is in question here is as follows. The grace of God has a double direction or movement. It is the grace of dying with Christ, a grace of the cross, of the downfall of the world, of being taken out of the aeon of the law, death, sin and also of all aims and purposes that belong to this world alone. All that is expressed in baptism as a descent into death with Christ; it takes place by being represented in sign. But at the same time the grace of Christ is the grace of incarnation, a grace of acceptance of the world for its transfiguration, a grace the victory of which will be visible in the world, in its healing, preservation, redemption from the nothingness to which it is subject, and such a grace is also one of mission to the world, work in the world, world-transformation. The particular function of the grace that is given more particularly to the individual as his special task, is decided by God's vocation and by the distribution of the charismata of the Spirit, which are nothing but the special directions in which one and the same Spirit unfolds its action. All receive it and with it all can and are to serve, even those who apparently have received the opposite grace. And because the second direction or tendency of the one grace of Christ, incarnate, crucified, and risen, is just as essential as the first, which is

273

that of death with Christ, it must be expressed in a sacramental rite of its own, although in a certain sense it is only a question in this sacrament of the same grace as in baptism becoming visibly apparent and manifest in history. This grace only "appears" under another aspect, and, of course, thereby, as through all sacramental manifestation, becomes deeper and increases. This second sacrament is confirmation, imposition of hands to receive the charismatic Spirit of a world-transforming mission in the accomplishment of the task proper to the Church as such, for she as holy Church, in the plenitude of her vitality and transfiguring power, is to be God's witness in the world that he does not abandon the whole mundane creation to its sinful nothingness, but redeems, preserves and transfigures it.

When we call confirmation the sacrament of strength in the faith and in professing the faith before the world, this must not be taken to mean only that the Christian receives in confirmation the grace of the Holy Spirit to keep his faith, to save it, but with great trouble, in a world hostile to it. The comprehensive sense is intended which we have indicated. It is in this light that the apostolate must be viewed, on which the Christian who is made an adult by confirmation, is sent. It is not so much ultimately an apostolate of defence and self-affirmation of the Church, as a mission to the task which the Church has been given, not to assert herself anxiously and save herself, but in order that the world should be saved through her. The task imposed on the Christian by confirmation is therefore the obligation of an apostolic mission into the world itself, as a part of the function and task of the Church to transform it and bring it into the kingdom of God which is at hand. It is not so much the grace of individual care for the salvation of one's own soul as the charismatic gift, that is, one rich in blessing for others, of collaborating in the mission of the Church, using all the gifts which may be of service to the salvation of all.

5. Penance

That the sacrament of penance[10] has an ecclesiological aspect requires no lengthy explanation. If with the whole of tradition down to the thirteenth century and in accordance with correct exegesis of the relevant texts, we give the words of Matthew chapters sixteen and eighteen about "binding and loosing" their full value, we have a reference to what we nowadays call the sacrament of penance. These passages concern the way Christ's holy community is to deal with a sinful member. If such a member of that sacred society which by her life is to announce the victory of grace and the coming of the kingdom of God sins contumaciously, grievously, this cannot be a matter of indifference to Christ's Church, for otherwise, of course, she would belie her nature. She must react against such a sin, through which the member of the community not only puts himself in contradiction to God but also to the Church of Christ, for the Church in her members and by their holiness must be the primal sacramental sign of the victorious grace of God. For that reason the Church "binds" this sinner, that is, she draws away from him "on earth" by some form of exclusion, not to be confused with excommunication as it is at present, but similar, for example, to the present-day exclusion from holy communion

[10] See K. Rahner, Bußsakrament, in *LThK* II² 826–838.

with the obligation of confession. The consequence is that the sinner is no longer regarded by God as belonging to that holy community and for that reason cannot share in the grace which is acknowledged by God in men to the degree in which they are members of the Church of Christ. If on the contrary the Church raises the ban "on earth and in heaven", she "looses" him on earth, through a renewed and full recognition of his reconciliation with the Church; to the extent, we may say, that this has a sacramentally symbolic value, the sinner is "loosed" in heaven too. God effectively regards him in the full sense as a member of that community which the Son has gathered on earth for heaven, as those who are his, the beloved of his Father, those who will possess the kingdom. And in that and by that God forgives him his sins.

From this it is at once clear that sin itself has an ecclesiological aspect. Reconciliation through the Church is also reconciliation with the Church. The *pax cum ecclesia* is *sacramentum et res* of reconciliation with God.

The ecclesiological aspect of the sacrament of penance becomes deeper and more extensive if we recall the Thomistic doctrine that the acts of the contrite penitent confessing to the Church are part of the sacramental sign itself. For that means that the contrite sinner and the Church together make up the sign in which in the public, social, historical domain of the Church (which is not necessarily *in foro externo*), both the act of the human being as a baptized member of the Church, and the reconciling act of God in the human being's regard, all attain visible and manifest expression. What happens here in the sacrament of penance is an actualization of the Church's own essence. She is manifested in the penitent himself (who co-operates in her liturgy), as the penitent Church of sinners ever bathing the feet of Christ with her tears and hearing his words, "Neither will I condemn thee". It is the Church's very nature in act, in as much as she, holy Church, withdraws in judgment from sin, (hearing the confession, judicial verdict, imposition of a penance), and so lifts again the darkness cast by her rejection of sin, the sin of one of her members. It is a vital expression of the Church's essence, as bearer of God's grace-giving words, which she addresses here to the individual and so effectually fulfils her own nature as the abiding sacrament of God's mercy in the world.

Thus in this sacrament again and again the Church's action manifests that the Church herself in the unity of her judicial holiness and of her ever renewed mercy to the sinner, is the indestructible sign of the grace of God that is irrevocably given in the world as long as this aeon lasts. Because there is this irrevocable grace of God, holding sin within its mercy during this epoch of the world, and because this grace has its historical presence in the Church, there is within the Church in regard to members of the Church herself a sacrament of the unconquerable readiness of God to forgive, the sacrament of penance. In the common action of the priest as the authorized spokesman of the Church, and of the penitent human being, the fundamental nature of the Church herself is manifested.

6. Holy Order

Before we can go on to examine the ecclesiological aspect of the sacrament of holy order considered as an event that sanctifies an individual, there remains a task to be completed which was left unfinished earlier. We indicated that with this sacrament, as with some others, words of institution uttered by Christ are not in all historical probability to be reckoned on, words that in this particular case would not only explicitly express the authority to transmit office and ministry but would also expressly affirm the sacramental nature of this transmission. We have not yet, however, explained how the sacramentality of this transmission of ministry in the Church follows from the principle that the Church is the primal and fundamental sacrament.

We can start with that basic axiom. When in respect to an individual, in situations decisive for his salvation, the Church accomplishes one of the actions proper to her, engaging her responsibility fully, and actualizing her essence as the primal sacrament of grace, there we have a sacrament. Consequently the existence of the sacrament has its ground in the existence of the Church as primal sacrament, and when no express words of institution have been handed down to us, the establishment of the Church by Christ can be regarded as the institution of such an action and therefore of a sacrament. The recognition by the Church of her own nature as she fulfils it in this way, can be the gnoseological ground for her recognition of the sacramentality of a sacrament. And as the Church is never without this means of recognizing a particular sacrament, and her reflection on her own intrinsic nature lasts through history, there is no need to postulate that the explicit recognition of the sacramentality of such an actuation of her essence (which we call a sacrament), must always have been present or else, without a new revelation, be lacking in any legitimate source or origin.

The question we have to propound and answer in greater detail is a double one. Why is the handing on of spiritual power in the Church a fundamental action for her, radically involving her own very nature? And why is the end and purpose of this act not the office and ministry itself, but also, and necessarily, a special grace of state which sanctifies the bearer of the office? These two questions are to be distinguished. Not every fundamental action of the Church is, as such, a sacrament. An infallible definition is such an action in which the Church's very nature, but in another direction, is involved, yet it is not a sacrament. Conversely an act of the Church, for example, a prayer in the ordinary course of the liturgy or in a sacramental, can have as its purpose a grace and yet not be a sacrament in the strict sense. We have the same thing when a Christian says something convincing to another in his personal circumstances which awakens his faith and trust in forgiveness; it is quite possible to regard this in a true sense not as the words of a "private individual" but as the words of the Church too; for, of course, they can be spoken by a baptized and confirmed Christian, or by a teacher authorized by the Church, or by parents in a sacramental marriage, valid in the eyes of the Church and symbolizing the Church. The two questions must not, accordingly, be confused, although we shall see in any case that both can be answered from a proper understanding of the Church.

A positive answer to the first is not far to seek. The really fundamental offices in the Church are the most indispensable constituents of the Church herself. She only exists by possessing and transmitting the functions given her by Christ, and the powers bound up with and serving them. By the transmission of office, especially when this gives power to exercise the fundamental functions of the Church, to bear witness to Christ's message, to celebrate the eucharist, and, we must add, conversely, to hand

279

on these powers which are constitutive of the Church, the Church in one important respect keeps on re-constituting herself anew. So that is quite definitely an indispensable fundamental function of the Church, provided the Church is not thought to spring into existence afresh perpetually in an ever actual charismatic beginning but is recognized to have both an historically visible and tangible form and likewise an historically manifest temporal continuity. And this is in fact the case. For historical form and temporal continuity are not to be separated in a reality that has existence in time. And the idea of succession is directly present and discernible in the New Testament and in the world of that time.

Why, however, is this fundamental act of the Church handing on her ministry and by so doing constituting herself anew, an act which also has as its purpose, the sanctification of the man who receives the ministry, and so merits the name of sacrament? Here too the answer is to be sought in the nature of the Church. This shows that it is not a matter of indifference to the meaning and nature of ministry in the Church whether it is exercised and administered with holiness or not. To be sure the ministry keeps its validity and its bearer his authority and power, even if as an individual he is a sinner and exercises his office itself in a sinful way. This teaching in condemnation of that of the Donatists and Wycliff is well known. Viewed in the present context it is not surprising either. For the validity of a sacrament in the individual case is not identical with its fruitful reception. In the sacraments there can truly be a proffer of grace by God, actually promised by God on his part to men, and suspended over them in this period of the history of redemption as promise and summons, without by that very fact effecting their sanctification, by being applied and accepted and ratified by human freedom. Of course, this latter is again a grace of God, so that in the ultimate resort the institutional grace of the sacraments is not a matter of administration. The teaching concerning the baptism conferred by heretics is a classic example, especially as the "heretic" in the third century was always presumed to be culpably heterodox whether as dispenser or recipient of the sacrament.

The ultimate theological ground of this difference between validity and fruitfulness is on the one hand the circumstance that, in adults, grace as in fact effecting sanctification can only occur in a way that includes human freedom, while on the other hand this freedom itself must remain inaccessible to ultimate evaluation, before the coming of the judgment of God which alone will make all things known. The individual cannot promise himself from a sacrament the indefectible holiness of the Church as unambiguously his own; he must remain a pilgrim in fear and trembling leaving all to the judgment of God. This is precisely the reason why an actual official action of an individual minister cannot depend on his holiness, for otherwise the Church as represented in the acts of her minister would not be the invincible manifestation of redemptive grace, if such an act could be invalidated by the individual's guilt; or else the minister would know, as if by a sacrament that could not be without fruit, that he as an individual was justified by grace when he validly carried out an act of his office, and then he at least thanks to his office would have escaped from the condition of a pilgrim, not yet "justified" (1 Cor. 4:4).

But this distinction between possession of official authority and the holiness of ministry does not sufficiently describe the relation between office and grace. The fact is that the same relation holds here as in the question whether individual human beings who remain members of the Church can remain and be sinners, without detriment to the holiness of the Church. An affirmative answer must be given straightaway. But that does not mean that the personal holiness of her members is a matter of no importance to the Church's essence. The Church herself only exists by existing in her members. The holiness of "holy Church", which necessarily follows from the eschatological victory of grace, can therefore only consist in a personal holiness of her members. If all were sinners who had fallen away from the grace of God, holy Church herself would no longer exist. Despite the possibility, therefore, that individual human beings in the Church are sinners, and despite the fact that for that reason it remains uncertain in general until the death of the individual in which members of the Church of any age her holiness is realized, which members are in fact the bearers of the indefectible holiness of the Church, nevertheless God's will to bestow efficacious grace (the very will which gave the Church her being) rules over her, infallibly sanctifies her members, even if we do not know in detail which ones, and preserves them in grace, so that the Church never ceases to be holy. That same will must be operative too in regard to the Church's ministry if she is to be indefectibly holy and remain the presence and manifestation of the eschatologically victorious grace of Christ. A ministry impious throughout its exercise and a holy Church are incompatibles. If it were supposed that the ministry in its totality could accomplish its task without holiness, neither the holiness of the Church's members would essentially depend on the exercise of the ministry, which however it does, nor would the ministry remain what nevertheless it is, a ministry of sanctification for men.

At first sight it might, of course, occur to someone to ask why the members of the Church should not receive from her ministers what the ministry can and is there to give them, and receive this *ex opere operato,* that is to say, independently of the holiness of the ministers dispensing the sacraments, and yet at the same time these ministers fail in their own lives to carry out in faith and love, what they do in their official capacity. The Church as a whole would still be a holy Church, even if she (or rather the one Church in so far as she was holy) consisted only of the "poor in spirit", the laity humbly receiving from the hierarchy. Let us leave out of account the fact that such a supposition imagines something impossible in real practice. For how could it be really possible for absolutely all bearers of office to reject the holiness which *ex supposito* is present in the Church, and which necessarily finds expression, is manifest, and consequently has a social and human and personal character and produces effects by inviting and convincing and bearing witness. Even apart from that, such a separation of office and holiness and its distribution between two subjects, is impossible. The ministry certainly has a power which is exercised *ex opere operato.* But if this *opus operatum* is in fact to be exercised in the Church (and it must be if the Church is to be and remain sanctified by the sacraments), God must not only ensure that if sacraments are administered, they are what they should be, but he must absolutely ensure that they are administered. God must will absolutely that in the Church (which is to be indefectible), the administration of the sacraments should take place. This, however, is inescapably and necessarily dependent on the subjective dispositions of men who administer them. In other words, the Church's rite must not only carry God's promise of inalienable validity if it is performed, because it is an

283

expression of the Church's inalienable validity as primal sacrament of grace, but God's formal and constitutive will must provide that the sacraments are actually administered, if the Church is to be what she is and if this essence of hers is to be actually realized. For not only the essence but also the existence of the Church are unconditionally willed by God. Consequently, if the sacraments belong to the Church's essence, the sacraments' actual existence in practice must be unconditionally willed by God.

But this existence of the sacraments does essentially depend on the holiness of those who dispense them. Of course, the individual minister can in fact carry out a sacramental rite in this or that instance without holiness, for alien motives, without its losing its essence or ceasing to exist. But that is impossible if applied to the whole of the Church's sacramental activity. It is not the efficacy of a sacrament actually administered that depends on its minister's being in a state of grace, but the perpetuation of sacraments in the Church as a whole and in the long run. If all the ministers were unbelieving and void of divine love and consequently if the gentle power were to disappear from the whole Church by which believing love induces even the faithless and the loveless in the Church to deeds which essentially really spring from faith and love (the administration of the sacraments is of that kind), could the administration of the sacraments itself survive in the long run? What reason would a body of ministers of that kind have still to remain true to their office? Is it thinkable that a reality should remain when its hold on existence has disappeared not only in this or that human being, but universally, as such? That would amount to explaining one and the same effect as capable of deriving from two disparate causes, which is impossible. So if God absolutely wills the existence of the sacraments in the whole Church, he must also absolutely will the holiness of the hierarchy as a whole, otherwise he would not will, what the actual factual existence of the administration of the sacraments depends on.

For the sake of closer consideration, it must be repeated that the typical instance of administration of the sacraments is not the baptism of infants, but the baptism of adults and the eucharist with an adult congregation. If anything of the kind is to take place, it can only be (looking at the totality of cases) when faith and receptiveness are found in the recipients. Otherwise there will be no one there to whom baptism can be administered or with whom the eucharist can be celebrated. The words of these sacraments can therefore only ever really be spoken in the context of the preaching of the faith. Those who have the power and authority to address God's sacramental words to men, have also the right and obligation to produce that context of affirmation of faith, in which alone these sacramental words *ex opere operato* encounter that disposition which is a situation within which the sacramental words can be uttered at all and heard with faith, and within which they have the power to produce their effect.[11] Now even though, once again, an individual instance of preaching of the faith is not dependent for its truth and claim on the faith of the hearers, simply on the faith and holiness of the individual who is preaching, nevertheless from the nature of the case, and according to the testimony of Scripture, testifying to the faith is in general essentially connected with the preacher's genuine

---

[11] From this it can be seen too that an absolute separation between power of order and power of jurisdiction, between *potestas ordinis* and *iurisdictionis,* is impossible in the Church.

witness in his own life, in other words, with his holiness. It has to be based on the "shewing of the Spirit and power" (1 Cor. 2:4) and a "spirit of power, of love and of sobriety" (2 Tim. 1:6–7). This proof of the inseparable connection between mission and authority to preach and personal and sanctifying charisma according to the testimony of Scripture, cannot be expounded in detail here.[12] Yet so that it is clear that this principle involves no element of Donatism, it should be noticed that every preacher of the faith bears witness, not to his own "private opinion", but to the belief of the Church. What he says, therefore, does not refer back to the fact that he, as a private person, is actually giving this testimony, but to the testimony of the Church as a whole. The Church, however, according to defined doctrine, is necessarily and indefectibly holy and as such is a motive of faith (Denzinger 1794). So what we have added to this teaching of the First Vatican Council in what we have been saying (which seems to us simply to expound what the Vatican Council taught), is only to say that it is not a merely factual relationship between the holiness of the Church and the motivation of faith, but an intrinsic and necessary one. The word of faith that calls for practical acceptance in faith and love, can only rightly be preached by the exercise of this faith and love, nor is it preached in any other way, for this is not possible in preaching that is done in the name of holy Church. Only in that way is such preaching really "witness", which is and must always be more than the communication of mere thought content. Consequently those who are entrusted with the power of the sacramental word are by the nature of the case (because this word can only be spoken in the context of the

---

[12] See K. Rahner, *Schriften zur Theologie* III (Einsiedeln ³1959) 306f.

words of faith as a whole), in principle also entrusted with giving
testimony to the faith. But it is only really possible to bear witness to the faith by being a Christian oneself, that is, by one's
own "holiness". For although the individual preacher by his
preaching points to the holiness of the Church as a motive of
faith and not merely or in the first place or expressly to his own,
nevertheless this holiness of the Church is only present and
existent in the holiness of individuals, the multitude in fact who
actually form the Church which is holy. Such a necessary reference is consequently the affirmation that preaching is only
testimony that calls for belief, when it is supported by the
shewing of the Spirit; it implies, therefore, even when the individual preacher withdraws himself from the sanctifying power
of the Spirit, the admission that the truth of Christ (which demands faith), must be proclaimed in holiness, even on the part
of that individual preacher himself. For he cannot refuse as a
demand on himself, what he needs to find actually realized in
others, if his own preaching is to be possible, in others who are
Christians and human beings just as he is. (It could be noted in
addition here that someone who is publicly an unbeliever is
thereby absolutely incapable of preaching in the name of the
Church. Here again the final inseparability of office and life
makes itself evident.)

Now this holiness, necessary and present in the whole and
required of the individual, as testimony to the truth of the faith
that is preached, is only possible through grace. The conferring
by God of the office of administering the sacraments (which is
only possible in the context of bearing witness to the faith), must
therefore also necessarily imply the gift of grace, without which
the carrying out of the functions of the office would be impossi-

ble. Otherwise God would be requiring something to be done, and at the same time making it impossible, by refusing the necessary means. Gift of ministry is therefore necessarily a proffer of grace to exercise the office. As, however, this conferring of ministry is, in fact, always a fundamental act of the indefectible Church and therefore is and remains a valid and true transmission of office, and can never be emptied of its significance and become outward show of such a transmission of power, the gift of grace on God's side in the rite of handing on of ministry is absolutely promised, it is *opus operatum,* a sacrament.

That in itself makes clear the ecclesiological aspect of the individual sanctification that occurs in the reception of holy order. The recipient of order receives his office as a grace, for he receives the grace which enables him to exercise his ministry as one that sanctifies him, and the grace to achieve the holiness that is essential to the really adequate fulfilment of his functions. Priestly holiness is not a question of a requirement that the priest should be a "pious man" in addition to carrying out the duties of his ministry, because after all, that is suitable and proper. The connection between office and priestly holiness is much closer and gives the latter itself an intrinsically ecclesiological aspect. The holiness of a priest is the living assimilation of his office, made possible by grace, and this assimilation in its turn, is a necessary factor in this office as a whole, in as much as this office includes the ministry of the word, as the setting and the exposition of the sacramental words.

For the working out on this basis of the idea of a priestly life and its essentially ecclesiological aspect, we must refer to our earlier treatment.[13]

[13] K. Rahner, *Schriften zur Theologie* III (Einsiedeln ³1959) 285–312.

7. Matrimony

Here too as with the discussion of holy order, a postponed question has to be answered: Why marriage is a sacrament, and how this can be shewn from the sources or from the more comprehensive principles of theology. St. Paul says explicitly (Eph. 5) that marriage is and should be in a certain way an image and an echo of the love between Christ and the Church. The double aspect of a reality which is both fact and exigence is found in all profoundly human things and need not arouse remark here. Yet to understand the statement is more difficult than is usually thought. Of course, with a little ingenuity anything can be compared with anything else. If conjugal unity and love only served in some such vague sense as a simile for the loving union between Christ and the Church, if the two realities were only being related metaphorically, the whole matter would be a very incidental one. That cannot be the intention.[14] Marriage and the covenant between God and humanity in Christ can not only be compared by us, they stand objectively in such a relation that matrimony objectively represents this love of God in Christ for the Church; the relation and the attitude of Christ to the Church is the model for the relation and attitude that belongs to marriage, and is mirrored by imitation in marriage, so that the latter is something contained or involved in the former. But why this is so, is not very easy to say. Of course, one can appeal to Paul's testimony, and this testimony of an apostle is indubitably fundamental. One can say that it is thereby

[14] The reader is referred to the more detailed interpretations of the text by biblical scholars, e. g. H. Schlier, *Der Brief an die Epheser* (Düsseldorf 1957) 252—280.

evidenced that God from the beginning in the garden of Eden created marriage to be such an image of the relation between Christ and the Church. But unless this symbolism is to be explained in a purely juridical and nominalist way, through the will of God viewed as quite extrinsic to the reality itself, and transcendent to it, and unless we are to rest content with the apostle's testimony as a mere matter of fact, without aiming at any understanding of the faith, we must certainly say that this will of God is operative in the reality itself, in marriage, and gives it a definite intrinsic characteristic which fits it for the function of symbol.

But then we must also say in what this characteristic consists. Only the answer to this question will furnish the reason why Paul knew what he tells us. Various factors might perhaps be suggested in explanation, though much more inquiry is called for, which cannot be undertaken here, for it would involve a consideration of practically the whole of revelation, as will be clear from the pointers which are all that are possible. A starting-point might be, that the different kinds of human love which give rise to genuinely human and personal relationship, are not only extrinsically comparable, but have a real interconnection as condition and foundation of one another. They are more than merely species of a merely logical genus, and conjugal love has a quite special place among them. Then, that being understood, one might indicate that Christ established the Church as the one "people of God", by entering the unity of "monogenetic" humanity (which is one through conjugal love) as a member of it. He loves men with a genuine love, and this, by accomplishing the sacrifice of the Cross, is of significance for the formation of the Church, while its power to establish a community rests on factors that concern the structure of the human condition generally and consequently stand in real relation to matrimony. The attempt might then be made to show that marriage has a real capacity to represent or typify God's love in Christ for the "one" humanity which he hallows by that love, and which we call the Church. This representative value is not a merely conceptual one formed in our minds, nor is it merely extrinsic, decreed by God.

Then one might delve deeper and show the very idea of man has its original, ultimate ground and basis in the idea of the God-man, and try to make it intelligible that the very possibility of man rests on the possibility (not the fact) of the God-man; that man is by origin what emerges not as a possibility, but as the possibility, when God as it were comes forth from himself into what is other than himself.[15] It would then have to be added that man, human being, means: "Male and female he created them." One would further have to add that Christ, by being envisaged from the beginning as the son born of woman, is willed formally and not merely *de facto* as a human being in a humanity of two sexes. One would have to say as well that the will to humanity (incarnation) itself necessarily, formally and implicitly involved the willing of the Church. If all these things (to which it is only possible to direct attention here), were thought out, it might perhaps be possible to grasp why authentic matrimony at all times has a truly representative value for God's unitive love in Christ for mankind.

If that were grasped, two further steps would have to be taken. It would have to be shown that this rôle of representation of Christians in the Church has to be carried out as a function

---

[15] See K. Rahner, *Schriften zur Theologie* IV (Einsiedeln 1960).

291

of the Church, because the Church in her members and through everything of which such members are capable, must show herself visibly and manifestly to be the beloved bride of Christ. That is, it would have to be shown that this representative function has to be exercised not only by Christians in as much as they are human beings, but in a higher degree through their being Christians and members of the Church. That would show that this typifying rôle, once Church and Christians exist, belongs within the Church as such. Then finally the second and last step could be taken. In fact it has been, by what has been said. Such symbolism of a fundamental kind, established in the very essence of the Church, is truly a fundamental act in which the Church fulfils her very nature, and consequently, in the Church, is a sign which produces what it signifies, and therefore, since it signifies grace, a sacrament. From that it would follow that it is the contracting of marriage which constitutes the sacrament of matrimony, and the reason for this would emerge. It is because this conjugal consent is itself one of the acts in which the Church's own nature is brought into activity, because in this consent of her members, she herself manifests herself as the mystery of the union between Christ and mankind.

This is also another of the cases in which, as in baptism by a layman in case of necessity (which in the light of the sacramental nature of baptism has nothing unusual or abnormal about it), not a cleric, but this or that Christian accomplishes an act of the Church herself, by "administering" the sacrament. Another example of that kind is seen in the sacrament of penance, where the acts of the penitent himself belong to the sacramental sign.[16]

[16] It is impossible here to investigate how it is possible for an unbaptized person validly to baptize and so accomplish an act of the Church.

With all these considerations in mind, the ecclesiological aspect of the sacrament of matrimony would then be clearly envisaged. For it would have emerged from these proofs of the sacramentality of marriage, that it is not only possible to compare marriage to the union between Christ and the Church, but that marriage itself contributes to it and indeed in a quite special way; and that the visible Church even in its historical reality appears as the bride of Christ, through her existence and characteristics bearing witness that in the Church, Christ has espoused humanity irrevocably to himself. In other words, it would have to be shown that marriage has a definite function in the Church, belongs to her full constitution and the full accomplishment of her nature, so that this is the objective reason for the sacramentality of marriage, the sacramentality of marriage being for us, once its existence is established, the means whereby this function in the Church can be recognized.

Finally, in this connection the following would need to be considered. We have already said how remarkable the relation between individual parish (local community) and the whole Church is. The local community is not only a member, a province of the whole Church. The whole Church is not only the sum of the parishes. Rather in the local church and its active accomplishment and self-realization, the whole Church in a true sense is manifested as a totality. What happens in the individual parish, especially in the celebration of the eucharist, renders unmistakably and really present, in its ground (the redemptive death of the Lord), the existence of the whole Church as the grace-giving presence of God. It testifies unambiguously to it and guarantees her nature and reality in the world. In view of this, and seeing that matrimony is an image of the alliance between Christ and the Church, we can say in a true sense of marriage that in it the Church is present; to the extent to which marriage realizes its own nature, as a valid marriage, sanctified by grace and lived in holiness. It is the smallest community but, for all that, a genuine community of the redeemed and sanctified, whose unity can build on the same foundation as that on which the Church is founded, the smallest of local churches, but a true one, the Church in miniature.

8. *The Anointing of the Sick*

The ecclesiological aspect of extreme unction, last anointing, cannot be indicated so readily. It is not easy here to get beyond the analogy of faith that suggests that if all the other sacraments have such an aspect, extreme unction cannot be lacking in this universal fundamental sacramental structure, either. Perhaps the following offers an approach. The nature of the Church is the starting-point. She is not an eternal welfare institute delivering, as it were, in the next world, to God, the successful results of her care for the salvation of souls, but with no inclination to see an end put to herself and her activity by the consummation of all things. She is rather the community of those who wait expectantly, looking with longing for the coming of the Lord and the approach of his final and perfect kingly rule. She is the Church who wills to be transformed into the eternal kingdom of God. Eschatological expectation is an essential component of the Church. But when does the Church actually exercise and practise it? In reply, it must be remembered that the Church is not a substance, but is realized in and through the individual human beings who are her members. They, however, are defined by their mortality. They are subject to death, and in it they experience an exceptionally distinctive situation of their eschatological expectation, hope and courage to transcend the world and the limits of their senses. The ineluctable situation of approaching death, with its accompanying distress, summons them practically compellingly to make up their mind about the ultimate meaning of their existence, in faith and hope and self-transcending love. This climax in the individual's eschatological position, being a concrete instance of eschatological hope, must also be an act in which the very nature of the Church is fulfilled. For the Church herself is the community of those who are on pilgrimage to the Lord in faith and love, and she only exists in individual human beings. And this is so not only because she endures in hope the mortal peril in her individual member (actual death need not necessarily supervene), but she herself must be able to stand by the sick person's bedside in her official and visible form. A Church incapable of doing so and who took her leave in embarrassment at the approach of death, as the "world" does, inevitably, because it has no hope, would not be the Church of eschatological hope, visibly and manifestly. Either that fundamentally eschatological attitude and activity would be lacking, or it would be unable to find expression when most called for, where the world really threatens to collapse, and the human being, and in him the actual Church in the concrete, are challenged whether they really dare audibly to speak words of Christian hope.

That does not quite bring us to the sacrament of extreme unction, but we have, nevertheless, reached the point where we can expect an act of the Church in the sick person and in his regard, that manifests the Church as overcoming death and its darkness by her eschatological hope. And in view of our general considerations so far, we can say that because such an act is a symbolic proclamation of the fundamental nature of the Church as instituted by Christ, the symbol is not empty, but renders present what it proclaims and therefore gives the saving grace of hope amid the ruin of death, which in this way becomes, instead of a death of Adam, the coming of Christ in the life of an individual. We have still not attained the sacrament of extreme unction, however, because, of course, it might be held that everything we are postulating could take place by the Church's giving the sick person that Body which, delivered to death, gives eternal life to those that receive it. Such a supposition would not be without foundation. We do pray *Esto nobis praegustatum mortis in examine*. And Jesus himself, as St. John shows, links the meaning of the eucharist very directly to the hope of resurrection and eternal life. The φάρμακον ἀθανασίας (medicine of immortality) has indeed a very great deal to do with that death in which true life comes to birth. And its reception is so much a sacrament of the dying that the Christian has a definite obligation to receive viaticum, which cannot be said to the same degree of extreme unction. All this, which is correct, should, however, not lead to the conclusion that the eucharist is the sacrament of the dying, since there must be one, and that there cannot be, and is not, any other.

For we observe that the various sacraments do not all stand in the same relation to each other, and that the degree of independence and distinct significance is not the same in each. Confirmation, for example, as we have already seen, is particularly connected with baptism and is in fact the completion of the rite of initiation, which fundamentally is already fully applied in baptism. And yet that does not disprove the existence of a separate sacrament which also has its meaning, for a part of the reality which was present in the other sacrament as *res sacramenti* is more clearly manifest as *sacramentum* in the new rite, which because it more distinctly represents this, also confers more deeply and abundantly what it represents. Similarly the Church herself calls anointing of the sick *consummativum* of the sacrament of penance (D 907). On this basis, then, we can now say without hesitation that it is quite possible and indeed to be expected that there is a rite which makes plain what is already fundamentally present in the eucharist as viaticum, and yet which is a separate sacrament. For since the eucharist is the daily bread of Christians, it cannot manifest so unmistakably a special symbolism celebrating eschatological expectation and firm hope of eternity, that it would be pointless for the Church and the individual close to death to testify to this hope specially, in a separate visible and tangible way. But if this happens, we have precisely the sacrament of extreme unction.

If what we have said is correct, (it has only been possible to indicate a line of thought), it will follow, conversely, that extreme unction has an ecclesiological aspect. For both in the sick person who, endowed with free will, (infants are not proper subjects of this sacrament), allows this anointing by a consent in faith, as a baptized member of the Church, and also in the Church's action, which bears witness that she is without despair at the approach of mortal agony for her member, and expresses her solidarity with him, the Church's nature is accomplished as the one who, when night falls on this world, raises the lamp of faith and goes to meet the bridegroom, daring to say, "Let grace come, and this world pass away. Maranatha" (*Didache* I, 6).

There are many other things which might be considered in regard to the theme dealt with in this essay. It would be possible, for example, to reflect how, as the liturgy demonstrates, the person administering a particular sacrament need not only be a physical individual, but can also be a group associated in unity. In this way it becomes clearer than ever that the Church herself fulfils her own nature when she acts in the individual. One might recall in this connection the imposition of hands of the *presbyterium* in ordinations, the concelebration of mass, the administration of extreme unction by several priests and the custom of the early Church in the sacrament of penance, of imposition of hands by the whole *presbyterium* in conjunction with the bishop.

One could recall too that not the whole life of the Christian although he is always and everywhere a member of the Church and exercises in everything a representative and sanctifying function for her, can be lived in the official and public domain of the Church as though it belonged to this and was a part of the formal accomplishment of the Church's nature in magisterium and sacraments and so on. But the existence of such a "private" Christian life in the members of the Church does not prevent there being an intrinsic similarity and a very close connection between their "private" Christian life *(in foro conscientiae)* and their official, public life in the celebration of the liturgy and reception of the sacraments. If in addition we remember that even in sacramental life the personal element is not replaced or really made easy or diminished, but, in adults, should find expression in the sacraments; and that a sacrament visibly manifests in time, within the Church, before her eyes and for the world, not only the action of God and of the Church, but also the interior act of the recipient's faith; it is clear that the sacraments contain implicit directions for the structure of the whole of Christian life even in its private domain. It would in fact be possible to sketch out a theology of Christian life in the concrete, on the basis of the sacraments. And since they all have an ecclesiological aspect, it would become clearer from it, that no one lives to himself; that each must bear another's burden; and that those who love their neighbour have fulfilled the law. Even in the most private sphere we are still one another's debtors. We are saved when we have forgotten ourselves on account of others. We are in blessedness when we have become those who, in the eternal kingdom of love, have found the Church of eternity, the beginning and promise of which is the Church who accomplishes her own life in the sacraments of Christ.

THE EPISCOPATE
AND THE PRIMACY

I

THE EPISCOPATE AND THE PRIMACY

1. *The State of the Question*

Is IT permissible to feel that we could reflect more on the constitution of the Church than we have hitherto done? Since the Church and her theology are always aware of her nature, there is never any question of a leap from downright ignorance to knowledge, say, like the discovery of Australia, but rather of a growth in the reflex consciousness of a knowledge which, in substance, the Church has always possessed, as when, for example, after a long life of active and candid self-discovery, a person may additionally also come to know himself with the help of all available psychological tests and concepts.

Even today, this reflex knowledge of her own, permanent nature which the Church has, can grow. Deeper insight is possible not only into the actual mysteries of this Church which is the community of the faithful in the Spirit of God, the body of Christ, the beginning of the Kingdom of God, the primal sacrament of God's eschatological salvation. It can also embrace her constitution – that is to say, those juridical bonds which create and sustain her as a "perfect society". Here too, one may well think, the nature of the Church could be conceived in clearer and more conscious fashion. For if we consult one of the current theological textbooks, we learn that the Church has a "hierarchical" structure, in that Christ entrusted to the Apostolic college and to the bishops, the successors of the apostles, the power to preach the gospel, to administer the sacraments, and to give spiritual guidance. We learn that the Church is not a purely voluntary association of a democratic kind, established by men, but one whose fundamental rights, duties and powers were established by God.

We are further told that this hierarchically constituted Church has a "monarchical" summit in the immediate, universal primacy of jurisdiction of Peter and his successors, the popes. But with this the doctrine of the constitution of the Church, insofar as that constitution is of direct divine origin, is exhausted. It would seem to us that the relation between the hierarchic-episcopal and the monarchic–papal structure of the Church – a question which, as we know, the Vatican Council of 1870 was not allowed time to broach – is still not clear. Nor indeed is the one homogeneous nature of this constitution clarified, its ultimate basic idea, by merely affirming these two powers in the Church. A certain obscurity still shrouds the "metaphysics" of the Church's constitution.

When such a problem is raised one can, of course, say that in this matter an answer can hardly be expected beyond the clear and common teaching. After all, it can be argued, the Church is a juridical entity unique in history, instituted by a free disposition of God which cannot be deduced from necessary metaphysical principles, both of which facts – her uniqueness and her foundation through God's free will – render it unlikely that, by means of some sort of supernatural philosophy of law and constitutional metaphysics (which would always proceed from general and neccessary principles), much more could be said than is already explicitly known. One could indeed ask oneself whether there is such a thing as a written constitution of the Church; or, better, wonder that there is none. The Code of Canon Law is, in content, purpose and make-up, not a constitution of the Church, even though it can be said to contain the most important constitutional rules. It might be asked further, whether there could be such a thing as a comprehensive written constitution of the Church on the lines of a modern, written state constitution. But the question cannot be pursued here.

This scepticism may be justified. Those who profess it will certainly not be refuted by the modest observations that follow. The author does not presume to attempt a comprehensive solution to the problem that has been posed, but merely to set forth some tentative considerations prompted by the feeling that we can and should make progress in the theology of this constitution, which is more than a matter of articles. Such considerations may also have a practical import. For although the nature of the Church is of divine origin and indestructible, nevertheless its realization in every-day life, even when under the protection of the promised Holy Ghost, is still exposed to man's freedom, to his whims and to his errors. And therefore this nature can be manifested either to better or to worse effect. A deeper, more conscious knowledge of the Church's nature can also contribute towards the ever purer realization of this nature, even in her most ordinary activities, and it is precisely through this contribution that the Spirit of the Church affords her his own assistance.

We shall try to form a few ideas about the constitution of the

Church by comparing it with the constitutions of other societies. This method is perfectly legitimate. For, although we cannot thereby directly contemplate the ultimate mystery of the Church, still she is a visible society with legal powers and a juridical framework which belongs on the one hand to her divinely established essence (therefore not merely to the human law within the Church), and which on the other hand (because they are found within this world, incarnate) lend themselves to comparison with other human legal relationships just as the humanity of Christ can be compared with the nature of other men, because he became "consubstantial" with us.

2. The Constitution of the Church

It is commonly said that the Church has a monarchical constitution. If this is taken to mean that the pope, as an individual, has full, direct, ordinary and general episcopal primacy of jurisdiction over the whole Church and each of her parts and members – including the bishops – then the monarchical constitution of the Church is axiomatic for Catholics.[1] But a monarchical constitution is usually understood to mean an hereditary monarchy and not an elective one, whereas the pope is at least de facto elected.[2] This distinction is not insignificant. For where office and sovereign power are hereditary and where, therefore, their subject is designated by biological factors largely independent

[1] I Vatican Council; Denzinger, Enchiridion Symbolorum, no. 1831. CJC, can. 218.
[2] In the present context we cannot decide the question whether this must be so by divine law, or wheter per se a pope — since celibacy is only a

of the intellectual and moral decisions of men, the state or society in question is more stable and compact than where the bearer of supreme power is ever and again designated by election, *i.e.,* by a free, deliberate act of men themselves. This also holds true where the actual content of power subsists independent of the electors. Even here the *exercise* of this power is deeply influenced by the historical, the elective character of the chosen ruler, and therefore by the character of his electors as well. To define the Church as a monarchy is to fail to throw into relief the scope which, as history shows, here remains for the play of the charismatic and unexpected qualities of the Church's character, her perennial youthfulness, her vigour.

Furthermore, monarchy, when not reduced by an essentially extraneous element into constitutional monarchy, is of its own nature "absolute" monarchy. This need not mean tyranny or totalitarianism. An absolute monarchy may recognize that it is bound to observe the natural law as, for example, the better representatives of eighteenth century absolutism did; it may be enlightened or patriarchal absolutism; it may, because of pressing physical circumstances or by a policy consciously adopted (though not really consistent with the system as such), respect a defined and organically grown social order such as that of estates. Nevertheless, such a monarchy can be absolute to the extent that everything within the bounds of physical possibility and of morality — which can be realized in a given historical

positive church law – could set up the Church as an hereditary monarchy, or himself designate his successor in some other way. Cf. for example, A. Straub, *De Ecclesia Christi* (Innsbruck, 1912) n. 596; J. Salaverri, "De Ecclesia Christi", *Sacrae Theologiae Summa* 1⁴ (Madrid, 1958), p. 655, note 41.

situation—proceeds from the will of one man and of one man only. Now is the Church a monarchy in this sense? The answer is not easy. Is someone an absolute monarch in the sense defined if he possesses *suprema et plena potestas jurisdictionis vere episcopalis, ordinaria et immediata?*[3] The answer, of course, depends on terminological precisions which are always arbitrary to a certain extent, since they could be expressed differently regardless of the reality or the truth of the objects and propositions under consideration. But if we accept the meaning of an absolute monarchy according to the definition given above, then we must say that the pope is not a monarch[4] of the Church.

The reasons are clear. In an absolute monarchy there are no constitutional authorities beside the monarch, existing independent of the monarch's will. Indeed there may be facts and moral obligations which limit the will of the absolute monarch. But where his will is fundamentally limited by some legally binding reality which, as such, belongs to the constitutional structure of the society and not merely to the moral norms which stand above positive constitutional law, we can no longer speak of an absolute monarchy. But the Church is so constituted. The will of the pope, insofar as he has the highest authority in the Church, is limited by a reality which, according to the very will of God, belongs to the constitution of the Church, namely, the episcopate. Not only is the pope physically unable to abolish the episcopate (since in doing so he would rob himself of the means of administering his government of the universal Church), but he

[3] CJC, can. 218.
[4] The Vatican Council and the CJC therefore do not use this concept. When it does appear in theology it is used in a broader sense than that defined here.

308

also confronts an episcopate which, as such, is not his civil service instituted by himself which he could abolish, at least legally, if not in fact. For the episcopate itself is of divine right.[5] It is only conjoined with this episcopate – as immediately sprung from the institution of Christ as itself – that the papal primacy juridically constitutes the Church.

This does not exclude the pope from being above the individual bishop as an individual, even in his official capacity as bishop. The pope has direct and ordinary jurisdiction over each bishop as well. He determines which person shall possess the powers of a bishop,[6] and according to what is now the common teaching, gives that person his powers.[7] By that very fact it is open to the pope to fix the precise limits of these powers, to extend them, to restrict them by reserving certain elements of these powers to himself, even in principle, although, of their nature, they would fall within the bishop's competence. But it does not follow (quite the contrary) that the episcopate as a whole could be abolished by the pope, that it is only an instru-

---

[5] Cf. the Council of Trent: Dz. 960 and 966; Vatican Council: Dz. 1821 and 1826; CJC, can. 108. Accordingly, Leo XIII in his Encyclical *"Satis Cognitum"* expressly teaches that the bishops are not to be considered as representatives of the Roman pope, since they have their own proper authority; *"... nec tamen Vicarii Romanorum Pontificum putandi, quia potestatem gerunt sibi propriam ..."* ASS 28, 1895–96, p. 723; cf. also Dz. 1962. Hence they care for their flocks not in the name of the pope, but in Christ's and their own name, so that they are successors of the apostles by divine decree. Pius XII emphasized both of these points in *"Mystici Corporis"* (AAS 35, 1943, pp. 211ff.; Dz. 2287). Cf. also Pius XII in his allocution *"Si Diligis"* (AAS 46, 1954, p. 314).

[6] Dz. 968; 1750ff.; CJC, can. 329, § 2.

[7] Cf. J. Salaverri, *op. cit.,* p. 632, no. 374, where he refers to Pius XII's *"Mystici Corporis"* (AAS 35, 1943, pp. 211ff.; Dz. 2287) and *"Ad Sinarum*

ment of papal authority, that therefore the bishops are only the pope's officials, who, as his functionaries, are mere executive organs of the one absolute, monarchical power of the pope. As physical persons they receive their authority from the pope. But he does not confer on them a part of his own personal power to be exercised by them in his name. He gives them a power which, as distinct from that of the pope (even though subject to it), must exist in the Church according to the will of Christ himself, and forms one of the constituent elements of the Church and not of the papacy as such.

If it is true that the pope has a universal, supreme and direct episcopal jurisdiction over the whole Church and therefore over the bishops too, then it must be said that the authority of the bishops, whereby they are not mere functionaries of the pope, considered *materially* (that is, in its mere objectivity and through its subordination to the higher jurisdiction of the pope), cannot be separated from papal authority.[8] This means that there is nothing the bishops can do which the pope could not do, and that all they can do they can do in subordination to the pope. There is no

Gentem" (AAS 47, 1955, p. 9). In accordance with what has been said above, in conferring this office the pope does not delegate a part of his own authority to the bishop nominated by him, but grants him a share in that authority of the universal episcopate which Christ has entrusted to the Church. The ability to communicate a power and the ability to exercise the same power when it has not been communicated to another, are obviously not the same thing. Hence we cannot conclude that what the bishop receives is a delegated papal authority, he being thus a mere official of the pope, from the fact that he receives his authority through the pope.

[8] For this reason the Vatican Council uses the concept "episcopal" to describe the pope's authority. Dz. 1827.

doubt that this incontestable position, solemnly taught by the Vatican Council, gave the impression both inside and especially outside the Church, that the bishops are only officials, functionaries of the pope. When, however, it is pointed out that according to the equally definitive common doctrine the episcopate is of divine right, since the Church expressly teaches (Pius IX, Leo XIII, Pius XII) that even *after* the Vatican Council, the bishops are not mere officials of the pope, it still remains difficult to see how the two facts – the universal and direct primacy of jurisdiction of the pope on the one hand, and the divine institution and indissolubility of the episcopate on the other (as an irreducible, if not independent power), – can be reconciled with each other. Because this point remains obscure in practice the notion persists, both inside and outside the Church, that she is an absolute monarchy governed by the pope through his officials, the bishops. Why should we not openly and candidly admit that this unexpressed, but widespread and almost instinctive feeling can have involuntary but not insignificant effects in the life of the Church? One of these effects may be (and here we would pass no judgment on the existence and actual extent of this effect) that the "official" feels that the degree of his responsible initiative is very limited, since as the mere organ of a higher authority he must almost invariably wait for the initiative to come from above. It may be felt that the obscurity of the question we have been discussing could be clarified to better effect than hitherto.

3. Primacy and Episcopate
compared with the Relationship between Universal Church and Local Church

The non-Catholic legal historian who does not believe in the organic development of the Church's constitutional law will say that the doctrine of the divine institution of the episcopate and its peculiar rights and duties is a verbal residue from the time when such was the actual state of affairs in the Catholic Church; that her teaching on the universal and direct papal primacy of jurisdiction even over the bishops, as this has been understood and put into practice since the Vatican Council, cannot in fact be reconciled with the old doctrine, as is shown by usage, by people's feelings and by the admission that there is no legal power of any substance which the bishop could independently exercise in such a way that the pope could not withdraw the exercise of it from him by restricting his authority, or deposing him, or the like.

There are a number of ways in which we can try to shed light upon this obscurity. First of all the question arises: whence comes this remarkable duality, this interlocking of papal and episcopal authority? How can it be made clear that the concept here confronting us is not so involved, so impenetrable, so apparently tortuous as to indicate a merely verbal harmonization of two irreconcilables?

The historical and theological answer to this question seems to lie in the fact that an individual "church" is not just an administrative district of the whole Church, but bears a unique relationship to the universal Church, one based on the nature of the Church and on her differentiation from natural

312

territorial societies. It is in the light of this relationship that the relationship between pope and bishop can be understood and justified. What appeared to be the suspect complexity of this relation now reveals itself as a consequence of the Church's very character as a supernatural mystery.

These statements require elucidation. We could try to answer our question by referring to the apostles and their appointment by Christ as hierarchical leaders of the Church under Peter. Indeed ecclesiology rightly appeals to the foundation of the apostolic college by Christ in order to prove the existence in the Church of the episcopal office and its establishment by Christ, whilst clearly recognizing that the apostles were not simply the first bishops, (since they enjoyed prerogatives which bishops do not have, because they were not local bishops), and that it is not so easy as one would gather from many a textbook to determine whether a monarchical episcopate existed always and everywhere from the very beginning, or whether there was, here and there in the primitive Church, associate government of individual Christian communities, albeit authoritative and proceding from above. If, however, we merely cite the position of Peter and the apostles in the primitive Church in attempting to explain the seemingly remarkable relationship between primacy and episcopate, then we defer the question without answering it. For we still must explain why the other apostles are not reduced to the status of mere administrative organs and representatives of the Petrine authority, if we assign to Peter the same authority according to Scripture that the Vatican dogma predicates of the pope. Therefore we should not in the first instance fall back on the relation between Peter and the apostles, since the bishops, governing

313

as they do a limited territory, differ essentially from the apostles, even from the point of view of jurisdiction, so that it is not at all easy to say to what extent they are "successors" of the apostles, and it is best to understand this expression in the sense that the function of the apostolic college as a whole is continued in the Church primarily by the episcopal college as a whole,[9] and not in the sense that each bishop is the direct successor of a particular apostle, because in that case neither his confinement to one territory nor his more limited teaching power could be plausibly explained.

Therefore, as we were saying, the solution[10] should be sought in the fundamental relation which obtains between the local Church and the universal Church. It has long been acknowledged that this is a unique relation not found between other societies and their parts, at least not in this intensity and with this significance. The layman in these questions will see this most clearly if he remembers that one speaks of the universal Church and of the individual community, even in the New Testament, as the "Church". The Church which Christ redeemed by his blood is the universal Church; but the individual community at a certain place is also the "Church", in Ephesus, for example. This strange way of speaking cannot be explained by saying that the word for the whole is used to designate the part and that there is nothing strange about it. It is as strange as calling London the United Kingdom. Behind this usage lies a conviction and an intuition which are not at all self-explanatory, and which mean something quite different from the truism that a particular community is a member and an administrative district of the universal Church.

[9] We shall deal with this question in Part Two of this Study.
[10] To put it more cautiously, a partial solution of the question.

The idea at the root of this usage has a history going back far beyond New Testament times. It is rooted in the problem of pre-Christian Jewish theology as to where that holy people of God, to whom his promises were made, is palpably and conclusively to be found in history, since this same people in the concrete (according to the "flesh") remains recalcitrant to God's decree and unbelieving. The thought naturally arises that, since God's promises and faithfulness cannot come to nought, the "people", "Israel", still truly exists, even if it survives only in a "faithful remnant", in a brotherhood of a few loyal souls. A limited administrative district in one community cannot cause the totality of this community to live on, when the totality as such has disappeared, if the part was nothing more than a part, a mere organ, not endowed with the sensibility and the various faculties of the whole organism. On the other hand, if the whole is so present in the part that it can fully consummate itself there according to its nature, and if the whole cannot by any means disappear while the part still lives, then the part is indeed more than a mere part, and rightly bears the name of the whole. This is exactly how pre-Christian Jewish theology conceived the faithful remnant, the individual community of brethren, in which God was truly served in faith according to his law.

In order to develop this basic thought more systematically we can also say that the Church as a whole, where she becomes "event" in the full sense of the term, is necessarily a local Church. In the local Church the whole Church becomes tangible. Further explanation is needed to show exactly what this means.[11]

---

[11] In the next few paragraphs we repeat the ideas which we developed in *Die Pfarre,* edited by Hugo Rahner, S.J. (Freiburg i. B., 1956).

315

When asked what is this Church in its entirety, founded by Christ for all men, the answer we, as men of today, instinctively turn to is a "perfect society", an organization founded by Christ with its hierarchical structure of offices, with the powers pertaining to these offices, with the many men who, under particular conditions, gain membership in this social organization. All this, indeed, exists and is of the greatest importance for salvation. This society, like any other, has a permanent legal existence which is not discontinued even if we suppose that this Church at a particular time is not operative in any of her powers or in any of her members. A legally founded society has a type of existence different from that of substances. Nevertheless it cannot be denied that, when the Church acts, that is, teaches, confesses the faith, prays, celebrates the Sacrifice of Christ, etc., she reaches a higher degree of actuality than she does by her mere continuing existence. She is a visible society; as really visible she must continually realize her historical, spatio-temporal tangibility through the actions of men. She must become "event" over and over again.

It is not as if these "events" in their separated individuality in space and time founded the Church anew. An actualism of this sort, which would basically deny the social constitution of the Church, tradition, apostolic succession and any real church law of divine right, is foreign to Catholic ecclesiology. But the static and historical continuity of a permanently existing Church does not imply that this Church need not become "event" again and again at definite spatio-temporal points, that she need not pass from a certain potentiality to a particular actuality, and that the whole enduring essence of the Church is not ordered towards this event. If we distinguish in this way between the Church as a mere institution with an enduring social constitution on the one hand, and the Church as "event" on the other, then it follows that she becomes an actual "event", with a spatio-temporal tangibility, in the highest degree when she becomes "event" as the communion of saints, as a society. Naturally she is also present when an individual acts in the Church and for the Church by virtue of the authority of Christ and of an office in the Church. But it cannot be denied that where the Church appears as a communion, *i. e.,* as a plurality of men bound together by a visible occurrence and united by grace, she attains a higher degree of actuality as the Church, than she does when the individual holder of an office brings the Church to actuality by an action of his own in which the other members of the Church take no active part.

Now we ask where and when does the Church become, in the sense indicated above, an "event" in the most intense and actual way? Essentially the Church is the historically continuing presence in the world of the incarnate Word of God. She is the historical tangibility of the salvific will of God as revealed in Christ. Therefore the Church is most tangibly and intensively an "event" where (through the words of consecration) Christ himself is present in his own congregation as the crucified and resurrected Saviour, the fount of salvation; where the Redemption makes itself felt in the congregation by becoming sacramentally visible; where the "New and Eternal Testament" which he founded on the cross is most palpably and actually present in the holy remembrance of its first institution. Therefore the celebration of the Eucharist is the most intensive event of the Church. For by this celebration Christ is not only present in the Church's liturgical solemnity as the Redeemer of

317

his body, as the salvation and lord of the Church; but in the Eucharist the union of the faithful with Christ and with one another is also most tangibly visible, and at the Holy Table is most interiorly realized. Inasmuch as the celebration of the Eucharist is the sacramental anticipation of the heavenly marriage banquet, the final, eternal form of the community of saints shines forth even now in this solemnity just as the source of the Church, Christ's sacrifice on the cross, is present in it.

An essential characteristic of the Eucharistic celebration as a sacramental rite is that it must be localized. (The same holds true for the other sacraments, which are all essentially bound up with the corporeal). It can only be celebrated by one congregation gathered together in one place. But this means that the Church, without prejudice to her social constitution, permanency, universality and relation to all men, is by her inmost nature oriented towards a local concretization and actualization. Therefore the Eucharist as an event in a place not only occurs in the Church; the Church herself becomes in the fullest sense an event only in the local celebration of the Eucharist. That is the fundamental reason why Scripture calls the individual communities *ecclesia,* the same name that the unity of the faithful all over the world possesses. It is not only true that the Eucharist exists because the Church exists; it is also true, if rightly understood, that the Church exists because the Eucharist exists. The Church is and remains, even as a whole, only because she is actualized again and again in the one all-embracing "event" of herself, that is, in the Eucharist. Because this event is essentially localized at one point of time and space and in one local community, therefore the local Church is not only an agency of the universal Church, subsequently founded, and

318

which she could easily dispense with, but is the "event" itself of this universal Church.

If, by some historical catastrophe, a great nation were reduced to a village, then one could no longer correctly say that the nation still existed, that its nature as an historical entity was still realized. But if, *per impossibile,* the Church were reduced to one diocese with its bishop, its legitimate pastor would also be the pope of Rome, and – this is a decisive point – exactly as much would occur in it, as can occur in the universal Church and is the actualization of her nature.[12] She is the proclamation of the dominion of God revealed in the crucified and resurrected flesh of the Son of God as the tribunal of grace over the sins of the world. This proclamation takes place through the legitimate eucharistic celebration of the holy community subjecting itself to the redeeming dominion of God in the remembrance of the Lord's death.

Therefore a local Church is not brought about by an atomizing division of the world-territory of the universal Church, but by the concentration of the Church into her own nature as "event". For this reason, no doubt, the earliest local Church was a bishop's Church. And we might note that the presbyteroi (priests and pastors) originally were not those who were needed

[12] Properly to evaluate such an "actualistic" definition of the Church the following must be taken into consideration: a natural society can do or neglect to do many things and still exist; it can neglect to do many things (even though wrongly) that it ought to do; and there are not many things the neglect of which would destroy its existence. In the Church however, there are certain acts which were made a part of her very essence by her divine Founder and which he guaranteed would always take place. Hence the act here lies really in the potency and is not a mere accident of the Church.

because there were a number of local communities, but were from the first the senate of the local bishop. As a result the original (episcopal) local communities contained only elements of divine foundation: the holy cultic community of Christ with an apostle or his successor at its head.

What conclusions can be drawn from the relations we have briefly sketched between the universal Church and the local Church (or better, between the Church as she is everywhere and the same Church as she appears in one particular place), which can be applied to the relation between the primacy and the episcopate?

Since the Church is and is intended to be a world Church, insofar as there should be everywhere true adorers of the Father in the Spirit and in the name of Christ, and insofar as this Church, according to her historically perceptible constitution is intended to be one, to that extent the primacy exists. Inasmuch as the same one and universal Church is intended to appear in particular places and precisely in this way to achieve its full consummation, namely, in the celebration of the Eucharist and the rest of the sacraments, to this extent the episcopate exists of divine right.[13] This episcopacy must therefore have all the rights and powers that should belong to it if, on the one hand, the Church as a whole (which does not mean wholly) and in her highest act is to make an historical, tangible appearance

[13] Naturally this does not mean that we could of ourselves, and independent of positive revelation, deduce primacy and episcopate from this principle. But if we already know from positive sources about the positive institution of primacy and episcopate, then we can clearly see their essential connection with this fundamental concept of the Church. For even a positive free institution can conform to the fundamental nature of a thing and does not mean positivistic arbitrariness.

wherever an individual bishop rules; and if, on the other hand, this Church, though "appearing" locally, is the same one which is spread over the whole world and is represented in its catholicity by the pope. We can say that, in the sense and to the extent that the whole Church is completely present in the local Church, the Church's powers of jurisdiction and order are completely present in the local bishop. The papal authority is not more comprehensive in this respect, but in the sense that the pope alone, by divine right of course, represents the unity of the whole Church as the totality of the local Churches. This is quite simply demonstrated by the fact that the pope has no power of order beyond that of the ordinary bishop, although, from an absolute and comprehensive point of view, the *potestas ordinis* is a higher one than the power of jurisdiction.

It will not do merely to accept this equality as the result of an arbitrary divine decree; rather we may and must seek its essential basis, even though we may hold that this can be known only as a result of the express revelation of the fact. Since therefore the Church must make its appearance in particular places, "the episcopate exists in virtue of the same divine institution on which the papacy rests; it too has its rights and duties, which the pope has neither the right nor the power to change. It is therefore a complete misunderstanding . . . to suppose . . . that the bishops are only instruments of the pope, officials of his without personal responsibility." "According to the constant teaching of the Catholic Church, as expressly declared also by the Vatican Council, the bishops are not mere instruments of the pope, not papal officials without responsibility of their own, but, established by the Holy Spirit and taking the place of the apostles, as true shepherds they feed and rule

321

the flocks entrusted to them. . ."[14] Insofar as the local bishop by his own teaching represents the teaching of the universal Church (which always involves the supreme magisterium of the pope and belief in the unity of the Church), he does not merely relay the teaching of the universal Church or of the pope as if he were a loudspeaker, as though his listeners had to direct their attention past the bishop to what was being said elsewhere in the same connection. On the contrary, in the bishop the Church herself continues her authoritative witness to revealed truth.[15] The case of the powers of order and jurisdiction is similar.

4. The Episcopate and Charismata[16]

The sense of this expression (and by the same token the limits of the concept of the Church's "monarchical" constitution) will perhaps become clearer if we consider the following. In

[14] Therefore "the pope cannot be described as an absolute monarch, even with regard to Church affairs". From a collective Statement of the German bishops in 1875 which was expressly and solemnly approved by Pius IX. Cited with a German translation of this approbation in J. Neuner-H. Roos, *Der Glaube der Kirche in den Urkunden der Lehrverkündigung* (Regensburg, ⁵1958), n. 388 a. The complete text in *Katholik*, N. F. Bd. 33 (1875) pp. 209–213.
[15] Cf. D. Palmieri, *Tractatus de Romano Pontifice*² (Prati, 1891), pp. 666 ff. The bishops are *"magistri authentici verique judices, etsi non supremi, in causis fidei et cum singuli in suis sedibus docent, praesumendum est juridice, doctrinam eorum esse catholicam . . ."* For example, when a bishop proscribes the teaching of a particular book (CJC, can. 1395 n. 1), he thereby performs an act of the magisterium which by the nature of the case is not just a repetition of what has always and everywhere been said.
[16] This section will be discussed in a broader context and in more detail to our purpose in Part Three of this book.

the decision of any civil servant it is but the initiative of his superior that is expressed. He may and should indeed show some initiative in preparing this decision, but the content of it is wholly derived from the authority and resolve of his superior, so that whatever occurs in his decision was already "present" in his superior. Now a bishop's decisions are not of this kind. We have already pointed out elsewhere[17] that there is a "charismatic" structure in the Church besides the hierarchical, that is, that in the constitution of the Church the Spirit as Lord of the Church reserves to himself the power and the right to impart impulses to the Church without always and everywhere directing them through the official hierarchical organs of the Church. The same thing can expressly be said about the relation between the hierarchical organs themselves, that is, between the papacy and the bishops. Because the bishops embody the universal Church "on the spot", and insofar as they do so, being the direct representatives of Christ himself and not simply of the pope, they are indeed always dependent on, and responsible to, that unity of the Church in her diffusion which is embodied by the pope, and hence are subject to him; they must preserve "peace and communion" with the Apostolic See. But it does not follow that they are executors of the papal will alone. For they are also hierarchical channels for the impulses of the Holy Spirit, who in the first place accomplishes through them what he wishes done at this particular place in the Church, and furthermore possibly some new insight, a new vitality, new modes of Christian life, private or public, that he wishes to impart via this point to the Church as a whole.

[17] *The Dynamic Element in the Church,* Quaestiones Disputatae 12 (Freiburg - New York - London - Montreal 1964).

In his initiative, subject to the immediate guidance of the Spirit of God, the individual bishop must always assure himself of permanent unity and of the assent, at least tacitly given, of the universal Church and the pope. But he is not simply carrying out impulses which emanate from the highest echelon of the Church. Just as he is of divine right, to the extent that he shares in the divine right of the episcopate (even though he as an individual is appointed by the pope), so he is an official organ of such immediate guidance by the Holy Spirit. The approbation of the pope, and thus of the whole Church, is a criterion of his being and remaining a docile organ of this immediate guidance by the Holy Spirit. But this does not mean that his initiative is confined to carrying out an impulse received from the supreme human government of the Church. The pope must also exercise a continuous, official and normal authority over the individual bishop, since the bishop's Church is also a member and a part – though more than this – of the universal Church. To this extent the individual bishop is *also* an executive organ of the papal power. But since his bishop's Church is *the* Church, in that mysterious presence of the whole in the part, which is found only in the Church, impulses from above can directly manifest Christian and ecclesiastical life in him, and through him and his Church to the whole Church. These may be impulses which have not been transmitted through official channels from the higher reaches of the hierarchy.

In the openness to such impulses, to which the bishop (as opposed to the charismatic layman) is obliged by reason of his office, there is a dignity and an obligation which make him even "subjectively" more than a mere official of the pope. This immediate contact of the episcopate with God and his government, in the midst of its "ordinary" dependence on the papacy, may seem complicated, may elude a neat juridical formulation and a clear-cut demarcation of the respective powers of pope and bishop. But this very complexity, these imponderables in the delimitation of the two powers, are grounded in the unique essence of the Church. The Church's own nature shows that the problem of the inalienable powers of the bishops cannot possibly be solved by singling out certain powers and privileges of the bishops over which the pope has no control, as every sort of Gallicanism and Febronianism has always tried to do. The bishop has his most fundamental powers because *the* Church in its actuality appears in him and in his Church; and these same powers of *the* Church are fully vested in the person of the pope for the whole Church.

But the very fact that powers and privileges cannot be divided up between pope and bishop (in the sense of the pope's influence on the bishop having a legally determinable limit) does not mean that the bishop is only an executive official of the pope; and this for the very same reason that the bishop is subject to the pope. Ultimately he is subject to him not because the bishopric represents a small administrative sector of the universal Church, which the bishop administers merely in the name of the universal Church, but because the universal Church is manifest in his diocese. This makes him at once subordinate and independent. Therefore the bishop, too, has a responsibility for the whole Church. Not in the sense that he directly governs her, something which is reserved to the pope alone, but in the sense that he remains at the disposal of the universal Church and of God in such a way that whatever happens in his diocese happens in "communion" with the universal Church, and at the same

325

time happens in such a way that it can be a point of departure from which God's impulse can spread into the universal Church.

As a matter of fact, this has always been so in the history of the Church. If an Athanasius, an Ambrose, an Augustine, a Ketteler (as the pioneer of the Church's modern social teaching), a Cardinal Suhard and many others were not only good bishops of their own dioceses, but signified something irreplaceable for the whole Church, then this greater significance was not theirs as merely private persons (as great theologians, for example) but was essentially based on their quality as bishops. They could never have done what they did, if they had not been bishops; and what they did it was for them to do because they were bishops. The charismatic function of the individual bishops for the universal Church does not detract from the dignity and importance of the papacy. For there have also been many popes in whom office and charismatic mission were united to the blessing of the Church. Only a dictator, not a pope, could see in the free charismata in the Church, in the breathing of the Holy Spirit where it will anything to depreciate, to question or to threaten his permanent office. This is especially true where a charismatic bishop feeds his flock in the name of Christ under the direction of the Holy Spirit. Finally, the popes have constantly emphasized that the *solidus vigor* of the bishops is their honour.[18] This is especially true of that power and vitality which God's Spirit himself grants to the bishops.

Since the pope has the fulness of power, and since any particular jurisdictional power of an individual bishop can, in a given case, be withdrawn by the pope for good cause (or its

[18] Dz. 1828, where the Vatican Council quotes Gregory the Great.

exercise forbidden) – even though the episcopate as such must, as divinely instituted, remain intact – the respective spheres of papal and episcopal authority cannot be sharply delimited, and this very fact makes possible a *human* canon law, its development and modification in accordance with developments in the actual distribution of duties and ordinary powers between the two authorities; whilst the "right" delimitation of these powers (through positive human canon law), that is, appropriate to the matter, to the times and to the intellectual climate, is a process not always to be regulated by fixed constitutional norms. Therefore there is no *legal* tribunal which can ensure that the actual relation between primacy and episcopate, in the canonical delimitation of their respective competences, is proper and objective. Only the influence of the Holy Spirit can continuously assure that the practical balance in positive canon law and in the concrete administration of this law is effected in the manner most beneficial to the Church. If we consider the relation between the two powers from a purely *legal* point of view, then, there is no provision which would effectually prevent the pope so concentrating all power in himself as to leave an episcopate of divine right in name only. For, according to what has been said above, we cannot single out any one power which the pope cannot or may not assume for himself; there is no tribunal on earth which as the pope's superior could declare such action illicit, for the decisions of the Apostolic See are irreformable by any authority. The pope's is the supreme and final jurisdiction, and there is not and cannot be (because of the promised assistance of the Spirit) any ultimate right of resistance, which in practice would dissolve the Church. The continual assistance of the Spirit is the only, the final and decisive guarantee for the

Catholic, that on the whole the properly balanced relationship of a practical kind subsists between the two powers, that according to the exigencies of each successive age neither exaggerated centralization nor episcopalist disintegration, will prevail over the unity of the Church.

Since the solemn definition of the papal primacy there remains practically only one danger, which is the danger of overcentralization in the Church. It was given legal footing and opportunity by the Vatican Council while the decentralizing tendencies operate only through facts and habits.

Hence the ultimate bulwark against this danger can be found only in confidence in the assistance of the Spirit of the Church, which is not legally guaranteed. The Spirit of God is the final guarantee that the episcopate shall retain that scope which, by divine right, it must enjoy. But that is true everywhere: freedom is only where the Spirit is. The field of his free action can indeed be translated into legal norms, but in the last analysis he himself must protect these norms. This shows why the Church cannot have an adequate constitution. Part of herself is the Spirit who alone can guarantee the unity of the Church by the existence of two powers, one of which cannot be adequately reduced to the other in such a way that the Church could really be called a kind of absolute monarchy.

II

ON THE DIVINE RIGHT OF THE EPISCOPATE

1. Preliminary Remarks

THE theology of the relation between the papal primacy and the episcopate is undoubtedly one part of ecclesiology which has yet to find its final form. Even that degree of development possible in today's circumstances has not yet been reached. It is of course recognized that the Vatican Council could not treat this question systematically and thoroughly, after defining the universal and ordinary episcopal primacy of jurisdiction of the pope, because of the break–up of the Council. And not all questions about this relationship which arise in the practical life of the Church can be solved by dogmatic ecclesiology, since the concrete relationship between these two powers in the practical life of the Church cannot be unequivocally deduced from the Church's dogmatic nature *iuris divini* alone. It is also a matter of historical development, of practical experience, of *human* law in the Church, and must be continually thought through and regulated anew in her changing historical circumstances.

The plain fact that this concrete relationship has had a history is clear proof that it lawfully can and will have a history in the future as well, because the history of the Church will continue. From this fact alone, it would be false and naïve to think, consciously or unconsciously, that this relationship in the course of history has developed dogmatically, canonically and practically into its final form, which will now endure without any further change. If one were tacitly to assume, therefore, that even the slightest modification in this relationship (within the framework of the permanent *ius divinum,* of course) would amount to at least a secret attack either on this *ius divinum* or upon a form of the Church's *ius humanum* never to be improved upon, this would be to deny the basic truth that the Church is truly an historical thing. It would be to forget that the Church preserves and remains faithful to her Christ-given, permanent nature precisely by continually expressing it in a temporally conditioned form, in her *ius humanum* and in its practical application according to the needs of the time.

If the dogmatic theologian is not the only one called upon to consider this relationship in its concrete form, still we presume it will not be alleged that further dogmatic reflection on the nature of the Church and on the theological nature (that is, the divine right) of the relationship between primacy and episcopate has nothing more to contribute to the perennially necessary discussion about the form this relation takes in practice. This is the object of some of the dogmatic considerations that follow. They are not particularly systematic, nor do they pretend to exhaust the subject.[1]

According to defined Catholic doctrine, the pope personally possesses a full, immediate, ordinary and general episcopal primacy of jurisdiction over the whole Church and over her

---

[1] The reader is referred to the first part of this book for a fuller treatment of what will be repeated here only in brief.

every part and member, including the bishops.[1a] On the other hand it is definitive Catholic teaching (though not as yet defined in terms of such conscious clarity) that the episcopate exists of divine right[1b] in such a way that the pope, for all his jurisdictional primacy, cannot abolish it, that the bishops are not to be considered mere functionaries or representatives of the Roman Pontiff, that they have, rather, their own proper power to tend their flocks, not in the name of the pope, but in Christ's name and their own, and are therefore successors of the apostles by divine disposition. "The episcopate exists in virtue of the same divine institution on which the papacy rests; it too has its rights and duties, which the pope has neither the right nor the power to change. It is therefore a complete misunderstanding . . . to suppose . . . that the bishops are only instruments of the pope, officials of his without personal responsibility." "According to the constant teaching of the Catholic Church, as expressly declared also by the Vatican Council, the bishops are not mere instruments of the pope, not papal officials without responsibility of their own, but established by the Holy Spirit and taking the place of the apostles, as true shepherds they tend and rule the flocks entrusted to them . . ." Thus the already quoted statement of the German episcopate of 1875, which enjoyed the express and solemn approbation of Pius IX.[2] If we compare these two statements on the episcopate and the papal primacy, both no doubt correct, we shall not be able to say that their compatibility is immediately evident, either in theory or in practice.

[1a] Dz. 1831; CJC, can. 218.
[1b] Dz. 960, 966, 1821, 1828.
[2] Cf. J. Neuner – H. Roos, *Der Glaube der Kirche in den Urkunden der Lehrverkündigung* (Regensburg, 1958), n. 388a.

Not in theory: it is not easy to understand how it is that a bishop has inalienable rights *iuris divini* which the pope cannot take from him, how it is that he governs his flock in the name of Christ and his own name, and not in the name of the pope, how it is that he is no mere functionary, when nowhere in our ecclesiology are we able to lay down within definable limits which rights[3] the episcopate as a whole, and hence the individual bishop, inalienably and irrevocably possesses; when the pope has undoubted right, immediately and in any given case, and without having to observe any judicial process, to intervene directly in any diocese and in any of its affairs, to appoint or to depose any bishop. Our question cannot be adequately answered by emphasizing that the pope can dispose of all these rights of the bishop, but that in fact he will never do so. It is not a question of the mere practical relations between the episcopate and the papal primacy, but of the basic legal relationship as such. Nor is it sufficient to point out that the pope naturally needs in his government of the universal Church some such local subordinates to whom he must grant a certain measure of authority, just as in an absolute monarchy or a radically totalitarian system, because without them he would simply be physically unable personally to carry on the government of the universal Church in all its detailed dispositions and arrangements.

Such a presentation of the case would imply that we were still considering the bishops as nothing more than functionaries, whose power was only a portion of the papal jurisdiction granted them by the pope. It cannot be denied that many Christians, judging more from the external appearance of the administrative

---

[3] Disregarding of course, the mere *"potestas ordinis"*.

practice of the Church than from dogmatic considerations, view the matter in this way. They regard the bishops as officials of the pope, the sole true ruler of the one Church, whose unity is conceived on the model of the modern state in which the only regions recognized are administrative districts. But that does not justify this view. I do not intend here and now to take up afresh the question why the appearance is false that the bishop is but the commissioned functionary of the pope, directing in the name and *ad nutum* of the pope a territorially limited administrative district, even though it is impossible to adduce a definite sum of rights reserved in every case to the bishop. For the fundamental answer to this problem the reader is referred to the first part of this book. Here I intend to supplement those considerations in certain respects.

2. Necessity and Precise Definition of the Question

First a comparison: a large part of the natural law of social behaviour will find its way, in a well ordered state, into the civil code and become positive law as well. But it is not to be expected *a priori* that the whole content of the natural law concerning social conduct, even obligations in justice, will expressly be defined in such a code of law. The same can be true in the Church. The divine right of the episcopate, which flows from the very essence of the Church, need not, for all that, already be expressed in its full development and with all desirable clarity in the explicit statements of our dogmatic theology about the Church, or in canon law. This right as a whole (despite possible individual abuses) is always present in the Church, of course, but as something which is lived. Nevertheless, it is not at all impossible that much which *de facto* happens in the relation, for example, between pope and bishops, is *ius divinum* though not explicitly recognized as such, and is therefore occasionally infringed, at least in individual cases, even given good will on both sides.

When we consult the average tract on ecclesiology for its doctrine on the *ius divinum* of the episcopate, which cannot be abolished even by the pope, we learn hardly anything beyond the fact that the episcopate is *iuris divini* and that the pope therefore cannot abolish it altogether. No doubt this is much too general an answer for us to take as an adequate and articulated account of the *ius divinum* of the episcopate, as if everything but the nominal existence of the bishops were therefore mere *ius humanum;* something which the pope could grant the bishops or withhold as he alone thought best; something normal to the Church only in certain exigencies of which the pope alone could definitively judge.

The existence of an episcopate without any definable essence would be absurd. If the episcopate exists of divine right, the episcopate must have an essence of divine right. Now this essence of divine right cannot reasonably be based on those powers alone which we refer to as the episcopal power of order. For if one be of the perfectly legitimate, though not certain, opinion that even a simple priest can at times, with the authorization of the pope, ordain priests; and if one share the view, by no means censurable even today, that the episcopate represents no new sacramental order superior to the priesthood,[4]

---

[4] This does not mean to imply that the author of this article shares this opinion. Quite the contrary. His conviction is that the Church, even as to *potestas ordinis,* can distribute the sacred powers present in her by the will of her Founder, in that measure which she finds appropriate at any

but is merely a hierarchical degree distinguished *iure divino* from the priesthood because of its powers of jurisdiction, then one can no longer specify what absolute difference there is, as to the power of order, between priest and bishop. Therefore the *ius divinum* which must be attributed to the essence of the episcopate and the existence of which is certain (and therefore cannot be made to depend on uncertain, conflicting opinions about the difference in the power of order between priest and bishop) must be sought also and above all in the power of jurisdiction. Even if, according to the common doctrine today, the bishop receives his power of jurisdiction from the pope, yet the power thus received is *iuris divini,* not a portion of the pope's own power delegated to the bishop. Rather, the pope, in appointing the individual bishop, gives him a share in the power of the whole episcopate *iuris divini* which was granted the Church by Christ. This the pope can and must impart to the individual bishop, but it does not follow that he could withhold it for

given time. The possibility of passing on "in doses" the powers inherent in a "perfect society" seems to the author to follow directly from the nature of such a society, even though we can point to no express declaration about it by the founder of this society. If therefore the Church today almost universally holds (which seems to be the case) that she gives the priest less *potestas ordinis* at his ordination than she does to the bishop at his consecration, (e. g. with respect to the consecration of bishops) then we can safely conclude that she does not *intend* to give the priest more *potestas ordinis*, and that, since she does not intend to, she does not do so. But since this question has not yet been settled among theologians, (and is probably still left open by the Apostolic Constitution of Pius XII, *"Sacramentum ordinis")*, the consideration above is justified as an *"argumentum ad hominem"* to show that the *ius divinum* of the episcopate cannot consist in the *potestas ordinis* alone – insofar as this thesis has to be defended at all against some imaginary opponent.

himself, (in which case, of course, the bishop would be a mere official of the pope).

But this only raises in more urgent fashion the problem of the content of this episcopal power of jurisdiction which belongs to the whole episcopate by divine right and which the pope cannot retain for himself. No doubt it must be possible to say more about this content than theological textbooks and canon law expressly state. Much (not all!) that bishops do as a matter of course and that is also permitted by the Holy See as a matter of course is not mere *de facto* custom, something the pope could as well withdraw from the bishops, or has to give them merely because an official must have certain permanent powers if he is not to be useless, but is *iuris divini,* even when not explicitly so conceived. This is not to say (as has already been emphasized above) that concrete, definitely fixed individual rights of an *individual* bishop as an individual must be *iuris divini* in such a way that the pope could not deprive the bishop of one of these particular rights. Such a claim would be of no practical use and would really be senseless, because it could only fortify, and provide some content for, the episcopal jurisdiction if the bishop were declared legally irremovable. But since this is impossible, any attempt to define the content of the *ius divinum* in the bishops' jurisdiction by listing inalienable particular rights is futile from the start.

Nevertheless this is not to say that, apart from its general origin, the *ius divinum* of the bishop is impossible to define. Though the attempt to fix the material limits of the rights of the papacy and the episcopate is not feasible for the reasons indicated above, and though we cannot ascertain a residue of particular episcopal jurisdictional rights which escape papal supremacy, nevertheless the inalienable episcopal *ius divinum* need not be thought void of any real content.

3. The ius divinum *of the whole Episcopate* *is the Material and Cognitive Ground of the* ius divinum *of Individual Bishops*

Its exact definition must proceed on the one hand from the nature of the universal Church, and on the other from the nature of the episcopate as a college (the successor of the apostolic college, which as a college takes precedence over the individual apostles and their powers, and is not merely the sum of the individual apostles and their powers).

The first point of departure is obvious: the nature of the Church is always the permanent foundation of the nature of her governmental powers, even though we cannot deduce, from any abstract concept of the nature of the Church alone, her exact juridical structure, which is at least in part an additional positive institution of Christ, so that an exact concept of the Church entails some knowledge of her juridical constitution, of the authorities that govern her, and of their rights and duties. Yet recourse to the theological nature of the Church which underlies her juridical structure is always advisable, even necessary, if one is seeking an accurate notion of her organs of government.

But the second approach mentioned above is the decisive one in our case. The answer to the problem of the *ius divinum* of the individual bishop lies in the *ius divinum* of the universal episcopate. To understand our point, we must remember that

337

the papal power over the individual bishop, even to the point of deposing him, cannot and may not, by a simple extension, be exercised over the universal episcopate; that, therefore, the pope's rights over the universal episcopate are not the mere sum of his rights over the individual bishops. Therefore the papal rights over the individual bishop must be exercised in such a way that the divine right of the universal episcopate as a college is not, in effect, abolished or its nature threatened. The fact that a particular limitation of a bishop's episcopal rights by the pope happens to be canonically and dogmatically legitimate in a particular case, does not at all imply that the same limitation can by divine right be imposed on the rights of the universal episcopate. Because the universal episcopate, as the apostolic college living on in history, has *qua* college inalienable rights and duties *iuris divini,* the pope is obliged to take care, lest some of his measures, legitimate when imposed on an individual bishop, infringe the original right of the universal episcopate – for example, if the sum total of such measures taken against many bishops should make the rights (and duties) of the universal episcopate illusory in practice, or reduce them to a dimension where they might survive in practice, but without any clear juridical status.

Even if it cannot be said that the pope has only those rights over individual bishops which he has over the universal episcopate as such, neither can one conversely conclude from the papal right over the individual bishop to the existence of that same right over the bishops as a whole. A simple example, obvious and familiar: the pope could remove a particular bishop and install an apostolic vicar or administrator, that is, a papal official, in his place. Nobody can conclude from this that he could do this with all the bishops at one time. This would amount to abolishing the episcopate itself, which the pope cannot do. One can even go so far as to say that the full participation of a bishop in the rights and duties of the universal episcopate is *de iure* to be presumed, so that the contrary, in the case of a particular bishop or a particular measure, must be proved, even though the burden of proof and the actual proof is left to the conscience of the pope, against whom the individual bishop has no legal recourse. Therefore, *iuris divini,* the rights of the universal episcopate can be taken from an individual bishop only to the extent which the concrete circumstances show to be lawful and equitable.

But with this the problem is not solved, only transferred. The problem of the content of any single bishop's divinely given jurisdictional power becomes the problem of the jurisdiction of the episcopate as a whole. And, according to the history of the Church, which, on the whole, may be taken as a guide to what is legitimate, the divine right of the episcopate is not (materially, at least) bound to any absolutely fixed form as its realization in the concrete. Then again, the episcopate is obviously the subject of these divine rights only insofar as it is unified in the bishop of Rome, that is, it is not really a subject of rights as a college *vis-à-vis* the pope, but in unity with him.

But subject to these presuppositions and qualifications, the question can and must be put whether and how the content of the episcopate's rights *iuris divini* can be more precisely defined. The problem is a difficult one, one that theology to date can hardly claim to have properly posed, much less adequately answered. Our attempt here to pose the question more accurately and (as far as possible) to answer it can only be modest and fragmentary.

*4. The Theological Nature of
the College of Apostles*

We shall take as our point of departure a principle which will not be disputed, that the episcopate as a whole is the successor of the apostolic college. An individual bishop is not the successor of an individual apostle. He is only in the line of succession from an apostle insofar as he belongs to the Church's episcopate, which in turn, as a body, succeeds the corporate apostolic college. Theology emphasizes this point in the process of giving a detailed definition of "apostolic succession", or when it asks why an individual bishop is not automatically infallible though he is a successor of the apostles to whom theology ascribes infallibility, primarily as a body but also in their individual capacity. It is of paramount importance firmly to grasp the point that the apostolic college as a genuine *corporate body* holds the authority in the Church; and that the apostles as individuals[5] did not first receive

---

[5] This need not exclude an apostle's having certain authority, powers, charismata, etc. as an "individual" as well. We cannot go into this point here. Suffice it to say, first of all, that the point made in the text does not exclude a grant of such personal powers and privileges through a positive disposition of Christ. Nor is it, secondly, at all unthinkable that because of the function of the college of apostles in the "Apostolic Church" (cf. *Inspiration in the Bible,* the first Study in this book, **pp. 43–49** in a specifically theological sense of the term referring to the Church's beginnings as decisive and normative for all future times, never subject to revision) extraordinary powers belonged also to the individual apostle as such (even though they belong to him because of his membership in this college as the college of the Apostolic Church). These powers were not passed on to later bishops as members of the governing body of the later Church. Thirdly, the notion of membership in a college does not exclude but rather includes (at least with certain colleges) the possibility of rights and duties of the individual members as such deriving from the

their distinct powers from Christ separately and then afterwards bind themselves together to form a college. The ontological and juridical relationship is the other way round: Jesus founds a college. In it the apostles have power[6] insofar and only insofar as they are members of this college and are acting as such. From any other point of view it is impossible to understand how Peter can appear from the beginning as head of the apostolic college. If each apostle were first of all an individually authorized representative of Christ, then no subordination of the apostles to Peter (or rather, no subordination of the individual apostles to a college with Peter at its head) would ever be possible. The individual apostle would then have immediately from Christ an authority of such a kind that he would not possess it *qua* member of the college. He could not be held accountable to Peter or to the college, but only to Christ, the direct source of his authority.

Once again we are faced with the dilemma which in the case of the relationship between the primacy and the episcopate can

college, though the primary and basic function of a member of the college can only be exercised in an act of the whole body. A member of parliament can, for example, only legislate validly insofar as parliament itself (and he in it) legislates. But his function as a member of such a body may imply a right which he as an individual enjoys, his immunity, for example. In this sense it is possible that powers and rights of individual apostles as such did flow from their membership in the collegiate body of apostles which they could exercise as individuals, and which rights later passed to individual bishops, because and if they did not arise solely from the situation of the Church being the Apostolic Church. But even those rights and powers belonging to the apostles as individuals must have flowed ultimately from their membership in the college of apostles as such.

[6] The power meant here is the basic power that makes an apostle an apostle.

be resolved only by recognizing the college as such to be the prior entity, not subseqently composed of individuals already possessed of their own authority before entering the college; and that the primacy of the pope is a primacy *within* and not *vis-à-vis* this college. If the apostles had their authority first of all as individuals, they could hold this authority only by a mandate which Christ had given to them as individuals, or by a mandate from Peter. In the first case, they would no longer be subject to Peter; in the second, they would be apostles of Peter, not of Christ.[7] Only if Christ founds a college which as such has an authoritative head and yet as such possesses real power deriving from himself, so that from the outset Peter can never be thought of without the other apostles, nor the college without Peter, is an apostle really an apostle of Christ, come of Christ and of Christ's own mission. And yet he is such an apostle only within the college and consequently under Peter, because this college, according to Scripture once again, was set up by Christ with one part subordinate to the other. It did not autonomously choose this structure for itself. Such a procedure would only be conceivable if the apostles had each his own authority as an individual, whether from Christ or from the Church. But at best this would give the apostles as a college an

---

[7] To say that Christ bestows on each individual apostle his authority, but with the command to use it (under pain of invalidating his act) in subordination to Peter, is objectively correct. But this only circumvents the problem instead of answering it. How can a person be given an authority which is completely at the disposal of a third person, without this authority thereby being a delegated authority originally vested in this third person? However positive the institution of a right may be, the logic and facts of the case simply do not permit just any "combination". Rights cannot be granted and taken away at the same time.

organization that could be altered at will, and it would then be open to question *why* the individual apostles had to unite in a college at all.

To approach the problem from another angle: *non enim plura secundum se uniuntur*. A real unity is prior to its parts, not made up out of them as parts. If the individual apostles together founded a college according to their own notions, then it would be dependent on their will, and the individuals could not be dependent on Peter *iuris divini*. Or if unity originated with Peter as its proper and active cause (not only its representative, who realizes in the life of the Church the unity which already exists), then *he* would be affiliating a college to himself to be *his* agent, and its members would receive a power dependent upon him. (This is quite a different thing from having no power except insofar as they remain dependent on him; in the first case Peter would be the source of power, in the second he is the prerequisite for its lawful possession and exercise.) They would be his functionaries, entrusted with that portion of his own power which he thought fit to give them. As both these hypotheses break down, our only recourse is to conclude that what Christ founded was precisely a college from the outset, in which the individual apostle has an authority he derives from Christ because Christ endowed the college as such with its authority, and that Peter has his unique authority insofar as he is constituted head of this college from the outset.

Another indication that the apostles, in the thought of Jesus, were to be a college from the beginning is their function of tangibly representing the unity of the New Israel, mystically composed of twelve tribes. There is, accordingly, no mention in the New Testament of functions belonging to one apostle rather

343

than another, such as the administration of a particular territory (the *"divisio apostolorum"* is a typically late and apocryphal piece). Wherever the apostles appear on the scene after Pentecost it is always as a collegiate body.[7a] Where individual apostles (even Peter) emerge from the college and come into view they act by commission of the college; wherever they go, they go as representatives of the college (*e.g.,* Samaria). This permits us to say without hesitation: Peter is Peter, insofar as he is head of this college, *i. e.,* he has his position in the Church as vicar of the master of the household to the extent that he is head of the apostolic college. This does not mean, of course, that he is democratically commissioned from below to represent the college, as though the organization already had the full legal capacity to act, and then, for practical reasons, chose to act through a single head. The apostolic college itself exists inasmuch as and because it possesses its head, and this head is appointed by Christ. But equally the head is furnished with his powers by Christ insofar as he is appointed head. Ontologically and juridically, then, the apostolic college with Peter at its head forms one entity. The college cannot exist without Peter, nor he without it. One could say that Peter is the divinely ordained head of the Church insofar as he is head of the apostolic college, which he rules while ruling the Church with it. "With it", not "through it". Here again, without having made much progress, we meet the basic logical and juridical problem in the Church's constitution. She is ruled by a *college,* without its head thereby becoming the mere elected representative of the college; the head truly

---

[7a] Acts 15; Gal. 2:1–10; Acts 1:13 ff.; 2:42; 4:33; 5:2; 5:12; 5:18, 29, 40; 6:2; 8:1, 14; 9:27; 11:1; 15:6, 22, 23.

rules the college, without the college thereby becoming his mere executive organ.

This relationship is undoubtedly one which cannot be adequately reduced to legal terms. No axiomatic juridical principle can be laid down capable of materially governing the relationship between Peter and the other apostles once and for all, and of marking off their respective spheres of competence.[8] Such a state of affairs, which would, in the long run, prove the undoing of any secular body, flows from that unique relationship between whole and part peculiar to the Church.[9] It has proved juridically durable in the course of history because an absolute conflict between these two mutually restrictive elements of the Church's governing body, or a complete elimination of one by the other, is prevented by a supra–juridical authority, the assistance of the Holy Ghost.

The structure of the Church rests essentially on something

---

[8] The difficulty arises from the fact that we have a real ecclesiastical entity on each side only in so far as both sides are united to make up the one apostolic college under Peter, and that nonetheless, we can always wonder how the two are juridically related "to one another", because both Peter and the other apostles are real persons, free agents with their own ideas, who act upon one another. But precisely this right to reciprocal activity, which does exist, must be derived from the nature of their unity among one another. It is not something which the two parts have independently of and prior to this unity. In a purely physical structure there is no difficulty in understanding that the norm of one part's "activity" is the function it has in the whole. It is when this "part" is a conscious, free, responsible person, that we find it hard to grasp this clearly. From the unity of the personal agent, we almost automatically conclude to a "right" he has independent of and prior to the collegiate unity, and which thus governs his relationship to the college.

[9] Cf. above, pp. 312f.

supra-institutional, on the Nomos of the Spirit, which cannot and will not adequately be translated into institutional terms.[10] Yet this very fact makes it possible to ascertain more precisely the content of the authority of the whole apostolic college, and thus of the individual apostles. The college rules the Church. But this means that the apostles' function in the universal Church is an active one. They are not merely executive agents of Peter, doing his will. Precisely because within the college each apostle actively co-governs the universal Church as such, it is *a priori* impossible for any sphere to be reserved to him alone, whether territorially, materially or departmentally, beyond the governmental reach of the apostolic college or of Peter. But for this reason also each individual apostle has an active function of his own which originates with him and the exercise of which he cannot give up. How he brings this activity into operation in such a manner that (explicitly or implicitly) it becomes the activity of the whole college and thereby legitimate in the eyes of the Church, is not something to be regulated by canons, but is left to the apostle's own judgment, even with respect to its harmony with the activity of Peter and the other apostles. He knows, as it were, only two things: that he is obliged to be constantly active, exercising an initiative and responsibility which cannot be transferred to others or deduced from directives of theirs; and that the Holy Spirit, not some fixed rule setting limits to his competence, will see to it that this responsible initiative, which is both his right and his duty, will have the abiding influence

[10] This has its analogy in profane matters. No set of positive propositions for instance, can adequately express the natural law or replace and render superfluous formal principles such as equity, which can never be translated completely into the form of propositions.

346

and effect which the situation requires, at least on the whole and in the long run.

Such initiative can, from the nature of the college and its authority as both a unity and a composite thing, take either of two forms. Either an apostle tries to win the college for his line of action (though there is no legal procedure available to him for this purpose, since such a thing would destroy the supra-legal unity of the college and the full juridical power of its head) or he may represent the college where, so far as practical activity is concerned, it is not physically present but can be so.

The initiative of the individual apostle in regard to the college (without which a college as an acting body is unthinkable, since it can really act only in and through physical persons) implies in the other members a duty to listen, a basic readiness to remain open to such initiative. On the one hand, it is more fitting to qualify this duty as moral rather than legal, because the original subject of rights in the Church is the college as a whole, and so this duty has no corresponding concrete person to judge of its neglect or fulfilment, distinct from the body itself which owes this duty. On the other hand, this duty is legal insofar as it is an element necessarily implied in the rights each apostle has as an active member of the college. Nor is this duty limited depart-mentally, insofar as it signifies active participation in the authority of the one ruling college in the Church. Each apostle is (always within the college) competent in the entire government of the whole Church. He bears the whole burden together with Peter, he concerns himself with the whole Church in all her labours and necessities. Such authority may, of course, have a local objective. Peter and John travel to Samaria as represent-atives of the whole college, as Acts 8, 14 explicitly attests. Such a conception is quite unobjectionable from the point of view of the Church's teaching concerning the position of Peter. The apostolic college is not a body above Peter, it is itself only with him as its active head. In this capacity it commissions Peter to go to Samaria. Peter's whole function is to be head of the college – Peter, the keeper of the keys. His function is not territorial or departmental. He is not pope because he receives some commission from the apostolic college to work in Samaria or in Rome, but because he, with the college and as its head, commissions others and so also himself with a special function – as giving the special function, not receiving it. All these primatial rights are rights of the head of the college as such. They are based on the existence of the college, not as though given by the college conceived as a pre-existing thing capable of its own activity (to stress our point once again), but as rights which would cease really to exist unless the college existed in its entirety, acting as a unit with Peter, and founded as such by Christ. Hence it is most significant and altogether appropriate that the apostles act as a college, and do not postpone the realization of their apostolic character until (as later legends have it) they come to divide the world among themselves. They had no need to be predecessors of the bishops as rulers of the Church in certain restricted territories, nor were they such.

5. The College of Bishops as Successor of the Apostolic College

With this in mind, then, let us investigate more closely the thesis that the episcopate is the successor of the apostolic college.

348

a) Priority of the College of Bishops over the Individual Bishops

The college of bishops, as successsor of the apostolic college, takes priority over the individual bishops, their rights and responsibilities. The college of bishops is neither a logical sum of the individual bishops in the mind of some external observer, nor is it their subsequent incorporation, effected either by the bishops themselves or by the pope. The bishops' college is the primary entity, successor to the apostolic college, having in the pope its pre-ordained head, without whom it cannot be conceived, as the head of which alone the pope can be pope.

This follows first of all from the truth that the Church (even as visibly constituted) is primarily *one* (although, while one, she contains a basic pluralism in the differentiation of her members). And she is one, not merely through the activity of the individual faithful or individual churches (to which the nature of the Church is prior), as though these had created her unity by forming themselves into an association, but because she was originally founded as one and always so exists. And this holds even in the social and juridical order, because without such an order the Church does not exist. But if unity is prior and primordial, then the college of bishops is prior to the individual bishops, unless this unity is to be manifested only in the pope, which cannot be true because then the episcopate would not be of divine right.

That the primary unity of the episcopate takes precedence over the individual bishops and their power follows also from the fact that the episcopate succeeds the apostolic college, which, as a unity, ranks before the plurality of the individual apostles, as we have shown.

Our contention can also be clarified by another consideration. According to the CJC a council has supreme authority in the

Church. This principle must be *iuris divini,* for if it were human law in the Church, it would mean a legal curtailment of the divine right of the pope (of whom the same thing is said) and/or imply a concession on the pope's part. But neither can be correct, for the pope cannot relinquish the rights he has *iure divino,* and one could not say that a council had supreme authority in the Church, if it had this authority from the pope and therefore subject to revocation.

But if the council, being summoned by the pope, were nothing more than the purely conceptual sum of the individual bishops as such, then a council could never be termed the highest and sovereign subject of power in the Church. For the individual bishops as such cannot have this plenitude of power. The aggregation of individual bishops as such could not deprive the individual bishop of his own proper power, since it cannot curtail the power of those individuals by whose free decision, *ex supposito,* it has its very existence. The council as such, then, could have a sovereign power over the individual bishop, if at all, only in and through the power of the pope. But then, once more, the council could only be conceived as an organ of the pope. Its power would be, at best, part of the pope's power as such, since he, in delegating it, chooses to share it with the council; or else the council would be only the auxiliary and advisory organ of the pope. But by no means could one say that the council had supreme power in the Church. The council could not have such a supreme power if the pope not only called it and presided over it,[11] but also had to constitute it a subject of this power which

[11] This does not contradict the supreme power of the council, because that which here assembles in council, the episcopal college which always had this supreme power, has the pope as its summit.

previously did not exist. Then this subject could only be the subject of that power which the pope gives as his own. It would then be the subject of a power comprehended, supported and conditioned by the power of the pope insofar as he is distinct from the council and deals with it as such. A power of this description could hardly be called supreme.

We remain caught in this dilemma as long as we fail to realize that the college of bishops always exists as such in the Church and does not first come into being when the bishops gather in council, and that the college of bishops as such is always the subject of the *suprema potestas in Ecclesia,* even though this *potestas in Ecclesia* has remained, as it were, on a para-canonical level so far as our present canon law is concerned. Such a conception does not restrict or threaten the papal primacy, since the college of bishops always includes the pope as its head, without which it could not exist at all. It is the council itself that acts when the pope acts, by reason of his supreme jurisdiction, because the pope, precisely when he acts *ex sese,* acts not as a private person but as pope, that is, as head of a college of bishops *iuris divini.* In other words, in the canonical conception of the nature of the council as subject of the supreme power in the Church, the same thing is implicitly declared to be true of the college of bishops.[12] This leads, however, to the conclusion that the college of bishops, as such, exists as the supreme subject of governmental power in

[12] This is stated quite explicitly, by the way, in the doctrine on the *ordinary* magisterium of the college of bishops, for this magisterium of the episcopate as a whole possesses, according to the explicit teaching of all ecclesiologists, the same teaching authority as the extraordinary magisterium of a council. Only the manner of its exercise is different, but not its subject, competence or binding force.

the universal Church prior to the individual bishop as such. The individual bishop is primarily a member of the universal episcopate as the collegiate[13] ruling body of the Church, which *iure divino* finds in the pope its permanent unity and the possibility of lasting concrete activity.

b) Possible Objections

Against the proposed thesis the objection could be raised that the bishops were from the very beginning so much governors of territorially delimited communities that for this reason alone it seems improbable that they were originally conceived as a college, and that thus their college could have been the successor of the apostolic college. In other words, since the bishops did not first appear as a college, they cannot have been intended to form a college in succession to the apostolic college. And this function cannot, therefore, have been their primary one.

This objection, it must be pointed out first of all, is not directed against our thesis alone as proposed above, but against the general Catholic teaching that the bishops are the successors of the apostles. We can dispense, therefore, with a detailed rebuttal of the objection, recalling only what every ecclesiology has to say about the bishops as successors of the apostles. It

---

[13] The term "collegiate" does not, of course, in any way imply that the pope is only a *primus inter pares,* who elect him as an official of theirs. But it does mean that the subject of the supreme power in the Church is composed of many physical persons. If this were fundamentally impossible, then it would be equally impossible and false for the council to be the subject of supreme power in the Church. This latter, however, is not false, but true. And therefore it is true that the Church has, in the episcopate as a whole a collegiate "summit". This does not exclude the college itself having a personal summit in the pope.

suffices here to point out that from the beginning of the second century we find everywhere in the Church the monarchical episcopate, and the idea that these bishops derive their office and their authority "in apostolic succession" from the apostles. Or, to look at the question another way, if Christ's community was to be governed, according to his will, by the apostolic college united under Peter, if the Church was to last until the end of time, then this apostolic college *must* have a successor. But there is no institution to be seen in the ancient Church which could even lay claim to such a succession except the episcopal body. This succession must then be found in them.

The fact that this same argument is used for the successors of Peter is another sign of its pertinence for understanding the Catholic Church. While today there are a good many Protestant exegetes who admit a primacy of some sort during the lifetime of Peter, but deny that this institution must in principle have continued on in the Church even after the death (or departure) of Peter (from Jerusalem), Catholic ecclesiology is firmly convinced that (even without an explicit testimony from the lips of Jesus) the function of Peter must have continued in the Church. But then the same must be said of the apostolic college. But then this college as such must continue, and since one cannot seriously maintain that the individual apostle had an official, regular function in the Church independent of, and prior to, his membership in the college of the Twelve, there must be a permanent successor in the Church for this college. But this implies not only the general thesis about the bishops as the successors of the apostles, but also the more precise interpretation which we have given to this doctrine. Even at the risk of displaying his ignorance the author must say that he knows of no work in recent literature which systematically treats the question of the exact relation between the territorially limited power of the individual bishop, and his membership in the episcopal college. The only exception known to me is a contribution from Spain, by Bernardo Monsegú.[14]

A detailed theological discussion of this article is not possible here. We should like only to make one point. Insofar as this work (the title of which poses the very problem we have treated here, and which does attempt its treatment), comes to a negative conclusion which contradicts the view we propose, it strikes us as unsound. It tacitly assumes that the co-optation of an individual into the episcopal college by the pope is impossible. Thus when the pope, according to the common teaching today, bestows the episcopal power on an individual bishop (as the cause and not merely the condition of the episcopal powers), then this could only be understood to mean that the primary, indeed only, object of the papal act was the bestowal of the territorially limited episcopal powers as such, and that membership in the episcopal college was a purely secondary consequence of his installation as ruler of a diocese.

But why should the head of a college not have the power to receive someone into that college? And why could the primary object of the installation of a bishop, its ultimate theological signification, not be such a co-optation into the college? It makes no difference that this act is usually described by its effect on the territorially limited episcopal powers. If the two things (mem-

[14] B. Monsegú, "Los obispos ¿on sucesores de los Apóstoles directos inmediatamente como miembros del colegio, o más bien en cuanto personalmente consagrados o investidos de su oficio? XVI *Semana Española de Teología* (Sept. 17–22, 1956), (Madrid, 1957), p. 217–247.

bership in the episcopal college and the territorially limited episcopal office) are necessarily connected — at least according to present canon law and in the cases we here have in mind — then one can describe or designate the whole act according to either aspect. The mere fact that the territorial and not the collegiate aspect of the whole act of investiture occupies the foreground in the average canonical, religious and theological consciousness is no unequivocal indication of how these two things are objectively related to one another.[15]

We have so far always had in mind, in this whole question, "the normal bishop", that is, one who not only possesses the power of order through episcopal consecration, but also the power of jurisdiction over a certain diocese. This is the type we have studied, and considered as a member of the college of bishops. But there are others possessed of episcopal orders (because of the validity of their episcopal consecration) who, as heretics and schismatics, are not, according to the teaching of the Church, members of the Church (in the full sense); still less, then, can they be members of the college of bishops, the Catholic Church's supreme governing body. This being so, it is clear, on the one hand, that we have been correct up to now in looking on the power of jurisdiction over a part of the Catholic Church, in the full sense of "Catholic Church", as a condition, a sign, a part, and a consequence of membership in the college of bishops.

---

[15] We have the same kind of discrepancy between objective order and subjective emphasis in relation to two such elements, in the question whether the bishop of Rome is primarily bishop of Rome and therefore pope, or first pope and in addition also bishop of Rome, (even granting in the second case that the office of bishop is a condition and sign of possessing the primatial power in the whole Church).

But there remains, on the other hand, the question whether those Catholic bishops who are within the body of the Church but who do not rule any diocese of their own, are to be considered members of the college of bishops (that is, the college of bishops in the theological sense, as the supreme ruling body in the Church, not as the sum total of "bishops"). These bishops certainly cannot be regarded in the same way as those who through heresy or schism are separated from the one Church of Peter, because they are certainly full members of the Church. Yet they are hardly members of the college of bishops in the same sense as the *ordinarii loci*.

Membership of the supreme governing body of the Church entails the primary consequence that the apostles send one to "Samaria", that is, as a member of the supreme body there, to represent it by undertaking responsibility for a particular territory. And this definitely cannot be said of an auxiliary bishop. On the other hand, it follows from our considerations that it is not in principle impossible to belong to a college without having any authority or rôle to play apart from the college's own. This holds good in the case of the Church. One can certainly belong to the supreme governing body of the Church without possessing jurisdiction over any particular territory. There are ordinaries, in episcopal orders and otherwise, whose jurisdiction is personal. The question is thus not easy to answer. Perhaps we can say for the present that such bishops belong to the episcopal college by reason of their power of order – provided that we do not envisage this power as purely individualistic, but see it instead as part of the one episcopal power the proper subject of which is precisely the college of bishops under the pope. This can be done even if one grants that, because of the validity of

356

their sacraments, there are real bishops outside the Church (a point we cannot go into here). Besides, it is not *a priori* impossible that the Church considers auxiliary bishops to be members of the college on the grounds of some function beyond the mere power of order, even though they are able to exercise that function only within the college as such and in respect of the college. *If* the Church can call an auxiliary bishop to a general council as a voting member — something which she can do, and which she provides for[16] — then it is not inconceivable that she tacitly regards an auxiliary bishop as a co-governing member of the college even outside a council; and this even though she does not entrust to him, on the grounds of this function in the college, a special function of his own, as she normally does in making a man a local ordinary.

c) The Subject(s) of Infallible Teaching Authority

The knowledgeable reader has probably noticed before now that our remarks about the relation between pope and episcopate touch upon a matter which is treated in ecclesiology as the question whether there are *two* inadequately distinct subjects of the magisterium in the Church, that is, the pope himself and the council under the pope, or only one, that is, the pope, so that he alone is the subject of active infallibility directly supported by the divine assistance, the council being only indirectly a subject of active infallibility insofar as the bishops in council, concurring with the pope, participate in the papal infallibility. This question, as is well known, is still controverted among theologians, and was expressly left open at the First Vatican

[16] Cf. J. Hamer, "Note sur la collégialité épiscopale", *Revue des Sciences Philosophiques et Théologiques* 44 (1960), p. 40–50.

Council (when, however, a "papal" theologian of the stature of Gasser considered the papal view "regrettable"[16a]). What we have been trying to say up to now can perhaps be clarified if we briefly relate it to this controversy.

First of all, it is remarkable that this controversy is only discussed under the heading of conciliar and papal infallibility. It is easy enough to see, however, that the basic question here is that of the general relation of the episcopal college to the pope, with all its rights and powers. The basic question underlying this controversy should be discussed and settled under the heading of the Church's fundamental constitution. One society can contain only one supreme authority; a double supreme authority seems a metaphysical absurdity from the outset (even with the qualification that these "two" powers are only inadequately distinct). Two supreme powers (powers, that is, from which there is no appeal to a higher court in this world), if they are really two, can only rule two distinct bodies. The two may be associated, but never really united, without the dual sovereignty ceasing to exist. When one considers as well the certain fact that in the Church only the supreme governing power (which includes the magisterium) can enjoy infallibility, and further, that a mediate, derivative and yet active infallibility, for this and other reasons (as Gasser too emphasized) amounts to a contradiction in terms, one is led to the inescapable conclusion that the papal theory, in insisting that there can be only one infallible authority in the Church, is quite correct. It has, as Salaverri[17] stresses, the "speculative" arguments on its side. It

[16a] Mansi 52, 1216.
[17] Patres S. J. Facultatum theologicarum in Hispania professores, *Sacrae Theologiae Summa I*[4] (Madrid, 1958), p. 713, n. 640.

is impossible to speak of two infallibilities and therefore of two supreme teaching authorities and consequently of two supreme subjects of power in the Church. Whether one likes it or not, this would amount to denying the real unity of the Church, or to recognizing in one of the powers a merely nominal supremacy.

But at the same time we know from positive sources that the council too has an active infallibility, that in Council the bishops together with the pope are *judges* in matters of faith and not simply advisers to the pope or merely the first to express their assent to a papal decision which the pope has reached independently, something which would not transcend the "hearing" or passive infallibility possessed by all members of the hearing Church. Past councils, it must be admitted, never considered themselves to be mere sounding boards or "amplifiers" for papal infallibility. It would be absurd to envisage the early councils thus and no less absurd in the case of the later ones, even where no more doubts existed about the supreme papal primacy of jurisdiction and so about the pope's supreme magisterium. Many theologians,[18] even to the present day, point out that the promise of Christ to the apostolic college seems to signify an *immediate* divine assistance for the apostolic college as such,[18a] so that this apostolic college must be infallible directly, not "derivatively" from Peter. But if the pope (according to the promise to Peter) and the episcopal college as such (as united, of course, under its petrine head) are both infallible through immediate divine

---

[18] Cf. J. Salaverri, *Sacrae Theol. Summa* I , p. 713 ff., n. 641 ff. (and p. 686 ff., n. 561 ff.).

[18a] Matt. 18:18; 28:18–20; Mark 16:15; John 14:16; 17:26; 20:21; cf. Matt. 10:40; Luke 10:16.

assistance, then do we not after all have two supreme authorities in the Church, even if they are stated to be only inadequately distinct? It is precisely this dualism that is impossible. The dilemma seems inescapable. No wonder there has been no agreement on this question to this day.

The question to ask at this point is the following: Is the tacit assumption made by both sides correct, the assumption that the infallibility of the pope when he defines "alone" is in no way also the infallibility of the college of bishops? Grant the assumption, and either the pope alone must possess the immediate active infallibility (if there can be only one in the Church) or, if the council is also immediately infallible, then there must actually be two subjects of the infallible teaching authority, since the pope is also infallible "without" the council or the episcopal college. But the question is: Can the dilemma be judiciously avoided altogether by conceiving only one subject of supreme power from the start — the college of bishops united under the pope as its head, so that an act of the pope "alone" and an act of the council are only different forms and modes of the activity of this one subject of supreme ecclesiastical authority, but need not be derived from two different subjects? It is generally conceded that in the act of a council, and that as such, the act of the pope is always included. The terminology which speaks of papal "approbation" of conciliar decrees is to this extent unfortunate. This "approbation" is, after all, an intrinsic element of the conciliar decree itself, not the adventitious decree of a different authority, conceived as a check on the college, supervening from without as a condition for the validity of a decree, already fully constituted, of the council as a subject apart. The "approbation" is rather to be conceived as a constitutive element of the college itself. But can we say conversely that the episcopal college with its authority and its act (if not formally as concentrated in council) is included in the pope, in his authority and his act, so that when the pope acts "alone" he still acts *as* head of the episcopal college, and his act is also the act of the college?

If this question may be answered in the affirmative, then it is clear without more ado that there is only *one* subject of infallibility in the Church and that nevertheless the council as such possesses an immediate active infallibility. That has been our answer, and therefore we feel we have superseded the controversy. Of course this thesis of a mutual rather than unilateral inclusion of papacy and fully constituted episcopal college would need to be established more in detail than we have done here. But it is clear that, fundamentally and quite in general, it does not involve any contradiction for an individual physical person to posit the act of a collegiate moral person without the other physical members' being required to posit the act physically with him. It is also clear that such a possibility is not limited to the case where the members of the college delegate this person to act in the name of the college. The appointment of a physical person to represent a legal person can be conceived as happening in the most various ways (by God, by the nature of the case, etc.). It can quite definitely be conceived in such a way that the body represented cannot itself reject the appointment (consider, for example, Adam's representation of the human race, in many interpretations of original sin). Such a representation of the college by an individual physical person, effected by a third party and not subject to repudiation by the college, can, in its precise content and powers and without its act ceasing to be an act of the college, be such that in a very real sense one could call this act the act of this physical person "alone", if only because the college cannot annul it. Such an interpretation of the word "alone" does ample justice to the Vatican Council's *"ex sese"* and *"non ex consensu"* of the Church. We have already shown that actually such a papal act occurs as the act of the episcopal college in more than a legalistic sense, that actually (without prejudice to the primatial rights of the papacy as defined by the Vatican Council) the papal act always expresses the reality and initiative of the episcopate in a variety of ways, even though the two parties are not two different juridical entities in the sense that the episcopate as a separate juridical entity could take legal proceedings against the pope in defence of its rights. The fact that these two concepts mutually include each other does not of course mean that they are related to each other in exactly the same way.

When therefore the pope defines sometimes "alone" and sometimes together with the council, it is not a question of two acts of different subjects, but of two different procedures of one and the same subject, which differ only in the circumstance that in the one case the one moral subject is "dispersed throughout the world", and in the other is assembled in one place, where the co-operation and fraternity of the members of the college with the head is more clearly manifested. For a better grasp of this point it will be well to reconsider the "ordinary magisterium". It too has only one subject, the unit comprised by the college with the pope as its head; it can also act when "dispersed" over the earth. Its activity too can assume concrete form in a special act of the pope, so that the question has arisen whether and in what circumstances such a papal act (though not a solemn definition) possesses the infallibility proper to the "ordinary magisterium".[19]

The relationship between the function of the pope (Peter) as head of the episcopal (apostolic) college, and the powers ascribed to him as head of the Church by the Vatican Council (universal, supreme, episcopal, immediate, sovereign power over the whole Church and each of her parts) would require, of course, a more thorough treatment than this short essay can provide. We can only contribute a few observations to the subject. The proposition that the pope is pope insofar as he is head of the episcopal college, is, first of all, certainly correct, at least in the sense that, on the one hand, this episcopal college, although (because) *iuris divini,* cannot be conceived without the pope as its head and, on the other hand, the pope would not be pope of this concrete Church as *de facto* founded by Christ if the episcopal college did not exist or if the pope did not recognize it as such. It is also clear and beyond dispute that *if* the pope possesses his universal powers for the whole Church *qua* head of the episcopal college, he has this power from God and not from that college, and that therefore even in the supposition aforesaid, the actual competence of the pope as head of the episcopal college and so the concrete nature of his "presidency" in the college (which the above mentioned papal powers over the whole Church include) is *iuris divini,* given to him by Christ in Peter. The question is therefore only whether the conditional proposition suggested above corresponds to a reality

---

[19] J. Salaverri (*Sacrae Theol. Summa* I⁴, p. 714 ff., n. 645–648). We cannot enter into this question, though it too would show that to assume two different subjects of the ordinary or extraordinary magisterium would always lead to a dilemma.

or not. Which means: Is the relationship between the two papal functions to be understood formally as one of mutual inclusion (though, of course, only by divine positive institution) so that it is in the strictest of senses true to say: The pope is pope (supreme and immediate pastor of the whole Church) precisely *insofar* as he is head of the college of bishops; or do these two functions only by way of addition make up the full power of the pope? Is it only true that his position as supreme pastor over the Church implies his position in the episcopal college, or is the reverse also true?

Obviously the scope for serious dispute has been very much reduced. It seems to us that the remaining problem can be solved by assuming a reciprocal inclusion or mutual implication of both sides of the papal power (as we have, more or less, implicitly done in the preceding discussion). The reason is the following. If there were two wholly different powers ("adequately distinct", even if indissolubly bound together), then the pope would have to possess his (supreme, unrestricted) jurisdiction over the whole Church precisely in the same way[20] over the bishops as over other officials in the Church, or his jurisdictional primacy could not be called simply unrestricted.[21] The former is not true, because the primacy of jurisdiction is restricted by the *ius divinum* of the episcopacy, whose powers are not a participation in the papal power. The latter cannot be true, because this

[20] Please note this qualification. The pope obviously has powers of jurisdiction over the bishops.
[21] Of course this power is restricted in many respects, as is any power granted to a human being. The question is only whether or not it is limited in its own dimension and in its own nature by another *legal* authority adequately distinct from it. If not, then it is "unrestricted".

potestas is called *"plena"*. This is the dilemma one confronts in conceiving the two papal powers as adequately distinct. The one power is limited from outside by the "restrictedness" of the other[22] and can no longer be called "full", unlimited. But if the two papal powers are considered from the very beginning as two aspects of one and the same power, or as two concepts that formally include each other (as they are intended and exist in the present order of things), then the difficulty disappears. The pope's full jurisdiction over the whole Church and over all her members is precisely what is meant by "head of the college of bishops"[23] translated into concrete terms. And because this power is intrinsically implied in the concept of "being head of the college of bishops", it is not really limited through that inner "restrictedness" or, better, precise determination involved in the function of being head of the college of bishops.

[22] That is, by the "restrictedness" which, given a college, comes from the very nature of its function and therefore, in itself and in relation to this function, cannot really be called a restrictedness. Cf. footnote 2. But such a "restricted" function can quite definitely imply a genuine restriction for another power, if this other power is distinct from it and not intrinsically limited in the manner of the former.

[23] "Head of the episcopal college", that is, as found in the concrete order of things. The actual papal powers cannot, of course, be deduced from the abstract formal concept of "head of a society's ruling college" alone. To show whence and how these actual powers become recognized as such (Peter as the rock of the Church, as keeper of the keys, as "support of his brethren", as shepherd of the whole flock) in the context of the whole concrete historical evolution of the Church's understanding of herself, is not our task here. Here we have only to show how the two papal powers can be recognized as mutually inclusive. And this knowledge can be got otherwise than by deducing the one power from the abstract concept of the other. We can arrive at this knowledge even if no such deduction is possible.

THE EPISCOPATE AND THE PRIMACY

By this brief sketch of one argument, we do not suggest that no other arguments (perhaps more essential and pertinent) exist in favour of our view. But the above must suffice for the present.

d) "Para-Canonical" Influence of the Episcopate

Although (and because) what we have said under (a) is valid, we must be careful not to demand as a condition for the truth of our thesis, that there must be systematic, written legislation according to which the permanent co-operation of the whole episcopate in the government of the Church ought to be effected. There is no need for this simply because such legislation, the observance of which would be enforceable, would, if considered necessary, again presuppose that there could be a separate authority to control the conduct of individual bishops or the whole college, distinct from the pope or the college, and compatible with their rights and duties. Or it would presuppose that the individual persons who make up the college were vested with sovereign rights and duties outside and independently of the college, or that the college of bishops were, independent of the pope, a college with rights and powers, which could sit in judgment on the manner in which the pope respected these rights.[24] On the other hand, it would be an error to think that the whole episcopate as a college does not *de facto* rule the Church because there are no (or almost no) regulations in canon law

---

[24] We must also clearly note that for the same reason there are no material legal norms in canon law (cn. 218–221) which would really regulate the functions of the pope as such, except for the general formal norm that he has supreme authority in the Church and is subject to no other authority on earth.

according to which this government might be conducted. For first of all, if what we have said about the relation of the pope to the episcopal college is true, that is, that he is, in the first place, pope *insofar* as he is head of the college, then the college rules in the pope. (Anyone who feels that this is a subterfuge only shows that he has not grasped the basic unity of the bishops hierarchically united in the pope, outside of which unity neither pope nor college of bishops can formally exist as such.)

We should add that there are a thousand ways and means (which have always been efficacious) for the individual bishops in the college of bishops to influence the college itself and the pope, and thereby the government of the whole Church. It has never been true, not only because it is physically and psychologically impossible but also because it cannot lawfully be so, that the pope so rules the Church that impulses, directives and creative ideas only descend from the head, who in turn is inspired only by God. This is false, not only because of the "charismatic" structure of the Church, in virtue of which the charismatic impulses, as Pius XII explicitly stressed, originate at points freely chosen by the sovereign grace of God, and relatively seldom with the pope himself.[25]

Even within the hierarchical structure of the Church there is a constant give and take between pope and bishops. Never has a pope based any doctrinal judgment, preliminary or definitive, solely upon the teachings of earlier popes. The one solemn definition pronounced by a pope since the Vatican Council followed only after consultation with the entire episcopate. The permanent contact of the primacy with the universal episcopate,

[25] Cf. K. Rahner, *The Dynamic Element in the Church,* pp. 48–58.

though canonically it appears to have been established so that the pope can govern the individual bishops, also provides for the constant co-operation of the universal episcopate in the government of the Church, by example, suggestions, complaints, petitions, etc. – direct influence on the centre of the Church, and for indirect influence through the initiative of the individual bishop in his own diocese.

Though this influence "from below", from periphery to centre, may be acceptable to the pope and affect his government only on "moral" grounds (reason, fairness, sympathy, charity, forebearance, consideration for particular wishes and peculiarities, etc.), yet in such forms and ways the para-canonical but truly abiding right of the universal episcopate to rule the Church with and under the pope, is brought to bear. This right (and duty) is not the mere sum of the rights of the individual bishops in their own dioceses, though it may be realized in practice to a great extent through the individual bishop's right to govern his own diocese and the influence he thereby automatically exercises on the universal Church. If the right of the episcopate in the government of the universal Church cannot be adequately incorporated in a set of laws governing the relations of the individual members of the college with one another – that is, practically, between pope and individual bishops or even between pope and the rest of the episcopate, it does not by any means follow that some such individual, detailed regulations, of a more or less legal character, are not possible or desirable in addition to what we already have. Rules for conciliar procedure, which the pope issues alone[26] or with the express consent of the rest

[26] If the pope "alone" issues these procedural rules, he acts *as* pope, as head of the college of bishops which is in tacit agreement with him, an

of the council, are an example of such canonical regulations. But before we proceed further in this direction, we must consider another matter.

e) Why a "College" to Rule the Church?

If we ask why the Church has, by the will of Christ, a collegiate head in the above sense there are several possible answers, not necessarily mutually exclusive. We are dealing with a free act of the Church's Founder, and such a disposition may achieve many objects through a single decision or ordinance, especially if the institution he chooses to found (a college) has already existed elsewhere in theory and practice and therefore already has various traditional connotations. One can deduce the unity of primacy and episcopate from the idea of "communion".[27] One can start from the notion of apostolic succession, as J. Ratzinger does with considerable historical and speculative perspicacity.[28] One can also take the biblical notion of a body of many witnesses, and attack the problem from a "theology of the word", as H. Schauf attempts to do.[29] Such attempts need

agreement which through the assistance of the Holy Ghost can never fail him but will always exist (at least in a sufficient degree), even though the proof of this is no evident criterion whereby a third party could judge whether the pope has acted as head of the college of bishops. And conversely, the express consent of the college can only have a legal significance in the Church insofar as the college is constituted under the pope and not as an entity distinct from him and capable of independent action. Express consent (or the request for it) may, however, in a given situation, be morally, though not legally, imperative. Cf .§ 7 *infra*.

[27] As I have done in the first part of this Study.

[28] Joseph Ratzinger, "Primacy, Episcopate and Apostolic Succession" in *The Episcopate and the Primacy*. Rahner and Ratzinger. Quaestiones Disputatae 4.

[29] H. Schauf, *De Corpore Christi mystico* (Freiburg 1959), pp. 298–310.

not contradict one another. The idea of a college undoubtedly contains, inasmuch as it implies not a simple unity but a unity of many, the conviction that the Church, without prejudice to her unity, is rightly a diversity. This pluralism is thus not simply a feature which is later supplanted by unity, but is something which is to remain and to which we should aspire. And obviously not only in the sense that the Church is composed of many members numerically distinct from each other. The members are to be qualitatively distinct, and not merely through characteristics not pertinent to their membership as such,[30] but also through those which are important in and for the Church. The Church is to be constituted not simply of many members but of qualitatively different members. The variety is not only an irreducible fact but something to be cherished. The unity of the Church as a whole demands, of course, a certain homogeneity among her members, which is either presupposed, or when lacking must be created. It will always have to be preserved and defended against pluralistic tendencies incompatible with unity. But even though unity as well as a certain equality among the members is the object of the hierarchy's solicitude, yet pluralism in the Church is not merely something unavoidable or something to be overcome, but something requiring encouragement and protection. This follows simply from the Pauline teaching on the Body of Christ with its many members and their different spiritual gifts, which cannot all be realized in one and the same member.

This legitimate and necessary pluralism in the Church is not only a pluralism of the individual members, but also of the larger

[30] Provided that there could be such characteristics, which is doubtful, since the whole man in all his dimensions is to be saved.

groups, of local Churches, of countries and peoples, especially since these too, as such, have a "vocation" to the light of the Gospel. It would thus be preposterous to think, for example, that the existence of the Uniate Churches of the East, with their non-Latin rites, their own ecclesiastical law and theology, their own spirituality and piety, etc. is only tolerated by an indulgent Rome, as though Rome, for purely tactical reasons, had resigned itself to the virtually inevitable, as though an absolute uniformity of law, liturgy, etc. were really the ideal. Such a theory, if taken seriously, would be outright heresy. Obviously it is impossible to lay down once and for all exact, material norms for the proper proportion between necessary homogeneity and pluralism *iuris divini*. But in principle the Church also has the right and duty to encourage and to develop a genuine pluralism in all spheres of her existence and activity, in the manner appropriate to each sphere.

Neither in practice nor ideally is the Church a systematically administered unitary state.[31] Such a uniformity has never existed in the Church, even in the Latin Church. Even in the Roman, Western Church there has always been a pluralism in every sphere of liturgy, piety, theology, law (which is not simply identical with a Code of Canon Law), and the cure of souls, etc. If homogeneity is relatively strong here, the fact is to be explained less from the nature of the Church than from the

[31] Such a consideration is important, for example in the question of the conditions under which Protestant communities could and must be granted communion with the Roman Church. We cannot make it our aim to eradicate from such communities the whole history of Protestant Christianity, which after all was not illegitimate in every respect. To aspire to this, as a single, fundamental principle, would contradict the doctrine of the necessary pluralism in the Church.

historical origin and character of Western culture; and other imponderable factors are involved, such as the absent influence of the Eastern Church; the schism in Western Christianity, which forced or sometimes misled the Church to consider a militant uniformity necessary or unavoidable; a certain tendency of the Roman mind towards legal standardization, etc. At any rate, the present large measure of homogeneity does not mean that this is the ideal, or that it is not legitimate to allow or aspire to a greater pluralism even in the Latin part of the Church. (Here would be the historical and theological context for the contribution of Protestant Christianity to the plenitude of the Church were it to return, wholly or in part, to the household of the common Father.)

The significance of the college of bishops can also be seen from this point of view. Collegiate government of the Church ensures that the pluralism of divine right in the Church also becomes manifest in her head, and is valid and active there. If the Tribes of Israel as such were part of the very fabric of the "people of the covenant", and thus had a permanent significance (each in its own way, in distinction from the others; for example, the tribe of Levi); if the apostles in the college represent the tribes of the new "people of God" (though not according to the flesh, but according to the various charismata) then it becomes quite clear that the collegiate character of the Church's government derives from her permanent pluralism and is destined to serve it.

All this explains why the college of bishops, even though its unity is naturally prior to the individual bishops, does not (like the college of cardinals resident in Rome) remain assembled in one place (practically speaking, in Rome, as a sort of *pres-*

byterium for the pope), but is normally dispersed throughout the world. Only thus can it actually serve the pluralism necessary in the Church. The bishops are "local ordinaries" not merely because the pope for practical reasons needs administrative officials in various places for his personal rule of the Church (the purpose of apostolic vicars and prefects) but because a bishop can fulfil the function which he has in the college of bishops and indeed for the universal Church,[32] only when he authoritatively represents a particular member of the universal Church,[33] in which the differentiation from other members of the Church intended by the Spirit can really exist.[34]

[32] Thus M. Schmaus says quite correctly (*Lexikon für Theologie und Kirche* II², col. 492 and 493): The bishops "represent each in his own diocese the universal Church. . . It follows from the unity of the episcopate with the pope, that the bishops have, in a certain sense, a responsibility for the universal Church, over and above the territory of their own diocese." Schmaus does not necessarily contradict the opinion given here when he derives the function of the individual bishop for the universal Church from his unity with the pope. This unity with the pope is founded precisely on the unity of the college of bishops with the pope, just as the apostolic college may be understood only in its unity with the Petrine office, from which it receives its entire juridical structure.

[33] That this aspect could not be clearly seen in the apostolic college is a consequence of the small geographical size of the apostolic Church. But even in the apostolic age Paul and Barnabas felt they were representatives of the communities they founded and of their spirit vis-à-vis the mother community in Jerusalem and Peter and the original apostles.

[34] This should also make it clear that not only members who are distinguishable territorially can have this function, but also members who are only personally distinguishable. The highest superior of an exempt order can, for example, be an "ordinary" in the full canonical sense, and it is thus quite reasonable that he belongs to a general council as a member.

6. Conclusions from the Nature of the Episcopate

Finally I shall only attempt to say something about the feasibility of working out certain "rules" (without prejudice to the basic impossibility of an adequate material delimitation of the respective rights of the "primacy" and the "episcopate") for their relationship in practice, which either flow directly from the relationship or appear germane and desirable in its light.

a) The *ius divinum* of the Individual Bishop

First, some consequences from the legitimate pluralism in the Church. This pluralism not only forbids the suppression of the rights of the episcopate as a whole, since they are of divine right, or such a curtailment of the rights of the individual bishop[35] as, imposed on all individual bishops, would in practice subvert the essence of the episcopate *iuris divini,* and reduce the bishops to subordinate officials of the pope. It also implies that the rights of a bishop, as the concrete representation of and the *sine qua non* for this legitimate pluralism, are a reality in the Church which must be positively protected and fostered, even by the pope. In discussing the balance to be struck in the Church between furthering unity through homogeneity and encouraging pluralism through a self-reliant episcopate, the juridical notion of "presumption" is out of place. Thus it will be well to avoid saying that the "proper rights" of the bishop should be "presumed" and the right of the pope must be

---

[35] Without prejudice to what was said above, to the effect that the rights (in relation to the Holy See) of the episcopate must not be identified with those of the individual bishop, and therefore a restriction of the rights of an individual bishop can be legitimate, whereas it would not be if extended to the episcopate as a whole.

"proved" (if only in the pope's own conscience, and recognizing that even here the pope has the necessary competence). For both these realities which have to be protected, the unity and the pluralism, are equally fundamental,[36] and depend on one another. By the same token it would be wrong to describe as "subsidiary" the pope's power of intervening in favour of homogeneity, because it is also the duty of the individual bishop himself as a member of the universal episcopate, to promote Church unity and the homogeneity which it requires.[37] But it is clear nonetheless that each bishop should be left scope for the independent initiative necessary for his diocese to be a member with a character of its own, not simply in the Church, but for the Church as well. Only if the bishop, too, shows himself receptive to the sort of initiative that can arise in the Church even without a *Motu Proprio* from Rome, only if he is willing to take such initiative himself, if he notices and takes up questions not already answered by higher authority, if he has the ingenuous courage (like, say, Cardinal Suhard) to write a pastoral letter worthy to be an encyclical, and only if the necessary scope is allowed for the play of such initiative, can a bishop fully implement his office

[36] And ultimately guaranteed in their unity and mutual compatibility by a principle superior to law, which is the power of the Spirit in the Church.

[37] By the same token it is better to avoid talk of a "decentralization". For this notion means, in itself, nothing more than a technical administrative measure, that can also be applied in a totalitarian state, and thus has nothing to do with what we mean here, which is the essential and original pluralism of the Church. A certain decentralization can occur in the Church at most as the by-product of a conscious grasp of the genuinely Catholic principle of pluralism. Hence the pluralism of the rights of various supernatural gifts in the Church has nothing to do with "democratism".

within his own diocese for the good of the whole Church. When a bishop, by setting some example, by taking some initiative, by posing a new theological question yet to be formulated, by enacting legislation which serves as a model for other dioceses, by developing new ways of preaching the Gospel, does something destined to enrich the whole Church (were it only by a sort of unobtrusive spiritual osmosis), then this is not presumption or exceeding his competence, but a part of exercising his office and his duty.

Because of the legitimate and necessary pluralism in the Church, the same holds true when a bishop's words, acts or legislation cannot serve as a norm for other parts of the Church, but yet are recommended or required in the concrete situation of his Church (diocese) as in keeping with the principles of the Church and the urging of the Spirit. The correctness of an action is not always and in principle to be judged according to whether it could serve as a norm for the whole Church. It may well be that a bishop has the right and duty to use all legitimate means available to him, without contenting himself with the higher wisdom of Rome or the alleged necessity of uniform legislation, to win (through dispensation, indult and so on) a place within the law for some special ordinance in his diocese. Were he to refuse to do this on principle, he would be denying that the Church should be made up of different members, and implicitly asserting that his Church should be nothing but an absolutely uniform administrative area in an absolutely homogeneous religious "unitary state".

We always strive in practice, of course, to preserve the special character of the individual member Church. But it would perhaps be well to translate this practice into a more explicit principle. For in this way the practice itself will be supported at episcopal and again at papal level. The truth will stand out more clearly and resolutely in the consciousness of the Church that the intention of the Church's government can never be to strive only for the maximum of uniformity, or to consider all differences merely as "necessary evils" or variations irrelevant to religion. No, the charismata of the Spirit himself are varied. And this variety can work itself out territorially (in religious life, in the liturgy,[38] in theology, in modes of conventual life, in Christian education, etc.). The bishops can and should be the guardians of all this, today more than ever because of a certain paradoxical phenomenon to be observed simultaneously in the world and in the Church. A unity unknown before our century exists both in the world (because of the inter-relation in culture and power in the historical and political spheres, which no longer allows the existence of isolated national histories) and in the Church (in which the principle of the unity embodied in the

---

[38] This reference does not contradict the Church's legislation (CJC can. 1257) according to which the Holy See has reserved to itself the legislation over liturgy for the Latin Church. For (apart from the fact that such a juridical norm is not in principle unchangeable) this norm does not mean that Rome has really reserved to itself the regulation of everything "liturgical" in the *theological* sense. An afternoon devotion ordered by the bishop and conducted according to the diocesan prayer book, a procession carried out according to episcopal instruction, etc. are, in a theological sense, very much Catholic liturgy without Rome's really having reserved to itself the regulation of such services. Even if by a certain legalistic formalism the name "liturgy" is often reserved for those parts of the Church's divine service which are regulated from Rome and the regulation of which Rome has actually reserved to itself, without its being always evident that these parts are more important than those the control of which is left to the bishops.

Church has found its absolute dogmatic and juridical expression in the definition of the First Vatican Council).

At the same time, however, the differences within these unities have not diminished but increased, whether one regards these as "still extant", or as something that ought to have a permanent existence. For in the world, first of all, the consciousness of the varieties of national culture, of economic differences etc., has been sharpened precisely because of the influence of the one world culture, and changed from something merely known to something deliberately chosen. The end of colonialism is a sign of this. And in that the Western Church has become a world Church, she is confronted as never before with the task of coping with pluralism, which certainly cannot be done by abolishing the latter.

The Church today contains peoples, territories, civilizations, the differences of which are much greater, even within the life of the Church, than has ever been the case before in the Church. That these differences have so far remained para-canonical and para-liturgical, and can therefore escape the notice of the naïve and superficial observer, does not change the fact. The only difference in earlier times was between a Christianity in a single highly civilized area, and a Christianity among nations with less developed civilizations. Today for the first time a Christianity is needed for areas historically different but culturally equal. We can today no longer afford to identify Christianity with European and North American Christianity. This same pluralism is growing relentlessly even within the old Western world, for despite our unified civilization the underlying differences are awakening to clearer consciousness and more deliberate self-assertion. (Who today would really hold, for example, that it is absolutely necessary for the unity of the Church to have an

378

ordinary Low Mass in a small parish said in Latin, and largely to exclude the most highly developed and civilized modern languages from the sacramental sphere, while in the secular sphere the growing unity of Europe and of the world is by no means due to any common uniform language, but unabashedly accepts the plurality of languages?)

The stagnation of the Asian missions among the Far Eastern civilizations, and in awakening Africa, shows (if differently in each case) that a non-Western Christianity must be developed there, or the Gospel will not advance, because its success until now (whether it wished or no) has been in large part due to the preponderance of Western civilization. In the past, this may indeed have been an instrument of supernatural providence through which the force of the Gospel could be proclaimed, but today it is a means of declining efficacy. In this situation very much will depend on whether the Church unhesitatingly and confidently opens herself to such a pluralism, or whether, out of a cautious conservatism, she decides that unity must be maintained through the maximum possible uniformity. She can accept such a pluralism with perfect equanimity. She has systematically developed the principle of unity in her law and dogma for one hundred years past, she possesses in the Holy Ghost the most potent principle of unity, and she has in the history of the early Church and in the Uniate Churches of the Middle East a ready example in her own history to show that the unity of the Church is compatible with the pluralism of the churches. An episcopate of divine right should be the embodiment and guarantor of such a pluralism, which will be the more necessary in the future (though we must hope that this will not have to be brought about forcibly by yet other iron curtains).

We might also consider whether a good deal of what is actually granted to the individual bishop and the individual diocese by way of dispensation, indult, quinquennial powers etc., should not perhaps be left to the responsibility of the bishop from the start. Little would change in the concrete practice of the Church, but it would become clearer in principle that it is hardly the business of the supreme pastor to regulate the smallest diocesan affairs himself. (Has no one, for example, ever wondered – it is quite licit to do so – that Rome herself regulates and urges such petty details as the three Hail Mary's at the end of Mass, a detail, after all, quite problematical from a liturgical standpoint?)

Even where considerations of Church unity, sound doctrine, or concern about possible undesirable repercussions in other parts of the Church require that a certain diocesan or metro-politan measure should have a preliminary authorization and clearance and cannot automatically be left to local initiative, yet this need not mean that such a regulation is acceptable only if it is appropriate for the whole Church and could be universally imposed by Rome. For example, the question concerning the restoration of the ordained diaconate (with permission to marry) which according to prevailing law falls within the exclusive competence of Rome, should not be made to depend on whether it is advisable to introduce it in all parts of the world. It would be quite sufficient if Rome cleared the way for those bishops who feel that some such thing is necessary or useful for their territory, and promulgated certain skeleton laws accordingly.[39]

[39] The practice in Roman liturgical legislation of allowing a certain feast only to those dioceses which ask for it, provides a model for what we mean here. When we consider for example, that it was in this way (that is, leaving scope for charismatic initiative from below, while the

The whole question of such a legitimate pluralism subject to episcopal initiative and direction in the Church has another possible application which should not be overlooked, the ecumenical problem. We proceed on the assumption that there exist also (not only, of course) within the Christian communities separated by the Reformation legitimate developments and realizations of Christian faith, theology, prayer etc., which in fact are not, not yet, or not so clearly, to be found in the Catholic Church in the same particular way. We proceed on the assumption that a pluralism which had a quite legitimate place within the Catholic Church (a pluralism of supernatural gifts, of ways of living the Christian life) developed, through the fault of Christians, partly outside the Catholic Church, and thus also (not only!) with partly heretical, partly schismatic distortions. If this is so, then the question of reunion must be posed otherwise today than it was in the sixteenth century. That is, the Church today is asked the question whether and how and to what extent she is willing to accept and preserve that legitimate pluralism which the separated Christians of the Reformation could (and certainly wish to) bring into the Church as legitimate and as genuinely Christian, developed in the last four centuries outside the Catholic Church. If the Catholic Church fundamentally has a real duty to affirm pluralism, one cannot, at least *a priori,* deny some such duty toward the Protestant Christians. No matter how utopian the actual prospects (judging from the attitude of the Protestant Christians themselves) for a union (in

supreme authority followed a policy of "wait and see") that the devotion to the Sacred Heart became common to the whole Church, we may certainly wonder whether such a model could not be followed more courageously in other important questions.

contradistinction to individual conversions) between Protestant communities and the Catholic Church may seem to many Catholics, we must declare such a thing possible *in principle,* for to maintain the contrary would be to deny the pluralistic principle in the Church.

Of course many serious objections can be raised against such a union between Latin and Protestant communities in the same area, (which we cannot enter into here). But at this point one ought to ask whether these questions could not be brought closer to a real solution by affording the individual bishop or the episcopate of a country greater opportunities to work towards a union which he, in accordance with his Church's situation and spiritual vigour, considers possible and compatible with the preservation of the "Latin" heritage he administers (which has of course its justification, like the Protestant tradition). It is quite possible that the spiritual vigour of a charismatically gifted bishop might prove that in this matter things are possible by the grace of God which would seem impossible from a purely bureaucratic or legislative point of view. In any case, if the situation of Christendom mortally threatened as it is today is such that everything should be done for a reunion of Christians that does not definitely contradict dogma and conscience, and all other considerations should be put aside, then here too the principle of pluralism, responsibly borne by episcopal initiative, should not be forgotten.

b) Organization of "Para-Canonical" Customs according to this Divine Right

It would perhaps be advisable and necessary, towards a canonical clarification of episcopal rights which still exist in principle and have not become paralysed in practice, (and for the preservation of the influence of the episcopate on the whole Church and of its representation of the legitimate pluralism in the Church), if we were to examine the para-canonical customs both negatively and positively in the light of the relation between primacy and episcopate. By this we mean that there is much done in the Church which is not laid down in the Code of Canon Law and which is important, negatively or positively, for the function of the episcopate in the Church. Such a para-canonical reality ought to be brought under the light of a juridical consciousness and examined to see what should be dropped and what given legal form, the object in each case being to provide the function of the episcopate with the necessary room for development, and the sure and rapid means for it to come into its own and make itself felt. Very little, for example, is laid down in legislation for the practice of the Roman Congregations in their relations with the episcopate. That can be good, since it makes for flexible accommodation to the requirements of the particular situation. But it can also have bad effects by encouraging bureaucratic routine among the Roman authorities, who in practice, if not in theory, can be tempted to regard the bishops as their subordinate officials out in the provinces.

Another (positive) example is the German Bishops' Conference.[40] It is necessary and extremely important. But according to

[40] Its counterpart in other countries are the annual meeting of the Hierarchy of England and Wales, the Canadien Catholic Conference or the NCWC for North American Bishops. The situation, however, is the same everywhere. The natural (and thereby also the supernatural) unity of a certain territory in the Church (larger than a diocese) seeks (though the canonical framework for it is non-existent, or exists in atrophy in the metropolitan group etc.) to take on sharper outlines, to find an

official Canon Law, it does not exist. The question might be raised whether it ought not to exist canonically as well as actually. Behind this actual institution, which is indispensable,[41] stands the para-canonical reality of the old office of Primate of Germany[42] or what was intended to be such. But if the German Bishops' Conference also existed canonically, and not merely *de facto* and with rights the existence of which can at any time be challenged, then it would be — by its very existence — a more imposing factor in the influence of the universal episcopate on the welfare of the whole Church, than a single bishop. This is not at all meant as "power politics". All that is meant is that where the episcopate itself is juridically more concretely represented through canonically unified groups, so that it can become more active, it can exercise more effectively its function of co-operating with the highest office in the Church. This does not work to the detriment of the primacy or diminish its power, but to the good of that for which the primacy exists, that is the Church.

A further example: There is no legislation in the Code about the form in which a general council should take place. At the

organ whereby it may cope with this situation and the responsibility thus entailed – a responsibility always fraught with blessing or disaster for the universal Church.

[41] There are thousands of matters in any nation which simply cannot be regulated at diocesan level, but require a uniform nation-wide solution. But there is no legal means available (except the Holy See itself, which, again, ought to be the ultimate, not the first authority for such affairs) for effecting the uniformity of such solutions for a whole country.

[42] We may leave it an open question whether such a primate (with or without the name) should be envisaged in the chairman of the Bishops' Conference, existing canonically and making decisions binding for all Germany.

last council the outlines of its procedure were laid down by the pope.[43] Would it not correspond to the nature of the episcopate and of the council (which is derived from the nature of the episcopate) if a group — its size to be more exactly determined — of the Fathers of the council were able to make additions to the council's agenda as of right, so that such proposals could not be set aside by a purely papal commission? The right of the bishops to active participation and co-operation in a council need not necessarily find concrete expression precisely in such a legal regulation of procedure. But nobody can deny that such a legal provision would be a meaningful realization of the essential function of the episcopate at a council.

If it is clear that the episcopate is not merely the pope's counsellor, when he wants and asks for counsel, but that it possesses an active function, then at least we can pose the question whether councils in regular rotation would not be a sensible arrangement. In both the ancient and modern Church the council has been, to its detriment, somewhat mystified, in contra-distinction to the ordinary magisterial and pastoral office of the Church, as if only through it (abstracting from the pope, but from him alone) there were possible a collegiate expression of the Church's supreme power, forgetting that the council is one quite particular form of the real college, which even without the council, and with another *modus procedendi,* exists continuously in the Church. Thus the impression was created that a council is essentially a very "extraordinary" and therefore rare occurrence.

[43] Cf. H. Jedin, "Die Geschäftsordnungen der beiden letzten ökumenischen Konzilien in ekklesiologischer Sicht", *Catholica* 14 (1960), p. 105–118.

If we remember that a council is certainly not called for the sole purpose of pronouncing doctrinal decisions, and if we adopt the sober but correct idea of John XXIII that a council can be important and exercise a very essential function when it acts primarily as the highest *pastoral* office, then it is not easy to see why it could not assemble at regular, though not too brief, intervals.

The late Middle Ages had this bold idea.[44] That it was not put into effect is still no proof that it was false or unrealistic. The quicker tempo of life today will certainly ensure that the themes worth discussing in a council will not be lacking (unless one makes the unfair demand that one council solve everything). And the regularity of the rotation could be an incentive not to put off urgent problems (which has certainly happened in the history of the Church) and could at the same time guard against the temptation to try to decide at one council (since it is a unique opportunity that will not soon recur) something which would be ripe only at another council. Not every council would, then, have the same rank and weight as those of Chalcedon or Trent. But such regular councils would nevertheless not find it too difficult to become as important as many other councils (*e.g.*, the Lateran Councils) which we also customarily number among the ecumenical councils.

---

[44] The Council of Constance, in its thirty-ninth session (October 9, 1417) laid down, in the first reform decree, that a general council must meet regularly every ten years. (Cf. K. J. Hefele – H. Leclerq, *Histoire des Conciles,* VII/1 [Paris, 1916] p. 459.) Whatever be thought of the motives behind this decree and the brevity of the interval, the fact that it was never carried out is no proof that it was impracticable ot that the basic idea would not suit our times.

c) The Position of Auxiliary Bishops in the Universal Episcopate

The individual bishop, according to the nature of the episcopate, is first of all a member of the college of bishops, and only because of this the ruler of a particular territory of the Church (though possession of a territory, for reasons we have indicated, may follow as a natural if, for the individual bishop, not absolutely necessary consequence). Hence it is not at all inconceivable that there are members of the college of bishops who are not rulers of a particular diocese. Even such a bishop can have duties within the whole college, can participate in the college's one task of ruling the universal Church. It cannot therefore automatically be said that every episcopal consecration that is not "relative" is self-contradictory, because it does not assign the consecrated man to a particular diocese, or that it could allot him a participation only in the *potestas ordinis* of the bishops. If then auxiliary bishops are, for example, called to the council as voting members (CJC No. 223, 2), this is (or would be) only a reasonable consequence of the nature of the episcopal office (even if not a strictly necessary one).[45] This does not, of course, justify raising those who really are and are to be only officials of the pope (a high dignity and a great office!), to the episcopate *honoris causa* as it were, to betoken their dignity (something quite unnecessary, for this dignity speaks for itself) or to enable them to exercise the episcopal *potestas ordinis*. Real auxiliary bishops for whom there is a genuine need should according to our principle be looked on in every way as members

---

[45] And perhaps not to be recommended today for purely technical reasons (that is, too many participants at the council). It is to be noted that a council can also be made up of representatives of those who themselves compose the supreme governing body in the Church.

of the one universal episcopate, the one subject of universal power in the Church, even though their rights with respect to the individual diocese essentially differ from those of the local ordinary.

d) Some Consequences for the Structure of Dioceses

Our principle would also require a bold re-thinking of the concept and actual structure of a diocese. If the bishop is primarily a member of the supreme governing body of the Church, and yet on this ground is meant to rule a particular part of the Church, and if both tasks must be intimately connected, then a diocese must be of such a size (though the ideal will necessarily be only approximately attainable) that it can fulfil within its own life all the functions of the Church (except that of representing the unity of the whole Church through the Petrine office). Its life should be such that he who guides and rules it does something which can seem to be a function of the Church as such and as a whole, an example of the life of the universal Church. This should be the criterion of reasonable size for a diocese. Where only a quite limited part of the Church's life can be lived within it, there is really no diocese in the true sense of the word.[46]

[46] Of course it must be borne in mind that because of the divinely intended pluralism, each true diocese must or may live and represent the whole life of the Church in a different way, in a different style than another diocese, without thereby either ceasing to be true to its nature or to live and mirror the whole life of the Church; and this not only in the exercise of a Bishop's power of ordination (which is always present, and is an essential factor in a diocese's realizing the whole content of the Church within its own boundaries, and thus being "Church" in the Church), but also in other vital activites of the Church. Within the diocese

It must be kept in mind that this norm of the rôle and size of a diocese is realized differently in different ages and different cultural and political circumstances. Because an "ancient" *Polis* provided an adequate foundation for and representation of the whole of the Church's life, since within the city the whole of human life at that time could come into play, each "city" could also be a diocese. This is no longer true today, since a single city can no longer sustain and represent the whole of human life, and therefore the whole of the Church's life. The central-European and extra-European conception of a diocese is therefore the correct one today, and the ancient conception, which has primarily been preserved in Italy, is obsolete. An indication of this is seen in the fact that the Church promised in the Italian Concordat to suppress Italian dioceses which were too small (though this has still not been carried out) and that in para-canonical measures (*e.g.,* the setting up of inter-diocesan provincial seminaries, etc.) the modern conception of a diocese has made itself felt even in Italy.

From this point of view, the tendency discernible here and there in central Europe to make the diocese as small as possible lacks justification. The needs which such efforts are meant to fill should and can be met in other ways (*e.g.,* by deans clothed with wider powers etc.; some old institutions, like that of the arch-priest, etc., could be renewed in accordance with the times). A diocese which cannot support its own seminary, in which (as such!) the whole life of the Church cannot to some extent shine forth (in theology, liturgy, religious orders, art etc.) is really not

the plenitude of the world ought in some way (in quality, not quantity) manage to exist, to be lived and shaped in Christian fashion, so that Church may be manifested at all.

a diocese. Certainly a German bishopric, for example, has para-canonically an entirely different function from an Italian one, and recognizing this difference does not imply that one is merely counting heads. In an Italian diocese of say 40.000 souls, there can be today (in this diocese as such!) no independent theological tradition (in a human, not specifically theological sense of the word), no independent liturgical life (even if expressed para–canonically), no conscious attitude to the intellectual and social questions of the day, etc. The material and personal basis for these things is simply too narrow. Thus such a diocese cannot really be a member of the Church with a character of its own and its own special vocation in the Church. It can only represent what exists elsewhere.

The bishop of such a diocese personally may still be extremely important in the Church (more or less charismatically, through the weight of his spiritual personality and the special character of what it represents), he can to a certain extent be the representative of a particular "member of the Church" (or rather, the representative of a particular function or structure in the organism of the Church) that is not, and need not be, based on territory.[47] Such a bishop still represents the wholeness of the Church with respect to her power of order (since the whole Church has no more power in this respect than he), but as the responsible ruler and representative of his territorial diocese, he does not represent the life and being of the whole Church to such an extent that he should for this reason necessarily belong to her supreme governing body.

[47] Such "members" of the Church exist, of course. Otherwise each exemption would lack any theological and ecclesiological foundation.

Of course, in the Church just as in the state,[48] the actual situation will at best be able to approach the ideal only asymptotically. The actual dioceses will in very different degrees realize the ideal of an independent member of the Church with its own particular calling, destined to portray the life of the whole Church in its own way, and thus provide the basis for its own ruler's membership in the supreme governing body of the whole Church and *vice versa*. But that does not make it any less important to know what a diocese really is. To see it merely as a technically necessary "administrative area" of the one (ideally homogeneous) Church is to misunderstand its nature, and willy-nilly to make the bishop in fact an official of the pope, whose business he conducts in some provincial "outpost".

e) The Office of Bishop as Service of the Universal Church

The whole question of the permanent right of the universal episcopacy (united under the pope), as the subject of the one government of the Church, has another quite different side. What a right does, after all, is to provide scope for the fulfilment of a duty. If the individual bishop is primarily member of a college which is entrusted with the care if the whole Church, if he rules his diocese precisely insofar as it is a part of the whole

---

[48] How differently, and to what different degrees, is, for example, the concept of a "city" realized in actual cities, even if all have the rights of a city by positive legislation. Some are really less than sizeable villages, others approximate to the nature of provinces or states. Here too there exists a legal positivism, justified because inevitable, which regards as a city any entity acknowledged as such by positive law. And yet it is possible to consider a city according to its nature, which even positive law cannot ignore. It cannot, for example, effectively make two houses into a city by positive decree. Such a positivism would cancel itself out.

Church, and if he performs his local duties as one element of his primary and total duty — then he must fulfill it in the consciousness of his responsibility for the whole Church, instead of regarding this responsibility for the whole Church as an additional and less important part of his duty. He should think about the whole Church as much as about his own diocese. He can never look on the greater good of the whole Church as detrimental to his own diocese. He can never think that his only concern is with his own diocese. His priests are not ordained for his diocese so exclusively that they, and he in them, do not also have a function for the whole Church. If, for example, the shortage of priests in Latin America is five times as acute as in North America or Europe, can a bishop say that this is indeed regrettable and that he will gladly pray for Latin America, but that nothing more can be expected of him, since he must look after his own diocese, and his duties toward the missions do not extend beyond those which all pious Christians have? Or must he feel an immediate episcopal responsibility for such lands, even if this responsibility is not legally or morally the same as for his own diocese? If such questions raise awkward legislative and moral[49] problems, this is no reason to avoid them.[50]

[49] May, for example, a European bishop deny an individual priest permission, if he wants to volunteer for Latin America, merely because there is also a shortage of priests in Europe? And this although those who know say that Latin America will be lost to the Church in the next thirty years, if it does not receive tens of thousands of priests from elsewhere?

[50] The co-responsibility of the bishops with the pope for the whole mission work of the Church has been stressed by Pius XI (*"Rerum ecclesiae"* of February 18, 1926; AAS 18 [1926], pp. 68 ff.) and Pius XII (*"Fidei Donum"* of April 21, 1957; AAS 49 [1957], pp. 236 ff.), though it is not

f) Concerning the Possibility of an Election of the
Pope by the Whole Episcopate

From the manner in which the pope, for centuries now, has seen his role in the universal Church (both in practice and in principle), and from other considerations (some given above), it can be concluded that the Roman pope is primarily head of the Church and not just Bishop of Rome. This local office only indicates who the head of the whole Church is, it is not the reason for his headship. If one bears in mind what we have said about the existence and function of the universal episcopate in the Church, then the question arises whether it would not be most in keeping with the nature of both these institutions of divine right in the Church, if the universal episcopate were to elect the pope in some manner or other. Not as though such a thing were necessary, however,[51] nor as though this familiar idea were not sufficiently realized, in essence if not in form, in that the majority of the College of Cardinals is made up of diocesan bishops. But if the report be true that recent popes have considered altering the method of papal elections in this very sense, then it is certainly legitimate to call attention to the question here.

made clear why the duty towards the universal Church arising from their office and their "mission" is not sufficiently discharged merely by ruling their own dioceses, and why they do not simply share the missionary duty of all Christians (though in greater measure).

[51] Or that this idea should be linked with the consideration whether other nations besides the Italians might not also provide the popes. Our idea has nothing to do with such considerations and is quite compatible with the sober realization that it is best to exclude petty national jealousies from papal elections by the expedient of choosing the pope from among the Italians.

7. A Distinction: Legal and Moral Norms

In order to clarify what is to be said in this section, let us begin with a fictitious example, asking the reader to bear with its crudity for the sake of the point to be made. Imagine that the pope, as supreme pastor of the Church, issued a decree today requiring all the Uniate Churches of the Near East to give up their Oriental liturgy and adopt the Latin rite. Would the pope by such a decree overstep the limits of his supreme jurisdictional primacy, exceeding his legal competence, and would his decree therefore be legally null and void? Disregarding the question whether the pope would in fact always be hindered from publishing such a decree, for reasons which lie not in his legal jurisdictional primacy as such, but elsewhere (*e.g.,* because of the guidance of the Holy Ghost in the Church, which would prevent the pluralism that belongs to the essence of the one Church from being mortally endangered by a decree in favour of an absolute uniformism), disregarding, that is, the question whether we have proposed a hypothesis that could not be fulfilled, we would have to answer the question posed above with a clear "no".[52] The pope would not exceed the competence

---

[52] We must of course pass over the question whether the pope, in certain circumstances, is or can be so bound by an explicit or implicit contract entered into by the Oriental and Roman Churches at the time of their reunion, that a decree conflicting with this contract would be not only immoral, but also legally invalid as breach of contract. This question would lead in turn to the question whether a contract of the pope with another legal person in strictly ecclesiastical matters (*e.g.,* a concordat) is to be interpreted according to regular contract theory or to the theory of privileges. Depending upon that answer, the question of the legal validity of a unilateral denunciation of such an agreement by the pope, would also be susceptible of different answers.

of his jurisdictional primacy by such a decree, and the decree would be legally valid.

But we can also pose an entirely different question. Would it be morally licit for the pope to issue such a decree? Any reasonable man and any true Christian would have to answer "no". Any confessor of the pope would have to tell him that in the concrete situation of the Church today such a decree, despite its legal validity, would be subjectively and objectively an extremely grave moral offence against charity, against the unity of the Church rightly understood (which does not demand uniformity), against possible reunion of the Orthodox with the Roman Catholic Church etc., a mortal sin from which the pope could be absolved only if he revoked the decree.

From this example one can readily gather the heart of the matter. It can, of course, be worked out more fundamentally and abstractly in a theological demonstration:

1. The exercise of the papal jurisdictional primacy remains, even when it is legal, subject to moral norms, which are not necessarily satisfied merely because a given act of jurisdiction is legal. Even an act of jurisdiction which legally binds its subjects can offend against moral principles.

2. To point out and protest against the possible infringement against moral norms of an act which must respect these norms is not to deny or question the legal competence of the man possessing the jurisdiction.

3. Even if one assumes that the ultimate, most definitive acts of ecclesiastical superiors, so long as they are legal, are also practically and morally justified — that is, if one assumes that in the acts of the pope which decisively affect the good of the whole Church in absolutely essential matters, the guidance and

assistance of the Holy Ghost will prevent such acts from being, although legal, morally objectionable — nevertheless this assumption can hardly be extended to *all* acts of the pope or other ecclesiastical authorities which, though they do not formally exceed the legal competence of the concrete person holding power and thus cannot be looked on by his subjects as *legally* void, can still be disordered in reality, and therefore (at least objectively) morally wrong, and thus sinful. And this sin may not lie simply in the subjective attitude of the person performing the act, sufficient perhaps to ensure the content of the act itself, but the very content of the act may itself be morally disordered.[53]

4. If there is no court of appeal against the general jurisdictional primacy of the pope, before which a decree of this primacy could be contested and annulled against the will of the pope; if we, then, remain ultimately dependent upon the judgment and good will of the supreme pastor of the Church even in the legal sphere as such, and remain, so to speak, at his mercy, without a legal safeguard independent of him; if, in the necessary absence in this world of such a safeguard against possible abuse

---

[53] Take the case of a pope's deposing a competent and pious bishop in a diocese without any objective reason, merely in order to promote one of his relatives to the post. It could hardly be proved that such a deposition is legally invalid. There is no court of appeal before which the pope and his measure could be cited. The pope alone has the competence of competence, that is, he alone judges in the last juridical instance on earth whether in a given act he has observed those norms by which in his own view that act is to be judged. But for all the unassailable legal validity of such a measure, such a deposition would be immoral and an actual offence against the divine right of the episcopate, though not an offence extending to the proper sphere of doctrine.

of this power, we must remain trustingly dependent on the protection of the Holy Ghost, who, without such a human safeguard, will prevent abuse from destroying the essence of the Church as an institution, the embodiment of right and also of love (abuse being to a certain extent always possible, and to a certain extent indeed always present, given the sinfulness of all men); nevertheless it is not necessary to deny that there can be a right and even a duty to protest against the infraction of equity, of love, of the right of the individual, even where the legality of an act of ecclesiastical authority cannot be questioned.

What the proper forms might be for such a legitimate protest against an infraction of moral norms despite the observance of legal norms, cannot be discussed here. But in any case, the tacit view and consequent practice, according to which a disposition of an ecclesiastical superior is unobjectionable in every respect merely because it falls within his legal competence, should not prevail in the Church. Such a pernicious opinion, which definitely exists in practice, ignores the basic Catholic conviction that the sphere of law and the sphere of morality are not conterminous. Legality and morality are not identical, even in the measures of ecclesiastical superiors. Thus it is in principle quite conceivable that even papal officials, while remaining within their legal competence with respect to the bishops, might take steps within the possible legal limits of the papal jurisdictional primacy, and yet, at least objectively, act immorally. The moral impropriety of such measures might consist in restricting the rights of a bishop in a way which is legally possible, because of the papal jurisdictional primacy, yet not required by the nature of the case. Though the pope alone has the competence of competence in this matter, that is, though he alone decides, in the sphere of law, whether this restrictive measure (particular or general) is objectively justified or not, nevertheless, at the *moral* level, for the bishop to protest, much as the Epistle to the Galatians shows Paul protesting to Peter, is possible, justified and indeed in some circumstances a sacred duty. Since such objectively detrimental and thus often objectively immoral limitations of episcopal power, even by the human law of the Church cannot be considered *a priori* impossible, it cannot be maintained *a priori* that episcopal wishes regarding the arrangements of human law in the relations of the pope with the episcopate are always and necessarily irrelevant or unjustified. That is, it cannot be maintained that human law in the Church always and everywhere and in its every detail adequately corresponds to reality, that is, to the nature of the Church and to her ever changing historical situation. Nor can it be maintained that the desirable adaptations could never imply a moral duty but are always purely discretionary and not subject to moral judgment. It is also quite conceivable that such moral principles, even if they cannot yield codified legal norms, might be more exactly formulated and better adapted to the circumstances of our time and to the practical difficulties in the relationship between primacy and episcopate.

An example (if from a somewhat different sphere): If a pope wishes to issue a definition *de fide,* he is certainly not legally bound to follow any particular procedure in order to obtain moral certainty that the proposition in question is definable. Thus, for example, the definition could not be contested if he had not informed himself in the requisite manner. Nor is it denied, of course, that the pope's definition would remain infallible and binding in conscience should he not fulfil his moral duty to obtain enough information of a theological nature about the definability of the proposition in question. But neither fact prevents the pope having a moral duty thus to inform himself, nor can he dispense himself from that duty because he has the assistance of the Holy Ghost for such a definition in any case (the less so since the assistance of the Holy Ghost might operate to prevent the definition, *e.g.,* through the death of the pope, etc.). But if such a moral duty exists, then one can reasonably investigate in detail what this moral duty of the pope's involves for him in the particular circumstances of today, the present state of theology, the modern means for gathering information, the possibility of consulting the universal episcopate, etc.

Such an ethics of papal procedure in these affairs could (despite the moral variability of procedure which would still remain, and despite the incontestable legality of his actual procedure) be discussed and formulated even in public, and expressly acknowledged by the pope as the objectively valid norm for himself. Without in the least harming the position of the pope in matters of faith as an authority from whom there is no appeal to any authority on earth, such a thing might largely contribute to quieting the fears of Protestant Christians, who always suspect that the absolute magisterial primacy of the pope is an absolutely unlimited and arbitrary power, and that Catholics must at all times be prepared for new definitions at a moment's notice. It could thus be made more clear that there can well be a moral duty on the part of the pope to consult the whole Church, and that such a duty does not contradict the *"ex sese et non ex consensu Ecclesiae"* of papal infallibility. Such moral norms, which must preside over the relationship between primacy and episcopate, would of course often simply amount to rules of normal Christian charity, of courtesy, of objectivity, of respect for the personality of one's neighbour, of the obligation to consult others, of the principle of subsidiarity which does apply in the Church, even in particular cases and not simply in general. It might be thought that such moral norms were simply obvious, so that it would be pointless to formulate them anew for the context of the relations between primacy and episcopate, since they are valid generally for all human relations. That is, of course, in large part true, but still only in *part*. For it remains true that norms which in themselves and in the abstract are quite obvious are often difficult to apply in complex situations, so that it becomes necessary to work out more concrete "inter-mediate" norms that impress upon duller and more partisan folk what seemliness, willingness to seek advice, doing things through official channels, etc., mean concretely in particular circum-stances of one sort or another.

ON HERESY

I

THE CHRISTIAN ATTITUDE TOWARDS HERESY

THE history of Christianity is also a history of heresies and con-sequently of the attitudes adopted by Christianity and the Church towards heresy, and so involves a history of the concept of heresy itself. In all religions that possess any kind of definite doctrine, that is, in all the higher religions, there are differences of opinion about that doctrine and as a consequence quarrels and conflict about it and about the socially organized forms in which the different religious views find expression. To that extent we might say that the concept of heresy is exemplified in all the more highly developed religions. But caution is needed, nevertheless, for it is readily observed that religious wars are only found in Christendom. However much this assertion may call for qualification, and whatever more precise explanation is given, (for much that is involved may, of course, have little to do with Christianity itself), the assertion, though disputable, does draw attention to something. It is only in Christianity that a certain quite definite and very radical attitude to truth is found. This is the source of a quite specific view of heresy and that is why heresy is only really found here.

Two factors probably determine the attitude to truth to which we refer. One is the awareness that a revelation of truth by God himself has occurred as an event located quite precisely in space and time in certain quite definite human beings. The other is the awareness that this truth itself, as such, is important for salvation. In short, an awareness of the historical character of an absolute truth intrinsically important for salvation. In order to make clear why and how there follows from this a definite concept of heresy and a corresponding relation to it, both specifically Christian, what has been said will require elucidation.

First of all we must consider the character of revelation, as Christians understand it, as an event. We leave aside the question, important or even decisive as it may be in other connections, whether and how the essential of the Christian message in fact reaches all men – even where the historical revelation cannot plainly be observed to come to them, – from within, that is, through the offer of grace from God's universal salvific will, and in an implicit manner, without express formulation in propositions. Even if such is the case, it remains true, nevertheless, that this communication of truth from within which we are assuming to be granted and accepted, receives, in the Christian view, its full expression and definitively authentic conceptual expression, which also makes it unmistakable and applicable to the actual details of life, at quite definite places in historical space and time: through the prophets, through Jesus Christ, through the apostles, through authorized and appointed preachers and expounders of God's truth. He sends forth this truth to men as a free disclosure of his own nature and will. It is quite unattainable on a human basis.[1] What is funda-

---

[1] When we remember that this self-revelation and self-communication of God also takes place just as authentically in what we Christians call

mental to the idea of Christian truth, anterior even to any definite content of its message, is that here and now, in God's name, God's word went forth unambiguously demanding obedience, and continues to go forth perpetually, ever new. The reference back precisely to this event and to the authority that makes itself known in it belongs, therefore, to the essence of Christian truth. Christians may dispute who exactly is the bearer of that testimony to truth which occurred as an event, but no Christian concept of truth remains if that element is overlooked. Where it is only a case of different opinions regarding the actual contents of the message, one view cannot really regard another as a "heresy" in the proper sense. Only where in principle both sides have the will to take this occurrence and the authority that manifests itself in it as their point of reference can each party look upon the other as heretical, that is, as persons, who in their differences of opinion regarding matters of factual content, destroy, despite themselves, the authentic and direct relation to that authoritative event, though in itself this latter is maintained.

Heresy, therefore, is always a doctrine which despite itself threatens a whole spiritual existence, to the extent that this receives its foundation from the reference to the one complete revelation occurrence which the heretic himself affirms. Where he no longer does so, there can no longer be any question of heresy. Any such opinion then would from the Christian angle be apostasy from Christianity itself. Because and to the

participation in the divine nature by the grace of justification, we should perhaps phrase the above sentence more cautiously and precisely as follows: He sends forth this to men as one side, divinely authorized and expressed in human concepts, of the free disclosure he makes of his own nature and will. It is quite unattainable on a human basis.

extent that there scarcely exists for any other religion apart from Christianity such a point of reference from which the many affirmations were received and in regard to which they remain in permanent relation, there can hardly really be any such thing as heresy, or any real feeling against it as there is in Christianity. Heresy is only possible among brethren in the Spirit. But these are only possible when something absolutely common to all in the religious sphere expressly unites them. And among them a heresy that is more than a difference of opinion about something unimportant can only be present if one or both of those whose opinions differ see or think they see that the differences of opinion, contrary to the intention of the other, tend objectively speaking to destroy this ultimate foundation of Christianity and of its unity, and so threaten it at least subjectively. We shall have to consider in greater detail later what flows from this in regard to the nature of heresy and our attitude to it.

First, however, we must reflect on a point that has already been mentioned. For there to be any question of heresy, a truth must be involved which *as truth* is of importance for salvation. But in order to grasp how little this statement can be taken for granted, we must recall one of the deepest changes in outlook of the last three centuries. The coming of that change is perhaps only fully perceptible now that it is itself disappearing in its turn. What does the average European of today feel about truth, especially religious truth, the truth of a "view of the world"? His attitude might perhaps be described as follows. Apart from the simple facts of direct sense-experience which can be verified anew at any time by experiment, there are theories and opinions and nothing else. These opinions

406

may be correct in various ways. It is possible to concede to one or other of them a greater or less likelihood of approximating to reality and so to what would really be the truth. But more than such an approximation is never possible. As for a new view of the world, it is determined by national, individual, social and historical factors. In any case – and this is what is decisive, – the actual content of an opinion is of no account for passing any absolute moral judgment on the person who holds it, even before the judgment-seat of God if there is such a thing. For it is to be supposed that everyone forms his opinion to the best of his knowledge and in all conscience. It is true that some people will add that it is conceivable in itself and in principle for someone to have a false opinion through his own fault, because he culpably shut his ears to what was more correct and more adequate. But even in this case, what imperils salvation and determines a man's value absolutely is not his missing the truth and, consequently, reality as regards its definite content, but the unethical cause of this failure. The ultimate judgment on a man can never depend on the precise nature of his opinions. This, it is claimed, is self-evident. For even the worthiest people hold very varied views even in matters in themselves of the greatest importance. Consequently it is manifestly absurd to regard someone as a scoundrel simply because he holds a definite but different opinion.

Knowledge of truth, to the extent, that is, that it is constituted by a definite content has, therefore, moved from the centre of human existence to its periphery. It belongs with things like colour of the hair, taste, race, on which a man's absolute value cannot be made to depend. Once they think about it, people will concede that some errors may have disastrous consequences, even though they are held without guilt. For example, inculpable error about right of way may cost someone his life on the roads. But this is precisely what is not the case in regard to an absolute judgment that takes everything into account. Here it is indubitably only a matter of how well-meaning one was, not of what one thought. The premise that is tacitly assumed as the foundation of all this is, that any opinion may be held on good grounds and with a clear conscience. Consequently the question of what opinion someone held, does not enter into a complete evaluation, "provided they were decent people". The possibility that precisely this could perhaps be decided by the question of what opinion a person held, is to a large extent excluded from present-day mentality. To begin with, on democratic principles every opinion has equal rights. People are not given to reflecting very closely why this proposition may not, as a "rule of the game", itself be disputed. To put the matter in more theological terms, the content of the act of intellectual knowledge is no longer important for salvation *de necessitate medii* (as an indispensable means), but only the moral quality of its acquisition is vitally important: *necessitate praecepti* (it is necessary because prescribed).

In this view, therefore, God has arranged, if not for this earth, at least for the whole course of the world and for eternity, that nothing ultimately happens on account of an error as such. This view is based on a strange and excessively subjective "inwardness". Reality is "outside", thoughts are, after all, only "within", and not what matters. Only reality can do harm. But we are not really in touch with reality in what really matters, by what we think about it, for that makes no difference to reality in itself, but only through what reality does to us, apart from our own thoughts about it. The fact that precisely through what we think about things we enter into a very definite relation to them in themselves, so that things themselves become different for us according to how we think about them, – this fundamental truth regarding the actual nature of genuine cognition has to a great extent been lost to the contemporary mind. The current view of the ultimate indifference of truth is exactly what is rejected by Christianity and this rejection forms the second root of the feeling that can attach to the Christian rejection of error *qua* error. It is an intrinsic principle of the Christian understanding of man that there is truth which it is not possible, without guilt, to fail to attain. This affirmation, however, has, it seems, become so obscured even among Catholics (for reasons which will later be discussed), that we must first of all at least indicate what the grounds for it are, for them and on their premises. Only then can the attempt be made to remove the stumbling-block that this affirmation represents at the present time, and also with that principle in view understand Christian feeling against heresy and so the nature of heresy itself.

Catholic Christianity teaches that no human being who morally has come to the use of reason, can attain his true, authentic salvation without right belief in the true revelation of God. And what is meant is genuine theological faith in the actual truth of God's revelation. It is not our intention here to determine more precisely the sense of this thesis nor to inquire into its grounds. We take it for granted as indisputable for a Catholic. For our present purpose, it implies the fundamental principle, enunciated earlier, of the intrinsic importance for salvation of the knowledge of truth as such. For, of course, it affirms that what we believe – whether we have grasped genuine reality rightly, in truth, in knowledge – concerns the radically serious question of our final destiny definitively, decisively and absolutely, though not exclusively. It is not simply a matter of good will, noble striving, a decent attitude, but of whether we have in fact by knowledge laid hold of absolute reality itself, because in such a grasp, which is essentially, though not exclusively, an act of cognition, salvation itself consists.

Before the objection is raised that this is Greek intellectualism, it would be well to consider whether such a protest does not itself prove that cognition has not really been understood at all, if it is thought that this Christian doctrine must be rejected. Of course, the thesis presupposes that there exists a fundamental fulfilment of human life, a depth in human existence (not always and everywhere achieved), in which knowing and decision, truth and goodness are no longer separable but in which only the true have goodness and the good cannot fall away from truth. But precisely this radical and fundamental act in which cognition really achieves its true nature by being transformed into the decision of love without losing its own nature, and love becomes knowledge too, always remains an act of knowing truth. And it is of importance for salvation to the extent that it is such. For truth itself is one of the highest moral values. Consequently unless moral value is to be reduced to pure formalism, to a mere modality of how we act, in total indifference to what is done, the moral sphere itself is not attained unless genuine truth, and not merely well-meaning opinion, is achieved.

Of course, Christianity has always inquired in the reflection of her theologians how this basic idea of the decisive importance for salvation of truth as such is compatible with the observation that men appear to be at variance over the most decisive questions concerning truth. Unless, of course, someone were bold enough to regard all who did not expressly recognize the official Christian truth, as lost on that account. Now, of course, it is not to be denied that many have, in fact, been bold enough to do so, taking their stand on the Christian concept of truth. Francis Xavier himself told the Japanese whom he was trying to convert that all their ancestors were condemned to Hell. Even Augustine, to be consistent with his own theology, would have had to reply in the same sense. And as a matter of fact almost down to our own times such an attitude was one of the fundamental feelings about Christian missionary work among the heathen. But it cannot be disputed that one must not be so bold. In fact we may say that a Christian today, in the present stage of the development of dogma and of Christian awareness of the faith, *may* no longer be so absolute and so bold. Much theological thought has been devoted to the question how the thesis we have been considering, regarding the intrinsic value of truth as such for salvation, can be maintained without our needing to be so bold as to have this grim pessimism on the question of the salvation of the majority. Usually recourse has been had (with a reference to Heb. 11:6), to the principle that the absolutely decisive importance of the truth of revelation only concerns the ultimate and most fundamental truths. Consequently on this view anyone who denied or did not know the existence of God as the guardian of the moral order, certainly would not have that faith, that possession of truth which is decisive for salvation. But since it was clear that this basic truth is readily accessible and can only be missed, at least in the long run, through one's own fault, in the end it all really came back simply to moral factors. On this view inculpable error or ignorance regarding other truths is compatible with the possession of saving faith.

However important and correct this expedient is, it is not sufficient in itself today to reconcile our contemporaries to the thesis in question. For on the one hand, experience of the most radical differences of opinion among men has become more extensive and more profound, so that even the enlightened monotheist can no longer be considered as not seriously threatened with a further diminution of belief. On the other hand, a person today, however, egotistical in the actual life he leads, feels an almost inescapable solidarity with all men. He does not believe in, or want for himself, a heaven from which he sees others excluded whom he doesn't really think are any worse than he is, and who didn't have offered to them more or less an equal chance with himself of working out their salvation. Consequently, to the above-mentioned principle it will doubtless be necessary to add, that in certain circumstances a person may even be able to arrive at and affirm a truth, precisely as truth, in the depth of his actual accomplishment of life, even when he thinks himself obliged to deny it in his consciously formulated concepts, or knows nothing of it explicitly and expressly. In other words there can be people who consider themselves atheists whilst in truth they affirm God, for example by unconditional dedication to an honest search for truth, or by fidelity to the absolute judgment of conscience, just as there are Christians who on the plane of theoretical concepts

412

affirm the existence of God but deny him in the centre of their being where they know themselves as free.

However that may be, and whatever answers may be given to the questions inescapably raised by that thesis – which is not our theme here – nevertheless this fundamental Christian view is not to be denied or hazarded: Truth as such is even here on this earth so fundamentally important for life and salvation that it must be attained and accepted here if salvation is to be found at all. Even if an ultimate identity is affirmed between the possession of truth and moral quality or religious value, thus giving truth an ethical character and ethical values an intellectual one, and the thesis becomes thereby more intelligible to our contemporaries, it is not abandoned and cannot be. We can say to a contemporary that someone who truly affirms what is good does not radically fail to attain truth, because in his affirmation the decisive truths are asserted at least implicitly. But conversely, that means at the same time that a person would absolutely fail to attain what is good if he really were indifferent to truth as such and for that reason did not attain truth at all.

All this had to be said here, and defended against opposition, so that the Christian emotional reaction to heresy might be made intelligible. It, in fact, derives from the fundamental conviction of the importance for salvation of truth as such and as we can now immediately add, for it is, in fact, the same thing, from the essentially moral character of the finding of truth or of the failure to find it. This is the fundamental conviction that people of today have difficulty in grasping. When, of course, we say "people of today", we ought perhaps rather to say "those who are still people of today because they are still people of yesterday". For in the Communist view of human life the danger of any such cleavage between truth and ethical values obviously does not exist. For them anyone who diverges in theory from the party line, from the truth of the collectivity represented by the leaders of the state, reveals himself by that very fact to be a morally depraved person and consequently is treated on account of his "opinions" in exactly the same way as we in the West treat a thief or a murderer. Christians ought to avoid protesting against a false and crude application of a fundamentally true insight of the Communist East with an emotional reaction that is merely occidental and false.

It is only from this standpoint that the way in which Christendom has reacted to heresy in the course of its history becomes intelligible – which does not necessarily mean justified or even authorized in future. Indubitably the history of the persecution of heretics, of the Inquisition and of the wars of religion between Christians is a terrible chapter in the history of Christianity, full of dreadful things that are not to be defended, least of all in the name of Christianity. But an objective and historically just and discerning (not approving) attitude to the history of the Christian outlook on heresy can only be attained by those who recognize and share the permanent, essentially Christian and fundamentally indispensable sentiment: The untruth of heresy is much more of an absolute threat to human life than all other occurrences in face of which people today still feel the use of force to be justified – unless they hold a conception of non-violence of a kind that not even Gandhi and Nehru ever held or at least practised. For the Christian of former days the preacher of heresy was not someone who holds a different opinion that can be peacefully discussed, because the pattern of real life, common to all and only possible in common, is not seriously affected by these opinions. He is a person who with his proposition directs an immediate and deadly threat against what is more than physical life and earthly welfare, namely, eternal salvation.

Those who have no understanding for this profound feeling for truth or who have no sense of the direct and mortal seriousness of a decision whether this or that proposition is true, cannot understand the Christian estimation of heresy. That Christian judgment does not deny that in certain circumstances an implicit possession of truth may be found in a man who expressly rejects the truth in question, just as the converse is also possible. Nor does it of itself answer in principle and with precision the question whether on Christian and moral grounds there can in theory be a legitimate use of force against false teaching, and if so when and within what limits. This attitude of Christianity to heresy signifies that with truth as truth, and not merely or primarily with possible consequences distinct from it, as in the case of a true or false diagnosis of an illness, the issue is life and death here and in eternity. It is not a matter of opinions that can be debated in agreeable conversation. Christianity holds that this absolute truth which is salvation has communicated itself in a definitive and concrete manner, precisely as absolute truth, in Christianity: in Jesus Christ, in Scripture, in the Church, in the faith of this Church which can attain definitive awareness of itself in the authoritative pronouncements of the magisterium. This is why, we may quietly note, Christianity is most sensitive to heresy that arises among Christians. For then the absolute truth that was already present, expressed in an historically un-mistakable manner, is lost. It is not merely the provisional and undecided which has not yet reached its goal but what is final and definitive is again endangered or already lost.

Paganism can be regarded as the potentiality for and prelude to Christianity and judged benignly. Being provisional and of less importance it represents no danger to the Christian (unless it uses force itself), and he can regard himself as more advanced, superior, standing at a higher level of religious "development". But all that is different with the heretic. He is not merely someone who has not yet arrived. He abandons the end and claims that he alone attains it. Consequently it is more difficult for Christianity to attribute goodwill to him than to the unbeliever who has never been a Christian. This latter appears as the victim of the universal sinful history of mankind which has not yet reached its goal. The heretic has enjoyed the gift of truth that was promised. How could he, except by his fault, fail, despite this experience, to distinguish between true and falsified Christianity? He is the most dangerous. He combats the actual and definitive truth of Christianity in the name of Christian truth itself.

It is clear that Christianity stands in a special relation of its own to an error that arises in its own midst, and such an error is of a nature that cannot simply be reduced to the common denominator of "religious opinions rejected as incorrect by some other definite religious body". Heresy is rather, objectively speaking, the very failure to attain authentic existence at the precise point where, as God's truth, it is already absolutely present; and this under the attractive and illusory appearance of its fulfilment. Of course, that would all be simpler and more secure against heresy's being misunderstood as merely different, incorrect and non-ecclesiastical opinion in religious matters,

416

if Christianity could affirm at the same time that every objective error of a heretical kind is always in every case subjectively, in the actual individual professing it, culpable and consequently really a falling away of that person from absolute truth and therefore a loss of salvation. The anti-heretical feeling of Christianity is, of course, directed in the first place against the case in which the error as such is actually subjectively accomplished, accepted and taken into the centre of a human life, in other words, against religious error destructive of salvation, and threatening salvation.

We cannot deal here expressly with a question that is really overdue, that is, whether and how anything of such a kind is possible at all. How can an act of real knowledge itself be free, and so actually subject to moral evaluation? This, of course, at first sight seems impossible. An error that is seen to be such, one might think, is an error that is uncovered and overcome and no longer acceptable, while an unnoticed error precisely as such cannot be accepted with sufficient freedom to make the act of accepting it morally wrong. But the fact remains that the true and the good, knowledge and freedom are so close together in the root of their natures that we always have the one unity formed of both: truth that is accepted as a value, and conversely, knowledge that is only acquired by a free decision and can only reach its own true objectivity in that way.

But Christianity can never in principle and as it were as a matter of course take as a starting point the tacit, unexpressed but widespread opinion that it simply goes without saying that anyone who says something which on the face of it is false, "fundamentally" means what is correct and what one means oneself; that from the first and always, differences of opinion are only differences of terminology, obstacles to agreement which do not affect people's really profound convictions in the slightest. On the contrary the Christian attitude when authentically achieved has the same dialectical structure as the thing itself to which it refers. The proposition enunciated or theory expressed and what is really meant by it, and the fundamental conviction that embodies this meaning, are not simply identical, and it is possible that a man uttering a false statement has, nevertheless, apprehended the truth in the depth of his morally pure and truthful self. Consequently he is inculpably in error and his error is to be borne gently and tolerantly as a faulty formulation of a really apprehended truth.

But this distinction is not separation, and definitely does not mean a relation of mutual indifference and independence between the proposition expressed and what is "really meant" in the depths of the person; between the value of the opinion expressed and the value of the person himself. The final judgment on the relation between these two elements in the particular case, whether they are contradictory or synonymous (for they are, of course, not simply identical), belongs in principle to God alone and not to any outsider nor to a person's own introspection, a so-called "good conscience" or "honest conviction". But, if we may so formulate it, the opinion expressed is after all the "sacrament" of the inner activity and of the inner attitude, of the actual encounter with that truth which has not merely some slight relation to salvation but *is* salvation. Consequently a falsely stated proposition is itself a most dreadful possibility of the threat and temptation to that evil adherence to error in the depth of the soul, whereby a man to his own ruin accepts unreality and lying appearance as his truth and reality.

For that reason the merely false proposition cannot simply be met with indulgent tolerance, or regarded merely as one possible starting-point for a calculus of approximations in a perpetually open discussion, in which it is ultimately of little account in relation to the indefinitely distant final outcome, what point we start from among what are only more or less distant approximations. On the contrary, for Christianity even that error is terrible which does not yet pronounce unmistakably in our ears the final judgment on the person who is in error. For Christianity such a proposition is, objectively speaking, separated from truth by an infinity. It is not simply a slightly less well formulated truth than the doctrines of authentic Christianity are. Even if it is often very difficult in detail to say in regard to assertions that are not simply of a verifiable empirical kind, when and why they are not only inadequately and misleadingly expressed, or one-sided, but simply so false that they must meet with the full hatred that Christianity has for heresy, nevertheless, the distinction in principle must remain, if life is not to be an idle game, endless chatter and talk.

The following must also be noted with regard to this antiheretical feeling in Christianity. The Christian does not regard himself as more capable or cleverer than others, but as a sinner, and he holds that this latter self-appraisal has a pervasive influence in the realm of cognition, just as the former has, and all the more so as stupidity and sin are not without very direct connections. Consequently the Christian also recognizes in heresy a tempting, seductive, fascinating quality, in face of which he does not feel himself to be from the start immune. So he is aware that his instinct for real truth can be disturbed and numbed. He knows the temptation of modernity, of the over-obvious, facile solution, the charm of novelty. He is conscious in himself of the enemy from within going out treacherously to meet the untruth from without. Consequently he cannot simply meet with mild, distant and lofty impartiality the theses addressed to him that threaten his conviction, his faith. To put the same thing in more psychological terms, precisely because he knows that his conviction, in fact, is that of a corporeal creature exposed to innumerable influences of a non-logical kind, not built solely of theoretical and scientific considerations but containing factors of suggestion, custom, mass-instinct, subconscious compulsions and so on, he cannot treat heresy like a scientific theorem which can be gone over in the friendly neutrality of a learned discussion. Of course, this mistrust of himself and of the powers of darkness secretly at work in error can also lead to distorted reactions, to narrow-mindedness, witch-hunting, rejection of insights that are correct and important. These faulty responses may bring about the opposite result to that intended. They may promote the error despite themselves because they lend it the appearance of a truth narrowmindedly persecuted or because they prevent or delay the solution of questions without which in the long run the error cannot be averted. Fundamentally, however, the mistrust is justified because it is in accord with legitimate Christian self-appraisal, which is aware that in this aeon a seductive power is inherent in error as well as in other sin. Among human reactions in this sinful world, the instinct of self-defence has rightly a certain priority over respect and regard for "impartiality of thought", though this, too, is a Christian virtue.

II

THE TRADITIONAL CONCEPT OF HERESY
AND THE HERETIC,
AND THE PROBLEMS IT ENTAILS

WE ARE now in a position to understand the traditional concept of heresy and to evaluate it critically. This middle part of our essay forms a transition to the other section of the inquiry which concerns the changing pattern of heresy and latent or virtual heresy within the Church herself.

In Canon Law the heretic is defined as a person who after baptism and while retaining the name of Christian, pertinaciously denies or calls in doubt one of the truths that have to be believed with divine and Catholic faith (*Cod. Iur. Can.* 1325 § 2).

Consequently to be a heretic in the official ecclesiastical sense, a person must in the first place be baptized. By that alone heresy appears as an occurrence within Christianity, a contradiction not from outside on the part of those who have not yet accepted the message of Christianity at all by profession of faith and reception of the sacraments, but from within Christianity itself. To be sure even at this point difficulties appear. Is a heretic who, although baptized, was never a Catholic, and who, therefore, has never belonged to the true Church and her common belief, within the unity of the consciousness of the faith embodied in its socially constituted form, actually a heretic in

421

the same sense as a Catholic who becomes heretical? Can his heresy ever evoke the same protest from the Church, the same feeling of radical contradiction and self-defence against the inner threat to her own existence as do those who withdraw in separation from the Church themselves on their own spontaneous initiative? Of course, a distinction is drawn between formal, that is, subjectively guilty heretics, and material heretics who are inculpably implicated in error. So it might be said that the former are material heretics and the latter formal heretics and that the distinction aimed at is brought out by this conceptual differentiation. But fundamentally that is not so. For the possibility must definitely be reckoned with (notwithstanding the, of course, correct statement of the First Vatican Council, Denzinger 1794)[2], that people who belong to the Catholic Church as far as official statistics regarding the public, visible or denominational domain are concerned, may *inculpably* stray from the Church. They too in that case are merely material heretics and the above two distinctions do not, in fact, coincide. Consequently it is not possible to regard the difference indicated as insignificant, and so the attempt should be made to find a terminology to express it. Heresy such as arises now in the Church and goes out from it, is not the same thing as the now historical heresy of those who never belonged to the Church and cannot reject the Church and the truth she possesses in the same way as those who have once actually experienced it, or could have done.[3]

[2] See on this J. Trütsch, article "Glaubensabfall" in *LThK* IV[2], 931 ff.
[3] If it is assumed that on account of poor instruction, predominance of other influences of the world around, tepidity and superficiality of Church life, there are Catholics whose relation to the Catholic Church and the

At all events both kinds of heresy have this in common that the name of Christian is retained *(nomen retinens christianum)*, in contrast to apostasy.[4] That is a remarkable feature of the concept of heresy and the heretic. What it presupposes cannot surely be taken as a matter of course, namely that it is not necessarily the case that a person must either fall away from Christianity totally, as the apostate does, or possess it completely. For the attitude of faith, and so the virtue of faith as a divinely produced, grace-given, enduring capacity, is indivisible. Where its proper nature is really found, it cannot be only half present. Why and how can there, nevertheless, be human beings who are still Christians, and yet do not possess this one indivisible faith? Can there really be such people when *culpable* denial or doubt of a truth of faith is in question? Or is that not possible in this case? In other words is a formal heretic

truth preached and lived in her is just as tenuous, unreal and external as that of born non-Catholics – and this case cannot be held to be impossible *a priori* – then the distinction just worked out will not serve in these cases either. It is a matter there of Catholics of whom it can be said that from the point of view of their official registered status they are Catholics, but not that they accepted the faith *sub Ecclesiae magisterio,* as an institution effectively endowed with grace and salvation (Denz. 1794). Then quite definitely the alleged difference between non-Catholics by birth and "Catholics" who have become heretical will be, to say the least, of little account.

[4] An observation may assist understanding of what follows. Moral theologians emphasize (and by their standards and with their criteria they are right in doing so), that there is no difference in kind but at most one of degree between the sins of apostasy and heresy, because, of course, in both cases a truth revealed by God is denied. Nevertheless, very essential differences subsist, as the remarks which follow should make clear. The problems involved in these differences oblige us to obtain a better understanding of heresy.

always necessarily more than that, in fact an apostate? Does the definition then really only apply to the material heretic, to a person, that is, who without guilt contests a definite truth of the faith, even it may be "pertinaciously", but because he does this inculpably, preserves the fundamental attitude of belief and consequently does not reject the Christian faith in its root, at the point where all that is left is a plain Either – Or? Or does the *nomen retinere christianum* refer merely to the purely external situation, whether the heretic in question still wants to call himself a Christian or not, whether he still holds one or other of the doctrines which in the average view are regarded as specifically "Christian"? But on this basis where does the boundary lie between specifically Christian and non-Christian truths? For example, we shall not want to use the term heretic of a man who is still a theist but nothing more, even if he himself would still like to call himself a Christian because in his view the nature of Christianity simply consists in a mild belief in God.

The lack of precision in this element of the concept of heresy does not merely involve a question of theological subtlety, if only because it really decides whether the Church can not allow someone the name of Christian even in certain cases when the person himself calls himself one and sets store by it. In fact, it is only possible to solve this question correctly by placing the criterion for distinguishing between "partially" and "totally", neither exclusively in the domain of the inner attitude of belief, nor exclusively in what remains of specifically Christian doctrines. If we were completely to exclude from the criterion the question of inner attitude, it would really be impossible to see why the greater or lesser quantity of Christian doctrines still preserved could provide grounds for such an important distinction as that between heretical Christians (who are still Christians), and apostates (who are no longer Christians). For it is hard to indicate precisely when the residue of convictions that are still held in common with Christianity (viewed and judged purely in itself), is no longer sufficient for the "name of Christian". But if we were to take the inner attitude alone as criterion, a distinction betweeen heretics and apostates would no longer be possible in all cases, for there are certainly people who are generally regarded only as heretics and not as apostates despite just as complete a loss of the genuine attitude of faith as occurs with apostates, – that is, formal heretics.

In order, therefore, rightly to interpret the obscurity of the definition, we shall have to say that it is a question of heresy in contradistinction to apostasy when, on account of the greater extent of the Christian truths still acknowledged (and it may be still believed, at least with human faith), there is still sufficient likelihood and presumption (even of some juridical importance), that the person in question is, in the truths that he continues to retain, still in truth attaining the one saving reality which is signified both by the truths that are retained as well as by those that are denied.

Of course, even so the gradation between apostasy and heresy is only a fluid one and the outcome of material adherence to even a relatively large number of Christian truths is still very uncertain. The distinction is fluid because no one can really say precisely what adherence to certain truths of the faith continues to justify bearing the name of Christian.[5] In fact, it might be shown

---

[5] If we wanted to answer this question very systematically and on principle, drawing a theoretically clear dividing line, we should have

that there is probably no unmistakable boundary marking the distinction between this content and that.[6] Conversely in regard to its consequence for real faith the adherence to a greater number of Christian truths is uncertain, because even in such a case there can be an inner negation of the whole reality that is signified by faith. Otherwise it would not be possible to lose faith and justification by the denial of one, and even of only one, truth of faith. Nevertheless, it can be said that the full orderly unfolding of the articles of faith must have some meaning for the succesful achievement of the inner attitude of belief. This cannot reasonably be denied, even though faith, grace, justification – the whole reality that is signified by faith – can already be present even if

to say that anyone is still a Christian who affirms those truths which must be believed either *necessitate medii* or/and *necessitate praecepti,* in order to "believe" at all. Correct as this answer may be in itself, however, it is possible once again to dispute whether a person is still a heretic or already an apostate if he also rejects truths which are certainly explicitly to be believed *necessitate praecepti.* It can be disputed what explicitness is required, and this again is by no means an unambiguous concept. Above all, what truths are essentially necessary for Christian faith, and consequently must be believed explicitly *necessitate medii?* It is well-known that there is no unanimity in the theology of the schools on this point.
[6] Someone might certainly hold the arguable view that an act of Christian, supernatural and consequently (love of God being presupposed) justifying faith is perhaps possible if the content of belief is only the existence of God as the guarantor and ultimate meaning of the moral order and the bringer of salvation. It is very likely possible even to lay down very unexacting requirements in regard to what degree of explicitness is needed in this belief and so open up optimistic possibilities. On that view it would really be impossible to indicate any real boundary of belief, to cross which definitely makes a man cease to be justified, except the actual denial of God himself, really concretely and personally accomplished.

God is only believed in in the sense of Hebrews 11:6. Then it cannot be denied either that in principle and other things being equal, a greater chance of really believing in actual fact and so of attaining the whole saving reality is to be conceded to a man who adheres more expressly, plainly and systematically to a greater part of the Christian articles of faith. He also explicitly directs his attention to the Christian reality which he has encountered in actual life, and calls it by its name, and so has a real relation to it which is partially independent of how he interprets this reality in theory. We call a person a heretic, as opposed to an apostate, when such a possible chance is not indeed excluded for him but does not seem to be present to a readily perceptible degree.

From these problems regarding the retention of the name of Christian two further considerations follow, one concerning the possibility of apostasy or simply of heresy in a milieu and surroundings that bear in the details of life the stamp of Christianity; the other concerning the intrinsic ambiguity of heresy and the heretic.

In the first place the question may be raised whether it is possible at all in an historical milieu bearing the impress of Christianity for there to be people who are more than heretics, apostates in other words. We are here thinking in theological terms rather than in those of Canon Law, and assuming that the difference between apostasy and heresy does lie in the fluid and not perfectly plain, but, nevertheless, considerable difference in what doctrine is still retained, and in the degree of hope this offers of awakening the whole of faith and of regaining in a hidden manner the whole saving reality under the appearance of heresy. We are supposing, too, that the question is not being thought of as a matter of course in over-individualistic terms, but that the social factors that enter into everyone's manner of life are not being forgotten. And it is to be noted that it is not a question of whether the heretic possesses the faith that justifies and therefore a grace-giving contact with the saving reality or not. In that respect he can be an unbeliever, even if in the purely human elaboration of his theological convictions he still shares with the Christian many articles of the faith in the literal sense: as actual separately formulated propositions. Consequently the criterion for distinguishing between heretic and apostate does not consist in what actual influence the articles still retained in fact exercise in relation to grace and faith, but what in themselves, *per se,* they can have. If this is taken into account, it can be seen that there is a difference, which in practice is still considerable but which for theology is not an essential one, in whether someone accepts certain specifically Christian doctrines with what in itself is a purely human conviction,[7] or whether these doctrines for him are only contributory factors of the intellectual situation in which inescapably he is living. Where, when and as long as a person lives in surroundings which in innumerable ways, however anonymously and tacitly are impregnated and shaped by Christianity and the reality which finds express formulation in the articles of Christian belief, whether these be rejected or retained, he has always a chance of assenting to this reality, perhaps quite unreflectingly, and quite possibly of becoming a Christian without explicitly realizing it. Now, viewed theologically, this process does not differ from one in which

[7] The doctrines are not of themselves the object of such an assent, for by their nature they are intended to be heard with authentically grace-given faith. And in this it is the whole reality of faith which is and must always be indivisibly accepted, and consequently, at least implicitly, the objectively indivisible whole formed by the articles of faith.

a person lays hold of the essence of faith and saving reality because he yields to the inner dynamism of certain Christian doctrines which until then he had only held as human opinions. In the one case he is yielding to the force of the doctrines of his surroundings, of external, public opinion, in the other case to the force of the doctrines for his inner private opinion.

A case of apostasy in its pure form, therefore, would only be found where the falling away could take place in such a way that the person concerned would leave the historical milieu of Christianity and would no longer be involved (as regards the world of history), in a dialogue of assent and dissent with Christianity. Whether this case is possible in those civilizations that were once Christian is a question of fact and of theological principles. Moreover it is perhaps a question that events have already outdistanced. For today there exists something like a single world civilization extending over the whole planet and the elements and structures and history of every civilization have become contributory factors of this world civilization and so of all the other particular civilizations of the world, even if for the moment with varying degrees of intensity. So if Christianity persists in the world at all no-one can avoid from the start engaging in this dialogue with Christianity (however it may turn out), in differing degrees, of course, but nevertheless to a perpetually increasing extent viewed as a whole. To that extent no one can live in a purely withdrawn relation of *apo-stasis* to Christianity, but is compelled to contradict it and expressly dissociate himself from it in heresy. In a way, all that is not Christian and all non-Christians, in a theological sense assume in regard to Christianity the rôle of explicit contradiction and so of standing in permanent relation to it. For gradually everywhere in the world Christianity

429

is coming to belong to the roots of that universal history by which we are all living, even in contradiction. From that standpoint it is quite legitimate to prefer as a matter of terminology to call the world of today heretical rather than apostate. It remains forced to engage in dialogue with Christianity and cannot avoid the "name of Christian" always turning up even in its own activities, though the world avoids reflecting just how much is Christian in the material of the historical situation with which it is inevitably and perpetually engaged. That also implies, of course, that Christianity today is beginning to have no real paganism[8] to deal with in the sense of something simply apart, standing in no relation to itself, but has to see in it a partner in a discussion in the common historical frame of human life, and a partner that is taking on more or less the characteristics of the heretic.[9]

---

[8] It cannot, of course, be overlooked that the "gentiles", the "pagans", of the Old Testament were not only separated and characterized by a religious difference but also by a cultural and sociological one. For mediaeval Christianity and in modern times down to our own day, the pagan always had the appearance of living in a different historical and cultural domain apart, rejecting Christianity from outside, not from within, by a way of life and action which Christianity inevitably felt to be alien and as standing outside its own sphere. Precisely this, however, is now involved in a change that is becoming more and more rapid. The historical civilizations are penetrating one another and this is also altering the character of the encounter between Christianity and non-Christians. The latter are ceasing, even when they remain non-Christian, to be simply those untouched by Christianity. They are becoming, if the phrase be permitted, unbaptized heretics.

[9] This explains how the differences between the foreign missions and the home mission, between paganism and neo-paganism are becoming more and more blurred.

The second reflection is, however, more important: the ambiguity of heresy and the heretic that follows from the retention of the name of Christian. Before we can make clear what is meant by this, we must point out something that is fundamental for what we have to say. This is the unity of the reality of salvation, of saving reality, and consequently the unity of the doctrines of faith. The articles of faith as propositions are not just held together by the formal authority of the God who reveals them all and addresses them to man with a summons to belief. They belong together, describe from different sides one and the same saving reality. Certainly this one reality is not simply homogeneous; it indubitably is a unity in plurality, with many strata concerning persons, places, times and so forth. The connections between these various realities, God, Christ, grace, saints, sacraments, Church, times, places and so on, are sometimes intrinsic, sometimes freely posited. Nevertheless, they possess real unity and belong together, point to one another, are mutually dependent, form one meaningful pattern.

From this it follows that anyone who grasps in knowledge and love one of these various realities is drawn by his knowledge into the dynamism which belongs to the objective unity of this one manifold reality of salvation. One truth known points to another, trains comprehension of yet another, gives an understanding of the meaning and spirit of the whole and so makes it possible to grasp another part. Every question that is raised by one truth known leads immediately beyond the particular reality to the whole. Furthermore with every single act of knowing in faith the one grace of God is at work, at the very least in the sense of a saving grace that is offered, and this is one and the same thing as the very essence of the whole reality of salvation, for it is

431

the self-communication of the triune God in Christ. Consequently it has an intrinsic relation by its very nature to all the realities of salvation and the knowledge of them.

If this is correct, we must now add that anyone who, heretically picking and choosing, does not accept the whole of saving truth and yet *(retento christiano nomine)* holds fast to an important part of it, is in an indefinable fluctuating ambiguity in his mode of being, which is really only possible because this mode of existence of his is still involved in a process of change as yet incomplete. To the extent, therefore, that someone heretically rejects, he not only objectively and in some cases subjectively offends against the faith as a whole by contradicting the formal authority of God who reveals and guarantees his revelation in its entirety. Even more necessarily, by denying one truth he abandons himself to an immanent intellectual logic deriving from the nature of what is in question, and which as its final result must lead to denial of the whole truth of revelation. He takes up an attitude, even though it may only be explicitly in relation to one truth that serves as occasion for his attitude to take shape, which must, even if he does not yet notice and realize this, lead to the denial of the whole truth of revelation if carried through to its definitive and fully-developed completion. Conversely, too, in as much as he retains essential truths of the Christian revelation the contrary process is taking place. He is caught up in a movement directed towards the whole of Christianity. His situation is, therefore, ambiguous.

It may be that the heretic is accomplishing a truly supernatural and believing affirmation of the Christian truths that he retains, in grace, and by that, by the actual logic of those truths and by the grace of that act, is implicitly laying hold of the whole reality and truth of Christianity both theoretically and concretely, and his heretical opinions are by comparison only opinions – *opinio* in the Thomist sense. They are in fact held, their incompatibility with the much more profoundly personal act of acknowledgement, assimilation and faith is not seen, but in the concrete they are much more peripheral, uncertain and provisional than the person concerned is himself expressly aware. In this state of affairs there are always two things to be noted.

In the first place the recognition and assent to all the many propositions that a human being thinks he has recognized as correct is, both logically and in practice of quite a different order with regard to each individual proposition. On account ultimately of the conditioning of his cognition by corporeal, physiological and sense factors, man is a creature who can adhere to what is contradictory and opposed. But that again does not mean that these contradictory assertions can be made in acts of strictly the same kind and simultaneously. The fact is that in the structures of a man's logical and actually individual "system", such assertions have a different position and a different rank, and must inevitably have for this logical and concretely lived "schizophrenia" of the normal human being to be possible at all in actual experience, though, of course, the different valency of the various assertions need not be expressly known to the person concerned. One of the propositions will be affirmed with utter resolve as a rigorous judgment and made a really fixed point of the system and from it as far as may be the remaining assertions will be arranged. Another proposition is merely an opinion, a tentative hypothesis till something better turns up, always open to correction or rejection. Between such propositions the same logical and actual concrete relation holds as there can be between a man's moral acts. He loves God from the centre of his free nature, of his "heart" and yet at the periphery he commits a venial sin which is in contradiction to the fundamental decision, but only because, after all, as regards its content and intent (*quoad materiam*) and in actual terms of concrete experience, in relation to its centrality, it is qualitatively of less import than the fundamental act which it contradicts.

Furthermore, even in heresy itself there is concealed a dynamic relation to the whole of Christian truth. Not, of course, in as much as it is simply and formally an error and nothing else. But error does not exist in this abstract purity in individual heresies as they are actually propounded. Historically effective and powerful heresies are not simply assertions deriving from stupidity, obstinacy and inadequate information. Rather are they rooted in an authentic and original experience moulded by some reality and truth. It is quite possible, and it is probably so in most cases, that that reality and the truth it contains was not yet seen and experienced in orthodox Christianity with the same explicitness and intensity, depth and power (though, of course, it was not denied and was always perceived and expressed in some way), as it was given to and demanded of that person to see it at his moment in history. But he then brings this genuine experience to accomplishment in the form of an error. Just as evil lives by the power of good and can only be willed in virtue of the will to the residual good which persists in the evil, and without which it could not even be evil, but simply nothing, which cannot be the object of the will, so it is too in the relation between the truth affirmed and experienced and the error actually brought to expression. Even this error lives by the truth. And a great plenitude of error has undeniably a great content and possesses great motive

434

power, and these impel towards the one truth, the truth which the heretic has perhaps already, in fact, attained in the Christian truth which he expressly confesses by his retention of the name of Christian.

But the reverse is also possible. The error may be the really central, fundamental act for the heretic and the really systematizing principle of his whole intellectual structure. The Christian truths which are still present *(nomen christianum)* only survive as peripheral opinions, perpetually threatened with being recognized as contradictions to the fundamental intent whether abstract or concrete and of being in consequence "revised" and excluded. Despite the truths of Christianity still held as "opinions", the reality they signify is lost completely without grace, supplanted by the heretical error which has been radically accepted in the concrete into the centre of the personal life.

This ambiguity cannot be surmounted by introspective reflection. If it could be, a man would, of course, know with absolute certainty whether he really believes or not. But this is just as refused to introspection as absolute certainty about justification. Reflection, conceptually formulated propositions regarding oneself, never adequately expresses what a person is and what he makes of himself by direct unself-conscious action. This is so if for no other reason than that the act of introspection is itself another act that forms and changes a person and alters his intellectual system by trying to objectify it and determine what it is. Consequently the ambiguity itself is involved in a continual process both in the individual as well as in the social history of heresy. The decisive centre of the person can perpetually shift from the Christian truths taken as its own truth, and wander away into the heretical errors, and *vice versa*. It is never possible to say with absolute certainty whether the heretic despite his heresy is in the truth by reason of the Christian truths to which he adheres, or whether despite these truths he is really in error because of the heretical doctrines which he holds. This ambiguity cannot be removed, it is impossible to say what the state of affairs really is, because this historical process itself is not static but in motion and each observable element in this history can be supplanted by the next if it is fixed in a proposition. An error can long since be paralysed and expelled from the centre of the person yet still be held and defended with much verbal ingenuity in its theoretical and conceptual formulations. The same is true of the converse. An error apparently small in comparison to the mass of correct doctrines maintained, can already have mortally penetrated the very centre of the spiritual person and have become, though not yet fully operative, the really comprehensive law determining the relation of the person to all reality. Yet a great many doctrines may still be assented to which logically and in the concrete are fundamentally incompatible with it. And this vast array even gives the appearance of correctness and comprehensiveness, so that the deadly nature and heretical isolation of the error remains hidden from the reflection of the heretic himself and from others.

III

THE CHANGING PATTERN OF HERESY

OUR reflections on the problems connected with the traditional concept of heresy and the heretic provide a basis for understanding a phenomenon which may be called the changing pattern of heresy. Before we attempt to work out this pattern of heresy, we must note a characteristic of our intellectual situation today which did not exist in its present form or to the same extent in former times. This is the immeasurable wealth, quite beyond any individual's scope, of experience, knowledge, science, which precisely because of the impossibility of any individual's mastering them, contribute, paradoxical as it may seem, to determine the intellectual situation of the individual. Of course, men have never lived solely by what they knew or by what they had made the subject of express consideration. To that extent the intellectual situation of men today is not different from what it ever was. The world of man's intellectual life and its structures, antecedently presupposed to all his thinking, decisions and actions, is in part determined by what he does not know, for which he cannot really be answerable and does not need to be, yet which, nevertheless, is one of the forces of his mental existence. Formerly, however, these forces were not the knowledge, theories, opinions and postulates of men themselves. They were objective realities, country, race, abilities and so on, things which, taken as a whole, had the innocence of the things God has made. When human intellectual realities belonged to the forces determining his existence, they were not in principle beyond the possible scope of the individual's grasp. Each could learn them for himself, take up an attitude to them, bring them into harmony, form them into a system for which he could take responsibility. What he could not learn in that way did not essentially affect his mental world. What he did not know, though it was something that could be known, did not appear in his life, taking it as a whole, at all.

Today all that is different. We live in an age when the science of all has actual consequences for each; is operative, therefore, as a force in the mental world of each, yet can no longer be brought consciously before his mind. Has sufficient attention been paid to this characteristic of everyone's situation now? The known world, the world of the sciences, of experiences, theorems, hypotheses and of the things to which attention is directed, has become manifold, diversified,[10] in a way that was just not the case before. Of course, in earlier times everyone did

---

[10] We cannot here inquire more deeply into the ontological grounds for the very possibility of this heterogeneity. They have always been present. Man never possesses knowledge that derives from one source only and follows only one original and systematic pattern. What characterizes him rather from the start is a plurality of experiences which are only brought into relation subsequently in a temporal process of reflection and which only seek a synthesis through a process that is never closed. That has always been so. But what is new is that the diversity of possible experiences has developed to such an extent that nowadays no individual can any longer share with even approximate adequacy the experiences of those with whom he lives in direct contact biologically, socially and what is decisive, intellectually.

438

not know everything that was known by others. But in principle they could learn it. There was only a definite amount of accumulated knowledge to be mastered. In a few years of university study (where the whole universe of knowledge was available), it was possible to learn more or less everything, at least everything of importance for the world of what was known, not mere knowledge of details needed for some special professional function in society, but irrelevant to the constitution of a philosophical view of the world as a whole. The cobbler of the Middle Ages understood the actual human reality that comprised his world, and what he did not understand did not form part of his world.

Nowadays human reality has become heterogeneous. No one can consider that his "system" coincides even approximately or in mere extent with the present-day universe of knowledge. We reach a limit. What one individual in a single lifetime is physically capable of knowing even cursorily no longer even remotely corresponds to the whole of what is actually known. Of course, people seek a remedy for this, interpose intermediaries, collaborate. It is true, too, that every so often every science achieves a new advance with discoveries that affect its whole system and make it more simple and manageable. But none of that fundamentally alters the fact that the individual can no longer cope with the whole range of knowledge on which he depends and which contributes to determine his life, even as a spiritual person and not merely as a physical, biological and social reality. Of course, if this knowledge that others have and which exceeds the individual's power to master played no part in his own life, each could just leave it alone, in the same way as it was of no account to a Bavarian peasant in 1400 to what

Egyptian dynasty Thutmosis II belonged. And if this unknown and unknowable science had the merely factual character of, for example, the peristalsis of the intestines, of which we are also unconscious, it would be possible to take it on trust like children and leave it, like nature, to take care of itself.

But this knowledge is not, of course, the knowledge of indisputable facts, of the so-called results of science in which the men of the nineteenth century trusted much more naïvely than the theologian of the thirteenth century did in the Bible. This unmastered knowledge for which no responsibility can be taken is an amorphous and yet immeasurably influential mass of real results of the sciences, theorems, hypotheses, postulates, wishful thinking and utopias, one-sided tendencies, obscure impulses, in which intelligence and stupidity, every kind of human factor, guilt, the powers of darkness and divine inspiration from on high work themselves out. And this totality of the man-made mental world takes concrete form in technology, discoveries, social institutions, control over the attention through publicity, and innumerable other actual physical realities, and creates the very climate or atmosphere of the intellectual situation of every human being. Of course, in this amorphous mass of the "public mind" every so often adumbrations of structures, islands of meaning emerge, just as in a process of crystallization the first crystalline systems form in a flash in the solution. But such formations remain islands of meaning in an amorphous mass to which new material is added more quickly than its organization advances.

It is not adequate comfort in this situation – though this delusive solace is common among Christians – to say that the principles and general standards for the intellectual penetration, mastery and synthesis of all this shapeless *materia prima* of the mind are after all ready to hand, the principles of logic, of ontology, of natural law, of sociology. This reference could totally satisfy none but a rationalist, that is, a man who holds that abstract *a priori* principles in their immutable purity really are valid data antecedent purely and simply to the endlessly vast world of experience. In actual fact, adequate understanding of these principles itself only emerges in a slow process of encountering the stuff of historical experience, which has to be organized and mastered by means of them. The limitlessness and increasing complexity of the experiences which are no longer accessible to any single individual also makes these principles more obscure and less easy to apply. Though they indeed possess permanent validity in themselves antecedently to experience, they, nevertheless, only reveal precisely what they assert, contain, exclude, forbid and so on, in contact with experience. And precision is exactly what is in question. Experience, however, is manifold, diverse; and this heterogeneity is irreducible. The new situation we are referring to can be recognized by the often lamented fact that there is no one standard terminology any more, but instead, a Babel of tongues.

The experiences of the many, being no longer susceptible of unification in the individual,[11] bring about this confused Babel

---

[11] The heterogeneity of experiences does not only exist (to make this point quite explicitly), in regard to the physical and biological world, that is, in the natural sciences, the results of which are beyond the scope of any individual to survey, but also in the moral sciences of man, too. No one any longer, for instance, can have real contact at first hand with the whole length and breadth of the history of philosophy or with the entire available history of civilizations, of political life or music, law or other

of terminologies and also explain that a fundamental improvement of the situation is not to be expected, though, of course, improvements of a partial kind would be useful, worth attempting and also practicable. Formerly there was to some extent a uniform terminology in the field of the human and moral sciences, because the materials of sense-perception and the explanatory models and examples employed could be and were approximately the same for all, and their relative importance, vividness and so on more or less equal. Differences were merely individual or belonged to social structures which for other reasons did not come into contact at all and so could not provoke any confusion of tongues. It is to be noted all along in this that the insurmountable plurality of ways in which the world is now experienced is not one that is separated into particular elements by an intellectual and cultural No Man's Land stretching between particular social classes, civilizations and nations. It is a heterogeneity within the one same mental world which is inhabited by the innumerable members of the one world civilization comprising the whole planet in a classless society and all the technical and sociological structures to which this manifold and heterogeneous collective mind gives rise. Everyone is therefore immersed in, dependent on and influenced by a human mental world which none can bring under responsible control in his own knowledge and volition in the way men of earlier times could appropriate and make their mental universe their own.

human affairs. Each knows only segments. The heterogeneity of possible experiences forms human beings who have much greater difficulty in making themselves understood and of reaching agreement than in former times. And this situation is in principle irremediable, though ameliorations are conceivable.

This fundamental characteristic of the situation of mankind at the present day must now be brought into comparison with that ambiguity of Christian life which we envisaged in our reflections on the traditional concept of heresy. For this purpose we must draw attention to one circumstance which has not yet been expressly mentioned. The ambiguity of the heretic's situation as viewed from the standpoint of the orthodox Christian and judged by his standards, is particularly evident and disturbing. Yet in itself it is something that is also found in the orthodox Christian too. We have already noted that no one can say with absolute introspective certainty whether he himself actually believes. For nobody can bring to a conclusion the inquiry whether the articles of faith which he certainly wills to accept as his own, are accepted, even in his free and theoretical consciousness, in the concrete instance, with the depth and intensity of free personal decision. Now without such *free* assent there is no faith, at most a certain sympathy for doctrines that one has heard about. Nor can he say that these propositions are indubitably predominant and valid for him as opposed to the other guiding principles and ideals which everyone inevitably also possesses.[12] The individual system of values certainly present and freely constituted as his own is not fully and with absolute certainty accessible to introspection. If, however, objective conceptual expression were to be given to everything present in a man (even the most orthodox), all the judgments, prejudices, attitudes, preferences and opinions –

---

[12] There is not and cannot be any mental life which is nourished and based in a purely "fideist" way on revealed matters and their import. The experience of the individual as individual is itself diverse, deriving from revelation and from the world.

and taking all these, though ultimately inaccessible to introspection, in so far as they are the consequences of free decisions
and not merely as independent of and antecedent to them –
then as well as what objectively speaking are doctrines of faith,
there would be found propositions which in themselves are
heretical, though they are never expressly uttered in that objective form by the person in question. And even with an orthodox Christian, neither he nor anyone else could decide with
absolute certainty whether in him these "heresies" are only
"opinions", not of a kind to annul the radical personal decision
for the truths of faith (the real centre of gravity and seat of faith),
or whether on the contrary surviving convictions about articles
of faith apparently co-extensive with Christian doctrine as a
whole are, nevertheless, merely a residue and a façade hiding
quite a different world of convictions freely and even theoretically accepted though not equally clearly and explicitly
formulated.

After these preliminary considerations we can now state
and explain our contention regarding the changing pattern of
heresy. Nowadays, we may say, to a significantly greater
extent than in former times, hidden, latent heresy exists. This
tacit heresy exists even in the Church together with her explicit
orthodoxy. This heresy has the intrinsic tendency to remain
implicit. That is where its peculiar and exceptional danger lies.
The characteristically Christian attitude of anxiety, vigilance
and sensitivity towards heresy should chiefly be directed at the
present time against this cryptogamic heresy. This is particularly
difficult because this heresy is also found in members of the
Church and it is very difficult to distinguish it from legitimate
trends, a genuine contemporary style and so on.

We might start with the statement that latent heresy exists today to a significantly greater extent than formerly, and attempt an abstract theological proof. It might be said that there "must" always be heresies – a "must" that belongs to the history of redemption and which leaves intact the fact that there ought not to be any – and that this remains as a possibility which cannot be so averted from the first by the Church that the dutiful church-goer is thereby immune from any serious danger. Then it might be indicated that the development of the Church's awareness of her faith has gradually made the criterion of faith in its strictly formal, juridical rigour itself an object of faith. With the definition of the infallibility of the supreme teaching authority of the pope, this development has reached a certain finality. Consequently it is no longer as possible as it was in earlier days for there to be doubt or uncertainty whether some explicit doctrine is or is not in accordance with the Church's belief. From these two considerations it would follow that the heresy which even today threatens the Church and which "must" be, can no longer to the same extent, or solely, take the form of explicit propositions, but a more diffused, less explicit form, in fact that of latent heresy, and does do so, thus presenting a smaller area vulnerable to attack by the magisterium and having a better prospect of working itself out dangerously in the Church. This would be sufficient to enable us to point to certain phenomena in recent Church history since the days of Modernism, which add further light to the understanding obtained in this abstract way regarding the existence and nature of virtual or latent heresy.[13]

[13] See K. Rahner, *Gefahren im heutigen Katholizismus* (Einsiedeln, ³1955), pp. 63–80.

445

But an understanding of the nature and existence of latent heresy can also be attained inductively. Here we must recall what we have said about the heterogeneity, no longer totally reducible or surmountable, of the uncontrolled forces influencing the mental life of every human being, and about the ambiguity of everyone's life of faith, the possibility of being tacitly, implicitly, an unbeliever. People today live in a mental world which as individuals they cannot take the measure of and cannot be responsible for. This mental world is indubitably determined in part by attitude, doctrines and tendencies which must be characterized as heretical, as contradicting the teaching of the gospel. And all this heretical matter which contributes to determine the mental world of everyone, need not necessarily assume objective form in abstract assertions. No doubt it will often do so, but not necessarily or decisively. In fact, actual behaviour, concrete measures taken and so on, may be determined by a heretical attitude without this being consciously formulated in abstract theses. It is sufficient for them to be carried out in the details of actual life. It is to be noted that these actual realizations in the practice of life, in manner of living, – morals, customs, what is done and what is not done, the scale of values, what is given prominence and what is pushed into the background – are particularly suited not only to giving exterior expression to the fundamental heretical attitude, but also to concealing it. For often, if viewed simply in the abstract, they are not unmistakably only conceivable as external expressions of a heretical spirit, at least if we leave out of account their intensity, which often cannot easily be judged, or the place they occupy in the mental life as a whole. For example, respect for the body and idolatry of the body are outwardly difficult to distinguish,

446

especially when owing to the circumstances of earlier times there is a certain need to make up lost ground in regard to giving practical effect to Christian esteem for the body. So it can be very difficult to make out whether such esteem for the body is still Christian or already heretical. The motive of apparently Christian protest against such external manifestations may actually spring from Christian opposition to heresy or it may derive from a past, historically conditioned view of human life. And this may itself look Christian because of its long symbiosis with what is truly Christian but in reality is partly determined by latent heresies of earlier times. If, however, a heresy is very masked and implicit and yet is present and at the same time contributes to determine the mental world of modern men because of the insuperable heterogeneity of that world, and if this is so in such a way that people adopt no deliberate, conscious attitude towards it or even are not capable of doing so, at least expressly, we have the phenomenon that we are terming latent heresy.

It is to be noticed that with this concept, as with the traditional concept of heresy, the question can be left quite open whether the heresy is present formally or materially, consciously (though, of course, without deliberate advertence to what is heretical as such in it), or only concomitantly and implicitly, whether as a dangerous peripheral opinion or a decisive, radically central personal act. For the moment we can say that everyone nowadays is infected with the bacteria and viruses of latent heresy, even if they are not thereby to be declared to have caught an illness. Everyone adopts in the concrete, superficial attitudes of the world around him, at least unconsciously and as a loosely held opinion. Yet they, of course, spring from a fundamentally heretical attitude and supply sufficient *materia gravis* for the effective adoption of actually heretical attitudes. Each can only hope but not know with absolute reflex certainty that these heretical or quasi-heretical attitudes, practices, tendencies and so on, have not yet actually become incorporated into his fundamental decisions in an explicit theoretical manner but that his fundamental decisions, in fact, correspond to the principles of the gospel which he overtly and expressly holds.

This latent heresy also exists in the Church. For, of course, the Church is not an abstract entity, something apart from Christians but is the "host of believers" themselves, notwithstanding the fact that this "people of God" is socially constituted as a holy community under the direction of holders of office and led by the Holy Spirit. This Church as the host of believers lives in the mentally heterogeneous world of technology, of modern mass society, of the one world civilization, of constitutionally guaranteed freedom of thought, of propaganda, in short of all the characteristics that give its stamp to the mental world of the individual. She lives therefore in a world whose structures are heretical or quasi-heretical where heresies are latent. Consequently it is inevitable that her members should be infected with concealed or virtual heresy. For the Church is the Church of sinners. Now it is a fact that contradictory principles can co-exist in one and the same person (even if only by reason of the different levels of the actual assent given to them), especially when to some extent they are not expressly explicit and do not need to be in order to make their presence felt. This kind of heresy can be present in any members of the Church, even in members of the hierarchy. There is, of course, no principle in the

448

Church that would make it impossible for there to be unbelievers among them, if only hidden ones who do not admit the fact to themselves. This implicit, latent heresy need not, of course, be formal and culpable. Nowadays especially, it is less usual than in former times for what is found within the sphere of a man's mental world to coincide with what has passed the deliberate conscious scrutiny of his theoretical and personal responsibility.

Of course, the Church perpetually resists this hidden heresy within her. In her unity, in those who pray and bear the Cross, in those who are poor and abandoned but endure with patience, in short in all her saints great and small, known and unknown, she goes on living the true undistorted gospel with profoundly genuine determination, purity and authenticity, so that it is certain she does not yield to the heresy in her midst. Although she is the Church of sinners, she is also, through God's power and the grace of Christ promised to her as completely invincible despite all the weaknesses of men, the Church that abides in the truth. That certainly does not only mean that she bears witness always in her preaching to the truth of God in opposition to the declared or implicitly heretical error of the "world". It also means that the truth to which she testifies is put into practice in the really personal assent of many of her members if not all. Latent heresy remains present always and represents a perpetual mortal danger for every individual in the Church, but never attains such a preponderant force in the Church as a whole that she would only pay lip-service to the truth of the gospel, having fallen away at heart from the truth.

This makes clear what our second contention means, that latent heresy is found even in the Church besides her explicit

449

orthodoxy. To belong to the Church and expressly to accept her teaching is no absolute and automatically effective guarantee against heresy. Each, individually, even in the Church, is questioned by God in his own inalienable conscience whether perhaps at heart tacitly he is a heretic of this virtual kind. That is possible, for the appearance of orthodoxy can deceive not only others but also oneself. This assertion is not to be reduced to triviality by saying that it is only a matter in all this of the old familiar fact that a person's actual manner of life may contradict his theoretical principles, that theory and practice may not coincide. This phenomenon, of course, does exist and in the particular case may be difficult to distinguish from what we are referring to here as latent heresy and its danger in the Church. There is an implicit, tacit falsification of the standards of judgment themselves, not only an infringement in practice of the correct standards recognized to be valid in themselves. This unconscious falsification of the very criteria, this latent heresy, at first sight, of course, seems to concern more the domain of moral principles. It only appears to offend against principles of faith which do not seem directly relevant to morals, by indifference, uninterested avoidance and leaving alone. Yet it is quite possible for it to co-exist with a verbal orthodoxy and an anxious, "correct" care never to express views that might conflict with the official principles of the faith. It must be repeated once more, that not only practical heresy exists but theoretical heresy too, heresy in the proper sense, that is, even if latent, under the appearance of orthodoxy. This phenomenon must not be mistaken either for the other phenomenon which, to be sure, is also met with, that of deliberate pretence of the faith for social or similar reasons. In the case we are thinking of, a man deceives himself, not chiefly others, and this self-deception is an intrinsic constituent of the phenomenon of latent heresy as this may, and does, occur in the Church, so that we are not proof against it by well-meaning membership of the Church and explicit acknowledgment of her teaching.

The implicit, undeclared state of heresy in a member of the Church finds a strange ally in men of the present time, through their distaste for conceptual precision in religious matters. The man of today is more willing freely to discuss the most embarrassing details of his sexual life with a psychiatrist than to hold a purely theoretical conversation on religion, one in which he himself is in no way referred to, with someone whose absolute agreement he cannot reckon on from the start – because, for example, he is a representative of the official Church. The reasons for this strange phenomenon, at least in Central Europe, may well be various: The way some philosophers of today – and not merely in fashionable talk – think of the "absence of God"; the feeling of uncertainty in these matters in view of the disruption of the world and of our age into an innumerable multiplicity of views and standpoints which everyone meets with in his personal life with an acuity and emphasis that was not usual in former times. Especially there is a feeling which in itself is a perfectly correct one and positively estimable, but which is experienced almost as deadly, of the immeasurable disproportion between religious affirmations framed in human concepts and the reality they refer to. Whatever the particular reasons may be, the fact itself is not to be denied. Our contemporaries find religious and theological reflection difficult, and precise formulation in matters of belief easily strikes them as being irreverent, glib and typically clerical.

In itself that may not involve abandonment of the institu-
tionally organized practice of religion or even leaving the Church.
On the contrary, such a distaste for conceptual precision can
nowadays quite easily entail the consequence that people
instinctively avoid conceptual articulation of their own actual
concrete personal attitude in religion, and show themselves
"tolerant" towards the traditional conceptually formulated doctrine of the Church out of the feeling that after all they cannot
put "it" better themselves. And so we find among educated
people nowadays almost a feeling of taboo that avoids discussing
even the most childish formulations of belief. This attitude then
becomes a reason why someone's heretical attitude does not
become a heresy theoretically expressed and exactly formulated
as in former times. People live heresy but are averse to expressing
it as a doctrinal system and to opposing this in open debate to the
Church's teaching. For example, someone will actually live a
religious and metaphysical agnosticism but will be very careful
indeed not to assert that the First Vatican Council was incorrect
in teaching that men can know the existence of God by the light
of reason. They prefer not to inquire what this affirmation of the
Vatican Council really means and what it does not. They do not
formulate anything and so they do not come into conflict with
formularies. But in that case after all a person in the Church,
one who perhaps engages in quite an amount of ecclesiastical
practice of religion is in fact an unacknowledged, tacit heretic.

This explains the further assertion we made, that latent heresy
is not only *de facto* a heresy which is not deliberately and consciously formulated, but has a positive tendency to remain so.
Certainly there is in man, belonging in principle to the essentially
characteristic features of his mental life, the tendency to render

452

an account of himself to himself, to objectify what he is, to reduce what at first seems purely factual in his being and action to necessary essential principles. But there is also the opposite tendency. This is so not only in general because analytic reflection never really completely exhausts the whole of man's mental life and because a human being is always more, mentally and personally, than he can express in explicit propositions about himself through introspection. Nor is it because there is the phenomenon of self-deception, repression, false "clear conscience" and so on, all things that are only conceivable in relation to the tendency we are referring to. There are particular reasons for this phenomenon of positive clinging to the covert, unavowed mode of this fundamentally heretical attitude. One has already been mentioned, aversion from any thought about religion. But there are others as well. We can include a certain curious willingness to go to church possessed by not a few educated people of the twentieth century, greater than there was in the nineteenth. It is not to be explained, as it was then (where it did still persist), by a certain attachment to tradition of a social kind. Its roots are different today, though in themselves they have just as little to do with a genuine religious decision as the social traditionalism in religion of the upper and middle classes of the nineteenth century. In contrast to the age of self-conscious individualism and liberalism, people today have no longer the same confidence in their own opinion. In particular they are no longer convinced that a religious community can be built on such private opinions without its getting lost in hopeless sectarianism and fanaticism. But if people do not really trust their opinion, they are not really convinced either that anyone else will be right, in this case ecclesiastical authority. Yet they feel more or less clearly that to religion (which they want to have) there belongs in some way a religious community. And so the problem that these three considerations set is most simply "solved" by avoiding any conflict from the start. They do not give articulate form to their sceptical or otherwise heretical or quasi-heretical attitude and so they "get along all right". Furthermore, people perhaps also arrange things so as quite instinctively to engage in a certain forming of groups[14] within the universal Church, building a sort of special chapel in the great Church where they are more "at home", and so from the start the danger is less that themes might be mentioned which would compel them to abandon the attitude of leaving well alone.

The actual tactics employed by this hidden heresy in order to remain hidden are various. Often[15] they consist simply in an attitude of mistrust and resentful hostility towards the Church's teaching authority; or in that widespread feeling of being supervised suspiciously and narrowmindedly in research and teaching by her magisterium; or in the view that "one cannot say what one thinks" (and which one considers one is justified in thinking, with a "good conscience"). Don't we sometimes meet the attitude that more can be said, at least among friends, than can be written? Or we find people who are under the im-

---

[14] That, of course, in no way tells against the legitimate formation of groups in an open and confident relation to the Church as a whole and her hierarchy. Each religious order, for example, with its own spirit different from others, is a group formation in that sense, which makes life more tolerable for the individual within the Church as a whole.
[15] We repeat here a few pages composed earlier: *Gefahren im heutigen Katholizismus* (Einsieden, ³1955), pp. 75–8.

pression that they must be glad that this or that is expressed outside the Church by Protestant theologians, and that we must read it in their pages, for, of course, we could not say it ourselves without danger. Sometimes we may have the impression that the doctrinal views of a theologian are hidden behind the figures in his historical inquiry, in order to be perceptible without being tangible. Isn't there here and there even something like an esoteric doctrine only transmitted by word of mouth? Is there not an unformulated heresy that avoids theses, and works by mere omissions and one-sided views and by-passes a thesis but moves directly from false attitude into practice? Isn't something of that kind afoot when, for example, the doctrine of hell is deliberately avoided, when there is no longer any mention of the evangelical counsels, vows and the clerical state, or at the most with uncertainty and embarrassment, only when it is absolutely unavoidable? How often does a preacher addressing educated people in our countries still speak of the temporal punishment due to sin, indulgences, the angels, fasting, the devil (at most the "satanic element" in man may be mentioned), purgatory, prayer for the Holy Souls and similar old-fashioned things? When we find the "interior freedom" recommended to go on living positively in the Church and to treat the confessional as, in fact, incompetent, as long as the sacrament of forgiveness is there administered in the service of a legalistic "Moloch cult",[16] it is the practice of a concealed, unacknowledged heresy that is being recommended. By a strange paradox it can befall precisely those who are proudest of the assured orthodoxy of their longstanding views and doctrines – heresy in the form of indifference.

[16] We find this in E. Michel, *Die Ehe* (Stuttgart, 1949), p. 128.

God's truth is ever one and the same, definitive. It is proclaimed by the Church's magisterium. When and where that magisterium has expressed the truth entrusted to her by Christ in a form that binds the conscience of the faithful, that truth in that form is true and valid for all time. Theology and preaching will always refer back to such formularies of revealed truth drawn up in the course of the Church's history, secure in the knowledge that the truth meant was, in fact, rightly expressed in them. And this despite the fact that no formulation of the truths of faith in human words is ever adequate to the object referred to by them, and that at least in principle, any of them could be replaced by an even better, more comprehensive one. An intellectual, conceptual formulary is never merely the subsequent reflection of an experience of faith in itself irrational, as the modernist misconception of the intellectual element in faith would have it. But God's truth in human words is not, for all that, given merely in order to wander through the text books of dogmatic theology in printed propositions perpetually monotonous. It is intended rather for a vital encounter with the actual concrete individual, to penetrate into his mind and heart, become his very flesh and blood, bring him into the truth. That calls for a ceaselessly renewed assimilation by the individual. Just as he is, in his age, with his experiences, his lot, his intellectual situation, which is not only that of ecclesiastical Christianity but also that of the age generally, the individual must hear God's message ever anew, in all his own individuality. And since not the audible message, but only the message actually heard can be believed by a human being, and as the truth of revelation does not consist in a mere timeless intrinsic validity, but can only and is only intended to have an earthly existence by being actually believed in fact, the pure and ever identical truth of the gospel must bear the stamp of the age in the actual concrete accomplishment of being known and acknowledged in each successive epoch.

If it does not, or does so insufficiently, it does not become more timeless and more universally valid. It probably will merely bear the style of the mind of an earlier age which has become a habit, and which is wrongly regarded as an expression of the eternally identical validity of the truth of the gospel, because it is old and well-known. This hardening of the form in which the truth of the gospel is expressed is then itself nothing but the dangerous symptom of an indifference to this truth, from which the age is suffering whether consciously or not, and it is a symptom of the lack of strength to assimilate and effectively to make it their own from which such "traditionalists" are suffering. Who could deny that even at the present time the form of heresy exists in which lifeless orthodoxy is only the effect and expression of an inner indifference to truth, by which something is left alone because it is at bottom so much a matter of indifference that people even shrink from the trouble of clearing it out of the way or of contesting it?

It would be a complete misconception to suppose that all this has been said in order to make people start seeing heresies everywhere and hunting for secret heretics. We have pointed out the signs of the actual presence of such latent or virtual heresy simply in order to give factual verification of the theoretical contention that there must be some such change in the pattern of heresy nowadays. If anyone wishes to draw practical conclusions from this theological speculation, he must fear the danger for himself first of all and strive to escape it. For in the sense of heresy which we are using here, the mere good intention of being orthodox

457

and obedient to the teaching Church is not a complete safe-guard.

It follows that the Church's magisterium can do very little, with the means employed until now, against the danger of latent heresy. It can proclaim the truth, itself give conceptual formulation to heretical tendencies, as was first done in the Modernist encyclical of Pius X, and then reject them in this form. But it can do little against the tacit heresy itself. It is to a large extent helpless against heresy that only makes correct assertions and is silent on those that do not suit it, or against the heresy of indifference and of a theologically sterile integrism. The magisterium, in fact, inevitably lives in the temptation of exaggerating the difficulty, for the same reason that has caused the change in the pattern of heresy. Especially since the Vatican Council the magisterium knows its own authority to be express-ly recognized, even as an object of faith, and it can more easily be tempted to suppress heretical systems of ideas simply by its formal authority without making sure that they are overcome on principles relevant to the particular case. In this way the temptation arises to combat heresy to a certain extent only by administrative means, by putting books on the Index, dismissing suspect professors and so on, instead of by means of the *teaching* office, that is by such positive formulation of the true doctrine that the error is really supplanted. Or calm and silence are commanded without at the same time saying or allowing to be said what positively needs to be said, and that in such a way that it is not only true but really enters the minds and hearts of men. As we have remarked, the temptation is not insuperable but it exists, though not necessarily actually felt, and it too forms part of the situation created by the changing pattern of heresy. For that danger derives from the same causes as this change itself. For example, was silence not maintained far too long, in the days of Modernism, about many questions of Biblical theology?

At all events the danger is inevitably greater today than before that if theological theses and opinions which are over-hastily considered to look dubious or insufficiently mature, are officially suppressed, heresy is not destroyed but only assumes its new form and so really becomes unaffected by measures taken by the Church's magisterium. For as it seems to us, the development of the Church and the recognition of her formal teaching authority as an actual object of faith "must" introduce a form of heresy in the Church that was not known in earlier days on such a scale.

The battle against this implicit heresy of attitude is therefore chiefly a task incumbent on the conscience of the individual. When heresy does not find expression in theses but remains implicit, is never put forward for discussion, appearing blandly as a mere matter of course, it takes on more or less the nature of the insidious heresy of false proportions, in Christians who after all do really want to be such. That means that all or most of the things called for, postulated at the present time or for the immediate future, will have something quite correct or arguable or historically inevitable about them, even when they imply a departure from the style and manner of life of earlier generations, even Christian ones. In comparison with former times people may with good reason demand or simply tacitly assume in the concrete ordering of life, more tolerance, freedom, respect for the laity in the Church, more unaffectedness in regard to the body and to sexuality, more understanding of social factors, more emphasis on the principles of an ethics of the individual and of the formation of the individual conscience, greater distinction between the theological proposition in its historical and therefore conditioned "garb" and the reality it signifies, a more open and unembarrassed attitude towards the modern world in general. That can certainly be done in such a way that there can be no room for accusations of definite heresy. Yet, for all that, implicit heresy may be committed simply by the false proportions, the wrong dose of all these things, impossible as it may be exactly to check this.

"Dose" may sound crude and inappropriate. It may be said that the problems have not been properly thought out, otherwise the idea of using the image of the right dose could never have arisen. Of course, there are instances enough in which a problem cannot be solved by a compromise, by mutual give and take, avoidance of exaggerations on either side or by attitudes and measures of that kind, but only by an accurate, clear working out of a single principle by which right action can definitely be ascertained. Nevertheless, it remains true that because men are both finite and complex, they are inevitably forced to act on a plurality of principles the positive content of which they cannot reconcile and synthesize in the unity of a higher principle. Hence the problem of the right dose or relative proportions, that is, of simultaneously and genuinely respecting a number of requirements which are in content irreducible theoretically to a single higher criterion, whether principle or authority. This is an inescapable human task which by the nature of the case cannot be solved entirely on the plane of theory in a rationalistic way without regard for time and place, but only through direct action which is not entirely accessible to introspective analysis. That is to say it cannot be solved by knowledge and learning but only by prudence and wisdom. For that reason tacit heresy, precisely where it wishes to remain so, tends to be a heresy of false proportions, exaggeration, onesidedness. But it must be noted that it is a matter of false proportions difficult or even sometimes impossible to demonstrate theoretically. So it cannot be stigmatized by the Church's magisterium at all or only with great difficulty, subsequently or in very general terms which no one, of course, takes as referring to himself.

Who, for example, could say at what point present-day sport and athletics start to become an unavowed heresy altering the due proportions and relation between personality and body, a heresy of tacit idolatry of the physical? When general warnings are expressed in this connection every adherent of the heresy (when it does exist), considers that it is simply others who are meant, who are indulging in such idolatry even more onesidedly and radically, or else that some reactionary out-of-date bearer of office is taking advantage of the warning to treat with suspicion and to persecute as unchristian a pursuit of sport which nowadays is full of significance.

The following circumstance also complicates the situation. Even where modern heresy finds abstract expression, it will already have tested itself by a great number of people's experiences to far too great an extent for it to appear very onesided and rigid. In the expression of what it really means, in the praise of its idols, the necessary reserves, checks and balances, limitations and so on will be made, so that simple-minded people will only too easily be deceived and get the impression of a harmonious system. In every idolatrous praise of sport, to keep to our example, there will certainly nowadays also be a little incense offered to the "mind". And materialism will emphasize that it

461

must be understood to be "dialectical", so that the denial of spirit which it certainly contains is not at all easy to demonstrate.

It follows from all this how very much it is nowadays a matter of emphasis, of proportion and assignment of relative importance, and what a difficult task all this sets the Church's magisterium. This is where the individual Christian is assigned and called irreplaceably to a task and responsibility. For relative proportions in actual concrete attitudes in practical life cannot be sufficiently determined in the abstract. Yet they can be false and heretical. And the Christian is not relieved of responsibility for having committed such heresy by the mere fact that he received no protest from the magisterium. Isn't it possible, for example, that in the nineteenth and first half of the twentieth century, the magisterium stressed the legitimacy of patriotism *and* the integration of this principle with other higher principles, and Christians, while not denying this dialectical teaching in the abstract, in practice pursued a heretical nationalism against which the magisterium as judge of abstract principles did not and could not raise any really clear protest? So the Christians not being sufficiently vigilant and self-critical themselves, considered that all was well apart from a few exaggerations – other people's, that is. At the present day in nuclear weapons we have an example of a question which in the abstract, in theory, only leads to a dialectical exchange: On the one hand ... On the other ... The magisterium itself gets no further than this and may not, and so the whole question, in the historical circumstances in which a decision about definite action has to be made, actually remains an open one and yet it is a question of *conscience*.

This vigilance and distrust of latent heresy which are the indispensable task and duty of the individual, since they cannot be adequately taken over by the magisterium, are not, of course, to be regarded as an obligation for the individual conscience, of his individual ethic, in the sense that each would exist for himself alone, in isolation. The discovery of concrete prescriptions that go beyond the dialectical opposition of mutually balancing principles and lay down more definite demands is certainly something that can take place in the public life of the Church, for example in the formation of a charismatically inspired "public opinion". All great Christian movements in various spheres can be understood in that way, and quoted as examples of what is meant. But what will be decisive even for the ever new, living formation in the Church of such attitudes against latent heresy, will be the grace of God that gives individuals insight into that heresy and the resolution not simply to allow themselves to be "conformed to this world", as St. Paul already warned us (Rom. 12:2).